Gender and Natural Resource Management

Gender and Natural Resource Management

Livelihoods, Mobility and Interventions

Edited by
Bernadette P. Resurreccion and Rebecca Elmhirst

publishing for a sustainable future

London • New York

International Development Research Centre
Ottawa • Cairo • Dakar • Montevideo • Nairobi • New Delhi • Singapore

First published by Earthscan in the UK and USA in 2008

ISBN 13: 978-1-844-07580-5(hbk)
ISBN 13: 978-0-415-84791-9 (pbk)

IDRC publishes an e-book version of Gender and Natural Resource Management (ISBN 978-1-55250-398-0)

For further information, please contact:

International Development Research Centre
PO Box 8500
Ottawa, ON K1G 3H9
Canada
Email: info@idrc.ca
Web: www.idrc.ca

Typeset by MapSet Ltd, Gateshead, UK

Cover design by Yvonne Booth

For a full list of publications please contact:

Earthscan
2 Park Square, Milton Park, Abingdon, Oxfordshire OX14 4RN
Simultaneously published in the USA and Canada by Earthscan
711 Third Avenue, New York, NY 10017
Earthscan is an imprint of the Taylor & Francis Group, an informa business

First issued in paperback 2013

Earthscan publishes in association with the International Institute for Environment and Development

A catalogue record for this book is available from the British Library

Library of Congress Cataloging-in-Publication Data has been applied for

Contents

Introduction

Part I Contextualizing Gender and Natural Resource Governance in Neo-liberal Times

Part 2 Gender Interventions: Targeting Women in Sustainable Development Projects

Part 3 Responding to Intervention: Gender, Knowledge and Authority

List of Figures and Tables

Figures

Tables

Boxes

List of Contributors

Marlène Buchy is a senior lecturer in rural development, population and environmental studies at the Institute of Social Studies, The Hague, The Netherlands. She has worked for many years in South and Southeast Asia on community-based natural resource management issues from a gender and social equity perspective. She works within a participatory action research framework.

Barbara Earth is an independent scholar currently based in Honolulu, Hawaii after over 30 years of health-related research and teaching in the US, Africa and Asia. For the past ten years, she was a health social scientist in gender and development studies at the Asian Institute of Technology. She is now learning American Sign Language at Kapiolani Community College, a branch of the University of Hawaii that contains the Asia-Pacific regional centre of Gallaudet University.

Rebecca Elmhirst is senior lecturer in human geography at the University of Brighton, UK. Her research focuses on resource politics, migrant livelihoods and gender. She has worked closely with communities in resettlement areas of Lampung, Indonesia for many years. She is co-editor (with Ratna Saptari) of *Labour in Southeast Asia: Local Processes in a Globalised World* (2004).

Melinda Herrold-Menzies is assistant professor of environmental studies at Pitzer College, a member of the Claremont University Consortium in California. She completed her doctorate at the University of California, Berkeley in environmental science, policy and management and her masters at Yale University in international relations. Her research focuses on natural resource conflicts in China and Russia.

Soutthanome Keola is a 1999 graduate of gender and development studies at the Asian Institute of Technology (AIT), and is currently working towards a PhD in urban environmental management at AIT.

Patcharin Lapanun is a lecturer at the Department of Sociology and Anthropology, KKU, Thailand. Before joining the Department she was a researcher at the RDI, KKU. Her research is mainly in areas of gender and the socio-cultural aspects of natural resource management, and local organizations and networks in rural Thailand. Her PhD research (in progress) is on transnational marriages of rural Thai women and the consequences for local communities.

Hue Le Thi Van is a lecturer with the Faculty of Environmental Sciences at Hanoi University of Science in Vietnam. She is also a researcher with the Center for Natural Resources and Environmental Studies at the Vietnam National University in Hanoi. Her research interests are natural resource management, land tenure and gender. She has worked closely with ethnic groups in the north of Vietnam to improve their livelihoods while preserving their cultural identity and the local environment.

Chengfang Liu is a doctoral candidate in the Department of Agricultural and Resource Economics at the University of California, Davis. Her research interests include development economics, public economics and applied econometrics. Her current research work is on public goods investment, land tenure, education and gender.

Haomiao Liu is a senior research assistant with the Center for Chinese Agricultural Policy at the Chinese Academy of Sciences. Her major research area covers a wide range of rural development issues in China, including community governance and public goods investments, rural fiscal reform, and gender and tenure.

Benjawan Narasaj is a lecturer at the Department of History, Khon Kaen University (KKU), Thailand. Before joining the History Department she worked as a researcher at the Research and Development Institute (RDI), KKU. Her research work is mainly on the cultural and social aspects of economic activities in rural communities in Thailand.

Britta Ogle is a researcher and lecturer in nutrition and food security at the Swedish University of Agricultural Sciences. Her research interests focus on the dietary/nutritional role of traditional plants, especially wild plants, nutrition related to forestry, food security, agriculture and rural development. She is currently coordinator of the department's research collaboration in rural development with Vietnamese agricultural universities.

Kathleen O'Reilly teaches in the Department of Geography at Texas A&M University. She does research in political ecology and critical development geography. Her focus is on community participation in drinking water supply, women's development, and non-governmental organization (NGO) interventions in rural Rajasthan, India.

Lisa Leimar Price is an anthropologist and associate professor in gender studies in the Department of Social Sciences at Wageningen University in The

Netherlands. She has undertaken farm-level research throughout Asia and is the author of numerous publications on wild food plants and ethnoscience. She specializes in gender studies, agrobiodiversity, natural resource management, and ethnobiology and ethnoecology. She is co-editor (with Andrea Pieroni) of *Eating and Healing: Traditional Food as Medicine* (2006).

Bimala Rai (Paudyal) is a PhD participant in development studies at the Institute of Social Studies in The Hague, The Netherlands. Her doctoral research focuses on agrarian differentiation and distributive outcomes of common property resource management. She has worked closely with rural communities of Nepal for more than 15 years. Currently, she is working as a social development advisor with the Livelihoods and Forestry Programme (LFP), a forestry project of the Department for International Development (DFID) Nepal.

Bernadette P. Resurreccion is assistant professor and coordinator of gender and development studies at the Asian Institute of Technology in Pathum Thani, Thailand. Her areas of research include gender, natural resource management and migrant livelihoods. She is an associate editor of the journal *Gender, Technology and Development* and a member of the Consultative Group on International Agricultural Research (CGIAR) Challenge Program on Water and Food (CPWF) Management Team.

Patcharin Ruchuwararak is a researcher at the RDI, KKU, Thailand. Her research focuses on the social and cultural aspects of natural resource management, alternative energy, and local NGOs and networks in rural Thailand.

Nit Tassniyom is an associate professor in community nursing at KKU, Thailand. Her current work is in health promotion, community empowerment and primary health care.

Emma Tomalin is with the Department of Theology and Religious Studies at the University of Leeds in the UK. Her research interests focus on gender and religion; religion and international development; and religion and environmentalism, particularly with respect to South and Southeast Asia. Her current research is on women's ordination in Theravada Buddhism.

Carol Yong Ooi Lin is currently an independent researcher-consultant with over 20 years of research and NGO-related experience. She also has some teaching experience. Special interests include the rights of indigenous peoples, especially around dams and forced resettlement; gender and development; and issues relating to indigenous peoples' lands and forests. She is the author of *Flowed Over: The Babagon Dam and the Resettlement of Kadazandusun in Sabah* (2003).

Lerong Yu is a lecturer at the College of Humanities and Development, China Agricultural University. She has dedicated herself to research on China's rural development, especially on gender and land tenure. She also has some teaching responsibilities.

Linxiu Zhang is a professor and deputy director in the Center for Chinese Agricultural Policy at the Chinese Academy of Science. Her current research work is mainly on rural off-farm employment, poverty, land tenure and gender, community governance and public goods investment, and education in rural China.

Preface

The impetus for this book came from a growing sense of unease about the 'discursive landslide' of gender mainstreaming in natural resource management, which seemed to be at odds with our own research encounters and our engagement with emerging theoretical debates about gender in the social sciences more broadly. We observed a number of problematic and yet stubborn conceptual antecedents that continue to characterize the growing 'feminization' of natural resource management interventions. 'Gender' is persistently equated with the study of women and their roles, involving the application of a series of 'gender tools and techniques' that blunt its critical edge and place it a long way from its transformatory potential as a feminist concept. Our aim with this book is thus to initiate a response to recent calls to re-establish more politicized approaches to gender at the heart of environment–development debates. We accomplish this through exploration of the uneasy negotiations between theory, policy and practice that are evident within the realm of gender, environment and natural resource management across a range of contexts marked by hybridized neo-liberal and populist agendas of decentralization, community-based natural resource management and participation.

The book has evolved from a panel on gender, environment and natural resource management at the EU–Asia Link Project's International Conference on Gender, Globalization and Public Policy at the Asian Institute of Technology (AIT) in Thailand in May 2004. Several of the chapters here are substantially revised versions of papers presented in that panel, and discussions with other panel presenters whose work was not included helped shape the development of the book. Other contributions have grown out of an evolving network of specialists working on gender, environment and natural resource management who share a commitment to reinvigorating critical debate in this area. We would like to extend our appreciation to all our contributors for sharing their work, and for their careful and considered responses to the various rounds of revision that the chapters all underwent. Two of the chapters are revised versions of articles published in a special issue of *Gender, Technology and Development* and one is a substantially reworked version of a paper published in *Signs*. We are grateful to Sage and The University of Chicago Press, respectively, for granting us permission to reproduce these works in this collection. Financial support for some aspects of the project was given by the International Development Research

Centre (IDRC) in connection with their programme on social and gender analysis in natural resource management in Asia.

The book would thus not have been possible without colleagues from IDRC. We wish to sincerely thank Liz Fajber, then Senior Program Officer of the IDRC South Asian Regional Office (SARO), who was – and continues to be – keenly aware of the need to sustain the debates on social and gender dimensions of natural resource management, and thus together with Valthsala and Bill Carman of the Ottawa office, supported the production of the book until its completion. At AIT, Agnes Pardilla, Julaika Hossain and Mary Ann Pama of Gender and Development Studies, lightened the load of deadlines by attending to unstoppable, sometimes insurmountable, administrative challenges that would have otherwise slowed down the completion of the book. True to their mettle, Jonathan Shaw and Terry Clayton provided excellent editorial support. The unwavering friendship of Barbara Earth and her commitment to a feminist ethos within AIT is a reminder that keeping 'gender jobs' is not just about making a living, but that through them we actualize the most personal and the deeply political in us. At the University of Brighton, practical support for work on the book was provided through the School of the Environment Research Development Fund, whilst Jenny Elliott and other Geography colleagues provided a stimulating and supportive setting in which to pursue the project. We continue to draw intellectual inspiration from old friends and fellow feminist academics who, like us, traverse different worlds to engage with and challenge received wisdoms on gender, development and change: Thanh-dam Truong, Cecilia Ng, Ratna Saptari, Jeannette Gurung, Marlène Buchy, Jenny Elliott, Janet Momsen, Janet Townsend, Rachel Silvey and Ari Darmastuti. Huge, sometimes undeserving, quantities of laughter, love and care came generously from Edsel Sajor, Miela Sayo and Tony Resurreccion, and from Gordon, Angus and Shona Starks. This book is for them.

List of Acronyms and Abbreviations

AIT	Asian Institute of Technology
BAAC	Bank of Agriculture and Agricultural Cooperative
CBNRM	community-based natural resource management
CCD	Community Capacities Development
CDD	Community Development Department (Thailand)
CF	community fishery
CFP	Community Fisheries Co-Management Program (Cambodia)
CPRM	common property resource management
CTF	community trust fund
DOA	Department of Agriculture (Thailand)
DOAE	Department of Agricultural Extension (Thailand)
DFO	District Forest Office (Nepal)
DoF	Department of Fisheries (Cambodia)
DOF	Department of Forests (Nepal)
FECOFUN	Federation of Community Forest Users, Nepal
FHH	female-headed household
FPP	Forest Afforestation Partnership Project
FUG	forest user group
GAD	gender and development
GED	gender, environment and development
GOR	Government of Rajasthan
HRS	Household Responsibility System (China)
ICDP	integrated conservation and development project
IDRC	International Development Research Centre
IPGRI	International Plant Genetic Resources Institute
JHEOA	Department of Orang Asli Affairs (Malaysia)
JKKK	Village Security and Development Committee (Malaysia)
MoFSC	Ministry of Forests and Soil Conservation (Nepal)
NRM	natural resource management
NTFP	non-timber forest product
PRA	participatory rural appraisal
PSS	Project Social Side
SPLASH	Syarikat Pengeluar Air Sungai Selangor (Malaysia)
TUP	Trickle Up Program

UNCED   United Nations Conference on Environment and Development
UNDP   United Nations Development Programme
WCD   World Commission on Dams
WED   women, environment and development
WID   women in development

Introduction

Chapter One

Gender, Environment and Natural Resource Management: New Dimensions, New Debates

Rebecca Elmhirst and Bernadette P. Resurreccion

This book is about the gender dimensions of natural resource exploitation and management in Asia. It provides an exploration of the uneasy negotiations between theory, policy and practice that are often evident within the realm of gender, environment and natural resource management, especially where gender is understood as a political, negotiated and contested element of social relationships. In recent years, there has been some disquiet that, amidst efforts to mainstream gender into natural resource management interventions and into development policy more broadly, gender has lost its critical and politicized edge, having been institutionalized into a series of tools and techniques that are far removed from the transformatory potential of gender as a feminist concept (Kabeer, 2005; Molyneux and Razavi, 2005; Leach, 2007).

The tension between gender as a technical fix and a more politicized view of gender is examined in this book. The chapters touch on theory, policy and practice, all with a shared focus on gender as a critical analytical concept for understanding the social and political dimensions of natural resource management and governance across a range of empirical settings. In different ways, and with varying commitments to particular conceptualizations of gender, the authors explore how gender subjectivities, ideologies and identities are produced, employed and contested within natural resource governance, and how gender discourses shape exclusions and possibilities within environment/development processes.

The book focuses on environments in Asia as a realm in which new realities are producing significant challenges for natural resource management, livelihoods and the mitigation of social inequalities. Across the Asian region, natural resource exploitation is accelerating dramatically as countries, cities and small communities are ever more incorporated into the global economy. Economic reform programmes that favour domestic and global market expansion rather than a social welfare agenda, policy responses to climate change, pressures associated with population growth and intensified geographical mobility, and urbanization and commoditization, are reconfiguring patterns of natural resource use and governance at both a national and local level and are having complex effects on peoples' lives. These processes are themselves not innocent of gendered power relations: they are inflected with gender discourses that set in motion differentiated and unjust life opportunities and exclusions. At the same time, sustainable development policy initiatives that seek to ameliorate environmental degradation and its negative livelihood effects not only bring gendered impacts and responses, they also work through and produce particular framings of gender and gendered power relations. The impact of this is apparent in the unintended consequences associated with sustainable development initiatives that target women as a homogeneous and undifferentiated social category, at times exacerbating social and gender injustices.

In part, this book offers a response to recent calls to re-establish more politicized gender at the heart of environment–development debates (Leach, 2007) and we are encouraged by a recent wave of politically committed and theoretically sophisticated contributions to the 'gender agenda' in the development literature (Harris, 2006; Jackson, 2006; Nightingale, 2006; Cornwall, 2007; Cornwall et al, 2007). In contributing to this new wave of interest, we aim to provide a necessary corrective to the naturalized assumptions about men, women and power that underpin the widely held notion within sustainable development policy circles (and reiterated in the recent UN review of ten years of gender mainstreaming initiatives in Asia) that women play a central role as effective managers of resources, and therefore should be key actors in natural resource management programmes (UN-ESCAP, 2004). At the same time, and in line with a broadly conceived feminist political ecology, we conceptualize our endeavours within emerging political economies, globalizing conditions and changing cultural landscapes in the Asian region in contemporary times.

In this introduction, we develop three themes that link the discussions of gender, environment and natural resource management provided by our contributors, and around which the book is organized. First, we consider the changing global context with which approaches to gender and environment must engage, paying particular attention to macroeconomic policies and changes in governance associated with neo-liberalism. Second, we explore the ways 'gender' has been incorporated in environment and development practices, especially within interventions designed to accomplish sustainable development goals. Finally, we examine the realm of gender, knowledge and authority, offering a critical consideration of gendered subjectivities that problematize simplistic mappings of gendered agency and environmental actions. Within each of these themes, our contributors respond in various ways to longstanding debates around gender, environment and natural resource management, many of which resonate with developments in feminist social theory more generally. We begin, therefore, with an overview of debates around gender, environment and natural resource management as these have unfolded in response to a widening engagement with environmental concerns within development policy frameworks since the landmark World Commission on Environment and Development.

Theorizing gender and environment: Conceptual antecedents and new theoretical pathways

The genealogy of gender and environment debates is well documented in the literature. Broadly, two key strands may be identified that generally map onto (1) liberal correctives to gender-blind scholarship within development policy and practice, and (2) relational perspectives that emphasize binary power relations between men and women. Common to both is a sense in which experiences of the environment are differentiated by gender through the materially distinct daily work activities and responsibilities of men and women. Consequently, men and women hold gender-differentiated interests in natural resource management through their distinctive roles, responsibilities and knowledge. Gender is thus understood as a critical variable in shaping processes of ecological change, viable livelihoods and the prospects for sustainable development. However, relational perspectives on gender purport to give greater emphasis to the dynamics of gender, emphasizing power relations between men and women over resource access and control, and their concrete expressions in conflict, cooperation and coexistence over environments and livelihoods.

In recent years, new work in this area has been influenced by feminist and post-colonial theories that effectively destabilize 'gender' as a central analytical category and explore multidimensional subjectivities, emphasizing how gender is constituted through other kinds of social differences and axes of power such as race, sexuality, class and place, and practices of 'development' themselves. This type of thinking not only critiques 'development', but effectively challenges the representational strategy adopted initially by those concerned with overcoming differences among women by articulating a centred developing world woman subject in order to press for women's rights to inclusion in international agreements around sustainable development (Mohanty, 1988; Saunders, 2002). Such a strategy served a specific rhetorical purpose that was intensified through the United Nations' World Commission on Environment and Development (Brundtland) report in 1987, and the United Nations Conference on Environment and Development (UNCED) in Brazil in 1992, where alliances amongst feminist activists from across the world were forged to produce the Women's Action Agenda 21 (Leach, 2007). This effectively linked concerns with women and gender with environmentally sustainable development: both having been traditionally marginal issues on the development agenda (Dankelman and Davidson, 1988).

Exploration of the links between gender and the environment in the South began in Asia, stimulated largely by compelling narratives of rural and indigenous women saving trees and thwarting the destroyers of forests and forest livelihoods.[1] Two popular strands – a particular variant of ecofeminism from a Southern perspective and WED (or 'women, environment and development') – posited natural connections between women and environmental resources, positing rural women of the South as the unrecognized caretakers of the environment, and in whose care the Earth and its resources had better chances of surviving for future generations (Dankelman and Davidson, 1988; Shiva, 1989; Rodda, 1991; Sontheimer, 1991). All pre-colonial societies 'were based on an ontology of the feminine as the living principle', Vandana Shiva (1989) argued, 'where rural, indigenous women are the original givers of life and are therefore the rightful caretakers of nature' (p42; see Tomalin, Chapter 12 in this volume for a fuller discussion). WED's logic, unlike Shiva's more spiritualist–cultural premise, was that women were adversely affected by environmental degradation due to an *a priori* gender division of labour. In this division, women are usually assigned reproductive roles, explaining why they were chiefly responsible for the collection of forest products and food for daily household subsistence. Planners interpreted this to mean that women should then be targeted in conservation projects since their daily roles connected them more closely to natural resources. Early examples in this policy genre have been work on women, forests and energy resources (FAO, 1989; DGIS, 1990), especially in the light of the global energy crisis in the 1970s in the course of searches for rural energy alternatives.

Both in the exploration of the 'feminine principle' in human–nature relationships, or in the analysis of gender divisions of labour in natural resource management, the emphasis has been clearly on women and women's roles. Whilst this might well provide a corrective to gender-blind and androcentric environment–development policy, within the context of mainstream development policy it has been translated from the politicized category 'woman' into what Cornwall (2007) describes as a combination of 'gross essentialism' with 'patronising paternalism' (p71). A number of scholars have identified problems associated with WED approaches that inadvertently give rise to such a description. First, research has challenged the notion that women have fixed caretaker roles and that they may just end up being key assets to be 'harnessed' in resource conservation initiatives (Rocheleau, 1991; Leach, 1992, 1994). Planning on the basis of fixed and reified 'roles' may, in the end, turn out to be counterproductive for women. Policy translations of WED are implicitly founded on the rational choice stream in policy studies that rely on simplifications around women's care of natural resources as atomized individuals with fixed attributes, and with roles that are disassociated from wider relationships and webs of power.

Secondly, Rao (1991) has argued for the need to contextualize women as they dynamically respond to complex environmental realities, and to consider how they enter into and engage in social relationships with men within the institutions of their natural resource-dependent societies instead of *a priori* perceptions on women's roles. Thirdly, both ecofeminism and WED also connote a victim status of rural women from the South, conveying images of women walking longer distances in the daily collection of food, fuel and fodder for their households as resources are increasingly depleted. As the 'main victims' of environmental degradation, ecofeminism and WED position women as the 'most appropriate participants' in environmental conservation, and thus a natural constituency for donor-initiated resource protection, conservation and regeneration (Dankelman and Davidson, 1988; Shiva, 1989; Rodda, 1991).

Disquiet with the translation of WED thinking into policy has run in parallel with critiques levelled at 'women in development' or WID perspectives that saw women as a stand-alone homogeneous group with a set of static and predefined roles that translated into their disadvantaged social lives (Rathgeber, 1990). Arguments have been made for more context-specific and historically nuanced understandings of the relationship of specific groups of women with specific environmental resources, especially as these are mediated by their complex relations with men, kin and other social actors. In other words, greater emphasis is given to gender and its structuring, relational and power dimensions. An early proponent of gender analysis as a useful framework for unpacking environmental relations was Jackson (1993a, 1993b), who proposed that analysis should focus on power relations between women and men, and that women be treated as a disaggregated group of subjects as gender roles are socially and historically constructed and being continually reformulated. Like others before her, Jackson challenged the idea of 'women' as a natural constituency for environmental projects, underscoring the contingent nature and fluidity of gender interests, an approach that has been discussed more fully in debates regarding practical and strategic interests elsewhere in the wider field of gender and development (Molyneux, 1985; Moser, 1993; Wieringa, 1994).

A number of perspectives have subsequently emerged that share a concern to emphasize dynamic social and political relations and contextual analysis, rather than universal assumptions and essentialist views of men's and women's engagement with the environment. Alongside the gender analysis approach associated with gender, environment and development or GED (Leach, 1992, 1994; Jackson, 1993a; Joekes et al, 1996; Green et al, 1998), feminist environmentalism (Agarwal, 1992, 1994) emphasizes the material aspects of the gender–environment nexus, in particular gender divisions of resource-based labour and culturally specific gender roles. Finally, feminist political ecology draws on the field of political ecology to focus on resource access and control, gendered constructions of knowledge, and the embeddedness of local gendered environmental struggles in regional and global political economic contexts (Rocheleau et al, 1996; Schroeder, 1999). These debates and their policy counterparts are evident in an explosion of ethnographies and edited volumes that have sought to capture the gender–environment nexus in various geographical and resource use contexts, for example forests, land and agriculture, and water (Fortmann and Rocheleau, 1984; Leach, 1994; Carney, 1996; Sachs, 1996; van Koppen and Mahmud, 1996; Ireson, 1997; de Bruijn et al, 1997; Jarosz, 1997; Tinker, 1997; Zwarteveen, 1998; Schroeder, 1999; Cranney, 2001).

In locating gender within changing contexts of ecological change, economic dislocations and windfalls, as well as legal normative frameworks, gender, environment and natural resource management scholarship has engaged with a range of empirical concerns. Work has centred on gendered property rights (water and land) (Brunt, 1992; Agarwal, 1994; Meinzen-Dick et al, 1997; von Benda-Beckmann et al, 1997; Meinzen-Dick and Zwarteveen 1998); gender dynamics in local participation in development programmes and community-based institutions (Villareal, 1992; Mosse, 1994; Agarwal, 1997; Guijt and Shah, 1998; Cleaver, 2003; Colfer, 2005); the micro- and macro-politics of collective action (Rocheleau et al, 1996); geographical mobility (Elmhirst, 2001, 2002); gendered environmental knowledge (Fortmann, 1996; Jewitt, 2002; Howard, 2003; Momsen, 2007); livelihoods and resource use (Feldstein and Poats, 1989; Leach, 1994; Deere, 1995); history (Leach and Green, 1997; Resurreccion, 1999); and dynamics of gender in policy discourses and within environmental departments of development agencies (Crewe and Harrison, 1998; Kurian, 2000). In different ways, these studies hold a view of gender as relational: involving the interaction of men and women, structured through norms and institutions, reconfigured through individual agency. This is a view that is extended in different ways by contributors to this volume. Together, they also challenge the position that gender is primarily relevant only within households (a view that is often stated in mainstream environmental and political ecology research) and instead see gender as salient within policy and practice across a variety of scales, and within institutions central to natural resource governance, from gendered property relations to the gendered positions of actors within organizations charged with governing or managing natural resources.

In recent years, debates in GED and feminist political ecology have been taken in new directions through the influence of a performative approach to gender associated most notably with the feminist theorist Judith Butler (1990, 1994, 2004). Butler's work has had a profound impact on gender studies across the social science disciplines and holds a particular attraction for analyses that explore how gender is constituted in different contexts as a component of multiple and complex subjectivities. The performance of masculinities and femininities construct and reconstruct the gendered subject, as performativity is 'the vehicle through which ontological effects are established' (Butler, 1994, p33). This approach allows masculinities and femininities to be regarded as a process: fragmented, provisional and wrought through the interplay of culture, class, nationality and other fields of power, and, centrally for Butler, through regulatory frameworks such as normative heterosexuality. Those that subscribe to this kind of approach suggest that it challenges essentialist and binary views of relations between men and women that may overemphasize difference and opposition, and may essentialize particular patterns of gendered disadvantage (Jackson, 2006; Cornwall, 2007). Moreover, such an approach allows space to consider other kinds of gender relations that may be significant in people's lives beyond conjugal partnerships, for example seniority, status, co-sanguinity.

The significance of this view for gender, environment and natural resource management studies is that it shifts the direction and emphasis of analysis. Rather than seeing gender as structuring people's interactions with and responses to environmental change or shaping their roles in natural resource management, the emphasis is on the ways in which changing environmental conditions bring into existence categories of social difference including gender. In other words, gender itself is re-inscribed in and through practices, policies and responses associated with shifting environments and natural resource management, and whilst inherently unstable, through repeated acts, it comes to appear as natural and fixed. For example, work by Nightingale (2006) in Nepal and Harris (2006) in Turkey has shown how gendered subjectivities are defined and contested in relation to changing ecological conditions, becoming salient at particular moments through practices and discourses of gender associated with livelihoods, natural resources and wider development programmes and policies. Such frameworks, alongside the more politicized approaches to gender and natural resources outlined above, have been key to the development of a revitalized feminist political ecology that is being built around gender as an optic for analysing the power effects of the social constitution of difference (Cornwall, 2007). This has opened up new pathways for analysis that cross-cut the three key themes that are explored by the contributors to this book, and which we introduce below.

Gender, environment and natural resource management in neo-liberal times

Crucial to any contemporary consideration of gender issues in natural resource management is recognition of the ways that this is given shape by the processes and practices inherent in wider macroeconomic policies associated with neo-liberalism in its various guises. Following a feminist political ecology framework, which sees gendered natural resource management as embedded within wider political economic frameworks, our contributors examine a diversity of settings, from societies undergoing market transformation, albeit at different paces, such as India, China, Nepal and mainland Southeast Asia's 'societies in transition' (Vietnam and Cambodia), to those with a longer history of export-oriented growth and neo-liberal reform (Thailand and Indonesia). To a greater or lesser degree, these are countries blighted by poverty and increasing disparities of wealth, and governed by semi-authoritarian states or what Molyneux and Razavi (2005) have referred to as masculine democracies.

Notwithstanding diversities across the region, processes associated with globalization, economic efficiency and the rescaling of social reproduction are critical to any consideration of gender and natural resource management, particularly where these have directly intensified the feminization of production, reproduction and community management (Nagar et al, 2002). Globalization, trade liberalization and policies that support export production are rapidly drawing landscapes and livelihoods across Asia into global markets in various ways (Razavi, 2002). This may include extractive activities of various kinds, the expansion of large-scale commercial production of industrial crops such as oil palm, or the incorporation of smallholder producers into global markets through the production of cash crops such as coffee or cocoa. The processes through which marketization of this sort proceeds are reconfiguring nature–society relations and environmental conditions that not only produce gender-differenti-ated effects and responses, but reconfigure categories of social difference, including gender and class. In Chapter 2, Hue Le Thi Van demonstrates the links between economic reform (*doi moi*), natural resource management policies and gender in Vietnam, where privatization of coastal aquaculture has brought about a transformation of resource access and control. Because of gender biases that run through the new institutional arrangements associated with economic reform, this process has built on and reinforced social hierarchies within communities, and converged with a wider reassertion of patriarchal power and family ideologies in Vietnam to create gendered exclusions around access to natural resources. She shows how, despite women's expanded role during the war years, gender biases in the reform process itself, coupled with a revitalization of male-dominated kinship relations, are undermining any gains achieved. Her work shows how gendered power is multi-scalar and is at work in various ways and at various levels.

Related to this process of globalized marketization, natural resource manage-ment is embedded in the increasing diversification of livelihoods: a process buoyed by policies that support entrepreneurialism and appear to be producing individualized portfolio livelihood strategies across Asia (Rigg, 2006). In their chapter on the commoditization of silk production (sericulture) among ethnic minority groups in Thailand, Barbara Earth and her colleagues discuss the gendered effects of policies that have sought to develop this sector, in line with wider macroeconomic strategies to enhance non-farm production and expand rural industry (Chapter 3). In a nuanced analysis of variations in the gendering of changing technological and management processes, the authors show how osten-sibly gender-blind policies are not necessarily about gender exclusions but may be captured by particular groups – in this case, certain ethnic minority women – who are able to capitalize on their identifications with particular forms of local knowl-edge (traditional silk production) as these are revalued. This work is indicative of a need to avoid essentializing intra-household male–female gender relations: rather, gender is cast through the interplay between state and market systems, ethnicity and the wider realm of citizenship and belonging.

Associated with the diversification of farm livelihoods, enhanced geographical mobility is leading to the increasing engagement of rural people throughout Asia in urban and transnational labour circuits. A voluminous literature on migration reveals the gendering of this process, in terms of those who migrate, and those who are left behind (Resurreccion and Ha Thi Van Khanh, 2007). In Chapter 4, Elmhirst considers the disjunctures between mobile lives and livelihoods and the largely sedentarist, place-based assumptions that underpin the governance of natural resources. She examines the situation in Lampung province, Indonesia, where state-led displacement to facilitate commercial agriculture and forestry, coupled with the emergence of transnational migration as an aspect of rural liveli-hoods, has recast gender in particular ways, especially in instances where women migrate. In the context of migrant livelihoods, gender provides an optic for query-ing assumptions about de-agrarianization and the importance of land for the rural poor.

Whilst female-dominated migration in some parts of Asia has led to men negotiating productive and reproductive activities, perhaps even reconfiguring masculinities and femininities (Osella and Gardner, 2004; Resurreccion and Ha Thi Van Khanh, 2007), in other instances, male migration is associated with the feminization of agriculture. In Chapter 5, Linxiu Zhang and her colleagues explore how male-dominated rural–urban migration and the feminization of agriculture in China suggests the necessity of reconsidering the system through which the state contracts land out to farm households through male household heads, in circumstances where the key agents in agriculture are often women, whose dominion over land is dependent on their position in conjugal partner-ships.

Their discussion leads into a second dimension of neo-liberal macroeconomic policy in Asia, where one mechanism for achieving economic efficiency and environmental protection has been the expansion of private property, sometimes in the form of individualized land rights (Agarwal, 2003; Razavi, 2003). The neo-liberal 'commodity road to resource stabilization' is an issue that runs through a number of chapters in this volume, specifically Hue Le Thi Van (Chapter 2) and Elmhirst (Chapter 4) indicate the gendered exclusions that may be associated with programmes based on individualized and private property. In Chapter 6, Carol Yong Ooi Lin reveals the gender stereotypes and misplaced family ideolo-gies that have given shape to land titling processes associated with the displacement and resettlement of minority forest-dwelling Orang Asli groups in Malaysia, following the construction of hydropower dams to serve wider national economic imperatives. In a neat example of the 'simplifications of rule' associated with many development schemes, a combination of Islamization and Malay culture within state discourses and practices has erased the informal mechanisms through which Orang Asli women gain access to resources, producing hierarchies that combine gender and ethnic exclusions. Similar processes have been noted in other parts of Asia where land reform is taking place, prompting intense debate between those advocating land titling in women's name as a means of empower-ment (Agarwal, 2003) and those who call for greater recognition of what such programmes might erase (Jackson, 2003).

Gender interventions: The feminization of natural resource management

A longstanding feminist critique of neo-liberalism has demonstrated the negative gender impacts of the drive for economic efficiency and the scaling back of state services, demonstrating in various ways how macroeconomic policies have effectively rescaled social reproduction from the state to households and to individual women (Marchand and Runyan, 2000; Elson, 2002; Nagar et al, 2002). Whilst in recent times there has been a willingness to give social and political concerns greater emphasis (for example, through the World Bank's participatory poverty assessments and through the emphasis placed on issues such as social capital and good governance), this has not been translated into measures that tackle gender inequalities (Molyneux and Razavi, 2005). Indeed, a neo-liberal shift in the burden of care towards households and individual women is expressed in relation to the environment and natural resource management through the continued influence of programmes that draw upon the labour of women either directly or in unacknowledged ways. In some parts of Asia, women are being deliberately mobilized to constitute the unpaid labour force to meet the demands of conservation projects under the banner of 'women's participation', drawing on a view that women are the principal fixers of degraded environments (Kurian, 2000; Buchy and Rai, Chapter 7). Thus, a second theme of the book is the feminization of natural resource management; an issue that looms large in interventions seeking to enhance environmental governance in neo-liberal times. Within this particular realm of development policy, the twin objectives of efficiency and economic liberalization enshrined in the policies of multilateral lending agencies and government departments have entailed a rescaling of state power to the local level through a renewed interest in 'community' as a vehicle for achieving development objectives. As Meynen and Doornbos (2004) suggest, whilst the initial aim of decentralization of natural resource management was market deregulation and privatization, more recently the impetus has come from the so-called social face of neo-liberalism: empowering communities to deliver development objectives. Community-based natural resource management (CBNRM) is based on the premise that local populations have a greater interest in the sustainable use of resources than the state or disparate corporate interests, that local communities by virtue of their everyday practices have an enhanced knowledge of local ecological processes, and that communities are more able to effectively manage resources through local forms of access (Tsing et al, 2005). Despite a recognition that there are few if any instances of communities operating in this way (Agrawal and Gibson, 2001), the popularity of this approach has seen an unlikely convergence between grass-roots organizations, multilateral development agencies, transnational conservation organizations and the World Bank, all of whom share an overall 'will to improve' (Tsing et al, 2005; Li 2007a, 2007b).

As Mosse (2006) put it, simplified and idealized notions of community institutions readily comply with external visions of how natural resource management ought to proceed, but frequently the realities of social processes confound the models and modes of analysis that dominate within donor agencies. Such realities include the exigencies of gender and other forms of social power. Interest in CBNRM has coincided with specific efforts to target gender equity in policy interventions through gender mainstreaming, which theoretically inserts gender concerns across policies and development practices at a number of levels (McIlwaine and Datta, 2003; Molyneux, 2004; Radcliffe, 2006). Whilst gender mainstreaming itself is highly uneven, reflecting differing levels of commitment and resource investment, it has also been critiqued by those who regard it as a means by which gender has been depoliticized and made technical (Cornwall, 2003). Marlène Buchy and Bimala Rai (Chapter 7) examine the convergence of CBNRM and gender mainstreaming in women-only forest user groups (FUGs) in Nepal. This is an exemplary case of the institutionalization of gender, which as Jackson (2006) suggests, all too frequently sees gender slipping into a focus on women, often cast as a homogeneous group with undifferentiated interests. Women as a group are incorporated for largely instrumental reasons to realize conservation goals without addressing the 'messy' politics of gender equality. Whilst FUGs were devised to give space for women to negotiate their needs, gendered identities within them are constructed through caste hierarchies and economic class. The multifaceted nature of power within women-only FUGs means that general participatory exclusions (see for example, Agarwal 2001) are intensified for poor and low-caste women as powerful women exert their influence. In other words, 'elite capture' takes on gendered forms.

In Chapter 8, Bernadette Resurreccion offers a critique of the 'simplifications of rule' associated with institution building for the co-management of fisheries in the Tonle Sap Great Lake, Cambodia. She describes the embeddedness of new resource management institutions within social relations of kinship and patronage, and reveals the importance of backstage informal negotiations through which women legitimize their claims to resources. In a manner that parallels the problems researchers have identified in the formalization of women's title to land, she shows how well-intentioned state policies are effectively undermined through the reinforcement of traditionally male-dominated networks of patronage, especially in 'transition' contexts where 'shadow state' practices remain as vestiges of conflict-ridden, strongman societies in Southeast Asia. Melinda Herrold-Menzies (Chapter 9) also discusses gender in the context of CBNRM, this time in relation to an integrated conservation and development plan in Caohai, China, an initiative that sought to lessen the impact of local people on resources in an environmentally sensitive area. Specifically, the project involved a microcredit programme – another arm of neo-liberal development policy that effectively devolves responsibility for securing economic opportunity away from the state and onto individuals cast as agents responsible for their own well being but without challenging issues of resource redistribution (Rankin, 2001). Herrold-Menzies shows how women were incorporated in a standard WID framework, sidestepping the processes that have produced gendered divisions of labour, largely adding another burden to women. This has exacerbated rather than challenged existing social hierarchies, and done little to serve the purpose of environmental protection. Part of the problem is that such programmes are often cast through the political rationality of neo-liberalism that runs through many microcredit programmes, effectively cultivating particular kinds of gendered subjectivities, and seeking to align the personal goals of individual women with those set out by policy makers (Goetz and Gupta, 1996; Rankin 2001).

Gendered subjects: Knowledge and authority in natural resource management

Throughout the book, cases demonstrate the ambiguity of gender interests, recognizing that gender exists through other social identities, and that gendered subjectivities are, as a result, invariably fractured and in process. The final theme that we consider in the book concerns the issues of subjectivity, gendered agency and environmental actions: core concerns within early contributions to feminist political ecology (Rocheleau et al, 1996). Since Rocheleau and her colleagues outlined the principles of feminist political ecology in the early 1990s, post-structuralist approaches to power, subjectivity and women's agency have grown in influence, placing the 'decentred subject' at the heart of many debates (Radcliffe, 2006). This kind of perspective sees gender neither as analytically central nor as the end point of critique and analysis (Fraser, 2004). People are conceptualized as inhabiting multiple and fragmented identities, constituted through social relations that include gender, but also include class, religion, sexuality, race/ethnicity and post-coloniality, as well as in multiple networks for coping with, transforming or resisting development (Nagar ct al, 2002; Lawson, 2007). Of interest is how racialized/ethnic or religious subjects are co-produced as gendered, and how such complex subjects of development are formed and act in relation to the exercise of power.

The importance of this kind of approach lies in its power to problematize naturalized and undifferentiated categories of people and social relationships (men, women, gender relations), and critically in this context, relationships between people and the environment. It also places positionality – the subject positions of researchers, fieldworkers, farmers and other social actors – at the centre of analysis. Theoretical discussions around practice, politics and accountability inherent in the production of research and its associated texts have long held sway in debates regarding the politics of representation within academic scholarship (Chatterjee, 2002). Correspondingly, there is recognition, borne from similar theoretical premises, that issues of authority, authorial location and power are at work within development interventions, including those that are framed as participatory (Villareal, 1992). In Chapter 10, Kathleen O'Reilly takes up this analytical position in her discussion of gendered relations of power within a specific natural resource management project involving the delivery of clean drinking water to villages in northern Rajasthan, India. She offers a powerful critique of the dangers associated with assuming that mainstreaming gender into development projects is accomplished by appointing women as fieldworkers. As she puts it, this is based on a faulty assumption that there is a natural communication between all women. Her chapter explores the positionalities, knowledge and authority of women fieldworkers within the NGO charged with facilitating community and women's participation in the water project, all of which are complex and interwoven with class, insider/outsider and rural/urban relationships, negotiation of which either produces or subverts gendered power relations in natural resource management practices.

Whilst acknowledging that there is no essential connection between women and environmental knowledge, in Chapter 11, Lisa Price and Britta Ogle look at how work, activities and knowledge are constructed in socially differentiated ways and how this maps onto the landscape in complex ways that may be obscured in research, policy and practice that essentializes Asian rural landscapes into farms or forests. Working within a sustainable livelihoods framework that uses the languages of capital and economic metaphors to emphasize people's entitlements, assets and capabilities, they analyse women's roles, knowledge and authority in gathering indigenous wild vegetables that are scattered across the in-between spaces (field margins, roadsides and so on) in the agricultural landscapes of Lao PDR, Vietnam and Thailand. In their account, they demonstrate the complex intersections between knowledge, gender and power in relation to wild plants. They show that neo-liberal configurations of private property (and the power relations associated with such exclusions) prohibit gathering activities but not in obvious ways: exclusions may be negotiated according to the value of the species being collected and its end use (for home consumption or sale).

In the final chapter of the book (Chapter 12), Emma Tomalin revisits the refrain with which this introductory chapter began – critiques of the special relationship between women, religion and environmental resource use or management accorded by the powerful and compelling discourses of spiritual ecofeminism. The hegemony of discourses about women's primitive ecological wisdom have been influential, often in unacknowledged ways, across the field of natural resource management in Asia, and have served simultaneously as a powerful rallying cry for marginalized groups (Sturgeon, 1999) as well as for urban, middle-class environmentalist movements (Mawdsley, 2004). In adhering to an 'anti-development' perspective, ecofeminism has also chimed with post-colonial challenges to the 'Western' project of development itself (Saunders, 2002). Tomalin shows that whilst the criticisms of ecofeminism that have emanated from materialist perspectives on gender, environment and development have been important for puncturing the essentialism that may blight ecofeminist analyses (for example, Jackson, 1993a, 1993b; Leach, 2007), care must be taken not to jettison broader considerations of religion and religious identities from debates over gender, environment and natural resource management. In a conceptual and reflective discussion, Tomalin identifies a growing return to issues of religion within development studies generally, in part associated with a renewed interest on the part of Western governments and donors that may be motivated by wider geopolitical concerns. She outlines a possible research agenda for religion, gender and the environment that firstly uncovers how religious values may define and sustain gender roles and norms shaping control over resources, and secondly, that critically considers the ways in which religious attachment and participation in faith communities may serve as a source of social capital for collective action in the realm of natural resource management.

Together, the individual contributions to the book weave a multilayered and critical perspective on the intersection between gender, environment and natural resource management in Asia that speak within and across the three themes outlined in this chapter. Our aim is to explore gendered responses to shifting configurations of resource access and control wrought through processes associated with neo-liberalism and political decentralization in the region, through a combination of strong conceptual argument and empirical material drawn from a variety of geographical settings. There are many more stories to be told, and we hope that this book goes some way to open debate in this area at a time when a revitalized feminist political ecology is being articulated and as wider political economies of natural resource governance in Asia invite a vigorous analysis of gender across multiple sites and scales.

Notes

1   These narratives are derived from Vandana Shiva's (1989) use of the Chipko Movement in India to demonstrate the vanguard role of rural women in environmental protection. Both factual and conceptual assumptions have been put into question by a special collection of journal papers in the *Journal of Peasant Studies* (vol 25, no 4, 1998). The same iconization was applied to northern upland women in the Philippines who supposedly disrobed before a group of engineers to protest the construction of a dam in 1974.

References

Agarwal, B. (1992) 'The gender and environment debate: Lessons from India', *Feminist Studies* 18 (1): 119–158

Agarwal, B. (1994) *A Field of One's Own: Gender and Land Rights in South Asia*, Cambridge: Cambridge University Press

Agarwal, B. (1997). 'Gender, environment and poverty interlinks: Regional variations and temporal shifts in rural India, 1971–1991', *World Development* 25 (1): 23–52

Agarwal, B. (2001) 'Participatory exclusions, community forestry and gender: An analysis for South Asia and a conceptual framework', *World Development* 29: 1623–1648

Agarwal, B. (2003) 'Gender and land rights revisited: Exploring new prospects via the state, family and market', *Journal of Agrarian Change* 3 (1/2): 184–224

Agrawal, A. and C. Gibson (2001) 'Introduction: The role of community in natural resource conservation'. In A. Agrawal and C. Gibson (eds) *Communities and the Environment: Ethnicity, Gender and the State in Community-Based Conservation*, New Brunswick: Rutgers University Press, pp1–31

Brunt, D. (1992) *Mastering the Struggle: Gender, Actors and Agrarian Change in a Mexican Ejido*, Amsterdam: CEDLA Publications

Butler, J. (1990) *Gender Trouble: Feminism and the Subversion of Identity*, London: Routledge

Butler, J. (1994) 'Gender as performance: An interview with Judith Butler', *Radical Philosophy* 67: 32–39

Butler, J. (2004) *Undoing Gender*, London: Routledge

Carney, J. (1996) 'Converting the wetlands: Engendering the environment: The intersection of gender with agrarian change'. In R. Peet and M. Watts (eds) *Liberation Ecologies: Environment, Development, Social Movements*, London: Routledge, pp165–187

Chatterjee, P. (2002) 'Ethnographic acts: Writing women and other political fields'. In K. Saunders (ed.) *Feminist Post-Development Thought: Rethinking Modernity, Post-Colonialism and Representation*, London: Zed Books, pp243–262

Cleaver, F. (2003) 'Reinventing institutions: Bricolage and the social embeddedness of natural resource management'. In T. A. Benjaminsen and C. Lund (eds) *Securing Land Rights in Africa*, London: Frank Cass, pp11–30

Colfer, C. J. P. (ed.) (2005) *The Equitable Forest: Diversity, Community and Resource Management*, Washington DC: Resources for the Future

Cornwall, A. (2003) 'Whose voices? Whose choices? Reflections on gender and participatory development', *World Development* 31: 1325–1342

Cornwall. A. (2007) 'Revisiting the 'gender agenda', *IDS Bulletin* 38 (2): 69–78

Cornwall, A., E. Harrison and A. Whitehead (2007) 'Introduction: Feminisms in development: Contradictions, contestations and challenges'. In A. Cornwall, E. Harrison and A. Whitehead (eds), *Feminisms in Development: Contradictions, Contestations and Challenges*, London: Zed Books, pp1–20

Cranney, B. (2001) *Local Environment and Lived Experience: The Mountain Women of Himachal Pradesh*, New Delhi: Sage

Crewe, E. and E. Harrison (1998) *Whose Development? An Ethnography of Aid*, London and New York: Zed Books

Dankelman, I. and J. Davidson (eds) (1988) *Women and Environment in the Third World: Alliance for the Future*, London: Earthscan

de Bruijn, M., I. van Halsema and H. van den Hombergh (1997) 'Gender, land use and environmental management: Analysing trends and diversity'. In M. de Bruijn, I. van Halsema and H. van den Hombergh (eds) *Gender and Land Use, Diversity in Environmental Practices*, Amsterdam: Thela Publishers, pp1–8

Deere, C. D. (1995) 'What difference does gender make? Rethinking peasant studies', *Feminist Economics* 1 (1): 53–72

DGIS (1990) *Women, Energy, Forestry and Environment*, Sector Paper Women and Development No. 4, The Hague: Directorate General for International Cooperation, Ministry of Foreign Affairs, The Netherlands

Elmhirst, R. (2001) 'Resource struggles and the politics of place in North Lampung, Indonesia', *Singapore Journal of Tropical Geography* 22 (3): 284–306

Elmhirst, R. (2002) 'Daughters and displacement: Migration dynamics in an Indonesian transmigration area', *Journal of Development Studies* 38 (5): 138–166

Elson, D. (2002) 'Gender justice, human rights and neo-liberal economic policies'. In M. Molyneux and S. Razavi (eds) *Gender Justice, Development and Rights*, Oxford: Oxford University Press, pp78–114

FAO (1989) *Women in Community Forestry: A Field Guide for Project Design and Implementation*, Rome: UN Food and Agriculture Organization

Feldstein, H. and S. Poats (eds) (1989) *Working Together: Gender Analysis in Agriculture*, West Hartford: Kumarian Press

Fortmann, L. (1996) 'Gendered knowledge: Rights and space in two Zimbabwe villages: Reflections on methods and findings'. In D. Rocheleau, B. Thomas-Slayter and E. Wangari (eds) *Feminist Political Ecology: Global Lives and Local Experiences*, London: Routledge, pp211–223

Fortmann, L. and D. Rocheleau (1984) 'Women and agroforestry: Four myths and three case studies', *Agroforestry Systems* 2: 253–272

Fraser, N. (2004) 'To interpret the world and to change it: An interview with Nancy Fraser', *Signs* 29: 1103–1124

Goetz, A. M. and R. S. Gupta (1996) 'Who takes credit? Gender, power and control over loan use in rural credit programmes in Bangladesh', *World Development* 24: 45–63

Green, C., S. Joekes and M. Leach (1998) 'Questionable links: Approaches to gender in environmental research and policy'. In C. Jackson and R. Pearson (eds) *Feminist Visions of Development: Gender Analysis and Policy*, London: Routledge, pp259–283

Guijt, I. and M. K. Shah (1998) *The Myth of Community: Gender Issues in Participatory Development*, London: Intermediate Technology Publications

Harris, L. (2006) 'Irrigation, gender, and social geographies of the changing waterscapes of southeastern Anatolia', *Environment and Planning D: Society and Space* 24: 187–213

Howard, P. (ed.) (2003) *Women & Plants: Gender Relations in Biodiversity Management and Conservation*, London: Zed Books

Ireson, C. (1997) 'Women's forest work in Laos'. In C. Sachs (ed.) *Women Working in the Environment*, New York: Taylor and Francis, pp15–29

Jackson, C. (1993a) 'Doing what comes naturally? Women and environment in development', *World Development* 21 (12): 1947–1963

Jackson, C. (1993b) 'Environmentalisms and gender interests in the Third World', *Development and Change* 24: 649–677

Jackson, C. (2003) 'Gender analysis of land: Beyond land rights for women', *Journal of Agrarian Change* 3 (4): 453–480

Jackson, C. (2006) 'Feminism spoken here: Epistemologies for interdisciplinary development research', *Development and Change* 37 (3): 525–547

Jarosz, L. (1997) 'Women as rice sharecroppers in Madagascar'. In C. Sachs (ed.), *Women Working in the Environment*, New York: Taylor and Francis, pp127–138

Jewitt, S. (2002) *Environment, Knowledge and Gender: Local Development in India's Jharkhand*, Aldershot: Ashgate

Joekes, S., C. Green and M. Leach (1996). *Integrating Gender into Environmental Research and Policy*, IDS Working Paper 27, Brighton: Institute of Development Studies, University of Sussex

Kabeer, N. (2005). 'Gender equality and women's empowerment: A critical analysis of the third Millennium Development Goal', *Gender and Development* 13 (1): 13–24

Kurian, P. (2000) *Engendering the Environment? Gender in the World Bank's Environmental Policies*, Aldershot: Ashgate

Lawson, V. (2007) *Making Development Geography*, London: Hodder Arnold

Leach, M. (1992) 'Gender and the environment: Traps and opportunities', *Development in Practice* 2 (1): 12–22

Leach, M. (1994) *Rainforest Relations: Gender and Resource Use Among the Mende of Gola, Sierra Leone*, Edinburgh: Edinburgh University Press

Leach, M. (2007) 'Earth mother myths and other ecofeminist fables: How a strategic notion rose and fell', *Development and Change* 38 (1): 67–85

Leach, M. and C. Green (1997). 'Gender and environmental history: From representations of women and nature to gender analysis of ecology and politics', *Environment and History* 3 (3): 343–370

Li, T. M. (2007a) 'Practices of assemblage and community forest management', *Economy and Society* 36 (2): 263–293

Li, T. M. (2007b) *The Will to Improve: Governmentality, Development and the Practice of Politics*, Durham, NC: Duke University Press

Marchand, M. and A. Runyan (eds) (2000) *Gender and Global Restructuring*, London: Routledge

Mawdsley, E. (2004) 'India's middle classes and the environment', *Development and Change* 35 (1): 79–103

McIlwaine, C. and K. Datta (2003) 'From feminizing to engendering development', *Gender, Place and Culture* 10: 369–382

Meinzen-Dick, R. S., L. R. Brown, H. S. Feldstein and A. R. Quisumbing (1997) 'Gender and property rights: An overview', *World Development* 25 (8): 1299–1302

Meinzen-Dick, R. and M. Z. Zwarteveen (1998) 'Gender participation in water management: Issues and illustrations from water users' associations in South Asia', *Agriculture and Human Values* 15: 337–345

Meynen, W. and M. Doornbos (2004) 'Decentralizing natural resource management: A recipe for sustainability and equity?', *European Journal of Development Research* 16 (1): 235–254

Mohanty, C. T. (1988) 'Under Western eyes: Feminist scholarship and colonial discourses', *Feminist Review* 30: 61–88

Molyneux, M. (1985) 'Mobilization without emancipation? Women's interests, the state, and revolution in Nicaragua', *Feminist Studies* 11 (2): 227–254

Molyneux, M. (2004) 'The chimera of success', *IDS Bulletin* 35: 112–116

Molyneux, M. and S. Razavi (2005) 'Beijing Plus Ten: An ambivalent record on gender justice', *Development and Change* 36 (6): 983–1010

Momsen, J. (2007) 'Gender and agrobiodiversity: Introduction to the special issue', *Singapore Journal of Tropical Geography* 28: 1–6

Moser, C. (1993) *Gender Planning and Development: Theory, Practice and Training*, London: Routledge

Mosse, D. (1994) 'Authority, gender and knowledge: Theoretical reflections on the practice of participatory rural appraisal', *Development and Change* 25 (3): 497–526

Mosse, D. (2006) 'Collective action, common property and social capital in South India: An anthropological commentary', *Economic Development and Cultural Change* 54 (3): 685–724

Nagar, R., V. Lawson, L. McDowell and S. Hanson (2002) 'Locating globalization: Feminist (re)readings of the subjects and spaces of globalization', *Economic Geography* 78 (3): 285–306

Nightingale, A. (2006) 'The nature of gender: Work, gender, and environment', *Environment and Planning D: Society and Space* 24: 165–185

Osella, F. and K. Gardner (2004) *Migration, Modernity and Social Transformation in South Asia*, New Delhi: Sage

Radcliffe, S. A. (2006). 'Development and geography: Gendered subjects in development processes and interventions', *Progress in Human Geography* 30 (4): 524–532

Rankin, K. N. (2001) 'Governing development: Neoliberalism, microcredit and rational economic woman', *Economy and Society* 30 (1): 18–37

Rao, B. (1991) *Dominant Constructions of Women and Nature in the Social Science Literature*, CES/CNS Pamphlet 2, Santa Cruz: University of California

Razavi, S. (ed.) (2002) *Gender and Agrarian Change under Neoliberalism*, West Hartford: Kumarian Press

Razavi, S. (2003) 'Introduction: Agrarian change, gender and land rights', *Journal of Agrarian Change* 3 (1/2): 2–32

Rathgeber, E. M. (1990) 'WID, WAD, GAD: Trends in research and practice', *Journal of Developing Areas* 24: 489–502

Resurreccion, B. (1999) 'Engineering the Philippine uplands: Gender, ethnicity and scientific forestry in the U.S. colonial period', *Bulletin of Concerned Asian Scholars* 30 (1): 13–30

Resurreccion, B. and Ha Thi Van Khanh (2007) 'Able to come and go: Reproducing gender in female rural–urban migration in the Red River Delta', *Population, Space and Place* 32 (3): 211–224

Rigg, J. D. (2006) 'Land, farming, livelihoods and poverty: Rethinking the links in the rural South', *World Development* 34 (1): 180–202

Rocheleau, D. (1991). 'Gender, ecology and the science of survival', *Agriculture and Human Values* 8 (1): 156–165

Rocheleau, D., B. Thomas-Slayter and E. Wangari (eds) (1996) *Feminist Political Ecology: Global Issues and Local Experiences*, London: Routledge

Rodda, A. (1991) *Women and the Environment*, London: Zed Books

Sachs, C. (ed.) (1996) *Gendered Fields: Rural Women, Agriculture, and Environment*, Boulder, Colorado: Westview Press

Saunders, K. (2002) 'Towards a deconstructive post-development criticism'. In K. Saunders (ed.) *Feminist Post-Development Thought: Rethinking Modernity, Post-Colonialism and Representation*, London: Zed Books, pp1–38

Schroeder, R. A. (1999) *Shady Practices: Agroforestry and Gender Politics in The Gambia*, Berkeley: University of California Press

Shiva, V. (1989) *Staying Alive: Women, Ecology and Survival in India*, London: Zed Books

Sontheimer, S. (ed.) (1991) *Women and the Environment: A Reader*, London: Earthscan Publications

Sturgeon, N. (1999). 'Ecofeminist appropriations and transnational environmentalisms', *Identities: Global Studies in Culture and Power* 6 (2/3): 255–279

Tinker, I. (1997) 'Women and community forestry in Nepal: Expectations and realities'. In C. Sachs (ed.) *Women Working in the Environment*, New York: Taylor and Francis, pp277–291

Tsing, A. L., J. P. Brosius and C. Zerner (2005) 'Introduction: Raising questions about communities and conservation'. In A. L. Tsing, J. P. Brosius and C. Zerner (eds) *Communities and Conservation: Histories and Politics of Community Based Natural Resource Management*, Lanhan: Altamira Press, pp1–36

UN-ESCAP (2004) *Review of Regional Implementation of Beijing Platform for Action and its Outcomes*, Bangkok: UN Economic and Social Commission for Asia Pacific

van Koppen, B. and S. Mahmud (1996) *Women and Water-Pumps in Bangladesh: The Impact of Participation in Irrigation Groups on Women's Status*, London: Intermediate Technology Publications

Villareal, M. M. (1992) 'The poverty of practice: Power, gender and intervention from an actor-oriented perspective. In N. Long and A. Long (eds) *Battlefields of Knowledge: The Interlocking of Theory and Practice in Social Research and Development*, London: Routledge, pp247–267

von Benda-Beckmann, K., M. de Bruijn, H. van Dijk, G. Hesseling, B. van Koppen and L. Res (1997) *Women's Rights to Land and Water: Literature Review*, The Hague: The Special Program Women and Development, Department of International Cooperation (DGIS), Ministry of Foreign Affairs, The Government of The Netherlands

Wieringa, S. E. (1994) 'Women's interests and empowerment: Gender planning reconsidered', *Development and Change* 25 (6): 829–848

Zwarteveen, M. Z. (1998) 'Identifying gender aspects of new irrigation management policies', *Agriculture and Human Values* 15 (4): 301–312

Part 1

Contextualizing Gender and Natural Resource Governance in Neo-Liberal Times

Chapter 2

Gender, *Doi Moi* and Coastal Resource Management in the Red River Delta, Vietnam[1]

Hue Le Thi Van

Introduction

In Vietnam, economic reforms, known as *doi moi*, were introduced in 1986, and included the elimination of the state monopoly on agriculture and forestry, the introduction of short-term land use rights, and the encouragement of privatization and market liberalization. The reforms have dramatically improved living conditions in Vietnam and have been called 'one of the greatest success stories in economic development' (ADB et al, 2003, p11). It has been argued, however, that the *doi moi* economic reforms, while opening up economic opportunities for many, have not benefited women and men equally, and have resulted in an increasingly stratified distribution of income (Luong, 2003; Le, 2004). Others argue that rising inequality is associated with non-agricultural activities such as commercial aquaculture in lowland coastal north Vietnam, particularly where the distribution of land has been relatively equitable (Adger, 1999; Lutrell, 2002; Chant, 2004).

Using the case of a village in northern Vietnam, this chapter examines the ways in which policy reforms and other factors have affected villagers' management of mangrove forests, and how women and men have responded to national policy reforms. I argue that the *doi moi* economic reforms, while opening up economic opportunities for many, have not benefited the whole community. Specifically, women-headed households and women and girls more generally have been the most adversely affected, and they have become victims of both environmental degradation and the privatization process.

The analysis pays explicit attention to several areas: first, the different practices of women and men in resource use and management; second, changes in access to and control over mangrove resources; and third, the conflicts between those who have been able to capture nearly exclusive access and those who have lost access as a result of the privatization of coastal aquaculture resources. It explores how differing levels of access to and control over mangrove resources have caused inequality in household incomes, while the distribution of agricultural land has remained relatively equitable among households.

The chapter begins with an overview of the study site, and then provides a discussion of mangrove management in Giao Lac village. Next, it examines impacts of economic reforms and the Danish Red Cross Mangrove Plantation project on shrimp and clam management as well as marine product collection. The following section investigates how social differentiation has affected the ways in which different social groups defined by gender, class, age and social status use and manage mangrove resources within the community. It also examines inequality between income earned by women and men from the mangroves and intertidal mudflats. The concluding section suggests alternatives for Giao Lac's mangrove management, a mechanism that would promote social equity as well as productivity and sustainability.

The study area

Giao Lac village (see Figure 2.1) is a predominantly Roman Catholic coastal community. It is located in the Giao Thuy district of Nam Dinh province, which lies at the mouth of the Red River in northern Vietnam. The village land covers an area of about 744 hectares, of which 535 hectares is agricultural land. Its population during the period of this study (2000–2001) was about 9000. It is an agricultural community, farming mostly rice, but also engaging in animal husbandry and fisheries. It is bordered to the south by a dike, an intertidal area and the South China Sea. The dike is almost 3 kilometres (km) long. The intertidal area is more than 600 hectares (ha), of which 400ha have been planted with the mangroves *Kandelia candel, Sonneratia caseolaris* and *Rhizophora apiculata* (Phan and Hoang, 1993). There are also five shrimp ponds. Four of the five ponds and all of the intertidal area belong to the district, which, in turn, mandates the village to administer the ponds and the mudflats.

Giao Lac village has a long and rich history. Older members of the community have experienced life under three regimes: the French colonial government, the Japanese occupation and independent Vietnam. They have lived through the great famine of 1945, the war of liberation, post-independence land reforms, the struggle in the south to unify the country and the American bombing of the north, the post-1975 period of intensive collectivization and, more recently, the period of *doi moi* reform.

The study involved both library research and ethnographic fieldwork in Giao Lac village. Library research covered the historical development of Giao Lac and

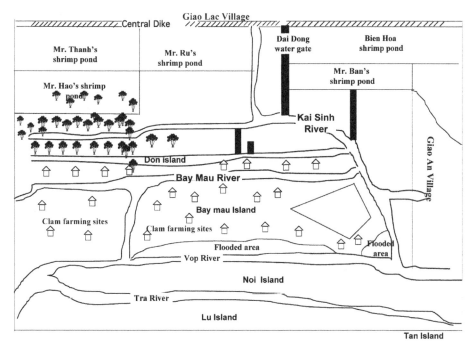

Source: Interview with Mr Tien at the People's Committee of Giao Lacin, 2001

Figure 2.1 *Mangrove and the intertidal areas of Giao Lac village*

the modes of access to and control over resources that changed during each historical period. The field research included the collection of household annual income and expenditure, household assets, houses and resource use and management in the village in a survey of 32 households randomly selected through semi-structured interviews with the male or female head of each household sampled. In the survey, the household was the unit of analysis since I wanted to examine the relationships of resource use and management within households that involved individual women and men. Also important was how gender relations within the household affected decisions on divisions of labour, budget management and access to and control over productive resources and products. In addition, interviews with local government and cooperative officials in Giao Lac, and with district and provincial officials provided insights into local implementation of national policy on land, specifically mangroves, the institutional setting and local power relations.

History of mangrove management in Giao Lac village

Giao Lac was established in 1843. Approximately 100ha of mangrove existed at the time. The mangrove included several tree species of 3 metres (m) or taller, including *Kandelia candel, Aegiceras corniculatum* and *Avicennia lanata* (Phan and

Hoang, 1993). From 1884 until 1945, the French colonial administration had authority over the mangrove forests, but no one was assigned to guard the forests. In 1939, the colonial administration supervised the construction of the central dike in Nam Dinh province. There were mangrove forests along the dike. There was a profusion of bees, fish, crabs, shrimp, snails and bivalves in the mangrove forests. Villagers collected bird eggs, crabs, fish and shrimp, and honey from the forest, either to eat or to sell at the Dai Dong market. According to elderly people, local people also collected firewood, but only the dry branches, both for domestic consumption and for sale. Although there was no law prohibiting forest exploitation and management, no one cut mangrove trees for firewood and no one shot birds for food. These accounts indicate the prevailing local practices of resource conservation.

The pre-colonial period in Giao Lac was characterized by a class-structured, kinship-centred and male-oriented hierarchy. This class-based and gender-based hierarchical framework dominated the village in all aspects from the household to the communal levels. Only males aged 18 and above were registered and allocated land. Women and children were not granted any land, because they were not registered adult men (*dinh*). Furthermore, women and girls were excluded from all institutions in the village, including the *giap*, an age-group organization within the village. They did not have any right to participate in any discussions of village affairs, to vote or to attend the village feasts. As a result, and despite their significant labour contribution, they were dependent on the registered male members of the family.

During the colonial period, village households varied greatly in wealth and status. During the French era, those who had several *mau* (a unit of area equal to 3600 square metres, m²) of land were better off, and those who had several dozen *mau* of land were considered wealthy. Men were engaged in collecting marine products. Because women and children were not granted any land, women had to go to the forests in the intertidal area to collect firewood and other marine products, all of which were sold at the local market to buy rice to support themselves and their families. Women were also in charge of selling their husbands' produce at the local market. They worked longer hours than men and took part in most production activities of their households. In addition, in a Confucian society, women were governed by the 'three obediences' (Luong, 2003). When they were girls, they were expected to obey their fathers. After they got married, they owed obedience to their husbands. Finally, when they were widowed, they were expected to obey their eldest sons. A man also had the right to have concubines. Wives and concubines were not given land, but they were required to contribute labour to their husband's family. Mrs Ngon recounted her experience:

> *I did not have any right to my husband's property. Instead, I was the property of my father or my husband. Women were bought and sold as part of that property. We were not allowed to go to school. We were prohibited from ownership and inheritance. Many women were beaten by*

their husbands. As a result, we were confined to the private sphere and household duties.

During the French colonial period, women had access to wage work. They were hired by the colonizers to construct the dike, but they were paid less than men. During the period of the resistance war (1946–1954), the villagers were severely exploited by the Japanese and suffered from shortages of rice, which later grew to become a famine. Landlords and rich peasants owned land, so no one from their families died of hunger during the famine. The highest death rate was among women and children. Women suffered the most. They worked very hard to earn a little cash to buy rice or to collect wild vegetables and mangrove fruits to support their families. Many women died during pregnancy.

After the August 1945 revolution, most landlords fled. New organizations, such as the Farmers' Association, were formed. In 1949, the French returned and supported a Catholic-led insurrection against the Vietnamese government. Houses of Buddhist families were burnt, and many relied on timber from mangrove forests to rebuild their houses when they returned. The new French administration promoted the harvesting of mangrove trees for firewood. The heads of villages granted timber concessions to outsiders who then hired local people to cut the forests for firewood. By and large, women were engaged in firewood collection. Buddhist women whose husbands were in hiding as professional soldiers or guerrillas were also engaged in collecting marine products to sell at the local market to buy rice for their families. At the same time, many women took part in clandestine activities, such as hiding Viet Minh cadres and digging tunnels for soldiers and villagers so they could hide from the French and the Catholics. Some women even served as secret agents, and some were arrested and tortured. In November 1953, the Viet Minh evicted the French from Giao Lac. In 1954, the entire area was liberated from French rule, and many Catholic people went to the south of Vietnam.

There was, however, no returning to the former ethic of mangrove conservation. Land reform in Giao Lac began in mid-1955 and was completed in mid-1956. All landlords and rich and middle-class peasants had to return to their land in the village if they had more than five *sao* (a unit of area equal to 360m^2) of land per head. For the first time since the village was established in 1843, everyone was allocated an equal amount of land. As mentioned earlier, women had not previously been allowed to participate in village administration. They had been excluded from all activities in the village. For the first time in their lives, they were now allocated land. This dramatically changed production relations in the village. In 1959, the first experimental cooperative was established in Giao Lac. High-level cooperatives were established and individual ownership was eliminated. All rice paddies and draught animals and other means of production contributed by villagers became common property and were managed by the cooperative. The amount each member worked for one day was measured in points. Male members received ten points and female members received eight points.

During the following 20-year period, the village managed the forests on behalf of the district. The local people were not allowed to go to the forests as before. They were told to protect the mangroves, which would in turn protect the dike, which would in turn protect their property. The village militia unit was mandated by the village to protect the mangroves while preserving peace and order in the coastal area, and it prevented firewood collection in the mangrove forests. However, people clandestinely cut big mangrove trees for firewood. It was reported that only men cut trees, while women collected dry branches. This role changed during the most difficult time under collective agriculture when villagers were generally excluded from the forests and the majority had trouble making ends meet. In this way, the government actually excluded the very people who knew best how to conserve the resources through their own conventions. The resulting depletion of the mangroves was Giao Lac's very own tragedy of the commons. Mrs Khau recounted her experience as a firewood collector at the time:

> *We did not like those who stopped us and confiscated our firewood. We were wondering how dry branches could protect the dike. If we did not collect them, the wind and the waves would carry them away. Firewood collectors like us worked very hard. It took us half of a day to collect a bundle of firewood, which weighed 15–20kg. It was so muddy in the forests that it was very difficult to walk with a bundle of firewood on your shoulder. When we carried the firewood to the dike, village cadres stopped us and confiscated our firewood, although we just collected dry branches. Both Catholic and Buddhist collectors had firewood confiscated from them. We went home with our empty hands after having spent half of a day working hard in the forests. We were very angry. But we could not do anything about it. We were like small fish and they were like big fish. Big fish always eat small fish. At the time, if someone had beaten us we would have suffered. Many collectors were brushing away their tears, while walking away and wondering what their children would have for the next meal.*

During the Vietnam–US war between 1964 and 1975, most young men joined the army, leaving the women and children home. As a result, women were engaged in ploughing rice fields, an activity that they had never been involved in before when men were at home, in addition to pulling up rice seedlings and transplantation. They even carried rice seedlings and paddy with a shoulder pole, another activity that traditionally they had never done. They became the heads of households and at the same time fulfilled their obligations as wives and daughters-in-law. They also encouraged husbands and sons to join the army when necessary. In such an exciting atmosphere of participating in combat, many young girls aged 18–20 in the village volunteered to be Vanguard Youth Women. Although they were not recruited to be professional soldiers, they were trained to be nurses and were involved in military support activities.

In the village, women were recruited for political leadership, which had never happened before in the history of Giao Lac, as other studies have documented (see Turley, 1972; White, 1982; Woodside, 1989). Previously, women were not allowed to register as *dinh*, and were therefore not allocated land. They were excluded from all activities in the village and they never had a chance to go to school. During the war with the US, Mrs Bong was elected as secretary of the Giao Lac Party Cell, and she later became the chairperson of the village, serving in the Party Executive Committee for 25 years. Other women were assigned to lead Giao Lac's Women's Union and production brigades. The village women took care of both public and family affairs while engaged in labour production equal to that of men (see also White, 1982). This pleased both those who were fighting at the battlefront and those who were at home. The song 'Women of Three Responsibilities' (*Phu nu ba dam dang*) was composed at the time to praise those women. In addition, the women were still making a living collecting firewood and marine produce.

In 1962, in response to ocean encroachment and the land reclamation policy of the district, Giao Lac officials opened up Bien Hoa pond, mobilizing local people to clear the mangrove area of 54ha lying between the pond and ocean. Sea grasses were planted in former mangrove habitat for weaving floor mats for export to the former Soviet Union and countries in Eastern European. However, by 1986–1987, this estuary margin habitat had become more saline, exports had weakened and mat production was abandoned. Villagers then turned to the more lucrative enterprise of shrimp farming.

In 1986, the government of Vietnam started its programme of economic reforms known as *doi moi*. In the late 1980s, a household-based economy increasingly displaced the cooperative-based economy (Le and Rambo, 1999). The government of Vietnam shifted responsibility for management of natural resources away from village cooperatives into the hands of individual farm households (Nguyen Cuc, 1995; Nguyen Huong, 2002). In 1988, each household received an allocation of agricultural land based on the number of members (1.2 *sao* per household member). Household heads, the majority of whom were men, signed the 'red book', documents that provided households with the right to use the land until 2013. Women did not receive individual rights to land, which were accorded only to men. Women were thus disadvantaged by legal policies regarding their ownership of resources such as land (Ha, 1997; Tran and Le, 1997).

Impact of economic reform: New institutions for shrimp and clam management and marine product collection

Shrimp management

During the *doi moi* period, China became the biggest importer of northern Vietnam's marine products. In Giao Lac, four additional shrimp ponds were constructed by the district. Households or entrepreneurs bid publicly to lease a shrimp pond, with five to ten households cooperating to manage a pond. Typically, each pond generated profits of at least 140 million Vietnamese Dong (VND) per year (US$10,000 in 2000). Although the bidding process was open to everyone, only the rich, who had sufficient capital, labour, management skills and access to political power, were able to participate in this process. Only the older Bien Hoa pond was managed locally by the Giao Lac Cooperative.

Only men are involved in shrimp aquaculture. According to shrimp pond owners, shrimp farming is a risky business and requires large amounts of capital, so women are unable to participate. Shrimp farming created a few full-time jobs for security personnel. Some poor men were recruited to guard shrimp ponds, earning VND150,000 (over $10) per month. Women were not hired for security work. They also did not have access to commercial coastal aquaculture resources and were totally excluded from shrimp farming. Women were only hired to collect seaweed for shrimp pond owners.

Clam farming

Prior to 1990, all villagers had access to the mudflats. In 1990, people in Giao Xuan village, Giao Lac's neighbouring village, began farming clams by putting in place a system of nets in the intertidal area. They were the first people to start this business, as they had connections with Chinese traders who sold clams to the bivalve markets in China. In the past, clams were so cheap that people substituted them for rice. Now clams have become a valuable commodity, about five times more expensive than in the past. One kilogram of clams was worth VND5000-6000 (36–42 cents) during the course of this fieldwork. Both central and local governments have encouraged clam farming, for example, National Decree 773-TTg (Orientation–Forecast–Prospect, 1995) stipulates that open coastal areas can be used for shrimp, crab and clam farming. In Giao Lac, there were only 15 farming sites in 1993. When this research was carried out in 2000–2001, there were 94 sites. Like shrimp farmers, all clam farmers were men, with the majority coming from Giao Xuan and the rest from Giao Lac.

Many people have become rich from farming bivalves and trading coastal products. Collectors, on the other hand, often suffer the impacts of price fluctuations. People began to acquire the use right to farm clams by setting up their own nets and claiming the mudflats as their own. The village officials measured the areas that the people claimed as their farming sites, and the farmers paid rent to the Village People's Committee based on the area measured by the officials.

This process of claiming land excluded poor and women-headed households, groups that had no access to productive resources such as the newly privatized coastal aquaculture and capital resources. Poor women and girls had to work on other people's mudflats and shrimp ponds, while the rich worked on their own land. Some collectors were hired to collect clams with somebody else's nets, and earned VND10,000 ($0.7) per day. Conflicts between those who had nets and those who had lost access to clams due to the privatization increased. In December 2000, the owner of a clam farming area in Giao Xuan beat a pregnant woman unconscious when he found her collecting clams in an area that he claimed as his property. By leasing previously common resources and having access to implements such as nets to collect marine products, well-off villagers have appropriated these resources and disenfranchised the poor.

When asked why people from Giao Xuan could come and farm clams on Giao Lac's intertidal mudflats, district officials replied that whatever land is situated beyond the dike, including the mudflats, belongs to the district, so Giao Lac does not have the right to exclude outsiders. After a year or two, people in Giao Lac learned from the Giao Xuan people how to farm clams. The intertidal area of 350ha, to which access had previously been open to all villagers, effectively became the property of those who had enough capital to invest in clam farming. The whole area was covered with nets and clam watch-houses.

The poor once again were excluded. To collect bivalves, they had to go further to 'unclaimed' coastal areas. Ten or 15 people would together hire a motorboat and spend a long day in distant mudflats, spending part of the money they earned to pay for the boat. Those who could not afford the boat had to stay at home, and therefore were dependent on wet rice production alone, which typically provided enough subsistence for only seven to eight months per year. This made poor people's lives even more difficult. Giao Lac was not exceptional in this respect. A similar situation was also observed in Nghia Hung district of Nam Dinh province (see Kleinen, 2002).

Danish Red Cross Mangrove Plantation Project

In 1997, the Danish Red Cross initiated a project in Giao Lac to plant mangroves for the protection of sea dikes and for the creation of jobs for a number of villagers. The district cleared the clam-farming site on Trong Island and enclosed an area of more than 400ha for mangrove plantation. As planned, one main household and another three supplemental households were to be chosen to each plant 5ha of new mangroves. To qualify, the district required that the main household had to be a 'poor' household with sufficient labour. The other three households were to be selected by the Giao Lac Red Cross and local leaders. For each hectare of mangrove planted, a group was to be paid VND360,000 ($26). In reality, few poor households were actually selected to participate. The majority were middle or upper-middle income households and were typically the relatives or friends of the heads of hamlets. The newly planted mangroves spawned shrimp and clams, which were potential sources of income for all the villagers. In practice, the rich and the upper-middle class households earned more from the mangroves and the mudflats than the middle and poor classes, as they had labour and management skills, the capital needed to invest and, more importantly, access to political power.

Differential control and access of resources

It appears that *doi moi* has not solved the problem of resource degradation and over-exploitation and that villagers have not benefited equally or equitably. Rapid changes in local land use systems, ownership, management practices of mangrove resources and institutional arrangements in response to *doi moi* appear to have weakened the livelihoods of poor households and marginalized women in particular, while opening up economic opportunities for others, especially well-off households and men. *Doi moi*, in effect, has built on and reinforced the older forms of social heterogeneity, and power and resource differences within communities (Sheridan, 1988; Durham and Painter, 1995; Leach et al, 1999). Differential relationships of power within and among communities mediate the exploitation, distribution and control of natural resources. People's relations within communities involve conflicts over access to the commons and over the definition of property rights and law and competition (McCay and Acheson, 1987; Leach et al, 1995). Gender, age, wealth and class all influence the ways in which villagers use and manage mangrove resources in the community. The market liberalization period opened up new opportunities for households that had management and entrepreneurial skills and capital, and were ready to work hard and take risks. The change in macroeconomic structure facilitated an acceleration of the accumulation process, thus causing further differentiation between those who could grasp the emerging market opportunities and those who were unprepared to do so.

Differentiation in the harvesting of intertidal coastal products

This section examines household cash income earned from the mangroves and mangrove-related resources by four different groups of households. We look at the main factors that cause differentiation, such as capital, labour, management and entrepreneurial skills, and access to market centres and towns where the market economy has become more developed (White, 1989; Ngo, 1993).

Hamlet 7, one of 22 hamlets in Giao Lac village seemed to be representative, being of average size, average income status and close to the central dike. This hamlet had 70 households with a total population of 270 people. Viewed from the perspective of annual income, the 70 households stratified into four groups, consisting of 5 'rich', 17 upper-middle, 40 middle and 8 'poor' households based on the results of a wealth-ranking exercise.

Distribution of households by shrimp pond area

Table 2.1 shows the distribution of households according to the area of shrimp pond that different groups of households had for shrimp farming. Only three households in the rich group and two households in the upper-middle group had shrimp ponds. One household in the rich group had less than 1ha of shrimp ponds, while one household in the upper-middle group had 1–2.5ha. The table also shows that one rich household and one upper-middle household had 2.5–5ha of fishponds. In addition, one household of the rich group had more than 5ha of

Table 2.1 *Distribution of sample households by access leased to shrimp pond area in 2000*

Area (m²)	Rich (n = 5)	Upper middle (n = 10)	Middle (n = 10)	Poor (n = 7)
0	2	8	10	7
≤ 10,000	1	0	0	0
10,001–25,000	0	1	0	0
25,001–50,000	1	1	0	0

Source: Author's field survey, 2000–2001

Table 2.2 *Distribution of sample households by access to clam farming area in 2000*

Area (m²)	Rich (n = 5)	Upper middle (n = 10)	Middle (n = 10)	Poor (n = 7)
0	3	8	8	7
< 3000	0	0	0	0
3001–5000	1	1	0	0
5001–7000	1	1	1	0
> 7001–9000	0	0	0	0

Source: Author's field survey, 2000–2001

pond for shrimp farming. The middle and the poor groups of households could not muster the required combination of access to capital, labour and management skill needed to become shrimp farmers.

Distribution of households by area of clam farming

Table 2.2 shows that one rich household and one upper-middle income household had clam farming sites of between 0.3 and 0.5ha. The table also shows that one household in the rich group, one household in the upper-middle income group and one household in the middle-income group had clam farming sites of between 0.5 and 0.7ha. Meanwhile, one household in the middle group had an area of more than 0.9ha. The rich household sites were better than those of the upper-middle and middle households. According to clam farmers, the ideal clam farming soil is one mixed with sand. Poor households did not have any bivalve farming sites because they did not have start-up capital.

Household cash income from mangroves and mangrove-related resources

The results of the analysis of household cash income earned by the four groups of households from the mangroves and the mudflats are shown in Table 2.3. These include shrimp, bivalves, crabs, fish collected from the intertidal mudflats and farmed shrimp and clams from ponds and clam farming sites.

Table 2.3 *Mean cash income per household in each category from mangroves and mangrove-related resources in 2000*

Types of households	Income from mangroves and mangrove-related resources (million VND)
Rich	8.7 ($621)
Upper Middle	5.5 ($393)
Middle	1.7 ($121)

Note: Income gained from trading of coastal products is also included.
Source: Author's field survey, 2000–2001

Table 2.4 shows the amounts earned by each social group from specific sources.

Table 2.4 *Sources of household income from mangroves and mudflats in 2000*

Sources of income	Rich		Upper middle		Middle		Poor	
	VND m	%	VND m	%	VND m	%	VND m	%
Shrimp farming	29.5 ($2107)	31	30.0 ($2143)	41	0.0	0	0.0	0
Clam farming	9.7 ($693)	10	5.0 ($357)	7	4.0 ($286)	18	0.0	0
Trade of intertidal coastal products	46.4 ($3314)	49	16.8 ($1200)	23	5.0 ($357)	23	0.0	0
Collection of bivalves, fish, crabs	4.1 ($293)	4	19.8 ($1414)	27	12.6 ($900)	58	5.7 ($407)	89
Project assistance	6.0 ($429)	6.0	0.97 ($69)	1.1	0.05 ($3.6)	0.2	0.7 ($50)	11.0

Source: Author's field survey, 2000–2001

In 2000, rich households earned VND29.5 million from shrimp farming, accounting for more than 31 per cent of household income, while the upper-middle class households gained VND30 million, accounting for 41 per cent of household income from mangroves and mudflats. The rich earned VND9.7 million from clam farming, constituting almost 10 per cent of their household income, while the upper-middle income households earned VND5 million, accounting for 7 per cent of their household income, and the middle-income households VND4 million, comprising more than 18 per cent of their household income.

Table 2.4 shows that the poor were hardly engaged in mangrove- and mudflat-based activities in 2000. Lack of access to capital and lack of management experience were formidable barriers to entry that the assisting NGO had not anticipated in their planning process. Regarding bivalve, fish, shrimp and baby crab collection, the upper-middle income households earned the most

(VND19.8 million), accounting for 27 per cent of overall household income earned from mangrove-related resources.

Collecting bivalves, fish, shrimp and baby crab does not require capital resources or management skills, but does require labour, which is available among the upper-middle and middle-income households, so just four groups benefited from the mangrove plantation project. The rich earned VND6 million, or 6 per cent of their household income; the upper-middle income households earned VND970,000, accounting for a small proportion of their household income (less than two per cent), and the middle-income households gained VND50,000, or 0.2 per cent of their household income. The poor earned VND700,000, accounting for 11 per cent of their household income. One of the rich households had planted mangroves in the early 1990s to protect its shrimp pond dikes. When the Danish Red Cross Project started, the household was willing to give their mangroves to the project and it was then considered as one of the households planting mangroves, like any other poor household in the village, and therefore earned VND6 million ($429).

By contrast, middle-income households were typically hired by the upper-middle income households to plant mangrove trees for two days, and were paid VND50,000 ($3.6) to do so. In principle, the project was designed to provide the poor with opportunities to improve their living standards. In reality, few poor households were actually selected to participate. The majority of households benefiting from the project were the upper-middle or middle-income households, often the hamlet head's relatives and friends (although these households did not have sufficient labour and they had to hire poor households to do the work). One was paid between VND16,000 and 25,000 ($1.1–1.8) per day, instead of the VND30,000 ($2.1) set by the project. But as the poor had no alternative forms of income, they had little choice but to participate on those terms.

In summary, the rich earn more and the poor earn the least from mangrove and mangrove-related resources. The average rich household earned 14 times more than the average poor household from mangroves and mangrove-related resources. However, the poor depend relatively more on mangroves, as they don't have access to alternatives. The rich earned the most from the mangroves and the intertidal mudflats because they had capital resources, labour, and management and entrepreneurial skills.

Analysis of sources of income from the mangroves and the mudflats confirms an inequality in the distribution of household income. It also demonstrates that these sources of income widen existing levels of inequality within the hamlets and the commune. The next section examines inequality between income earned by women and men, and provides insights into how different social groups of households and gender may influence household income distribution.

Class and gender distribution of income earned from mangroves and intertidal mudflats

Among the sample households, only five were involved in the trade of marine products. In three of these, both husbands and wives were engaged in the trade. In one household, the husband transacted business with clients and sold the products. In the other two households, only the wives were traders, since their husbands suffered from health problems. One was a veteran who had been injured during the Vietnam–US war. He was deaf and therefore could not communicate effectively. The other had a mental disorder and had been on medication for a long time. The disabilities of two of the five husbands compelled their spouses to rely on available natural resources for economic survival and to generate income through trading coastal products.

On the surface, the work seemed to generate large profits and did not require them to work too hard. Based on household records, on average, a trader had to work between eight and ten hours a day. The traders' working hours depended very much on the tide. Most of the time, shrimp were caught late at night, between 10 p.m. and 3 a.m., with the shrimp delivered to the purchasing agent between 3 a.m. and 4 a.m., and the trader only arriving home at 5–6 a.m. Table 2.5 shows how the amounts earned from trading coastal products varied between women and men.

Table 2.5 *Income earned by different groups of women and men*

Gender	Activity	Total hours	Amount of cash
Men	Trading of shrimp	8–10	VND90,000 ($6.4)
Men	Trading of crabs	8	VND33,000 ($2.4)
Men	Trading of all coastal products	8–10	VND40,000 ($2.9)
Women	Trading of all coastal products	8–10	VND13,000 ($0.8)

Source: Author's field survey, 2000–2001

In Table 2.5, women's activities are aggregated, as women usually traded clams, crabs, fish and shrimp at the same time, using motorized boats and push nets. The table shows that women earned much less than their male counterparts. The reason was that exclusion from the most lucrative activity, shrimp trading, could not be compensated for by trading other coastal products. According to one trader, there were around a hundred local traders in Giao Thien, Giao An and Giao Lac villages. All of these traders were men, each of them having signed a contract with the owner of a shrimp pond. Women were excluded from this work, principally because it was more stable and generated more profits than trading in other coastal products.

As shown in Table 2.5, women earned much less than men, although they worked as hard and as long as men. Due to the persistence of the biases against women, influenced by prevailing patriarchal values in Giao Lac, shrimp farmers did not want to sign a contract with a woman. Consequently, women's businesses were unstable and depended very much on the catch of their clients, the majority of whom were collectors of marginal marine products rather than shrimp and crabs.

Table 2.6 shows the monthly income of women and men. Women earned much less per month than their male counterparts engaged in the same activities.

Table 2.6 *Monthly income earned by different groups of women and men*

Gender	Activity	Amount of cash
Men	Trading of shrimp	VND2.7 m ($193)
Men	Trading of all coastal products	VND1.2 m ($86)
Men	Trading of crabs	VND1.0 m ($71)
Women	Trading of all coastal products	VND0.4 m ($25)

Source: Author's field survey, 2000–2001

There are several reasons for the inequity in earned income. First, the persistence of patriarchal values within rural society, which positions women normatively in the private sphere, conditions both women's and men's responsibilities and consequently limits women's access to highly lucrative jobs. Women have smaller trading networks than men, and networks play an important role in trading of intertidal coastal products. A Vietnamese saying is, 'Selling requires friends and buying requires associations'. One rich male shrimp trader said:

> *Connections play a very important role in providing the valuable information on who farms shrimp and who buys shrimp as well. I learn a great deal from my circle of friends who are all men from different villages through their success stories and also from whom I could get access to sources of capital.*

Women were totally excluded from the network of male shrimp traders. When these traders met, they drank and told stories among themselves. Women were never present. Because they were excluded from these networks, women depended on their immediate kin-based networks, which in turn prevented them from interacting with shrimp traders from different villages. Second, without motorbikes to transport shrimp to the purchasing agent in a neighbouring village, women were further constrained. A motorbike costs as much as a middle-income household's total annual income, thus only households producing large surpluses can afford to purchase one. Women from middle-income and poor households sold their products to the local fish markets and neighbouring households.

This demonstrates that the *doi moi* process is not driven by a neutral market (Werner, 2002), but is socially embedded and is characterized by unequal gender relations. As Luong (2003) notes, during the renovation process, kinship relations became more male-oriented and the rising of the male-oriented kinship relationships is to the disadvantage of women.

Capital resources, labour, management and entrepreneurial skills, social networks, education and age were also factors differentiating households within the community. Analysis provides insights into how social differentiation has affected women in poorer households. Apart from gender and social capital, finance capital was considered another important factor in differentiating households. No one could borrow money from the Vietnam Bank for Agriculture, and shrimp farming was considered a risky occupation by the government. Farmers then had to mobilize capital through family connections or borrow money from local moneylenders.

At the time of the study, there were two big moneylenders in Giao Lac. They had relatives who were traders elsewhere in the country and from whom they received large sums to invest in money lending to earn interest. These moneylenders provided loans to shrimp farmers. Unlike the government, moneylenders believed that background and labour capacity played an important role in successful shrimp and clam farming. First, family bonds helped to mobilize capital resources crucial in shrimp farming. Second, family labour played an important role in shrimp pond construction, especially at the initial stage when capital input is stretched thinly and available capital is insufficient to hire labourers. In this way, they could save money and invest in the business. Lastly, pond shareholders preferred to work with siblings as a way of avoiding distrust and preserving unity in tough or slack periods. Women were excluded from these shareholder groups. They were hired only to collect seaweed and clams from the owners of shrimp ponds and clam beds.

Educational attainment also differentiated households in the village. The mean number of years in school was eight years among heads of rich households, seven years in upper-middle income households and six years in poor households. Somewhat surprisingly, middle-income households had the lowest mean number of years of school attendance, but their economic situation was better than that of the poor. The explanation is that the majority (seven out of ten households) comprised of elderly couples who lived by themselves and their 'consumer/producer ratio' changed over the family cycle. Unlike younger households, the number of consumers did not exceed the number of producers. In older households, consumption, including food requirements, is usually less than that of younger households.

In contrast to Sikor's (2001) arguments on Black Thai villages of northern Vietnam, in Giao Lac, the contributions of older households to agricultural production did not decline at all with increasing age. They retained the agricultural land allocated to them by the village and continued to do some of the work themselves. Most of the time, their children helped them with the heavy work of transplanting and harvesting their rice. Older households had more cumulative savings than younger households. Further, it is important to note that people who were in their late 60s and 70s and whose children were all married were not obliged to contribute anything when they were invited to a wedding party or a house warming party in the village. Informants said that this was partly because elderly people could not earn as much as younger people and also because elderly villagers are no longer expected to contribute to their children's wedding parties or their house warming parties. Thus, elderly people could both save their money and continue to attend all ceremonies in the village. In rural villages, such contributions can comprise a significant portion of household income.

Male heads of the upper-middle income and rich households were younger than those of poor and middle-income households, and they were willing to take calculated risks. Some of them had inherited assets from their parents and continuously developed their businesses. Members of poor households had less household labour available and less ability to hire additional labour. Labour capacity is considered a primary determinant to the success of shrimp and clam farming as well as the ability to produce, save and reinvest wealth. In addition, poor households, which were mostly headed by women, were excluded from male-dominated networks that played a key role in the trade of coastal products, and they thus earned much less. Men in these households suffered from chronic health problems, and consequently medical expenses absorbed a large part of their savings and drove these households further into debt.

Conclusions

As the case of Giao Lac in this study illustrates, gender, age, wealth and class all influenced the ways in which villagers used and managed natural resources, with gender pervasively shaping the extent to which people benefited from their use of these resources. There were significant differences between women's and men's opportunities in resource use and management. This was due to the persistence of patriarchal values within the community, which resulted in differential access to power bases and support networks, especially among shrimp traders. Constraints on women date back to the pre-colonial and colonial eras. Women's roles and status were radically changed during the Vietnam–US war, when men went to the battlefields. The relative absence of men in the village during the war overturned traditional social relationships, although this did not completely alter the nature of unequal gender relations in the site under study. Evidence for this lies in the constraints women continue to face in coastal trade activities.

Following *doi moi*, women and men have had unequal access to the most productive coastal aquaculture resources, limiting their opportunities in the market economy. Consequently, access to resources is largely mediated by their relations with men, especially their husbands. Property rights are vested in the male head of household. In short, women usually do not gain legal rights to the land they farm, and therefore they do not have the right to sell or transfer use rights to others.

This study illustrates how the economic liberalization process, while opening up economic opportunities for many, has not benefited women and men equally. Changes in the macrostructure of state and economy have not resulted in changes in all aspects of life in a coastal village like Giao Lac. Consequently, it has led to a process of differentiation between classes, age groups and genders in the same village. Rapid changes in the allocation of private leaseholds in the coastal area and the legalization of private businesses have had the effect of progressively reducing the access of poor families to resources that were formerly under common access. Women-headed households and women and girls more generally have been the most adversely affected and they have become victims of both environmental degradation and the process of privatization, since they have less opportunity to engage in trade than men, and instead are confined to selling their labour to pond owners.

The social structure in Giao Lac remains highly complex. Neither the state nor the private sector alone can provide a viable solution to mangrove resource degradation. Likewise, it does not make sense to propose *only* community-based resource management, as the local community itself is highly heterogeneous and outsiders also use the resources. To manage the mangroves sustainably, more equitable policies are needed at the village and district levels. These policies must necessarily take into account factors such as political power, economic heterogeneity within the village, institutional arrangements for allocating resources, the implementation of property regimes, conflict resolution, economic and social incentives, and the cultural, historical and geographical specificity of local communities.

Local practices and conventions are not static but evolve over time. To make good rules, the government should understand local conventions and work to adapt them rather than imposing new rules from the outside. A central government agency could continue to manage the dike system, as a breach in the dike system could cause far-reaching damage to many communities. Households could manage individual shrimp ponds according to private sector principles, since the proceeds from the bidding process could be spent on the village infrastructure, such as roads, schools and health clinics. The whole community could oversee the management of the mangrove forests and be granted the right to require shrimp pond farmers to post environmental bonds, or otherwise pay money into a local fund that would be used to both offset loss of income to other villagers as a result of mangrove habitat destruction and subsequently to cover the cost of reclaiming abandoned shrimp ponds.

Notes

1   This chapter is based partly on an article that appeared in 2006 in a Special Issue entitled *Gender and Environmental Governance* of the journal *Gender, Technology and Development*, with permission of the publishers (Sage).

References

ADB, AusAID, DFID, GTZ, JICA, Save the Children UK, UNDP and the World Bank (2003) *Vietnam Development Report 2004: Poverty*, Joint Donor Report to the Vietnam Consultative Group Meeting, 2–3 December, Hanoi

Adger, N. (1999) 'Exploring income inequality in rural, coastal Vietnam', *Journal of Development Studies* 35 (5): 96–119

Chant, S. (2004) 'Dangerous equations? How female-headed households became the poorest of the poor', *IDS Bulletin* (35) 4: 19–26

Durham, W. and M. Painter (1995) *The Social Causes of Environmental Destruction in Latin America*, Michigan: University of Michigan Press

Ha, T. P. T. (1997) 'Some problems about land and rural women in the stage of restructuring', *Social Sciences* 2 (58): 56–64

Kleinen, J. (2002) 'Access to natural resources for whom? Aqua- and mariculture in Nam Dinh, Vietnam', paper presented at the International MARE conference 'People and the Sea II', 4–6 September 2003, University of Amsterdam

Le Hue (2004) 'Coastal resource use and management in a village of northern Vietnam', unpublished doctoral dissertation, The Hague: Institute of Social Studies

Le, T. C. and T. Rambo (1999) 'Composite swidden farmers of Ban Tat: A case study of the environmental and social conditions in a Tay ethnic minority community in Hoa Binh Province, Vietnam', paper presented at a Center for Natural Resources and Environmental Studies (CRES) seminar, Vietnam National University, 2 May 1999

Leach, M., R. Mearns and I. Scoones (1999) 'Environmental entitlements: Dynamics and institutions in community-based natural resource management', *World Development* 28 (4): 225–247

Leach, M., S. Joekes and C. Green (1995) 'Gender relations and environmental change', *IDS Bulletin* 26 (1): 1–8

Luong, H. (2003) 'Gender relations: Ideologies, kinship practices, and political economy'. In H. Luong (ed.) *Postwar Vietnam: Dynamics of a Transforming Society*, Singapore: Institute of Southeast Asian Studies, pp201–223

Lutrell, C. (2002) 'Embracing and resisting the global shrimp boom: Shifting access to resources in the Vietnamese renovation', paper presented at the Ninth Conference of the International Associations for the Study of Common Property (IASCP), 17–21 June, Victoria Falls, Zimbabwe

McCay, B. and J. Acheson (1987) *The Question of the Commons*, Tucson: University of Arizona Press

Ngo, L. V. (1993) 'Reform and rural development: Impact on class, sectoral and regional inequalities'. In W. S. Turley and M. Selden (eds) *Reinventing Vietnamese Socialism*, Boulder: Westview Press, pp165–207

Nguyen Cuc (1995) *Agriculture of Vietnam 1945–1995*, Hanoi: Statistical Publishing House

Nguyen Huong (2002) 'Exploring the role and status of women in the fish trading activities in Nam Dinh Province', paper presented at the workshop of The Netherlands–Vietnam Global Change Research in the Red River Delta (Vietnam): Working Group No. 4 'Local Use of Natural Resources and Environmental Change in the Ba Lat Estuary', Hanoi, Vietnam, 28–30 July 2002

Orientation–Forecast–Prospect (*Dinh Huong – Du Bao – Trien Vong*) (1995) *Chuong trinh Khai Thac, Su Dung Dat Hoang Hoa, Bai Boi Ven Song, Ven Bien Va Mat Nuoc o Cac Vung Dong Bang*, (Program on Reclamation and Use of Wasteland, Riverine and Coastal Areas and Water Fronts in the Delta), 3: 7–9, Hanoi: Agricultural Publishing House

Phan Hong and Hoang San (1993) *Vai Tro Cua Rung Ngap Man Viet Nam* [Mangroves of Vietnam], Hanoi: Nha Xuat Ban Nong Nghiep [Agricultural Publishing House]

Sheridan, T. (1988) *Where the Dove Calls: The Political Ecology of a Peasant Corporate Community in Northwestern Mexico*, Tucson: University of Arizona Press

Sikor, T. (2001) 'Agrarian differentiation in post-socialist societies: Evidence from three upland villages in north-western Vietnam', *Development and Change* 32 (5): 923–949

Tran Thi Van Anh and Le Ngoc Hung (1997) *Women and Doi Moi in Vietnam*, Hanoi: Women Publishing House

Turley, W. (1972) 'Women in the communist revolution in Vietnam', *Asian Survey* 12 (7): 793–805

Werner, J. (2002) 'Gender, household, and state: Renovation (*doi moi*) as social process in Vietnam'. In J. Werner and D. Belanger (eds) *Gender, Household, State: Doi Moi in Vietnam*, Ithaca: Cornell Southeast Asia Program, pp29–47

White, B. (1989) 'Problems in the empirical analysis of agrarian differentiation'. In G. Hart, A. Turton and B. White (eds) *Agrarian Transformations: Local Processes and the State in Southeast Asia*, Berkeley: University of California Press, pp15–30

White, C. P. (1982) 'Socialist transformation of agriculture and gender relations: The Vietnamese case', *IDS Bulletin* 13 (4): 44–51

Woodside, A. (1989) 'Peasants and the state in the aftermath of the Vietnamese revolution', *Peasant Studies* 16 (4): 283–297

Chapter 3

Intensification Regimes in Village-Based Silk Production, Northeast Thailand: Boosts (and Challenges) to Women's Authority

*Barbara Earth, Patcharin Lapanun, Nit Tassniyom,
Benjawan Narasaj, Patcharin Ruchuwararak
and Soutthanome Keola*

Introduction

This chapter is about changes in the gendered organization of sericulture and silk production in the northeast of Thailand, a region known as Isan. Silk is an animal fibre produced by caterpillars belonging to the moth genus *Bombyx*. During its lifetime, the domesticated silkworm, *Bombyx mori*, feeds exclusively on the leaves of mulberry trees, which like silkworms, are biotic attributes of the natural environment in Isan. Sericulture is the system of managing these natural resources that results in silk products suitable for consumption and exchange.

Since the 1960s, Thailand has undergone profound changes as a result of a modernization approach to development that aims to boost economic growth by shifting the economy from an agricultural to an industrial base. Changes in society have been far-reaching, entailing massive rural–urban migration and fundamental changes in livelihoods. As Thailand's economy became more integrated into the world economy, silk production was increasingly targeted for development. Until very recently, Isan people conformed to a subsistence farming economy, and produced their basic necessities, food and clothes. Sericulture and silk weaving were an integral part of that economy, and were always defined primarily as women's activities.

The government sector has had a prominent role in the technological transformation of sericulture through the development of new silkworm species and technical support provided through extension. Private companies have also radically changed the traditional mode of production by introducing a subcontracting system to rural villages in which imported silkworm eggs and specialized inputs for sericulture are sold to villagers, and then silk cocoons are bought back from them to supply factory-based mass production. Finally, NGOs have supported sericulture and weaving by providing access to markets. Through all of these outside agents, traditional village-based silk production has been intensified and commoditized.

State and market mechanisms of surplus extraction that accompany capitalization of the countryside have been theorized by Marxist scholars to increase rural social differentiation. The relationship of favoured groups with the state – and the exclusion of other groups – is central to understanding rural differentiation (Hart, 1989). The ways that sericulture is being promoted by the state on the one hand, and industry on the other, may include mechanisms of rural differentiation that have not yet been identified. At the same time, the way that market-led and state-led development affects material conditions at the micro-level may alter gender relations in the household and community (Heyzer, 1994). It is important to combine a Marxist focus on rural differentiation with a feminist focus on gender and power because women silk producers may differentiate *within* their group as well as relative to men as a group.

In the transition from a subsistence farming economy based on rice to a cash economy, Isan households employ a diverse set of livelihood strategies that include wage work, cash crop (sugar cane) plantations, vegetable farming, animal husbandry and sericulture, in addition to rice cultivation. In practice, all the studied villages currently have four to six livelihood strategies. In only one study village is rice cultivation still the primary source of income. Six out of seven study villages ranked wage work as the primary or secondary source of income, while in three study villages, sericulture was the primary or secondary source of income. All households pursue more than one livelihood strategy. In this context, sericulture has developed in distinct ways depending on the specific technology and support provided by government, non-government and industry stakeholders.

Three production systems are now found in the villages. These vary with the species of silkworm in use: local species, Thai hybrid species or imported species. All the species in use have been scientifically bred over time and are the property of the various stakeholders; we therefore consider the silkworm species to be both a natural resource and a technology. Alongside silkworm technologies, improved species of mulberry have been developed and introduced to keep pace with the feeding demands of more productive silkworms. Relations of production and the gender division of labour are specific to the species in use and the concomitant scale and outputs of production.

This chapter focuses on the changes in resources control and management and associated changes in power relations corresponding to each production system. Specifically, we examine changes in the gendered organization of sericulture and silk production in the context of neo-liberal economic development.

Methods

A qualitative research approach was used to study the dynamics of silk production in Isan. A multi-step selection process was applied to identify a cross section of silk-producing communities. First, nine provinces in Isan that mentioned silk in the province motto were selected. Second, the top three highest silk-producing provinces were identified on the basis of land used for mulberry cultivation. These provinces are Khon Kaen, Maha Sarakham and Buriram. In the third step, study villages were selected on the advice of staff of the Provincial Agricultural Extension Offices in the three provinces, the Sericulture Promotion Center at Khon Kaen and NGOs supporting sericulture and weaving. The villages were selected to get a cross-section of production systems in use, as shown in Table 3.1. The names of villages have been changed to respect the privacy of the informants.

Table 3.1 *Sampling frame of silk villages*

Technology (silkworm species)	Number of villages	Village	Province
Local species	3	Mai Baan	Khon Kaen
		Nong Deang	Maha Sarakham
		Baan Khmer	Buriram
Thai hybrid species	2	Mai Thai	Maha Sarakham
		Kang Kho	Maha Sarakham
Imported species	2	Nong Noi	Khon Kaen
		Sakham	Buriram

Data collection employed a three-step process. Information on the background and development of the villages was obtained by interviewing community leaders and key informants in each village. These semi-structured interviews generated questions for further investigation in focus group discussions with 10–15 participants in each village. Focus group discussion participants included leaders such as village heads, chairpersons and committee members of sericulture groups, villagers involved in sericulture, and the elderly who had been or are currently participating in sericulture. Finally, four household interviews were conducted in each village to understand how households have adjusted themselves in each system, especially their gendered production activities. Selected households included those engaging in sericulture on different scales and those whose members are the leaders of sericulture groups or mediators between producers and companies.

Research questions focused on production history, especially sericulture in relation to other productive activities; socio-cultural, ecological and natural resource systems and their changes in relation to production system; consequences of changes on income; health correlates of the technologies in use; and gender issues including control over resources. Fieldwork was conducted from June to September 2003, with follow-up visits to three villages (one in each species system) in June 2006.

Theory

Social differentiation in rural capitalization

Rural differentiation is a dynamic process in which social differences emerge among the rural population in the context of the development of commodity relations in the rural economy. It is primarily about the *quality* of changing relations and may not be income-related in the short term. It involves a cumulative process of change in the ways that different groups gain access to the products of their own or others' labour, based on their differentiated control over production resources (White, 1989).

The development of Isan sericulture in many ways parallels worldwide technological advances in agriculture that, beginning in the 1960s, vastly improved productivity of crops and contributed to widespread rural capitalization. This technology-driven movement, known as the Green Revolution, included new seed varieties to be used in combination with fertilizers, pesticides and machinery, a process that was furthered by state policies and mechanisms.

Contemporary scholars debate the fate of peasant societies undergoing capitalization. One view holds that new technologies bring higher yields for farmers who have sufficient resources, but fail to benefit poor farmers who don't have the resources to take advantage of the new technologies (Sachs, 1996). The inequalities in access to production resources leads to increased reliance on wage labour by poor peasants (Deere, 1995) and intensification of agricultural production is seen by critics to result in growing social disparity. Mechanisms of exclusion, new layers of middlemen and employer control of non-labour inputs create 'preferred but dependent' groups who come to occupy an improved social location relative to their neighbours (Hart, 1989; Turton, 1989). Impersonal market relations between neighbours gradually replace traditional social modes of income sharing (Hart, 1989). Production systems accompanying new technologies in sericulture similarly involve select groups, and state and industry ownership of resources. Like agricultural intensification, in which reliance on fertilizer and pesticide use has had devastating effects on land and water resources (Sachs, 1996), advanced technologies in sericulture also use toxic chemicals that affect health and environment.

An alternative view holds that new technologies for agricultural intensification have a successful distributive impact by increasing production of small as well as large farms. This more positive view argues that small farmers have been able to access inputs and institutional support from governmental, quasi-governmental and non-governmental agencies. Resource-poor households with surplus labour have been able to survive through sale of labour (Ghee and Said, 1989). Factors intrinsic to peasant communities may mitigate inequalities such that class differentiation is not clear-cut (Deere, 1995). White (1989) suggests that Marxist 'two-class polarization' being the inevitable result of commodity production and capital penetration simply does not fit. Hart (1989) casts doubt on the distinction between 'personalized' traditional social modes and 'impersonal' market relations. Theoretical flexibility is therefore needed to analyse how political-economic forces act on rural societies, and how internally generated processes in turn act on larger forces (Hart, 1989; White, 1989).

As can be seen in the pattern found in our study villages, one factor confounding a neat class categorization of households is the way that rural families construct a diverse portfolio of activities in their struggle for survival and improvement in their living standard (Ellis, 1998). Silk production is one of many livelihood strategies being pursued in response to the available opportunities. The class content of each livelihood activity may confer different class positions for different household members. Thus, the household may be the site of multiple class identities and relations (Deere, 1995). In the area under study, Earth (2005) found varying types of employment with local factories to be complicating an already mixed portfolio of Isan household economic strategies, and gender relations vary according to employment status of husband and wife.

Gender, technology and capitalism at the micro-level

Rural differentiation theory, like the Green Revolution itself, was gender blind. Limited attention to women's agricultural work contributed to inadequate analysis of effects as well as to poor results of policies. Technology change may affect women negatively and create new forms of gender inequality (Sachs, 1996). Sen and Grown (1987) address how technology development may place women's economic activities under male control and perpetuate unequal gender relations. Cockburn (1985) analyses how (in Western societies) men as toolmakers accrue skills that are defined as male property, and how these yield power over women.

Heyzer (1994) points out that state-led development often incorporates gender stereotypes that affect women negatively when operationalized at the micro-level. Due to stereotypes, men are more likely than women to get training in new technologies, both in formal and non-formal educational contexts. This training positions men to get the jobs that use advanced technologies (Ponniah and Reardon, 1999). Policies assume a unified household that is rarely the case, and even when they are instrumental in improving women's condition, may subordinate women in production and reproduction (Heyzer, 1994).

Overall, women's relationships to the means of production differ from men's, depending on the gender system operating in the society (Custers, 1997). Patriarchal farming systems are characterized by women's participation in agricultural work and animal-raising but male control over production decision making. Egalitarian farming systems, in contrast, are those in which there is a correspondence between men's and women's labour contributions, decision making over production and decision-making over income. Gender analysis has brought out the significant relationship between women's participation in production and women's status in the household (Deere, 1995). For example, income pooling for pooled household consumption is more likely in egalitarian farming systems. The specialization of household members in given occupations greatly influences the extent to which control over income is individualized or socialized. When income is generated individually, it is much more likely that women will pool their income earned from independent activities with their spouse and children, compared to men (Deere, 1995).

In Isan, the farming system is traditionally egalitarian; income is pooled and decisions are made jointly. As household managers, women control the purse; however, men with wage salaries are now exerting more influence over expenditures, especially large ones (Earth, 2005). Although silk was traditionally produced for personal use, it could be used as cash when needed and women's productive role as silk producers has always been recognized (Pattana, 1989; Smuthkup et al, 1994). However, the situation has fundamentally changed with the demands of capitalization and intensified production.

Evolution of the Thai silk industry

Market promotion of silk began at the turn of the 20th century when the Thai government became involved in what had previously been a subsistence occupation. The government's promotion of silk centred on technological improvement of the silkworm species to increase the volume of silk that silkworms could produce. Japanese experts have periodically assisted government development of improved species. Since 1961, four National Economic and Social Development Plans, with parallel plans for the Northeast, have emphasized sericulture. In 1972, sericulture research was placed under the Department of Agriculture (DOA), while the Department of Agricultural Extension (DOAE) focused on outreach and training. From 1993 to 2000, a government project, Devsilk, aimed to build sericulture groups in the villages. At the end of the project, Devsilk became an NGO, Silk Net.

The government-led transition from production-for-use to production-for-exchange encouraged the private sector to become involved. One of the main companies active in silk promotion is the Jim Thompson Thai Silk Company, which was established in 1948. The company runs a weaving factory with more than 1000 labourers in Nakhon Ratchasima. It promotes sericulture by raising silkworms in the factory and working with village producers under a subcontracting system. In recent years, the number of village producers has risen to 2200 households (DOAE, 2001, pp23–24). In addition to Jim Thompson, there other large, medium and small private companies owned by local entrepreneurs.

The way private companies have worked with farmers to promote sericulture differs from the approach of the government. The government focuses on boosting production but leaves marketing to agents. The private companies integrate both production and marketing. Under subcontracting systems, companies provide inputs to farmers on credit, including imported species silkworm eggs and materials necessary for their care. Producers are then required to sell their cocoons back to the company as raw material. These companies prefer producers in the communities to work together as a group and to deal with them through a representative. Other parties such as banks and government organizations may be brought into this system to provide loans and other support.

Different silkworm species require different management systems. The three types of silk production currently operating in Isan are outlined below.

1   Traditional sericulture: households keep local species. Production is usually done in parallel with rice cultivation and animal husbandry and was traditionally conducted in every part of the northeast. Local silk varieties are easy to take care of and are disease-tolerant. Farm women[1] can generate silkworm eggs by themselves.

2   Modified sericulture: sericulturists use Thai hybrid species of silkworm and apply what they have learned from training by DOAE. The Thai hybrid silkworm eggs are bred by DOA and distributed free to producers.

3   Modern sericulture: compared to the traditional and modified species, 'modern' sericulture requires more land to grow mulberry trees to generate the volume of food required. Farm families conducting this type of production need training and have to do it as a full-time job. Private companies import bivoltine[2] silkworm eggs and breed two imported varieties. The eggs are verified by the Silk Research and Training Center at Nakhon Ratchasima before being sold to households under contract (Siam DHV Co. Ltd, 1991).

Because of the different qualities of the silkworm species in use, the three production systems are quite different. The traditional system dealing with the hardy local species involves local technology and local knowledge passed from mother to daughter. The modified system promoted by the government requires an intermediate technology (Thai hybrid species), more specialized care and a certain amount of investment. Lastly, the system promoted by private companies involves advanced technology (imported species) and highly specialized care requiring high investment. The products of the systems vary with the technology in use. Organic silk thread and hand-woven silk textiles are the main products of the local species varieties. Thai hybrid species silk can be sold as raw material (cocoons), thread or woven silk textile. Imported species produce cocoons that are most suitable as raw material to be processed in a factory and machine-woven. The number of producers in each system is fluid depending on the market and other factors.

The Thai silk industry is subject to fluctuations in the world price of silk and faces intense competition from other silk-producing countries. Thus, efforts to

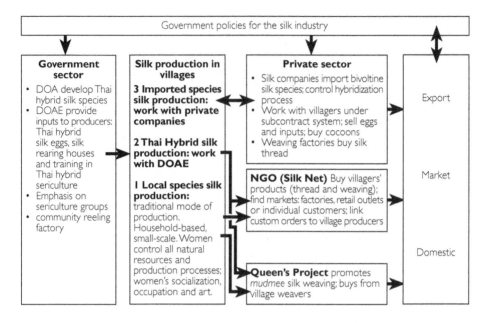

Figure 3.1 *Overview of the Thai silk industry*

increase the supply of silk for the international market are not always met with corresponding demand, having a disastrous effect on the industry-promoted system in particular. The Thai hybrid system is geared toward producing cocoons for reeling into silk thread for weaving by either factories or women weavers. The local species system is supported by a smaller but more dependable demand for woven organic silk. Actors in the promotion of local species and Thai hybrid species silk production are Silk Net and the Queen's Project. Figure 3.1 shows the various stakeholders and their relationships.

From this brief history, it can be said that the way in which sericulture has been promoted by both the government and the private sector has geared the industry towards increasing the scale of production through new technologies. The purpose of these changes has been to feed factory-based mass production. Early government involvement in silk production focused completely on research on technical aspects of sericulture that would increase the productivity of silkworms. Extension to rural producers eventually followed. Social infrastructure to support increased village productivity was not a focus until 1993. Gender equality has never been a consideration in any of these initiatives; however, silk is well established as a women's realm. A gender analysis of the three scenarios as revealed in the study villages illuminates the gendered effects taking place in association with the three management systems.

Traditional local species silk production

Traditional Isan culture is matrilineal and matrilocal, ensuring women a strong position in the family. In the past, men were primarily rice cultivators and public actors, while women performed a range of reproductive and productive work. In the traditional context, silk production was small scale. Daughters were socialized early to help their mothers with every aspect of production, including taking care of mulberry plants, picking leaves, feeding silkworms, reeling cocoons into thread and, the most difficult job, weaving. Men's contribution to silk production was ploughing the mulberry fields, assisting in mulberry cultivation and making wooden looms, bamboo trays, spools and other implements to be used by women.

Local species silkworms have a cycle of 45 days from mating of moths to reeling of silk cocoons. Women produce silkworm eggs themselves by selecting good specimens from the previous generation. Men symbolically assist in effecting high production by stepping over the bamboo tray while moths are mating. The young silkworms are placed in bamboo trays and fed mulberry through four stages of growth. Shelving is made to hold the bamboo trays in an area under the house that is protected by mosquito netting. When the silkworms reach a translucent colour, they are ready to spin and are placed one by one onto the *jor*, a large, round, flat bamboo tray. When cocoons are fully spun, they are removed from the *jor* and boiled in water. As the cocoons unravel in the boiling water, filaments from a number of cocoons are drawn together and pulled from the pot using a long wooden two-pronged tool. This rough thread is wound onto a fast-moving reel into three qualities of thread (quality depends on whether the filaments were from the outer, middle or inner portion of the cocoons). Re-reeling of the thread onto a large wooden spool makes it more standardized. Re-reeled thread is presented as a loosely coiled rope. It can be sold at this stage as silk thread, or dyed and spun onto small spools for weaving. Prior to 1980, villagers in all study villages raised only local species of silkworms, used local species of mulberry and followed traditional methods. Now, improved species of mulberry can be found alongside local varieties in every village. Production systems are more varied than in the past, and sericulture in some villages has become much more prominent in the household economy.

At the time of the study, villagers of Nong Deang, Mai Baan and Baan Khmer raised only local silkworm species. Nong Deang villagers' livelihoods have changed drastically during the past decade as large numbers of young women and men now work in a nearby electronics factory. Others have migrated to work in Bangkok. Households purchase fish and vegetables rather than cultivating them as they did previously. In this context, sericulture is ranked fourth as a source of household income, behind wage work, food-selling at the factory and rice cultivation. In the past, silk was traded for rice in times of drought. Now, 33 per cent of households engage in sericulture for market purposes. Sericulture is often undertaken in households where husbands are working outside for wages, and women producers remain at home performing a wide range of activities. Working for a wage constrains men's time and effort in the household, leaving women with almost all the work of sericulture. In this context, the scale of production is small and the traditional gender division of labour in sericulture and weaving is maintained. Women said that income earned from this activity is less than 5000 Thai Baht (TBH) ($145) per year. Some producers continue sericulture and weaving for their cultural and spiritual value, and lament the loss of traditional skills as young women take up factory work. This village is representative of many Isan villages in which sericulture remains traditional and small scale.

In sharp contrast to Nong Daeng, Mai Baan is an exceptional case of local species production, since sericulture and weaving are the major source of cash income, with 67 per cent of the households engaging in these activities. Until 2002, women of Mai Baan did sericulture and weaving only during the dry season for household use and for trading for rice and other necessities. Silk has now become the major source of family income. Producers earn up to THB50,000 ($1450) annually from selling silk thread and fabric. The income is used for daily household expenses and children's education.

The sericulture boom started in 2002 when Silk Net began working with villagers in Mai Baan to promote local species hand-reeled organic silk thread for sale to factories. Silk Net supports the idea that social infrastructure alone can improve productivity (as opposed to moving to advanced technologies). Approximately 80 households are now working with Silk Net. Production has doubled due to the presence of an effective marketing agent. Village women also engage in weaving, some with purchased thread, some with thread produced by themselves. Silk Net may assist in finding markets for woven fabrics and match custom orders to producers in the village.

Since the late 1970s, the women of Mai Baan have also sold their products to the Queen's Project. This is Her Majesty's project to preserve local knowledge, especially traditional Isan tying, dyeing and weaving techniques known as *mudmee*. An estimated 180 women weavers from Mai Baan are presently registered members. The visible trend in Mai Baan is men's involvement in sericulture increases as the scale of production increases. Men are involved in almost all activities in an unprecedented way. Because of its significance for household income, men's labour is essential. Men take responsibility for keeping the mulberry garden and picking mulberry leaves to feed the silkworms, especially when silkworms are in the fourth stage when feeding frequency is high. Men also take on heavy work such as lifting trays of silkworms. Men may also transfer worms to the *jor* for spinning, take cocoons from the *jor* and clean them before reeling, find firewood for reeling, re-reel and prepare warp thread for dyeing.

Some activities remain strictly women's work. Women are responsible for the critical task of feeding mulberry leaves to the silkworms, as they are the experts, and being centred near to home, can manage the frequent feedings. Hand reeling and weaving also remain exclusively women's work. Silk weaving requires patience and elegant skill that only women are considered to possess. Mai Baan women appreciate their husbands' help in sericulture and are glad to have them as partners in production. They were happy about two important things coming together: a secure livelihood *and* the household members working together.

Sericulture and silk production are regarded as women's particular expertise; therefore women control the process and determine the work that must be done. Men are their assistants.

Men are the innovators on equipment and have always made implements such as bamboo trays, looms, spools and bobbins. Recently, men have invented mechanized tools to use in the production process. Improvements are based on the information and instruction provided by women, but men have the technical confidence and experience that enable them to tinker with parts and create technical improvements. Women feel intimidated by mechanics and consider technology to be out of their realm.

In Mai Baan, there is one automatic re-reeling machine, which, although the property of the sericulture group, is under the control of a man who has become the leader of the group. He was able to get training in use of the machine, after which the local government bought a machine for the group. Now this man has created a supplemental job for himself (in addition to mulberry and rice cultivation) by re-reeling all the raw silk produced by the members. He and his wife manage the group's business. In spite of a heavy workload, husband and wife keep a monopoly on the machine. They have used their silk income to purchase two motorbikes. Their gain is not perceived as problematic by the women members, as they believe that all are working together for a common cause. But it appeared that the machine was now the personal property of this family. The fact that local species silk rearing is an organic process opens up further possibilities for surplus appropriation on the managers' part. In an unexpected turn of events, organic silkworm manure has recently become a commodity as valuable as the silk itself, now doubling the income of sericulturalists in Mai Baan.[3]

Another major change in Mai Baan is that the intensification of sericulture has resulted in corresponding changes in weaving, all involving acceleration in production. Women are economically motivated to weave for extended periods to produce more. With high market demand, they may push themselves to weave all day, interspersing household tasks with weaving. This is a reverse pattern from the past in which weaving was fitted in around the edges of more primary activities. The traditional meditative quality of weaving has been transformed into a frenetic activity. For the first time, weaving is being hired out and broken down into production steps that are compensated separately. A woman may do some steps herself in order to save money, for example design and weave her own piece, but hire workers to do the *mudmee* tying and dyeing. Women who do not have cash to invest in silk inputs may instead work for a wage.

In the past, silk cloth was sold to merchants in town or to those who commuted to the village to buy it. Now, some village women have developed themselves to be middlepersons who take products from other weavers to sell in the cities or at fairs and exhibitions that promote local wares. Normally, these women are also weavers, but expand their earnings by buying women's products for resale. This pattern follows the Marxist prediction that producers will differentiate, some to rise above the others. But weavers themselves seem not to perceive this as problematic, but rather as a service.

The situation in Baan Khmer is different from the other villages using local species, in part because the village is of Khmer origin. These people are indigenous to the area, but were separated from the Khmer majority in Cambodia by colonial, then national borders. The traditional silk-making processes and designs are of Khmer origin and the villagers have conserved their traditions. The village has had less outside intervention or support in sericulture, and production remains small scale. Women and men in Baan Khmer explained that men do not help much in sericulture because they take major roles in rice cultivation, which is the major source of income in this village. Over the past ten years, young women and men have migrated out to work in the cities. Wage work is the second highest source of income here. Sericulture and weaving are left to married and older women. The villagers explained that during the dry season, women may engage in sericulture and weaving, but there are no jobs in the village for men except taking care of buffaloes and cows, which can be done by the elderly or children. Therefore, men are expected to seek waged work to earn income to support their families.

Sixty per cent of households in Baan Khmer engage in silk production (ranked fourth as a source of income). Based on four in-depth interviews, income earned from sericulture and weaving ranges from THB4000–8000 ($116–232) per year but can reach THB14,000 ($406) per year. Cloth is sold when households are in need of money for health care, customary ceremonies or children's schooling. Products are sold through traders who travel from village to village to buy silk or through four village women who sell products outside. Some women sell their cloth through their daughters or relatives who have migrated.

Although many women are involved in silk, there is no group in the village. In 1995, staff of the Community Development Department (CDD) worked with women to form a group. The group was given nine weaving machines. However, the machines were not complete and did not work; furthermore there was no training. Reportedly, the CDD staff did not work with them seriously.

The Khmer silk of Baan Khmer does not use Isan *mudmee* designs, but rather has a distinctive shimmery look that is achieved by the winding together of two different colours of silk thread. The lack of attention to Khmer silk by the Thai government and business groups, on the one hand, has helped to preserve its distinctive style. On the other hand, Baan Khmer is not prosperous like Mai Baan. The worst possibility is that Thai designs and techniques will be promoted here and destroy indigenous Khmer silk knowledge. We observed an example of Isan dyeing colours being promoted over Khmer colours, to hideous effect. In June 2006, we learned that DOAE is intending to introduce Thai hybrid silkworms to Baan Khmer to enhance their production.

Government-promoted Thai hybrid species production

Unlike local species, home-based breeding of silkworms is not possible in the Thai hybrid system because silk eggs are distributed by DOAE officers. The main difference between traditional local species of silkworms and Thai hybrid species is that Thai hybrid has a shorter maturation cycle and much higher yield. These qualities allow for the scale of production to be increased, which in turn leads to economy of scale in a more centralized process. Thus, government promotion of this system has emphasized community groups, preferably with a community-owned silk reeling factory that purchases cocoons from households for reeling. The thread produced is sold to Silk Net for further distribution. This is the situation in Mai Thai village.

Women sericulturalists in Mai Thai have a tradition of mutual self-help and have been organized as a group since 1983. An original impetus for their organization was to resist exploitation by a middleman who used to buy their thread at a very low price to resell to large factories in Nakhon Ratchasima. The sericulture group, all women, began buying thread from producers in other villages at a fair price, and then selling in bulk at a fair price, thus excluding the middleman. All profits are returned to members of the network, which has grown to 17 groups across three districts, and some individual producers in other provinces as well. The network serves as a source of social security for members, including payments to families when a member dies. The leader of the sericulture group is also the village head.

In 1992, women in the group began to get government training in Thai hybrid silk rearing. Four women were supported to attend a one-month training programme at Nang Rong Sericultural Center. After the training, women were provided with materials to build silk rearing houses, a stock of promoted mulberry and fertilizers. They found that Thai hybrid silk eggs provided higher yields than the local species, so they wanted to switch to Thai hybrid. In 1994 and 1995, the second and third groups of women were trained. Sericulture has been the major source of household income in Mai Thai since the village joined the government project, Devsilk, in 1996. During 1996–2001, they received assistance from the project, including improvements in group structure as well as management and accounting. Courses relating to sericulture, such as mulberry management, silkworm rearing, cocoon reeling and marketing were provided to members of the group. The community reeling factory was established in 1999 with Devsilk support.

Raising Thai hybrid silkworms, unlike local species, requires some investment. Silk rearing houses are needed to protect the more sensitive Thai hybrid silkworms from flies and diseases. Chemicals and lime are applied. After each crop, silk houses have to be fumigated with chlorine. Although silk eggs are provided without charge, sericulturalists have to invest in these other inputs. Moreover, those who did not receive government support to build silk houses had to invest themselves. Informants reported that rearing Thai hybrid species is more complex and intensive than rearing local species. Some women who tried Thai hybrid found the process to be too complicated and if they are not able to follow the procedures exactly, the yield is very low or they may lose the entire crop. For these reasons, they returned to local species. Others returned to local species because they had allergic reactions to the chemicals. However, those who continued working with the Thai hybrid species were satisfied with the high yield.

Due to government promotion, almost all households in Mai Thai turned to raising silkworms and selling cocoons to the village reeling factory operated by the sericulture group. The factory processes cocoons from the entire network. Reeling of first quality thread is done in the factory, while rougher thread is reeled by women in their homes. When the factory is in full operation, there are three reeling machines and 16 women rotating work as reeling staff. These women are paid THB100 ($2.9) per six hours. In addition, there are women working in the selection, weighing and pricing processes. The rest of the tasks, except hand reeling, are done by one full-time male staff member. Men do not reel but they do help in re-reeling. Since the new reeling machine is available and also performs the re-reeling function, help from men on this task is no longer needed. This shows that mechanization does not always result in a takeover by men. Men still help with re-reeling at home, where there is no machine.

Although the volume of household production expanded, it ran into difficulties. After 11 September 2001, the price of silk in the world market fell and in 2002 there was an epidemic of root rot disease in the mulberry gardens. Therefore, a large number of households had to stop sericulture and engage in other income-generating activities, including agricultural wage labour. Mulberry fields were turned to sugar cane. Some women returned to the local species, which needs less mulberry and is more resistant to disease. Those who continued rearing Thai hybrid had to scale down their production. Some concentrated on weaving to earn income. Although members of the sericulture group at Mai Thai have faced this difficult situation, they anticipate that when the problems are alleviated they can resume raising Thai hybrid species and earn good incomes again.

During a return visit in June 2006, the village reeling factory was still closed but undergoing expansion. Mai Thai was slowly recovering from mulberry disease. At this time, only seven or eight women were engaged in sericulture, all of them in local species; however, production of Thai hybrid was strong enough in other network villages to justify the factory expansion. Three producers said that even when production is low, they prefer sericulture to agricultural wage work because they can control their own time, they feel proud of their skills and they are more free working for themselves. They admire and emulate richer neighbours. The gap in wealth had arisen in the past when some villagers were able to invest in land while others could not, they said. Differentiation is not perceived as resting on exploitation. The village head herself wore more gold jewellery than the others, but worked tirelessly for the well being of the village.

The case of Mai Thai village shows that benefits resulting from gender-blind government policies could be realized by women because of their traditional identification with sericulture. Women were encouraged in forming groups, trained in new skills, and supported with material inputs to succeed in the new technology. This case shows that women can be enthusiastic toward new technologies and had no problem operating machines. When production is undisturbed by mulberry disease, they experience great pride in their accomplishments. According to them, when production and incomes are down, men are sympathetic. Women's authority on silk is solid. The leader of the sericulture group related meetings in which men had to run home to consult their wives because they did not have the knowledge. Moreover, women retain leadership in a business venture that spans seven communities.

The village of Kang Kho, unlike Mai Thai, was not part of the Devsilk project and has no reeling factory. Yet women here too have accessed and benefited from government training since they organized as a group in 1993. They use the Thai hybrid species to produce silk thread, weave fabrics from their own thread and sell fabric by the piece. For those families in sericulture, it is the major source of cash income. According to the leader of the sericulture group, producers have been supported in terms of training and resource inputs since 1998 when Thai hybrid silkworms and improved mulberry species were firmly established in this village.

Women said that their husbands began helping in silk rearing after the sericulture group was officially established in 1998 and silk became the best economic option for their households. Men generally help women when they rear a large quantity of silk and more labour is required. They make decisions together about ordering silkworm eggs because they have to consult on the availability of mulberry for feeding the growing worms. Silk reeling and selling thread are women's responsibilities, according to a male informant; however, on one occasion, he drove to Mai Thai village to sell their cocoons to the factory. In this family, he is the money keeper because his wife 'spends money easily'. He added that he has never spent money without her permission.

The Thai hybrid system departs from the traditional system in several ways. It requires many more specialized inputs and higher investment. It also entails health effects from chemical exposures. After a period of success and high incomes, rearing the Thai hybrid species declined due to villagers' allergies to fungicide and reactions to formalin spraying. The current situation of Thai hybrid species is not good due to the low price of silk in the world market. Many producers have moved to other jobs. However, it is possible for women to recoup their losses by reverting to weaving and selling woven silk in the local market. In the best of circumstances, with a community re-reeling factory in operation, the Thai hybrid species production system provides silk producers with a market and a shorter period of production with frequent payments. Alternatively, the use of a re-reeling factory to process thread for sale as the end product has affected the ability of local women to maintain their knowledge of weaving. The increased mechanization involved in the Thai hybrid production process creates another type of limitation for women in that more complicated machines are used. This has created a situation in which women have to rely more on men. Although women use the machines, they have little or no confidence in building, repairing or maintaining them.

Industry-promoted silk production using imported species

Bivoltine silk species produce long, white and even silk filaments, easily reeled and with desirable characteristics for materials made on power looms. Silk produced by bivoltine silkworms is regarded in the industry as international grade A silk, known for its neatness, cleanliness and flawlessness, while having high tensile strength (Krishiworld, undated).

Although the private sector has been engaged in the silk business since the 1940s, it was not until the 1980s that they began to work with villagers on a subcontracting basis. Some companies produce bivoltine silkworm eggs themselves, while others import from China or Taiwan. Silkworm eggs are sold to producers through a group representative. Raising bivoltine species requires more investment and intensive care than Thai hybrid species and far more than local species. However, it provides higher yields because the size of imported species cocoons is bigger. The production system of bivoltine silk is much simplified compared to traditional silk production because the end product to be sold is the cocoons. The work is a segment of the traditional process, but is done on such a large scale that it requires intensive time and effort. Bivoltines require more investment than local and Thai hybrid species, more labour, and advanced skills and technology. They also require more land for mulberry plantation. However, if conditions are right, they provide higher yields and incomes.

Jim Thompson (The Thai Silk Company) has been intermittently involved with Sakham village since 1994, and like other silk companies, has greatly benefited from the efforts of DOAE during 1996–2000 to train producers in Thai hybrid sericulture. Devsilk organized a sericulture group in this village in 1999 (headed by a man). The agricultural extension officer advised the group to set up the community mulberry farm using community land near to the reeling factory, also funded by DOAE. Thus, the government extension services established an infrastructural as well as human resource base that private companies built upon. Sakham villagers have recently worked with two companies, Udonsaengrung and The Thai Silk Company. In the past, they also worked with a Chinese company under a collaborative project involving four parties: the villagers, DOAE, the Bank of Agriculture and Agricultural Cooperative (BAAC) and the company. Under that project, BAAC loaned money to sericulturalists to build silk houses and buy equipment. Besides silkworm eggs, the company promoted and sold improved mulberry stock to villagers. This project resulted in the expansion of sericulture and mulberry plantations in Sakham, but the company could not buy cocoons at the required rate. According to informants, producers were paid the promised amount of THB120 ($3.5) per kg for only the first crop; after that the company paid only THB60 ($1.7) per kg. For this reason, villagers stopped working with the Chinese company within one year of the project's inception. From the end of 2000 to 2002, the sericulture group worked with Udonsaengrung; however, their cocoon price was also low, so some villagers turned to rear silk for The Thai Silk Company, or 'Jim' as they called it. This arrangement operated through a woman agent who had previously worked for Devsilk. However, when the world silk price fell in early 2003, the village factory closed, and 'Jim' stopped providing eggs to the group.

Since 'modern' sericulture was a bad experience, many households changed their mulberry land into sugar cane plantations. There are now only seven producers who get eggs but 'Jim' will not buy cocoons from them, so they have to market their products on their own. Therefore, women have to reel their cocoons and sell the thread; others weave and sell the fabric. Though they can earn income this way, it is less cost-effective than large-scale sale of cocoons.

We visited Sakham at the time the village factory was closed and production volume was low. Though most Sakham villagers have not had a good experience with bivoltine, there is one success story: the woman agent who has worked with 'Jim' since the beginning. She became skilled at imported species production and then began working as an intermediary between the company and the villagers, earning a share of sales of cocoons produced by others. She was able to buy a pick-up truck from her earnings. Informants always referred to her as a success and respected her for her business acumen. This woman offered advice to her peers individually but never provided any training to the group, and if the failed producers felt any resentment about this, they did not express it to us.

In terms of gender, an interesting finding emerged. As in the other scenarios, men started participating in silk rearing when the companies became involved. Men's help was necessary to avoid hiring labour. What is new with bivoltines is that men take over the chemical applications, as women reportedly get allergic reactions more severely than men. Women avoid the chemicals entirely during pregnancy and following birth. As in the other systems, income from silk rearing is normally spent on daily expenditures, all of which are managed by women. Decisions on larger expenditures are made jointly.

Villagers of Nong Noi have worked only with 'Jim', but their experience is similar to that of Sakham village. During a return visit in June 2006, only ten households (out of 60 previously) were still working with imported species. When the world price fell, the company stopped buying their cocoons. Some households lost a lot of money. Many households at that time switched to raising cows. Mulberry land was converted to pasture and silk rearing houses became cowsheds. Now that the price of silk is high again, many households are contemplating returning to silk; however, conversion back to silk would be expensive.

The gender division of labour in sericulture was the same as found in Sakham village. Men increase their involvement during the fourth stage of the cocoon spinning process when silkworms need intensive feeding. After harvest, cleaning of silk houses and equipment is done by women but men, considered to be physically stronger, do the chemical disinfection. An in-depth interview with one couple captured intra-household dynamics. They had been doing imported species sericulture for 12 years. The husband had quit working in construction in Bangkok to come home and help his wife in the enterprise; however, he continued earning locally in construction and as a security guard, while she took charge of the sericulture business with the help of their son. She keeps all the books for the household. When silkworm feeding intensity is high, he helps in the house, especially with cooking. He also takes responsibility for dealing with the company, as the village no longer has a sericulture group. On one occasion, he had to confront the company representatives over inaccurate weighing of cocoons and was successful in the confrontation. The wife's role in the matter was to spread the word to other villagers about the company's questionable practices.

This couple works hard on a range of livelihood activities and are satisfied, especially with sericulture. Though they know that 'Jim' will profit from their labour, they are satisfied with the amount they get. The wife is proud of herself because of her earning power. Both resisted any suggestion that sericulture improved her position relative to her husband; rather they insisted that sericulture benefits them as a family – that they can buy whatever they want, buy land, renovate their house. Family relations are better than before because there is no need to migrate to Bangkok for work and family members can now stay together.

Sericulture and selling cocoons is advantageous in that it can provide cash every one to two months. This regular cash income is better than that from other crops, such as sugar cane and rice, which provide income only once a year. This explains why some households continue to engage in bivoltine production even though it is risky. The company never guarantees prices. Some producers have lost a whole crop of silkworms. They were not able to pay the company for the materials used in that crop cycle so they became indebted to the company. Another problem with the imported species is that they require more hygienic conditions than other species and people experienced allergies to chlorine, formalin, lime and anti-fungus drugs. Symptoms included headaches, eye pain, nausea, vomiting, fatigue, fainting, dyspnoea, coughing, numbness, skin rashes, itching and eye swelling. People applying the chemicals wear masks and long-sleeve shirts. Usually men do this work, but women may also come into contact with the chemicals. Some households avoid exposure to the chemicals by hiring labour. Recently, a company has been hired for fumigation, presumably with expertise in risk management. One woman who had been told by her doctor to avoid the chemicals was attempting to raise imported species silkworms quasi-organically. Anxiety and depression can occur during the process of raising imported species silkworms due to the potential or real loss of investment. Overall, raising imported species silkworms has requirements too exact to fit the village context, although with experience, some women producers can surmount the obstacles and succeed.

Overall comparisons and conclusions

All three contemporary production systems are countryside manifestations of state- and market-led development of the Thai silk industry. Through its macroeconomic policies as well as extension, the government has laid the ground for expanded production through three systems championed by different actors: local species by NGOs, Thai hybrid species by government and imported species by industry. We focused on how these intensified production systems are impacting gender roles and relations in sericulture and influencing social differentiation in the rural economy.

Intensification in all the systems results in silk occupying a more prominent place in producers' household economies. This transforms an unpaid, low-priority women's occupation into a rigorous livelihood strategy that requires men's as well as women's labour. In the context of Isan, women's identification with sericulture has kept them central to all three production systems. Feeding silkworms, reeling raw silk and weaving are strongly identified with women, even seen as innate qualities of women. Thus, industry development has had to incorporate women, always as resource managers and often as leaders.

Because of the different qualities of the silk species and their corresponding silk products, the three systems occupy distinct niches in the Isan rural economy. There is no coordination among the separate niches except through market trends. All three systems can be viewed as positive for women because they add livelihood options to the rural economy in which women take the primary role. When production increases, so does women's economic role in the household and therefore their status. When the silk enterprise requires the contributions of both spouses, women's status is doubly enhanced because they supervise the enterprise. Thus, with regard to Isan sericulture and silk production, advanced technologies do not place women's economic activities under male control, nor have policies negatively affected women producers.

Because of the strong Isan ideology that men and women 'work together' and 'decide together' for the well being of the family, informants did not speak of improvements in the status of women; rather they talked about the status of the family. Silk income is used especially for children's education and for household expenditures, reflecting Deere's (1995) view that women invest their earnings in their children. Even though informants maintained that decisions are made jointly, whatever the sources of income, we noticed women's greater satisfaction with themselves when silk is the basis of household well being.

The local species technology is accessible to all women because it is an indigenous natural resource. The importance of this management system is that it preserves the entire range of local knowledge on silk production, from breeding of silkworms to weaving of cloth. Moreover, it sustains and strengthens women's control and autonomy in silk production and trade. Local species use an organic process that ensures there will be a special market for organic thread as well as organic by-products. With NGO marketing support, women can expand the quality and quantity of their production. Though traditional *mudmee* weaving caters to a local market (imposing limits to growth), the organic silk thread has potential for growth. This potential has yet to be realized by Silk Net or other NGOs, and women sericulturalists cannot scale up their production without such support. In villages such as Nong Deang and Baan Khmer, where the traditional local species system enjoys no outside support, men are not called on to increase their contribution to women's silk production but are instead drawn into factory work. An outside wage would tend to boost men's position in the household and diminish women's position vis-à-vis their husbands, as was noted in another Isan context (Earth, 2005). Furthermore, when husbands migrate for wage work, women have to perform all the roles previously done by men: animal raising, rice cultivation and other agricultural activities, as well as reproductive work and sericulture. Silk production cannot expand in these circumstances.

In contrast to small-scale NGO support for local species production, government extension of Thai hybrid technology has been widespread. We feel that this has had a successful distributive impact because many small producers have been able to access training and sericulture inputs through the extension. Loans have been provided and support given, making Thai hybrid widely used. These government inputs have increased production, in line with theorists who look positively at agricultural intensification.

The local species system and the Thai hybrid system share commonalities because the government project Devsilk evolved into the NGO Silk Net, which now markets products from both systems. Due to the foundational principles of Devsilk, then Silk Net, sericulture groups have been strengthened in both systems. But there is a significant difference. Devsilk supported the Thai hybrid system to work on a larger scale in conjunction with a community reeling factory. This aspect makes the Thai hybrid system potentially more far-reaching as well as the most 'communitarian' of the three systems, perhaps facilitating a greater space for women to exercise their social, managerial and technical skills. If there are problems with Thai hybrid, producers can revert to the local species, which makes Thai hybrid a reasonable risk.

The imported species system is far more controversial. It is controlled by private companies that require and create 'preferred but dependent' producers. The system is highly differentiating, as few households have the land and training to even begin working with imported species, and of those who do, few succeed. If the world market is down, sericulturalists using this system are dropped by the companies and must scramble to find alternative income sources. The use of toxic chemicals in the imported species system mirrors the Green Revolution, and has similar contradictory results. Unlike the other systems, the industry-promoted imported species system does not promote women's business leadership. Because men are regarded as stronger in representing the interests of producers in negotiations with companies, men are often made the leaders of sericulture groups. This follows the traditional Isan gender system in which men are public actors. Women can negotiate the more socially embedded markets common to the local species and Thai hybrid systems, but external market transactions should be done by men. However, within the household, women continue running the business and authority on production rests with them. Though for the present, men's leadership is largely tactical, some men might like to claim this space and it might become easy for women to concede it.

All of the systems contain elements of social differentiation. Now some women are rising above others by becoming middlepersons. In the case of an imported species producer who became an agent for The Thai Silk Company, surplus appropriation could be large. The local species system has organic by-products that increase the potential for surplus extraction by group representatives. Although wages have entered silk production, labour relations have a 'softer' quality than in agricultural work. For example, a woman who is too poor to purchase inputs for weaving may be hired (thus helped) by friends and neighbours, or elderly women may be paid to remove dirt from cocoons. Thus some traditional 'social modes' of income sharing (Hart, 1989) are in evidence. However, most families in all the systems limit their production to what their own labour can accomplish rather than hiring workers.

Over time, mechanisms of extraction may alter traditional equal relations among producers, as predicted by Marxist scholars. However, producers themselves seem not to experience such events as exploitive or differentiating. It is regarded as natural that some will have the time, opportunity and ambition to improve themselves and rise above the others. Those who are able to do so are admired. Arrangements are made on a mutual basis that is seen as fair to both sides. Although rural differentiation is taking place both in the quality of relations as well as in the level of income (White, 1989), the subjective dimensions of relationships are less affected.

Sericulture is primarily the activity of mature and/or married women, as young women tend to migrate out for wages. Success is enhanced by their cohesiveness as an organized group, which invites support from government and NGOs. However, factors outside their control, such as blights in mulberry gardens, silkworm diseases and a fluctuating world market, make silk production always an uncertain venture, especially for Thai hybrid and imported species systems. Silk can never be a constant and sole livelihood strategy, thus setting a limit to the improvement of women's status that is possible to be earned through their expertise and management of silk. At best, silk-producing households can maximize their gains by taking advantage of favourable conditions, but scaling back their production when conditions change. Economic rationality determines the strategies adopted by Isan households. Livelihoods can be optimized through flexibility, both in resources management and gender expectations.

The major challenge to women's traditional authority in silk may lie in the increasing use of machines, which are an aspect of intensification in all the systems. Theorists have noted that compared to women, men are more comfortable with machines (Cockburn, 1985) and are able to access training on machines (Ponniah and Reardon, 1999). These trends are strongly evident in this study. Increasing mechanization associated with higher production volume is contradictory for women. On the one hand, household income is increased, which raises women's status, but on the other hand, women are dependent on men for building, repairing and maintaining machines. This dependence could eventually erode their power over the process while raising the importance of men. With regard to the continuing development of village-based silk production, an explicit gender equality approach would increase women's competence with machines and encourage their inventiveness. Silk Net and DOAE can take up this role. Mechanical competence will add to women's skills and give them full confidence to keep their rightful authority over silk production.

Acknowledgements

The authors appreciate the reviews and theoretical contributions of the editors of this collection, as well as those of Edsel Sajor.

Notes

1   Sachs (1996) discusses farm wives, housewives, farm women and women farmers. Rural Isan women are ideally farm wives (like housewives, they perform reproductive activities including childbearing, child-rearing, cooking, cleaning and washing. Like housewives, they are expected to express their sexuality in monogamous, heterosexual relationships with their husbands. In addition, they perform various activities related to farm enterprise such as bookkeeping and animal keeping). However, in reality, Isan farm wives are farmers as well, contributing to household-based rice cultivation as well as to cash crops such as cassava and sugar cane as wage labour. Perhaps they are best referred to as farm women. Isan gender ideology is egalitarian but overlooks intimate inequality, which is very rarely discussed. Domestic violence is an emerging issue, according to the Isan Women's Network.
2   Bivoltine silkworm species have only two generations in a year, but this fact is not relevant to our case because companies provide eggs as demand requires.
3   A Lao pharmaceutical company uses organic silkworm manure as an ingredient in high blood pressure medication, and pays the group THB50($1.4)/kg for 'hygienic' excrement. The wife buys the 'unhygienic' manure from group members at THB30($0.9)/kg to 'use as fertilizer on household plants. We thought it possible that she might clean the manure and re-sell it for a significant profit'.

References

Cockburn, C. (1985) *Machinery of Dominance: Women, Men and Technical Know-How*, London: Pluto Press

Custers, P. (1997) *Capital Accumulation and Women's Labour in Asian Economies*, London: Zed Books

Deere, C. D. (1995) 'What difference does gender make? Rethinking peasant studies', *Feminist Economics* 1 (1): 53–72

DOAE (2001) *Department of Agriculture Extension, Seminar Report on Marketing of Thai Silk and Its Products*, Bangkok: Department of Agriculture Extension

Earth, B. (2005) 'Globalization and human rights as gendered ideologies: Case of Phoenix Pulp Mill, N.E. Thailand', *Gender, Technology and Development* 9 (1): 103–123

Ellis, F. (1998) 'Household strategies and rural livelihood diversification', *Journal of Development Studies*, 35 (1): 1–38

Ghee, Lim Teck and M. I. Said (1989) 'Malaysia: Rice peasants and political priorities in an economy undergoing restructuring'. In G. Hart, A. Turton and B. White with B. Fegan and Lim Teck Ghee (eds) *Agrarian Transformations: Local Processes and the State in Southeast Asia*, Berkeley: University of California Press, pp181–192

Hart, G. (1989) 'Agrarian change in the context of state patronage'. In G. Hart, A. Turton and B. White with B. Fegan and Lim Teck Ghee (eds) *Agrarian Transformations: Local Processes and the State in Southeast Asia*, Berkeley: University of California Press, pp31–49

Heyzer, N. (1994) 'Introduction: Market, state and gender equity'. In N. Heyzer and G. Sen (eds) *Gender, Economic Growth and Poverty: Market Growth and State Planning in Asia and the Pacific*, New Delhi: Kali for Women and Utrecht: International Books in collaboration with Asian and Pacific Development Centre, Kuala Lumpur, pp3–27

Krishiworld (undated) 'The pulse of Indian agriculture', *Sericulture*, www.krishiworld.com/html/seri_ind2.html (accessed 4 July 2007)

Pattana Kiti-asa (1989) *Isan Cloth: An Anthropological Perspective*, Khon Kaen: Khon Kaen University

Ponniah, G. and G. Reardon (1999). 'Women's labour in Bangladesh and Sri Lanka: The trade-off with technology', *Gender, Technology and Development* 3 (1): 85–102.

Sachs, C. (1996) *Gendered Fields: Rural Women, Agriculture, and Environment*, Boulder: Westview Press

Sen, G. and C. Grown (1987) *Development, Crisis and Alternative Visions: Third World Women's Perspectives*, New York: Monthly Review Press

Siam DHV Co. Ltd (1991) *Sericulture Production Development in the Northeast: A Preliminary Survey*, Bangkok: Siam DHV Co. Ltd

Smuthkup, Suriya, Pattana Kitiasa and Nuntiya Phutta (1994) *Ways of Isan Weavers: The Development of Textile Production and the Changing Roles of Women in Contemporary Isan Villages*, Nakhon Ratchasima, Thailand: Suranaree University of Technology

Turton, A. (1989) 'Local powers and rural differentiation'. In G. Hart, A. Turton and B. White with B. Fegan and Lim Teck Ghee (eds) *Agrarian Transformations: Local Processes and the State in Southeast Asia*, Berkeley: University of California Press, pp70–97

White, B. (1989) 'Problems in the empirical analysis of agrarian differentiation'. In G. Hart, A. Turton and B. White with B. Fegan and Lim Teck Ghee (eds) *Agrarian Transformations: Local Processes and the State in Southeast Asia*, Berkeley: University of California Press, pp15–30

Multi-Local Livelihoods, Natural Resource Management and Gender in Upland Indonesia

Rebecca Elmhirst

Introduction

In the context of globalization and intensified market expansion, there is compelling evidence across the developing world that migration is of growing significance for rural people seeking to diversify agrarian livelihoods (Ellis, 2000; Adger et al, 2002; de Haan and Rogaly, 2002; Rigg 2006). As rural lives and livelihoods become increasingly multi-local, even transnational, marked by links that cut across the boundaries of localities, considerable challenges are posed for the ways in which rural development and natural resource management (NRM) is conventionally envisioned. In particular, migration and mobility are (perhaps deliberately) at odds with the spatial dynamic normally associated with natural resource management interventions (Black and Watson, 2006). Such interventions, whether associated with the state or with NGOs, generally attach resource management institutions to geographical territories (areas of land, forest and water) and thus implicitly carry assumptions about the geographical boundedness of communities and their relationship to particular spaces.

The relationship between migration, multi-local livelihoods and natural resource management is complex: a multiplicity of views held by researchers points to the need to take a contextual approach that distinguishes between migration as a response to crisis and livelihood failure, and migration as an accumulation strategy, in which social and economic remittances may play an important transformative role in people–environment relationships (Deshingkar, 2004). On the one hand, migration may be regarded as bearing negative consequences for natural resource management, disrupting community institutions, either through the arrival of migrants into protected areas (Curran and Agardy, 2002) or through labour shortages linked to outmigration (Mutersbaugh, 2002). In addition, there is also a concern that the growing individualization of livelihoods associated with migration undermines the efficacy of collective institutions associated with sustainable natural resource management (Durand and Landa, 2004). On the other hand, migrant remittances may strengthen natural resource management institutions in various ways (Jokisch, 2002; Nyberg Sørenson, 2004; VanWey et al, 2005), or mitigate the vulnerability of resource-poor rural people by offsetting shortfalls in access to various forms of capital assets, thus bringing positive environmental effects (Adger et al, 2002).

One area that remains relatively unexamined is the role of gender in the relationship between migration, multi-local livelihoods and natural resource management. Much of the attention on gender in the natural resource management literature has focused on deconstructing 'community' in natural resource management (for example, Rocheleau et al, 1996, Agarwal, 2001; Agrawal and Gibson, 2001; Cornwall, 2003), resting on an emphasis upon 'communities in place', which accepts the premise of territorially attached institutions and people–environment relations as spatially bounded. Far less is understood about the links between gender and natural resource management in multi-local settings, notwithstanding a recognition that migration patterns and processes within multi-local livelihoods are inherently gendered (Nyberg Sørensen, 2004).

Across a variety of contexts, the links between migration and gender are expressed in different ways, but in many instances, women are highlighted as holding a particular position within the dynamics of mobility. On the one hand, this may be through the pressures on women's reproductive roles associated with displacement (Townsend et al, 1995; Yong, 2007), or on the other, through women being drawn into highly feminized rural–urban and transnational migration networks associated with rural accumulation strategies in Southeast Asia (McKay, 2003; Resurreccion and Ha Thi Van Khanh, 2007). In a multiplicity of ways, whether in the realm of reproduction or production/income generation, women are critical to livelihood diversification, play an important role as migrants, or, when men migrate, mediate its effects on families and communities through their reproductive activities and through the feminization of agriculture (Razavi, 2003). The implications of women's and men's different engagements in migration and multi-local livelihoods thus points to an area in which an appreciation of gender is key for understanding people–environment relationships and the prospects for sustainable natural resource governance.

This chapter takes a particular view on this question by exploring the ways in which specific understandings of gender difference and gender identity become salient to the issue of natural resource management in the context of multi-local livelihoods. The empirical focus of the study is the link between multi-local livelihoods and natural resource governance in Lampung province, Indonesia, particularly as each is played out through the province's local transmigration resettlement programme, known as Translok. Translok has had a major impact on regional development in the province, transforming the ethnic structure of the population ('original' Lampung people now constitute just a third of the total provincial population), 'bureaucratizing' formerly remote areas and the governance structures of the Lampungese, bringing extensively cultivated areas into intensive cultivation, and diversifying and developing the regional economy in line with national economic objectives. The study focuses on the displacements associated with Translok, and the charged people–environment relationships associated with the gendered dynamics of resource access and control in the province, through which multi-local livelihoods are cast.

Multi-locality is understood in two senses: (1) in a temporal sense in terms of 'life geographies' and movements through different spaces; and (2) in a spatial sense, in terms of networks that (usually) link household members as they each seek livelihoods in different places. Analysis is woven around three critical concepts. First, gendered livelihoods are understood in spatial terms in a manner similar to Krishna's (2004) idea of a *genderscape*: interconnected networks of relations traversing the scales of household, community and society, which, as she points out, is very different from the 'imagined landscape of self-contained village communities living picturesquely close to the land' (p51), a powerful image in the literature on community-based natural resource management (see also Li, 2001).

Secondly, analysis draws on de Haan and Zoomers' (2005) concept of livelihood trajectories, which brings to the fore temporality and the transforming structures, institutions and organizations that give (changing) shape to access to opportunities, and that produce multifarious forms of social and geographical mobility. Their concept owes much to the sustainable livelihoods and 'environmental entitlements' framework developed by Leach et al (1999), but rather than focusing on peoples' capitals (for example, Bebbington, 1999), emphasizes how individual strategic behaviour is embedded both in a historical repertoire and in social differentiation. This provides a much more flexible conceptual platform for analysing livelihoods as pathways, explicitly focusing on access to opportunities and the workings of power.

Finally, rather than conceptualizing gender as a linear or structuring relation, the chapter draws on performative theorizations of gender that consider how gender difference is materialized through practices (Butler, 1990, 1994, 2004). Recently, performative approaches to gender have been applied in relation to natural resource management to illuminate how gendered subjectivities are defined and contested in relation to particular ecological conditions, becoming salient at particular moments through work, discourses of gender and the performance of subjectivities (Harris, 2006; Nightingale, 2006).

In this view, therefore, gender is re-inscribed through discursive and material struggles around livelihoods and natural resources, and whilst inherently unstable, through iterative repetition, it comes to appear as natural and fixed. The advantage of this conceptualization is that it emphasizes the processes and practices through which gender comes to matter in people–environment relations, at a variety of scales (household, community and in the wider political economy). Together, these three concepts make an implicit nod towards philosophical ideas about 'becoming'. Viewed performatively, as Clark (2003) puts it, 'bodies and their environment are construed as mutually conditioning and mutually transformative. "Constrained contingency", by this logic, inheres deep in the workings of the living world' (p169). This provides a lens through which to analyse the way in which gendered power relations emerge as salient within the power plays associated with natural resource governance and multi-local livelihoods, most specifically, through the dynamics of resource conflict, displacement and marginality.

Analysis centres on a group of people whose lives and livelihoods have long been inherently 'multi-local': Javanese migrant farmers in the Indonesian province of Lampung, located on Sumatra's southernmost tip. Their shifting circumstances are interlinked with the historical political ecology of the province, which has been a destination for landless people resettled from the crowded neighbouring island of Java since the early 1900s through the Dutch colonial authorities' Kolonisatie and the post-independence transmigration resettlement programme. More recently, many spontaneous migrants heralding from Java – cast as forest squatters – have been resettled through 'local transmigration' (Translok) programmes conducted at provincial level, and this provides a focus for the study. Resettlement in its various guises ostensibly reflects shifting patterns of natural resource governance and ideas about citizenship and entitlement as these are embedded in the Indonesian government's strategies of economic development and political reform.

A randomly selected sample of 40 local transmigrant (Translok) households from a transmigration settlement in the subdistrict of Pakuon Ratu provided the starting point for the study. When the research began in 1994, this was one of the poorest subdistricts in Lampung, with 39 of its 41 villages classified as poor (*miskin*) and therefore eligible for the highest form of government assistance (Kantor Wilayah Departemen Tenaga Kerja Propinsi Lampung (Provincial Manpower Office), 1993). The transmigration settlement, which is spread over a wide area, comprises approximately 900 households, the majority of which work the 2ha of land allocated at the time of their resettlement in 1982. Soils are poor and prone to weed invasions, drought and floods, and transmigrants struggle to eke a livelihood from agriculture, requiring them to diversify their livelihoods in a number of ways.

With a few gaps when household members were absent, intensive semi-structured interviews were conducted with men, women and teenage children from the 40 case study households in 1994–1995, 1998 and 2005 to assess their unfolding livelihood geographies over their life course, across particular years, and over the ten-year duration of the study. In addition, interviews were conducted at district and provincial level with key authorities associated with resource governance and rural development. In a manner similar to that suggested by de Haan and Zoomers (2005), particular efforts were made to tease out individuals' priorities and reflections on their livelihoods, in an attempt to highlight how past experiences had shaped subsequent courses of action. At the same time, shifting institutions and social arrangements were observed for their implications for gender. An important dimension of the study was the changing regional political ecology of Lampung (and indeed, Indonesia), which provides the political context and gives shape to gender and livelihoods. The chapter begins by outlining the conceptual framework through which the analysis proceeds, before moving on to explore the linkages between shifting configurations of territorial power associated with local transmigration and Lampung's changing political ecology, and the reconfiguration of gendered subjectivities within migrants' livelihood trajectories.

Gender performed in migrant livelihoods

Whilst the Indonesian government's transmigration programme has received considerable attention from scholars and environmental activists, much less attention has been paid to the local transmigration programme (Translok), perhaps because it has been conducted at a provincial level and away from international scrutiny. Studies that have been undertaken have tended to conclude that Translok in Lampung has been marked by similar problems to those associated with general transmigration, bringing displacement, further resettlement and spontaneous mobility, shifting problems of unsustainable resource use elsewhere and creating a category of marginal farmers, many of whom have moved on to protected areas elsewhere in the province (Levang, 1989; Charras and Pain, 1993; Levang et al, 1999; Witasari et al, 2006). Whilst many of these studies have detailed the complex relationships between state and civil society (migrants), missing from these accounts is a discussion of gender: migrants are either considered as an undifferentiated category, or else the focus is on horizontal distinctions related to notions of ethnic identity (Tajima, 2004). Accounts concerning migrants in the uplands elsewhere in Indonesia have also tended to focus on other dimensions of power and inequality, including differentiations around urban and rural, upland and lowland, newcomer (*pendatang*) and 'original' (*asli*) inhabitants, and between those whose livelihoods are more or less market-oriented (for example, Li, 2002; Tsing, 2005), rather than foregrounding gender.

Perhaps because of the ways resource concerns have been articulated around these other axes, gender has slipped out of view (Elmhirst, 2002), despite a vibrant literature on gender in other spheres of Indonesian life (for example see Ong and Peletz, 1995; Koning et al, 2000; Robinson and Bessel, 2002). Migration research, for example, has shown how the social costs of mobility are particularly felt by women, whilst at the same time exclusionary and disciplinary techniques are applied to specific bodies, denoting which gendered bodies belong where (Silvey, 2006; Purwani Williams, 2007). The question remains as to how gender is both displaced and becomes salient as a category of social relationships at different moments through multi-local livelihood trajectories and within the power plays of natural resource governance in Lampung province.

The work of Butler is instructive in showing how the performance of masculinities and femininities construct and reconstruct the gendered subject, as performativity is 'the vehicle through which ontological effects are established'

(Butler, 1994, p33). This approach allows masculinities and femininities to be regarded as in process: fragmented, provisional and wrought through the interplay of culture, class, nationality and other fields of power, and, centrally for Butler, through regulatory frameworks such as normative heterosexuality. The efficacy of performativity is enhanced when it is complemented by a focus on materiality and where material oppressions are brought into view (Pratt, 2004), or, as Butler (2004) herself has recently acknowledged, where gendered performances are regarded as 'not finally dissociable from the ways in which material life is organized' (p214).

A performative approach to gender has been influential within a number of recent gender and natural resource management studies, which have demonstrated its potential for illuminating the ways in which gender is produced and inscribed through discourses and practices, and through its reiteration or citation, comes to appear as fixed, given or natural. Nightingale (2006), for example, in her study of community forestry in Nepal, considers how gender has been sedimented in particular ways through the performances of subjectivities associated with labour practices and local ecologies. Others have focused on the potential instability of gender categories in the context of environmental interventions. Harris (2006) suggests that the dramatic landscape changes associated with a major irrigation scheme in southeast Turkey offered a particular moment when the form of gendered subjectivities could be renegotiated. Similar points of instability may be associated with migration and mobility, which are also laden with possibility for gender to be nudged into new forms (Silvey, 2006). Changes in Lampung's political ecology, coupled with the processes and disruptions accompanying the livelihood trajectories of migrants also redefine the terms of social difference, inviting consideration of the resilience, malleability and translatability of gender as labour, household conditions and political ecological contexts significantly shift (Harris, 2006). In other words, migration and the multi-localization of livelihoods provide a context in which gender may be unstable and reworked through the 'constrained contingencies' associated, in this case, with shifting patterns of natural resource governance in Lampung.

Resource governance, livelihood trajectories and gender in Lampung

In Indonesia's forest margins, both colonial and post-colonial codes of governance have long been associated with a somewhat uneven expansion and reworking of authority over people and space, creating what Peluso and Vandergeest (2002) have referred to as 'the political forest'. Drawing on Foucaultian notions of governmentality, this concept has been adopted in various ways to illuminate the processes and tactics through which both colonial government and the modern state have attempted to achieve control over people and territories, and which include strategies for increased control embracing the privatization of natural resources or direct state management (the formation of state forests, for example), the encouragement of settlement in unpopulated areas (transmigration), exclusion from particular areas (resettlement for conservation purposes), and the centralization of authority or its devolution to community levels (Li, 2002).

Within Lampung, efforts to reconcile natural resource management, produce governable citizens and foster economic growth have, in various ways, invoked exclusionary forms of spatialized power with critical impacts on those people whose lives and livelihoods are both forged and marginalized by the negotiations and power plays that produce Lampung's 'political forests'. This echoes a theme within the literature on natural resource management in which migrants and the process of migration are seen to pose a demographic or social threat to resource stability, and must therefore be managed (Curran and Agardy, 2002; de Haan and Rogaly, 2002; Deshingkar, 2004). At the same time, the history of migration and resource governance in Lampung province points to the ways in which vulnerable rural migrants are themselves produced through uneven and inequitable processes of governmentality and resource control, as people have been targeted and chased out of particular areas, usually through policies framed within a discourse of environmental protection, and through the tactics of resource control exacted by large-scale state and private agricultural capital (Li, 2002). As this chapter argues, these shifting configurations of territorial power are associated with the reconfiguration of gendered subjectivities within migrants' livelihood trajectories.

In outlining their concept of livelihood trajectories, de Haan and Zoomers (2005) point out the social nature of individual livelihoods, which are conditioned by social relationships within communities and beyond. The livelihood trajectories of people in this study were remarkably similar, reflecting to a large measure a commonality of class and cultural position (all were landless Javanese migrants prior to their resettlement) and a common experience in terms of relationships with structures of power associated with the local state. Thus, whilst Table 4.1 is a simplified version of a more complex reality, it conveys the three important phases that have marked out livelihood trajectories for most people within the study group. These correspond with shifting ideas within government about the control of people and the control of territory within Lampung, and through which individuals have negotiated displacement, resettlement, and most recently, increasingly multi-local livelihoods. Through the practices associated with each of these phases, gender has been re-inscribed to produce particular notions of gendered subjectivity.

Phase 1: Agricultural pioneers to Lampung's uplands

Recent migration into Lampung from Java on a large scale is usually traced back to the coffee boom of the late 1960s and 1970s, a period when rural Java was itself undergoing intense restructuring, particularly as the newly installed New Order government of Soeharto sought to achieve economic stability and national self-sufficiency in food crop production through Green Revolution technologies (Hüsken and White, 1989). This process was accompanied by intensified differ-

Table 4.1 *Migrant livelihoods in Lampung: A schematic trajectory*

	Place of birth	First phase	Second phase	Third phase
Location	Java or Lampung	To upland and protected forest areas in South and Central Lampung	To North Lampung either as Translok or as spontaneous migrants	Multi-local (protected forest in West Lampung), urban and transnational
Entitlement status	Landless or sharecropper, to become a 'pioneer farmer'	Sharecropper, some ownership, no certification, 'forest squatter'	Eligibility for state assistance, 'transmigrant', relatively secure tenure	Varies between localities
Livelihood	Sharecropping and wage work	Sharecropping, subsistence agriculture, cash cropping of coffee	Subsistence agriculture, cash crops, plantation wage labour or illegal logging	Diverse: sharecropping, subsistence agriculture, tree-based cash cropping, remittance income
Key gender issue		Women as brokers of official recognition and resource entitlements	Gender ideologies in Translok policy place women as dependants. Reinforced through encounters with state functionaries	Gender reworked through family obligations across diverse locations, practice of 'ethnic' gender ideologies

Source: Based on interviews with migrant men and women in 1994–19 95, 1998 and 2005

entiation and a lessening of paid work for the landless and landed poor, prompting livelihood diversification and, for some, migration to other parts of Indonesia, including Lampung. Javanese migrants coming to Lampung took advantage of confusion over land control in Lampung. Community resource regulation mechanisms associated with the Lampungese population and codified by the Dutch colonial authorities had officially been dismantled and 'unoccupied' areas appropriated by the state. A laissez-faire approach to land clearance and settlement, particularly in logged-over and previously cultivated areas within 'government forest' prevailed, and indeed at this time, there was tacit support from local government for spontaneous migration into forest areas – migrants were described as 'pioneers', a progressive force – partly because at this point land was perceived as being relatively abundant (Utomo, 1967).

Most of the older migrants interviewed in this study had moved either from Java or from the early transmigration settlements of South and Central Lampung and into areas officially under the control of the state, whilst the remaining individuals in the sample had been born in these recently opened forest areas (87 per cent had lived experience of what came to be 'protected forest'). Here, access to land was brokered through more established Javanese migrants who had been able to foster relations with Lampungese elites, who effectively controlled many of these areas. Often, these early migrants acted as a liaison point between newcomers from Java and the indigenous Lampungese elites, and (at least to a degree) controlled the distribution and settlement of land. Later, many were given formal recognition as village leaders in the forest settlements of central Lampung, and later on, as leaders in local transmigration (Translok) settlements (see below).

That men dominated this process is clear from the narratives of migrants, in their descriptions of their initial movement and the ensuing negotiations with other migrants and local Lampung people. Gender categories emerge in their stories through the importance attached to women as a stabilizing force in migrant communities, where their presence was deemed necessary for communities of migrants to demonstrate some sort of permanence. Whilst many initial forays into new areas were undertaken by men alone, the establishment of 'village communities' and qualification for state recognition rested on the capacity of migrant leaders to attract additional migrants and more specifically, those with wives and families. Women, therefore, whilst invisible as pioneer farmers per se, were critical for solidifying communities: their presence necessary for community recognition, generally granted to those areas with stable populations of established households, and for the entitlements that accompanied this. However, the process recast gender in specific ways. The pioneer narrative of Ibu Maliki, a 67-year-old woman migrant, illustrates many of these themes:

> *I was living in Java with my parents; we were sharecropping a small area of* sawah *[irrigated rice]. My brother had gone to Lampung with some other relatives. When he returned he told us how much land there was, that it was very fertile. I was just a young girl. Then I married my husband, and followed my husband to where my brother lived. Other wives also followed at this time. We borrowed land from other migrants, and planted rice, corn and later on, coffee. There were not so many women at first but after a few years many Javanese had followed and the area was busy (*ramai*). I felt at home there, though life was hard, the land was good and we always had a harvest.*

As women's practices as migrants coalesced around that of 'migrant wife' and through the practice of community that early settlement involved, gender was inscribed around the performance of migrant conjugal relationships, built around the necessity for successful pioneer farmers to be in possession of a 'stabilizing' wife, with little room for those (especially women) whose subject positions elided this.

Phase 2: Displacement and the resettlement of 'forest squatters' through transmigration

In the late 1970s, as migrants were consolidating their livelihoods in upland Lampung, government attitudes towards cultivation within protected areas began to harden, reflecting the entrenchment of Soeharto's authoritarian New Order government whose legitimacy was forged through state patronage and alliances with large-scale capital. This marked a shift in policies towards governance that favoured large-scale forest exploiters, concession holders and plantation development. The Basic Forestry Law of 1967 (UUK No 5/1967) ended the freedom of local people and migrants to convert forest, ostensibly opening the way for foreign investment in large-scale logging, whilst at the same time establishing protected areas (critical watersheds) that could be replanted with industrial tree crops (Sajogyo, 1993).

Inventories to count population dwelling in 'protected areas' were carried out by the provincial authorities, and migrants were told they must leave. The Translok resettlement programme was initiated as attitudes towards spontaneous settlement in *kawasan* (state-controlled) forests hardened, and land was closed by the Ministry of Forests, forbidding access to nearly 300,000ha of the most fertile land in the province (Levang, 1989), and prompting the resettlement of more than 74,000 households by 1992. Through a particular version of ecological authoritarianism, land was effectively appropriated by the state to serve watershed functions and to protect commercial enterprises downstream. For example, the construction of the Way Jepara irrigation scheme led to the designation of Gunung Balak as a protection forest (*hutan lindung*), forcing the removal of nearly all spontaneous settlers in the 1980s. As environmental protection became government priority and a sensitive issue, views about spontaneous migrants became increasingly negative and had the effect of redefining 'pioneers' as 'forest squatters'. As is typical of environmental interventions that often involve 'the assertion of sweeping property claims and the reconfiguring of associated livelihood and accumulation strategies' (Schroeder and Neumann, 1995, p321; see also Li, 2002), as environmental organizations and donors assert control over remote territories in new ways, spontaneous settlers found themselves to be 'out of place'. The impacts of displacement were harsh as people were resettled in areas in the north of the province with very poor soil fertility and that were poorly integrated into the province's infrastructure, serving to bring impoverishment and vulnerability to those resettled.

Gender emerges as salient and gender categories are inscribed through practices associated with three overlapping dimensions of the resettlement process, each of which invokes or, to use Butler's (1994) terminology, cites gender difference. First, resettlement itself, coordinated and administered by the provincial government in Lampung, conditioned the practices of migrants in ways that heightened gender divisions of labour and gender inequalities in terms of access to resources. In a manner similar to Indonesia's better-known transmigration programme, families included in Translok were provided with 2ha of land in the name of the male household head, a house and support for one year. While the provincial transmigration department had charge of the transmigration settlement at the beginning, after one year, the settlements were incorporated into the normal provincial government structure, and the migrant leader (identified as leading 'forest squatters' in Gunung Balak, the protected forest from where those in the sample were moved) was appointed as village head.

In interviews, migrants described the rules and regulations that governed their livelihoods in the new settlement. Translok migrants were obliged to cultivate the land they had been given, maintain their houses, maintain religious observance, keep the settlement orderly, follow any instructions given to them by settlement officials and observe good relations with the local Lampung population. They were forbidden from selling land or their houses within ten years of arrival, and from leaving the settlement without permission from settlement authorities (Kanwil Transmigrasi, 1986). In this way, their activities were controlled and contained, and 'order' restored to those who had hitherto carved out their lives with minimal regulation from government authorities. Livelihood repertoires that emerged from this include upland food cropping (rice and cassava), and sustained efforts to carve wet rice fields from the many streams that traversed the settlement. Through the politics and practices associated with Translok, a particular refrain of gender emerges that very much reflects the discourses of citizenship associated with Soeharto's New Order, at its height during that period. As a microcosm of New Order development policy, the Translok village was coloured by state discourses that, to use Butler's phraseology (1994), cited gender difference in particular ways: men were regarded as farmer-breadwinners, women were positioned as housewives or mothers of development. Practices of resettlement, agricultural assistance and access to credit rested on assumptions about nuclear, male-headed households through which all resources flowed via the titular male head. However, men did not qualify for the programme unless they were married. This meant that men's and women's control over and access to resources hinged on their marital status, reinforcing the importance of conjugal status for both men's and women's subjectivities.

Moreover, in the context of extremely poor agro-ecological conditions, livelihoods very much depend on the labour inputs of all household members. In interviews it was common to hear people describe how tasks normally associated with men (heavy ploughing, for example) were undertaken by women. Since the settlement was opened in 1982, it has not been possible for households to meet subsistence needs through own-account agriculture. Until the late 1990s, incomes were supplemented to a large degree by wage work at a nearby sugar plantation, for which women were recruited as day labourers for year-round crop maintenance, and men for work in the harvest. Together, their wages comprised up to 70 per cent of household income. The necessity of men and women working collectively in this way had the effect of reinforcing the unity of the household in most cases: '*gotong royong keluarga*' (family mutual assistance) being one way this was reflected upon in interviews. 'If we don't work, we don't eat' has been a familiar refrain for women, and indeed family success was very much measured, particularly by men, by the hard work and physical prowess of migrant women. Appropriate femininity was that associated with hard agricultural work, coupled with an unerring ability to mother and care for families, roles that were not always reconcilable.

A second dimension of the resettlement process concerns the effects trans-migration had on social networks: the practices that enabled migrants to build social capital and reciprocal relationships that traversed village power structures and that facilitated access to resources including land, capital and off-farm work opportunities. The importance of such networking practices was heightened by the process of displacement, which effectively severed or weakened many family support networks, particularly those associated with family remaining in Java. Gender was invoked in various different kinds of networking activities. Within formal structures of village authority, networking with the wives of the village political leadership was an important means by which migrant households could secure access to informal loans and labour opportunities at the plantation for example. Practices were thus moulded around Soeharto's New Order parallel hierarchies of male leaders and their wives that were common within the state bureaucracy up to the late 1990s. Effectively this meant engaging in practices such as rotating credit meetings and hygiene lessons, which reinforced idealized subjectivities of women as mothers and carers of the family – a position not realizable for the majority of migrant women in circumstances where demands for their productive labour were heavy. Again, this reinforced gender along the lines of women's relational subjectivity – a positioning that strengthened depend-ence on husbands. The potential for creative slippages in these gender citations might have been apparent in the case of divorced or widowed women, whose positionality was at odds with the gender discourses of resettlement and where alternative subjectivities might have emerged. However, the stability of this version of gender was notable even in such cases, as is illustrated by the story of Ibu Ani, widowed with young children. In her case, the village head effectively took on the position of husband/patriarch, securing a small plot of communal land for her to cultivate, and, over the course of the next few years, exerting an extraordinary amount of paternalistic power over her life, dictating various life decisions (he refused to authorize her marriage to another migrant on the grounds that this man had been involved in anti-government activities in the late 1960s), where she was allowed to work, and effectively he prevented her from heading to Jakarta to work as a maid.

Thirdly, livelihood and family practices in the resettlement process were conditioned in part through an awareness of cultural identity that was strength-ened by uneasy relationships between migrants and local Lampungese people. In circumstances of mutual suspicion and fear, women's practices became an object of moral regard within both communities, with migrants at pains to demonstrate their difference in terms of religious observance, gendered codes of behaviour within the family, and permissible or valued livelihood activities for men and women. Female labour is an important area from which cultural value is drawn. The proper behaviour of women young and old includes hard physical work and an unerring capacity to contribute responsibly to their families. Amongst migrants this was contrasted with negative (and false) stereotypes concerning their Lampung neighbours as 'lazy' men and 'oppressed' economically inactive women. Women's practices, even where women complain about their lot in life, also reinforce this version of gender. In complaining about her daughter's failings, Ibu Anik evokes the gender positions that Translok hardships and livelihood repertoires have produced:

> *All she wants to do is play. She hates to go to the plantation [to work as a labourer]. I tell her how hard we have to work to give her a good life. She doesn't realize how hard it has been for us. If she doesn't help, then there will be even less for us all. Life is very hard here, to live you need a system of family mutual assistance.*

Within these three dimensions of resettlement, through migrant's practices and through social interactions associated with work, reproductive and community activities, gender differences and inequalities were re-inscribed in ways that hinged around normatives of family and the material and moral obligations associated with conjugal partnerships.

Phase 3: Multi-local livelihoods

Since the downfall of Soeharto's presidency in the late 1990s, an emerging repertoire of livelihood diversification across localities has been given renewed impetus by wider processes associated with political disorder, reform and a reconfiguration of livelihood entitlements across Lampung. The political and economic ramifications of the unravelling of Soeharto's capitalist bureaucratic authoritarianism and the ensuing 'transition period' are complex (Samuel and Schulte Nordholt, 2004). However, key elements include a commitment to decentralization, compelled in part by the neo-liberal objectives of multilateral donors and lending agencies, and measures that support regional autonomy. Whilst many aspects of resource control (for example forestry) remain resolutely centralized, there have been shifts in local configurations of power, not least those associated with the rise of so-called ethnic elites (Samuel and Schulte Nordholt, 2004). Once again, these have shifted the territorial status of migrants, producing a landscape of differentiated access to and control of resources, including land, political influence and access to particular sources of income. Broadly, livelihood trajectories are now extremely dynamic, shaped by a volatile mix of political struggle and by globalization. First, land conflicts in the area became commonplace after 2000, as the local Lampung population began to assert their resource claims more forcefully, buoyed by wider movements to give recognition to 'original' populations (Li, 2000) and by changes in provincial-level politics where leadership has come to be associated with the capacity to demonstrate their original (*asli*) status. Changes in the political landscape have largely been associated with a desire to reverse the 'Javanese colonialism' (*penjaja*) that transmigration is seen to have represented in the province. In terms of access to power and material resources, this has brought challenges to the taken-for-granted structural advantage of transmigration settlements compared to their Lampungese neighbours. The effects of these processes on migrants have largely been indirect; this is not a province marked by profound ethnic conflict, and indeed differentiations tend to be subtle and along the lines of people's relative 'newcomer' status, rather than their ethnicity per se. Rather, violence has been expressed through class relations in the form of farmers' struggles over land against corporate interests. Whilst indirect, escalating violence in the study area in 2000 when 'whoever held the pistol held the power' had a profound impact on migrant livelihoods when the plantation on which they depended for wage work was forced to cease operations. Arson and damage to road infrastructure effectively cut off this important source of work, especially for women, as labour recruiters were no longer able to access the Translok settlement.

At the same time that localized labour recruitment networks linking the village with the plantation were collapsing, others were opening up and becoming more institutionalized in ways that again contributed to the production of gender. First, whilst the local production of sugar cane to the south of the settlement had been irrevocably damaged during the violent conflicts, investments in infrastructure linking the Translok settlement with Lampung centres of commerce to the north east had the effect of opening up new labour recruitment networks in other sugar plantation areas. Labour recruiters singled out male contract workers from the Translok settlement, who were housed in dormitories, returning periodically to their homes. Because of the nature of this arrangement, women were excluded from participating in plantation wage work. Second, and in the context of wider confusion over province-level resource control, it became significantly easier for migrants to work in newly cleared coffee plantations in protected areas to the west of the province. Men and their older sons with access to sufficient capital made such journeys, returning either when they had been chased out of areas by the authorities (a regular occurrence) or as necessary to help wives and mothers on their land at times when labour demands in the coffee gardens were relatively low. Third, globalizing forces of the kind seen in other parts of the world became strongly apparent in the early 2000s, with the appearance of labour brokers from outside to recruit women as domestic workers in Malaysia, Hong Kong and Saudi Arabia. Women's exclusion from other forms of income generation (i.e. plantation work) made them a ready 'reserve army', once such networks had become sufficiently institutionalized and trusted within the community. A contributing factor towards the massive scale of this migration was the availability of credit to pay for women to make the journey overseas as this was deducted from their first three month's wages, making this an attainable livelihood option for even the poorest of households, compared to other forms of migration. Finally, political instability and concerns over shifting resource entitlements have also been conducive to a reassertion of settled agriculture amongst migrants, contrary to what might be predicted by the literature on de-agrarianization and the management of risk. Of the original 40 families surveyed in 1994–1995, in 1998 at the height of Indonesia's political and economic crisis, more than a third of families were entirely absent from the Translok settlement. By 2005, nearly all had returned, the exception being a landless family with close ties to the redundant sugar plantation, and two others who had sold their land in 1998 to invest in their children's education. Not all of the returnees were land owners either: some had made use of social networks to secure access to land belonging to wealthier transmigrants. As part of a wider repertoire of multi-locality, this rural foothold is perceived as being less tenuous than other extra-local sources of livelihood, particularly where memories of economic crisis and recent experiences of exclusions from protected areas colour livelihood decisions. This accords with Winkels' (2004) observation that increased vulnerability is often itself an outcome of the uncertainties associated with serial mobility (see also Prowse, 2003). As one migrant put it: 'I'm tired of moving. Every time we move, we just seem to get poorer.' Their relative newcomer (*pendatang*) status in the Translok settlement was more secure than an absolute newcomer status elsewhere in the province.

A common pattern for livelihoods therefore, was for older women to remain in the settlement, involved in the year-round cultivation of food crops, men and older sons to spend part of their time either in coffee-growing areas to the west of the province or as plantation workers in the north east, whilst women from their late teens onwards were on two-year contracts as domestic workers in Malaysia, Hong Kong and Saudi Arabia. In some instances, very young children were left in the care of grandparents. Recurring in this increasing individualization of livelihoods is a number of practices and it is through these that gender is being expressed. First, the collective welfare of household members is regarded as being conditional on retaining a foothold in the Translok settlement for reasons outlined above. That this is built upon the agricultural labour practices of (older) women concretizes gendered subjectivities of hard-working women caring for their families. Second, gender is cast through the spatial imaginaries of these multi-local households, produced through a multi-local dynamics of obligation, guilt, shame and fear, which disciplines gendered bodies across space in a process others have described within the literature on transnational families (for example, Velayutham and Wise, 2005; Yeoh et al, 2005). Whilst the precise nature of conjugal arrangements has changed, the meanings and obligations associated with this have, if anything, strengthened. The contingencies of new resource-based livelihood practices that might have challenged gender have been constrained in ways that reveal the stability of gender across space and time. What emerges as apparent, therefore, is the resilience of gender categories, despite the changing experiences of migrants and the potential for gender to be recast or renegotiated.

Conclusions

Drawing on performative approaches to gender and the environment, this chapter began by suggesting that shifting resource entitlements, displacement and migration produce a dynamic and uncertain context in which gender differences and gender subjectivities may potentially be reconstructed. Yet despite this theoretical insistence that gender difference is neither natural nor given, what emerges from the livelihood trajectories of migrants in Lampung is a persistency and continuity of gender categories that appear to cement women's subjectivity in relational terms, primarily through conjugal and intra-familial relationships. Analysis of the stability of gender in the context of rapidly transforming environments and livelihoods invites the following conclusions.

First, rather than bringing about a disruption of gender, migrant practices associated with displacement and shifting livelihood possibilities have in effect led to its solidification. Specifically, this has been accomplished through the strengthening of conjugal relations and women's positionality as wives or dependents of men. Equally, men's subjectivities are conditioned by similar processes of governance that mean the securing of resources is best accomplished if men are part of a conjugal partnership. It appears that one line of continuity in an otherwise fractured picture of resource governance in Lampung is that successful livelihoods are conditional on a successful conjugal partnership. Somewhat counter-intuitively, rather than disrupting this pattern through an individualization of livelihoods, migration and multi-local livelihood trajectories encompass practices that re-cite gender in this way, particularly through women's work practices that maintain a family presence in the Translok settlement as a safety net of entitlement.

Second, the politicization of land and livelihoods in Lampung has heightened class divisions (between small-scale farmers and agro-industries) and configured a hierarchy of belonging and entitlement, extending from those who can demonstrate their original inhabitant status (*asli*) through complex genealogies, through to those with various degrees of 'newcomer' (*pendatang*) status. Practices associated with these distinctions generally coalesce around labour and livelihood, and have simultaneously displaced and marked gender. Gender is outweighed by lines of difference along which people organize and represent themselves, whilst at the same time 'gender' – in the form of comparative masculinities and femininities – is a site through which communal boundaries and cultural differences are drawn. The citations associated with social differentiation and resource entitlements again mark and solidify gender categories, specifically around a subject position associated with women's agricultural labour.

Finally, the empirical substance of the chapter concurs with gender theorists who have sought to show the material dimensions of performed gender, and suggests that wider processes of governmentality, including those associated with natural resources and livelihoods, also materialize and solidify gender differences in ways that go beyond Butler's original notion of normative heterosexuality (Butler, 1994). This provides a useful vantage point from which to caution against overly optimistic views of the transformative potential commonly granted to migration and mobility in the feminist literature, and instead to point out the need to specify the terms in which such transformations might be possible. For migrants in rural Lampung, there is a long way to go.

References

Adger, W., P. Kelly, A. Winkels, Luong Quang Huy and C. Locke (2002) 'Migration, remittances, livelihood trajectories and social resilience', *Ambio* 31 (4): 351–357

Agarwal, B. (2001) 'Participatory exclusions, community forestry and gender: An analysis for South Asia and a conceptual framework', *World Development* 29: 1623–1648

Agrawal, A. and C. Gibson (eds) (2001). *Communities and the Environment: Ethnicity, Gender, and the State in Community-Based Conservation*, New Brunswick: Rutgers University Press

Bebbington, A. (1999) 'Capitals and capabilities: A framework for analysing peasant viability, rural livelihoods and poverty', *World Development* 27 (12): 2021–2044.

Black, R. and E. Watson (2006) 'Local community, legitimacy and cultural authenticity in post-conflict natural resource management: Ethiopia and Mozambique', *Environment and Planning D: Society and Space* 24: 263–282

Butler, J. (1990) *Gender Trouble: Feminism and the Subversion of Identity*, London: Routledge

Butler, J. (1994) 'Gender as performance: An interview with Judith Butler', *Radical Philosophy* 67: 32–39

Butler, J. (2004) *Undoing Gender*, London: Routledge

Charras, M. and M. Pain (1993) 'Spontaneous agricultural settlement in Indonesia'. In M. Charras and M. Pain (eds) *Spontaneous Settlements in Indonesia: Agricultural Pioneers in Southern Sumatra*, Bondy: ORSTOM-CNRS and Jakarta: Department of Transmigration, pp13–34

Clark, N. (2003) 'Feral ecologies: Performing life on the colonial periphery'. In B. Szersynski, W. Heim and C. Waterton (eds) *Nature Performed: Environment, Culture and Performance*, Oxford: Blackwell, pp163–182

Cornwall, A. (2003) 'Whose voices? Whose choices? Reflections on gender and participatory development', *World Development* 31: 1325–1342

Curran, S. R. and T. Agardy (2002) 'Common property systems, migration and coastal ecosystems', *Ambio* 31 (4): 303–305

de Haan, A. and B. Rogaly (2002) 'Migrant workers and their role in rural change', *Journal of Development Studies* 38 (5): 1–14

de Haan, L. and A. Zoomers (2005) 'Exploring the frontiers of livelihoods research', *Development and Change* 36 (1): 27–47

Deshingkar, P. (2004) 'Improved livelihoods in improved watersheds: Can migration be mitigated?', paper presented at International Workshop on Watershed Management Challenges organized by the Indian Council of Agricultural Research, International Water Management Institute, International Crops Research Institute for the Semi-Arid Tropics, 3–4 November 2004, New Delhi

Durand, L. and R. Landa (2004) 'Demographic change and commons management: A focus on migration', *Common Property Resource Digest* 69: 1–4

Ellis, F. (2000) *Rural Livelihoods and Diversity in Developing Countries*, Oxford: Oxford University Press

Elmhirst, R. (2002) 'Negotiating land and livelihood: Agency and identities in Indonesia's transmigration programme'. In B. Yeoh, S. Huang and P. Teo (eds) *Gender Politics in the Asia-Pacific Region*, London: Routledge, pp79–98

Harris, L. M. (2006) 'Irrigation, gender and social geographies of the changing water-scapes of south eastern Anatolia', *Environment and Planning D: Society and Space* 24: 187–213

Hüsken, F. and B. White (1989) 'Java: Social differentiation, food production and agrarian control'. In G. Hart, A. Turton and B. White (eds) *Agrarian Transformations: Local*

Processes and the State in Southeast Asia, Berkeley: University of California Press, pp235–265

Jokisch, B. (2002) 'Migration and agricultural change: The case of smallholder agriculture in Highland Ecuador', *Human Ecology* 30 (4): 523–550

Kantor Wilayah Departemen Tenaga Kerja Propinsi Lampung (Provincial Manpower Office) (1993) *Kebutuhan Fisik Minimum* [Basic Physical Needs], Bandar Lampung: Province of Lampung, Kantor Wilayah Departemen Tenaga Kerja

Kanwil Transmigrasi (1986) *Statistik Translok, Propinsi Lampung [Local Transmigration Statistics, Lampung Province]*, Bandar Lampung: Kantor Wilayah Transmigrasi [Area Transmigration Office]

Koning, J., M. Nolten, J. Rodenburg and R. Saptari (eds) (2000) *Women and Households in Indonesia: Cultural Notions and Social Practices*, London: Curzon

Krishna, S. (2004) 'A "genderscape" of community rights in natural resource management'. In S. Krishna (ed.) *Livelihood and Gender: Equity in Community Resource Management*, New Delhi: Sage Publications, pp17–63

Leach, M., R. Mearns and I. Scoones (1999) 'Environmental entitlements: Dynamics and institutions in community-based natural resource management', *World Development* 27 (2): 225–247

Levang, P. (1989) 'Farming systems and household incomes'. In M. Pain (ed.) *Transmigration and Spontaneous Migrations in Indonesia*, Bondy: ORSTOM and Jakarta: Department of Transmigration, pp193–284

Levang, P., B. K. Yoza, D. Etty and H. Etty (1999) 'Not every cloud has a silver lining: Crop farmers in transmigration areas', Working Paper 99.16, ACIAR Indonesia Research Project, Australia Centre for International Agricultural Research

Li, T. (2000) 'Articulating indigenous identity in Indonesia: Resource politics and the tribal slot', *Comparative Studies in Society and History* 42(1): 149–179

Li, T. (2001) 'Boundary work: Community, market and state reconsidered'. In A. Agrawal and C. Gibson (eds) *Communities and the Environment: Ethnicity, Gender and the State in Community-Based Conservation*, New Brunswick: Rutgers University Press, pp157–179

Li, T. (2002) 'Engaging simplifications: Community based resource management, market processes and state agendas in upland Southeast Asia', *World Development* 30 (2): 265–283

McKay, D. (2003) 'Cultivating new local futures: Remittance economies and land use patterns in Ifugao, Philippines', *Journal of Southeast Asian Studies* 34 (2): 285–306

Mutersbaugh, T. (2002) 'Migration, common property and communal labor: Cultural politics and agency in a Mexican village', *Political Geography* 21 (4): 473–494

Nightingale, A. (2006) 'The nature of gender: Work, gender and environment', *Environment and Planning D: Society and Space* 24: 165–185

Nyberg Sørensen, N. (2004) *The Development Dimension of Migrant Transfers*, Working Paper no. 2004/16, Copenhagen: Danish Institute for Development Studies

Ong, A. and M. Peletz (1995) 'Introduction'. In A. Ong and M. Peletz (eds) *Bewitching Women, Pious Men: Gender and Body Politics in Southeast Asia*, Berkeley: University of California Press, pp1–18

Peluso, N. L. and P. Vandergeest (2002) 'Genealogies of the political forest and customary rights in Indonesia, Malaysia and Thailand', *Journal of Asian Studies* 60 (3): 761–812

Pratt, G. (2004) *Working Feminism*, Edinburgh: Edinburgh University Press

Prowse, M. (2003) *Towards a Clearer Understanding of 'Vulnerability' in Relation to Chronic Poverty*, CPRC Working Paper 24, Manchester: Chronic Poverty Research Centre

Purwani Williams, C. (2007) *Maiden Voyages: Eastern Indonesian Women on the Move*, Singapore: ISEAS Publishing

Razavi, S. (2003) 'Introduction: Agrarian change, gender and land rights', *Journal of Agrarian Change* 3 (1/2): 2–32

Resurreccion, B. and Ha Thi Van Khanh (2007) 'Able to come and go: Reproducing gender in female rural–urban migration in the Red River Delta', *Population, Space and Place* 32 (3): 211–224

Rigg, J. D. (2006) 'Land, farming, livelihoods and poverty: Rethinking the links in the rural South', *World Development* 34 (1): 180–202

Robinson, K. and S. Bessel (2002) *Women in Indonesia: Gender, Equity and Development*, Singapore: ISEAS Publications

Rocheleau, D., B. Thomas-Slayter and E. Wangari (eds) (1996) *Feminist Political Ecology. Global Issues and Local Experiences*, London: Routledge

Sajogyo (1993) 'Agriculture and industrialisation in rural development'. In J. P. Dirkse, F. Hüsken and M. Rutten (eds) *Development and Social Welfare: Indonesia's Experiences Under the New Order*, Leiden: Koninklijk Instituut voor Taal-, Land- en Volkenkunde, pp45–60

Samuel, H. and H. Schulte Nordholt (eds) (2004) *Indonesia in Transition: Rethinking 'Civil Society', 'Region' and 'Crisis'*, Yogyakarta: Pustaka Pelajar

Schroeder, R. A. and R. P. Neumann (1995) 'Manifest ecological destinies: Local rights and global environmental agendas', *Antipode* 27 (4): 321–324

Silvey, R. (2006) Geographies of gender and migration: Spatializing social difference', *International Migration Review* XL (1): 64–81

Tajima, Y. (2004) *Mobilising for Violence: The Escalation and Limitation of Identity Conflicts: The Case of Lampung, Indonesia*, Jakarta: World Bank

Townsend, J. in collaboration with U. Arrevillaga, J. Bain, S. C. Cordova, S. F. Frenk, S. Pacheco and E. Perez (1995) *Women's Voices from the Rainforest*, London: Routledge

Tsing, A. L. (2005) *Friction*, Durham, NC: Duke University Press

Utomo, K. (1967) 'Villages of unplanned resettlers in the subdistrict Kaliredjo, Central Lampung'. In Koentjaraningrat (ed.) *Villages in Indonesia*, Ithaca: Cornell University Press, pp281–298

Van Wey, L. K., C. M. Tucker and E. McConnell (2005) 'Community organisation, migration and remittances in Oaxaca', *Latin American Research Review* 40 (1): 83–108

Velayutham, S. and A. Wise (2005) 'Moral economics of a translocal village: Obligation and shame among South Indian transnational migrants', *Global Networks* 5 (1): 27–47

Winkels, A. (2004) 'Migratory livelihoods in Vietnam: Vulnerability and the role of social networks', unpublished doctoral thesis, Norwich: University of East Anglia

Witasari, A., R. Beilin, S. Batterbury and R. Nettle (2006) 'How does social capital matter in managing protected forest? A case of Indonesia', paper presented at the 11th Biennial Conference on Common Property: 'Survival of the Commons: Mounting Challenges and New Realities' 19–23 June 2006, Bali, Indonesia

Yeoh, B. S. A., S. Huang and T. Lam (2005) 'Transnationalizing the "Asian" family: Imaginaries, intimacies and strategic intents', *Global Networks* 5 (4), 307–315

Yong Ooi Lin, C. (2006) 'Autonomy reconstituted: Social and gendered implications of dam resettlement on the Orang Asli of Peninsular Malaysia', *Gender, Technology and Development* 10 (1): 77–100

Chapter 5

Women's Land Rights in Rural China: Current Situation and Likely Trends

Linxiu Zhang, Chengfang Liu, Haomiao Liu and Lerong Yu

Introduction

Women's land rights have become an issue in China's drive for a modernized and harmonious society. Despite the absence of large-scale studies, researchers have documented situations where women who are out-married (meaning that they are married to a man from a village other than that in which they were born), divorced or widowed, or girls who are above the customary marriage age but remain single, have difficulty getting land either in their out-married village or in their village of birth (Li, 2002).

There is a great deal of anecdotal evidence and numerous case studies about women who lose land during land reallocations, or as a result of changes in marital status. Li (2002) outlines five situations where women might lose their land. First, most villages in rural China are patrilocal, that is, women move to their husband's village on marriage. Married-in women (meaning women who have married a man from the same village) create a need for additional land for the new household. Second, due to policy and legal restrictions against land reallocations, women have increasing difficulty either obtaining land in their husband's village or retaining land in the village of their birth. Third, in the absence of land reallocations, the position of women is different from that of men. Unlike men, who can inherit land use rights in their village of birth, women cannot do so, since they move to their husband's village upon marriage, and hence upon marriage effectively become landless. Fourth, in many villages, girls who do not marry at the customary age face growing discrimination in land allocations. They are allocated a smaller share of land than men or no land at all. Finally, women who are widowed or divorced face growing difficulty in retaining land in their husband's village or being allocated land in their village of birth.

Few researchers have yet attempted to document or quantify key issues, such as how women have been affected during land reallocations, especially relative to men. There have been few studies that seek to understand what factors might contribute to or constrain women's land rights. The 'bits and pieces' in the literature on women's land rights in rural China are often incomplete. Hence, the aim of this chapter is to provide a better understanding of the current status of women's land rights in rural China and likely trends, in the hope that such information will inform actions taken to protect women's land rights. Specifically, we have three objectives. First, we provide a profile of women's land rights in rural China. Second, we examine how leaders of villages, the grass-roots governing body, perceive women's land rights. Finally, we investigate the factors ensuring or constraining rural women's land rights.

Land arrangements in China

Over the past three decades, China's rural land system has undergone three major changes: the Household Responsibility System (HRS), the 1998 Land Management Law and the 2003 Land Contracting Law. In this section, we briefly describe these three policy arrangements and their implications for women.

Household Responsibility System

Before the economic reforms started in the late 1970s, land was owned and managed by collectives and all activities were under the commune system. Between 1979 and 1983, China's land system shifted completely from collective ownership and cultivation to the household contract system, also known as the HRS, by granting households individual use rights to land for terms of 15 years. This change was based on an equitable distribution per household size of contracted land within production teams. The HRS implied that every member of a farm household would receive a piece of land of the same area. This shift to more individualized rights brought changes to rural women's lives, although the specific and differentiated impacts have not been widely studied. The HRS transferred authority over women's labour from the production team back to the head of the household. The HRS also allowed families to increase their revenues from agricultural production, resulting in marked increases in average household income. Although it is unclear how evenly distributed these increases in income were within households, it is probable that women gained some benefits. The HRS remains in place to this day.

The 1998 Land Management Law

The Land Management Law, which came into effect in 1998, strengthened individual farm household rights to land. There are several provisions in the law that could change women's land rights by providing for greater household land tenure security and by altering the way in which land is allocated to farm households through reallocations. The law attempts to increase land tenure security for farm households in three ways. First, the law extends the length of a term of use to 30 years. Second, the law requires written land use contracts that specify the duration and scope of household rights to land. Finally, the law reduces the frequency and scope of land reallocations. Village cadres had undertaken to maintain egalitarian per capita land distribution by periodically taking back and redistributing household land within the village to account for population changes within households. By constraining village reallocations, the law sought to eliminate a significant source of land tenure insecurity in China. This implies that over the next 30 years (assuming that the patrilocal marriage system remains in place), families with sons will have to support new daughters-in-law without additional land. Families with daughters, however, will retain 'excess' land when their daughters leave the household or village to marry.

The 2003 Land Contracting Law

The Land Contracting Law that came into effect in 2003 further strengthens the rights of households. This law states unequivocally that women and men have equal rights in respect to contracting land. Further, Article 30 stipulates that when a woman marries during the land contract term, the contract-issuing party cannot take away her original contracted land unless she receives land in her marriage village. When a woman is divorced or widowed, the contract-issuing party cannot take away her land if she still lives at her current place of residence or moves to a new place of residence where she cannot get land. Under this law, a woman should be given land in her marriage village instead of waiting for another round of land reallocations. Until a married woman has obtained land from her marriage village, her village of birth must keep land available for her.

Land rights and women's participation in agriculture

Under the HRS, although households do not own the land and cannot sell it, the use rights and residual income rights that have been extended to farm households offer benefits in several forms, such as the return-to-land as a factor of production, insurance and food security. Moreover, despite the rapid growth in off-farm employment in China, working off-farm is highly insecure and highly correlated with gender, age and education (Parish et al, 1995; Giles, 1998; Benjamin et al, 2000). Since it is typically older, less educated women who have less chance to work off-farm, land rights are relatively more valuable for this group. Land gives them a means to earn a return on their labour.

Meanwhile, there is a debate about the increasing participation of women in agriculture occurring in rural China. Both Judd (1990) and Song and Jiggins

(2000) describe women as 'taking over' farming in specific villages. Jacka (1997) quotes county officials in Sichuan talking about the 'feminization' of the agricultural labour force. Similarly, Rawski and Mead (1998) use aggregate provincial trends to suggest that women are taking over farm work in China. However, De Brauw et al (forthcoming) debunk the myth that China's agriculture is becoming feminized, concluding that agricultural feminization is not occurring in rural China. Based on employment history data for individuals from a representative sample of households, de Brauw et al examine the proportion of farm work done by women between 1990 and 2000. Their data show that the proportion of farm work done by women appears to have increased slightly during the early 1990s, peaking in 1995 and then declining thereafter, falling by nearly 5 per cent between 1995 and 2000. A drop in the percentage of farm work being done by women, on average, is not consistent with a story of agricultural feminization in China (see Figure 5.1). Feminization of agriculture would be a significant social trend with far-reaching implications. Hence, it is crucial for policy makers and for women to understand the current status of women's land rights.

Data

In this study, we use two sets of data on land management and tenure arrangements in rural China collected by the authors and their collaborators in 2003 and 2005. One set of data was collected at the village level ('the village data set'); the other data set was collected at the small group level ('the small group dataset').

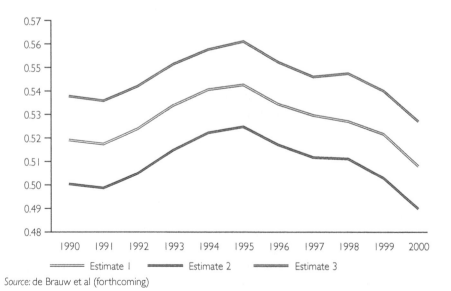

Source: de Brauw et al (forthcoming)

Figure 5.1 *Estimated proportion of household farm labour force that is female, 1990–2000*

The village data set was first collected at the end of 2003, with a follow-up survey in early 2005. The authors and several collaborators designed the sampling procedure and final survey instrument. The fieldwork team, made up of the four authors and 30 graduate students and research fellows, selected the sample and implemented the survey in five provinces and 25 counties in a nearly national representative sample in major agro-ecological zones.[1]

To accurately reflect varying income distributions within each province, we randomly selected five counties, one from each income quintile of a list of counties arranged in descending order of per capita gross value of industrial output. Within each county, we chose two townships, following the same procedure as the county selection. The survey team also randomly selected two villages within each county. In total, the survey covered 101 sample villages with data for the years 1998 and 2004.[2]

The survey collected a wide range of information on village characteristics, including land, population, labour, geographical location and economic development, with a particular focus on changes in women's land rights. For the purposes of verification and gathering effective information, interviews were carried out among several groups of people, including village leaders (village heads, party secretaries and village accountants), small group leaders and villagers (both men and women). For survey instruments, we used both formal interviews (based on pre-designed questionnaires) and participatory rural appraisals (PRAs), using focus group discussions. We also included information on land reallocation, such as reallocation time and the scale of households involved.

The small group data set was collected together with the village survey in 2005. The samples were within the sample framework of all the sample villages described above. To examine land reallocation in the village, we randomly selected three small groups in the sample village. Altogether we have data from 262 small groups and land readjustment information covering the period from 1991 to 2004.

A major focus of the small group survey was to understand land management practices at the community level. Land-related information includes population changes at small group level over time, who decides how and when to carry out land readjustment, and whether higher levels of government intervene in land readjustment decisions.

Land reallocation in rural China

Although the HRS stated that individual households would have at least 15 years of user rights to the land, evidence shows that land reallocations have happened in many villages. The 1998 Land Management Law further strengthened individual household rights to land by extending the length of the use term to 30 years. Under this new policy, one would expect that the frequency of land adjustments would decrease. However, evidence shows that land reallocation has actually increased in some areas.

Frequency of land reallocations

Our small group survey shows that more than half the small groups had experienced land reallocations during the study period and that there is some heterogeneity in the frequency of land reallocation. In response to our question on small group land readjustment between 1991 and 2004, 172 out of 262 small groups reported land reallocations. Some groups readjusted land more than once, other groups had as many as nine reallocations. On average, each small group had 1.6 land adjustments during the survey period (see Table 5.1). Moreover, there appears to be some regional heterogeneity in the frequency of land reallocation. For example, small groups in Sichuan had 2.3 land reallocations whereas those in Hebei and Shaanxi had only one (see Table 5.1).

The time lapse between two land reallocations decreased gradually over the study period. Our data show that in small groups where only two land reallocations were undertaken, the average time interval between two reallocations was 4.6 years. In contrast, in small groups where three land reallocations were undertaken, the average time interval between two reallocations was 1.5 years, and in groups where four reallocations occurred, the time interval was closer to one year (see Table 5.1).

Table 5.1 *Time lapse between two land reallocations*

Number of land adjustments per small group	Number of small groups	Time lapse between two land reallocations (years)
Two	60	4.6
Three	60	1.5
Four	28	1.1

Source: Authors' survey

Decision maker of land reallocations

Our data also show that local governing bodies above the county level and officials at the village level exercise a major influence over land reallocation. Between 1991 and 2004, village officials or governments above the county level made nearly half of all of land reallocation decisions. There was some regional heterogeneity in this regard, with interventions from higher levels of government ranging from nearly 70 per cent in Hebei province to less than 7 per cent in Shaanxi. Specifically, 46 per cent and 44 per cent of land reallocations were decided by villages or governments higher than the county level, respectively (see Table 5.2).

However, the data also reveal significant regional heterogeneity. While small groups in Jilin noted that 52 per cent of their land reallocation decisions were made by villages, in Hebei the proportion was only 30 per cent. By contrast, small groups in Hebei see almost 67 per cent of land reallocation decisions made by governing bodies above the county level, whereas in Shaanxi the number was less than 7 per cent. While township or county governments made few, if any, land

Table 5.2 *Decision makers for land reallocations in rural China, 1991–2004*

Province	Which level of government decided the land adjustment? (%)			
	Small group	Village	Township or county	Government above the county level
	(1)	(2)	(3)	(4)
Jiangsu	0	50.9	0	49.2
Sichuan	0	47.5	3.3	49.2
Shaanxi	23.3	40.0	30.0	6.7
Jilin	3.5	51.7	20.7	24.1
Hebei	0	30.3	3.0	66.7
China	3.0	45.8	7.4	43.9

Note: (1) + (2) + (3) + (4) = 100; any summation different from 100 is due to rounding error.

Source: Authors' survey

reallocation decisions in Jiangsu, Sichuan or Hebei, they made 21 per cent and 30 per cent of land reallocation decisions in small groups in Jilin and Shaanxi, respectively.

Changes in land area before and after land reallocations

By comparing the land area before and after reallocation (see Table 5.3), our data show that nearly all small groups, except those in Hebei, experienced a reduction in land area in absolute terms after land reallocations. Before land reallocation, the total land area in a small group was on average 383.3 *mu* (1 *mu* = 0.0667ha). This number dropped slightly to 377 *mu* after reallocation, a reduction of 6.3 *mu* on average. Again there is regional heterogeneity, with decreases ranging from 20.7 *mu* in Jiangsu to 1.1 *mu* in Sichuan. Although we have little information to determine the causal relations between land reallocation and reduction in land area, we can, at least, establish it as a fact.

Table 5.3 *Changes in land area in small groups after land reallocations* (mu)

Province	Before land adjustment (1)	After land adjustment (2)	Change in land area (3) = (2) – (1)
Jiangsu	719.0	698.4	-20.6
Sichuan	138.3	137.2	-1.1
Shaanxi	237.8	232.9	-4.8
Jilin	803.4	796.1	-7.3
Hebei	428.5	428.5	0
China	383.3	377.0	-6.3

Source: Authors' survey

Table 5.4 *Percentage of households whose plots and area changed after land reallocations*

	Households whose plots changed hands (%) (1)	Households whose land area changed (%) (2)	Households whose land area increased (%) (3)	Households whose land area decreased (%) (4) = (2) – (3)
Jiangsu	66.0	45.5	16.0	29.4
Sichuan	47.4	43.3	16.2	28.1
Shaanxi	38.2	43.7	22.3	21.5
Jilin	23.1	55.9	21.1	32.7
Hebei	81.8	46.6	26.9	19.1
China	52.3	45.6	18.6	27.2

Source: Authors' survey

Our data also show that plots of land change hands among households (Table 5.4). On the whole, 52 per cent of farm households no longer farm the same plots they farmed before land reallocation. However, averages disguise large variations across provinces. While almost 82 per cent of farm households in Hebei no longer farm the same plots as they used to farm before reallocation, this percentage is only 23 per cent in Jilin.

Consistent with the general decline in land area at the small group level, the percentage of households whose land area decreased exceeds the proportion of

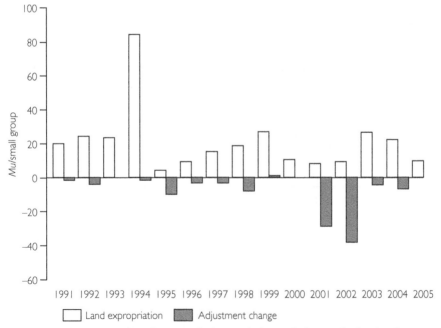

Figure 5.2 *Land expropriation and change before and after land adjustment in the small group*

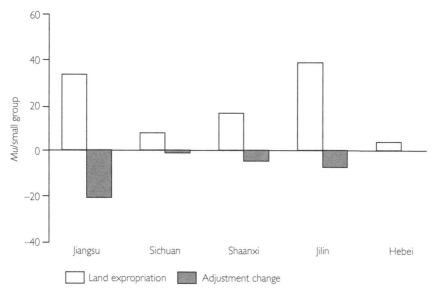

Figure 5.3 *Land expropriation and change before and after adjustment in small group by province*

households whose land area increased. Whereas nearly 27 per cent of farm households experienced a decrease in land area, nearly 19 per cent of farm households saw an increase. Again, there is variation across provinces. While 27 per cent of farm households in Hebei saw an increase in land area, this percentage is only 16 per cent in Jiangsu and Sichuan. While 20 per cent of farm households in Hebei saw a decrease in land area, this number is 33 per cent in Jilin.

What is behind the changes in land areas and plots in rural China? We attempted to find the answer by looking at land expropriations in small groups. Field observations revealed that sometimes land is expropriated for purposes such as roads, residential building or urbanization. Our data show that nearly all small groups experienced land expropriation between 1991 and 2005. The average expropriated land area was 21 *mu* (see Figure 5.2), more than three times the reduction in land area, which is 6.3 *mu* (see Table 5.3). The situation is similar across provinces (see Figure 5.3). Clearly, land expropriation is an important explanation for the reduction in land area after reallocations.

Women's land rights at the village level

Who are the landless in rural China? A gender perspective

One widely held public perception is that more rural women are losing their land rights due to either changes in their marital status or because of land conversion. Our data show that there has been a trend towards landlessness among villagers,

Table 5.5 *Landless villagers at the village level, 1998 and 2004 (%)*

Province	No.	Landless villagers		Landless female villagers		Among all landless villagers, % female	
		1998	2004	1998	2004	1998	2004
		(1)	(2)	(3)	(4)	(5) =	(6) =
						(3)/(1)×100	(4)/(2)×100
Jiangsu	20	7.1	11.0	3.4	5.3	47.9	48.2
Sichuan	20	7.3	8.6	3.8	4.4	52.1	51.2
Shaanxi	20	3.0	6.2	1.5	3.2	50.0	51.6
Jilin	21	8.3	8.9	3.6	4.0	43.4	44.9
Hebei	20	5.1	8.4	3.0	5.2	58.8	61.9
China	101	6.2	8.6	3.1	4.4	50.0	51.2

Source: Authors' survey

with 6.2 per cent of villagers landless in 1998 and 8.6 per cent in 2004 (see Table 5.5). Again, averages disguise heterogeneity across provinces. During the same period, while the percentage of landless villagers more than doubled in villages in Shaanxi (from 3.0 per cent to 6.2 per cent), it increased much less in Jilin (from 8.3 per cent to 8.9 per cent).

When looking at gender in landless villagers, we observed a slight increase in the proportion of landless female villagers from 3.1 per cent in 1998 to 4.4 per cent in 2004. Similarly, there is heterogeneity in changes in the percentage of landless women across provinces during this period. While the percentage of landless women more than doubled (from 1.5 per cent to 3.2 per cent) in villages in Shaanxi, the percentage of landless women increased only slightly in Jilin (from 3.6 per cent to 4.0 per cent). The percentage of landless women in 1998 was the highest in villages in Sichuan (3.8 per cent). By 2004, Jiangsu had the highest percentage of landless women (5.3 per cent). Villages in Shaanxi were lowest in both 1998 and 2004.

Overall, the percentage of landless women increased slightly at the village level during the period 1998–2004, from 50 per cent to 51.2 per cent. Almost all villages in all sample provinces (the exception being Sichuan) witnessed slight increases. Similarly, there are differences in the magnitude of change. While the percentage of landless women increased the least in villages in Jiangsu (from 47.9 per cent to 48.2 per cent), it increased the most in Hebei (from 58.8 per cent to 61.9 per cent). The percentage of landless women was highest in villages in Hebei, and lowest in Jilin in 1998; the same pattern was found in 2004.

Confirming popular perceptions, our survey shows that most villages did not provide any subsidy for women who did not have land rights in their marriage villages (see Table 5.6). Villages in Shaanxi are the only exceptions in that during the sample period they provided subsidies for women who did not have land rights in their marriages. Jilin is an extreme case, since no villages provided any landless subsidy to women at all in either 1998 or 2004. For villages in Jiangsu,

Table 5.6 *Availability of subsidies for landless women (%)*

Province	No.	Yes		No		Do not know	
		1998	2004	1998	2004	1998	2004
		(1)	(2)	(3)	(4)	(5) =	(6) =
						100–(1)–(3)	100–(2)–(4)
Jiangsu	20	0	0	70	90	30	10
Sichuan	20	0	0	85	95	15	5
Shaanxi	20	5	5	80	85	15	10
Jilin	21	0	0	100	100	0	0
Hebei	20	0	0	95	100	5	0
China	101	1	1	86	94	13	5

Source: Authors' survey

Sichuan, Shaanxi and Hebei, an overwhelming majority did not provide the landless with any subsidy at all. Constrained by traditional customs and the distance between their village of birth and their marriage village, it is difficult for landless women to ask for a share of land or any benefits associated with land rights.

Village leaders' perception about women's land rights

In rural China, village leaders are in charge of the management of the village and are a major influence on land reallocation. Thus, it is necessary to explore how village leaders perceive the issue of land accessibility and women. In this subsection, we focus on the land rights of three sub-groups of women: newly married, divorced and widowed.

Land rights of newly married women

It has become increasingly difficult for newly married women to get land in their marriage villages in rural China. In our survey, 48 per cent of village leaders claim that in their villages newly married women could not get any land at all in 1998. This percentage increased to 55 per cent by 2004. The percentage of village leaders who claimed that they did not allocate land to newly married women in their villages until the next land reallocation was the same (43.1 per cent) in 1998 and 2004. By contrast, during the sample period, no more than 2 per cent of villagers said that they allocate land to newly married women in their villages if the village has collective land. Overall, 6 per cent of village leaders said that they allocated land to newly married women immediately after their marriage in 1998 whereas no village did so in 2004.

Again, there exist regional differences in village leaders' perception of women's land rights. For example, in Jiangsu, Shaanxi and Hebei, at least 75 per cent of village leaders said that women could not get land in their villages in both 1998 and 2004, while in Sichuan and Jilin, at least 75 per cent village leaders said that newly married women in their villages had to wait until the next land realloca-

Table 5.7 *Village leaders, can newly married women get land in your village? (%)*

Province	No.	No		Yes, if the village has collective land		Yes, but they have to wait until the next land reallocation		Yes, immediately after marriage		Others	
		1998 (1)	2004 (2)	1998 (3)	2004 (4)	1998 (5)	2004 (6)	1998 (7)	2004 (8)	1998 (9)	2004 (10)
Jiangsu	20	80	80	0	0	20	20	0	0	0	0
Sichuan	20	5	5	5	5	75	90	15	0	0	0
Shaanxi	20	75	100	5	0	5	0	15	0	0	0
Jilin	21	4.8	4.8	0	0	90.5	90.5	0	0	4.8	4.8
Hebei	20	75	85	0	0	25	15	0	0	0	0
China	101	48	55	2	1	43.1	43.1	6	0	1	1

Source: Authors' survey

tion to get land. In 1998, in both Sichuan and Shaanxi, 15 per cent of village leaders said that newly married women could receive land immediately after marriage, whereas no village did so in 2004. In general, it appears that married women are facing increasing difficulty getting land rights (see Table 5.7).

Married women also have difficulty retaining their land in their natal villages. Here, we draw on case studies conducted by one of the authors in Guangdong, a coastal province in the southeast that is experiencing one of the fastest rates of industrialization and urbanization in China. In the 1990s, Guangdong introduced a land shareholding cooperative system. Under the shareholding system, the land use rights of individual farm households were converted into shares. After receiving land shares, individual farm households return their land use rights to the village. The village is now in charge of land use. As land shareholders, farm households are able to share dividends.

However, in Guangdong province alone, tens of thousands of married women who do not physically live in their village of birth get no shares or few shares or dividends, even though their household registration permit is still in their village of birth. In Beiting village in Panyu district of Guangzhou City, for example, by 2005 about 100 married women had lost their land shares and dividends in their village of birth, even though their land registration was still in the village. Consequently, these married women do not share the benefits associated with land use nor do they get land in their marriage village. Without this land-based social welfare and insurance, married women find it more difficult to make a living.

Our village survey shows that when a woman is either divorced or widowed, her share of land is treated in one of three ways: either it is retained by the woman automatically, or it is taken back by the village, or it is treated along with her residence registration. If her residence registration was transferred to her former husband's village, she may be able to keep land that is owned collectively by the

Table 5.8 *How village leaders deal with divorced women's land (%)*

Province	No.	She retains her land		Village takes back her land		Depending on her Hukou		Nothing to deal with since she did not get land here when she married in		Do not know	
		1998 (1)	2004 (2)	1998 (3)	2004 (4)	1998 (5)	2004 (6)	1998 (7)	2004 (8)	1998 (9)	2004 (10)
Jiangsu	20	60	50	5	5	0	0	25	30	10	15
Sichuan	20	65	80	20	0	0	0	15	20	0	0
Shaanxi	20	75	95	20	0	0	5	0	0	5	0
Jilin	21	100	95.2	0	0	0	4.8	0	0	0	0
Hebei	20	70	90	10	0	5	5	10	5	5	0
China	101	74	82	11	1	1	3	10	11	4	3

Source: Authors' survey

village.[3] In general, the land rights of divorced women who were already allocated land in their marriage village are better ensured than those of married women who live in their marriage villages.

Land rights of divorced women

In our village survey, 74 per cent of village leaders responded that divorced women retained their land in 1998 (see Table 5.8). This percentage went up to 82 per cent in 2004. Meanwhile, 11 per cent of village leaders said that in 1998, the village took back the land when a woman was divorced, whereas only 1 per cent did so in 2004. There is variation in divorced women's land rights across provinces. Over the sample period, more and more villages in Sichuan, Shaanxi and Hebei let divorced women retain their land. In contrast, in Jiangsu and Jilin, the two richer provinces in our sample, fewer villages let divorced women retain their land. Furthermore, an increasing percentage of villages in Jiangsu and Sichuan said that they had no land for divorced women, since these women did not get land when they married. Thus, although more than half of divorced women can retain their land, other divorced women had not had land at all since the start of their marriages. How to better ensure the land rights of divorced women poses a challenge for the government.

Land rights of widowed women

Are widows discriminated against in keeping their land after their husbands pass away? Clearly, they are not (see Table 5.9). Our data show that during the sample period, in almost all villages (98 per cent), widowed women kept their land. The only exception is Sichuan, where some villages took back widows' land in 1998, though none did so in 2004.

Table 5.9 *How village leaders deal with widowed women's land (%)*

Province	No.	She retains her land		Village takes back her land		Other	
		1998 (1)	2004 (2)	1998 (3)	2004 (4)	1998 (5)	2004 (6)
Jiangsu	20	100	100	0	0	0	0
Sichuan	20	90	95	5	0	5	5
Shaanxi	20	100	100	0	0	0	0
Jilin	21	100	100	0	0	0	0
Hebei	20	100	100	0	0	0	0
China	101	98	99	1	0	1	1

Source: Authors' survey

Explaining inter-village differences in women's land rights

While we have so far shown that women's land rights are better in some villages than in others, there are still some unanswered questions. For example, do village land endowment and structure matter? Are women's land rights better secured in poor villages? How does off-farm employment affect women's land rights? During the policy expansion of good community governance, does direct election of village leaders help secure women's land rights? Does the presence of women in the village committee help secure women's land rights? In this section, we identify some of the determinants of women's land rights. To do so, we employ both descriptive statistics and multivariate analysis.

Descriptive statistics

One of the empirically interesting factors correlated with women's land rights in our descriptive statistics is the level of net per capita income in the village. Our data also allow us to classify villages into poor, middle and rich, based on net per capita income in the village. When we cross-tabulate the percentage of landless women villagers and income level, two clear patterns emerge. First, villages in all income groups experienced increases in the percentage of landless women villagers from 1998 to 2004, with some variations. While the percentage of landless women villagers increased the least in middle-income villages (from 3.3 per cent to 4.4 per cent), it increased the most in poorer villages (from 2.2 per cent to 3.7 per cent). Second, the richer a village is, the more landless female villagers there are in the village. For example, when a village went from the poor category to the rich category in 1998, the percentage of landless villagers increased from 2.2 per cent to 3.7 per cent. Similarly in 2004, when a village went from the poor category to the rich category, the percentage of landless villagers increased from 3.7 per cent to 5.1 per cent (see Table 5.10).

Table 5.10 *Cross-tabulations between covariates and percentage of landless female villagers*

Income categories	1998	2004
Poorer	2.2	3.7
Middle	3.3	4.4
Richer	3.7	5.1

Off-farm employed village labour force	1998	2004
0–20%	2.4	3.9
20–40%	3.4	4.3
>40%	5.3	4.8

Source: Authors' survey

Descriptive correlates between women's land rights and off-farm employment can also be identified through cross-tabulations. Our descriptive data show that the more the village labour force is employed off-farm, the higher the percentage of landless female villagers. As villages move from the category with 0–20 per cent labour force off-farm employed to the category with more than 40 per cent labour force employed, the percentage of landless women villagers increased from 2.4 per cent to 5.3 per cent in 1998. A similar increase applied in 2004, from 3.9 per cent to 4.8 per cent. While villages with more than 40 per cent labour force employed off-farm saw a slight decrease in the percentage of women landless during the study period (from 5.3 per cent in 1998 to 4.8 per cent 2004), villages in the other two off-farm employment categories saw increases in these percentages. Moreover, villages with less than 20 per cent labour force employed off-farm experienced a much greater increase in the percentage of landless women villagers than villages with 20–40 per cent labour force employed off-farm (68 per cent vs. 33 per cent) (see Table 5.10).

Multivariate analysis

To further examine the determinants of women's land rights, we used a series of regressions to examine the factors that lead to better women's land rights in some villages than in others. To implement the multivariate analysis, we examine the effect of a number of factors on the percentage of landless women villagers in the total village population. The explanatory variables are of four types:

1   *Village land endowment factors,* including per capita land area and the percentage of collectively managed land. Per capita land area captures both population pressure and land availability in a village. We would expect that the more land a village has, the fewer landless women there are in the village.
2   *Economic development factors,* including per capita income and the percentage of the village labour force employed off-farm. We would expect that the more economically developed a village, the more difficult it is for women to get

land, thus the higher the percentage of landless women villagers.

3   *Land reallocation factors*, including the frequency of land reallocation. This is a dummy variable indicating whether the village land reallocation needs approval by the township government. We would expect that if a village needs approval, the percentage of landless female villagers would be higher. Our intuition is that given the current policy circumstances, the permission requirement means villages cannot reallocate land among households to account for demographic changes, thus those landless women remain landless, as do newly married-in women.

4   *Governance factors*, including a dummy variable indicating whether the village leader was directly elected and the lagged percentage of women members on the village committee. We would expect that the better village governance, the lower the percentage of landless women villagers. In other words, we expect the percentage of landless women villagers to be lower in villages with directly elected village leaders, and with relatively more women on village committees.

In addition, we introduce province and year dummies to account for unobservable factors at the province and year levels that might affect women's land rights. The mean, standard error and range of the main variables used in the regression analysis are in Table 5.11.

As one of the governance factors (percentage of female village committee members) entered our specification with its lags, we ran two empirical specifications: one without governance variables that uses all samples for years 1998 and

Table 5.11 *Summary statistics of main variables*

Variables	No.	Mean	S.D.	Min.	Max.
Dependent variable					
Percentage of landless female villagers in the village population	202	3.74	5.75	0	40.10
Explanatory variables					
Per capita land area (*mu*)	202	1.91	1.56	0	8.10
Percentage of collectively managed land	198	3.41	5.96	0	37.50
Net per capita income (yuan)	202	2092.70	1301.56	200	6596
% of village labour force employed off-farm	202	29.88	21.67	0.67	95.12
Does village land reallocation need approval by the township government? (1 = yes, 0 = no)	202	0.92	0.28	0	1
Was the village leader directly elected? (1 = yes, 0 = no)	202	0.51	0.50	0	1
% of female village committee members	101	23.37	25.13	0	100

Source: Authors' survey

Table 5.12 *Determinants of women's land rights at the village level*

	Dependent variable: percentage of landless female villagers	
	All sample	*Subsample of 2004*
1. Village land endowment factors		
Per capita land area (*mu*)	−1.187 (−3.52)***	−0.965 (−2.86)***
% of collectively managed land	−0.125 (−2.32)**	−0.132 (−2.08)**
2. Economic development factors		
Middle-income village? (1 = yes, 0 = no)	0.101 (0.12)	1.338 (1.13)
Richer village? (1 = yes, 0 = no)	0.558 (0.33)	2.711 (1.53)
% of labour force employed off-farm	0.023 (1.02)	0.017 (0.49)
3. Land reallocation factor		
Does village land reallocation need approval by township government? (1 = yes, 0 = no)	3.099 (2.85)***	4.077 (2.16)**
Frequency of land reallocation (times)	−1.096 (−1.54)*	−1.452 (−2.73)**
4. Governance factors		
Was village leader directly elected? (1 = yes, 0 = no)	0.366 (0.47)	−0.152 (−0.13)
% of female village committee members	No	−0.045 (−2.91)***
5. Province dummy variables	Yes	No
6. Year dummy variable	Yes	No
Constant	0.989 (0.64)	3.591 (1.10)
No. of observations	198	99
R-squared	0.15	0.18

Note: t-statistic in parentheses. *significant at 10 per cent, ** significant at 5 per cent, *** significant at 1 per cent.

Source. Authors' survey

2004; the other with governance variables that uses observations for the year 2004 only. On the whole, results from running these two specifications are similar and are presented in Table 5.12.

Although there are a number of exceptions, the results of the multivariate analysis lend supporting evidence for our hypotheses. For example, we find empirical evidence in support of our village land endowment hypothesis. In villages with more land on a per capita basis and more of that land managed by the village collective, there is a relatively lower percentage of women who are landless. It is possible that since villages have more land resource under their own control, they will take steps to allocate a share of land to women.

Our women's participation hypothesis is also supported by results from the multivariate analysis. Women's participation in village governance is important. In fact, villages with more women committee members have a smaller proportion of landless women. One plausible explanation is that since villages are major decision makers in village land reallocations, more women on the village committee (the village governing body) can be translated into more voices for women's land rights.

The multivariate analysis also lends supporting evidence to our land realloca- tion hypothesis. In villages with fewer land reallocations, and where approval by the township government is needed for land reallocations, there are relatively fewer landless women villagers. It is possible that since getting land adjustment approval from the township government is costly in terms of time and effort, that villages will not take steps towards reallocating land to landless villagers. In terms of the frequency of land reallocations, the more frequently the land has been reallocated among farm households, the land rights of more landless villagers having been taken care of, the lower the proportion of landless women villagers. By contrast, in the multivariate analysis, we did not find any of the economic development variables to be statistically significant.

Hence, we can surmise that villages with relatively more land, a larger part of land under collective management, a larger number of women on the village committee and more frequent land reallocations have relatively fewer landless women. Villages that need land reallocation approval from the township govern- ment have a relatively higher proportion of landless women.

Summary and conclusions

In this chapter, we used two primary data sets to create a profile of women's land rights at the village level in rural China. In doing so, we found that, overall, there is little statistically significant evidence that women in rural Chinese villages are discriminated against in terms of land rights. This is in contrast to the popular perception that women are losing land during economic transitions, and more so when land management policies are targeted at the household level rather than at the individual level. In fact, among landless villagers, approximately half are women and half are men, indicating no significant gender difference.

Our results show, however, that there has been a slight increase in the percentage of landless people, both men and women, in rural China. Moreover, it appears very unlikely for women who become landless due to changes in marital status to obtain land again. Losing land rights means a loss of those benefits associated with land rights, such as returning to the land, an opportunity to use one's own labour, insurance and food security. However, in the context of rural China, it is difficult to measure the impacts of women's land loss since the land distribution unit is the farm household rather than the individual. Some cases studies have shown that having no land exerts a negative effect on women's life security and their children's education. For a significant majority of rural households, land is the single most important source of security against poverty (Agarwal, 2002).

When assessing the determinants of women's land rights, we found that population pressure and limited land endowments are critical factors. Huang (1992) uses the same arguments (high population density and limited land resources) to explain rural development patterns and land use patterns in the Yangtze Delta in the last century. Thus, if women in rural Chinese villages, especially married women living in their marriage villages, want to obtain land in their husbands' villages, it will, to a large extent, depend on the amount of collectively managed land set aside by the village collective when the HRS was initiated in late 1970s. If the amount of collectively managed land is limited, these women cannot obtain land until the next land reallocation. On the one hand, land is limited relative to the continually increasing population in rural China. On the other hand, land tenure is limited in that land is owned by collectives, and no individual or rural collective organization has any right to dispose of the land without permission from the state. In such circumstances, promoting economic development, generating more off-farm jobs and improving social security would be rational policy options for the government. With more off-farm job opportunities and better social security, rural women would not need to rely so much on land.

Although our results show that villages with frequent land reallocations had a lower percentage of landless women during the sample period, it should be noted that frequent land adjustment is not a viable option to ensure women's land rights, since the term of land contracts is 30 years and policy enforcement is getting stricter. Thus, compensations other than land reallocation should be considered to ensure women's welfare associated with land rights.

Our results also show that increasing women's participation in village governance is an effective way of protecting women's land rights. Hence, government and individual women should try to increase their participation in community management. Through participation, women can voice their needs to protect their land rights. Unfortunately, the current picture of women's' participation in rural China is not promising. A recent study by Ye et al (2006) shows that few woman become leaders in rural Chinese villages. In fact, in 101 sample villages, only one village head was a woman and there were no women party secretaries. Undoubtedly, there is still a long way to go towards increasing women's participation in village governance. One way to strengthen women's participation might be group-based programmes. These groups help women to access critical support services and strengthen their participation in social activities. However, it is necessary to remember that women are not a homogeneous group, and particular attention should be given to different sub-groups of women to ensure that all women can participate effectively in such programmes. Involving more women in development processes may require special outreach and training for older, poorer and less educated women and for those who hesitate to voice their needs in front of men. At the same time, raising the gender consciousness of the public, especially leaders, will be useful for the development of women and society.

Notes

1   The sample villages come from five representative provinces: Jiangsu represents the eastern coastal areas (Jiangsu, Shandong, Shanghai, Zhejiang, Fujian, Guangdong and Hainan); Sichuan represents the southwestern provinces (Sichuan, Chongqing, Guizhou and Yunnan) plus Guangxi; Shaanxi represents the provinces on the Loess Plateau (Gansu, Ningxia, Qinghai, Shaanxi and Shanxi) and neighbouring Inner Mongolia; Hebei represents the north and central provinces (Hebei, Beijing, Tianjin, Henan, Anhui, Hubei, Jiangxi and Hunan); and Jilin represents the northeastern provinces (Jilin, Liaoning and Heilongjiang).

2   There were 20 sample villages in each province, except for Jilin, from which 21 sample villages were selected.

3   Every individual is given a residence registration record when they are born. This is transferable among rural areas, but it is difficult to transfer between rural and urban areas. This is the famous separated rural/urban registration system, which has prevailed for more than five decades in China.

References

Agarwal, B. (2002) *Are We Not Peasants Too? Land Rights and Women's Claims in India*, SEEDS 21, New York: Population Council

Benjamin, D., L. Brandt and S. Rozelle (2000) 'Aging, well-being, and social security in rural north China', *Population and Development* 26 (Supplement 2000): 89–116

De Brauw, A., Qiang Li, Chengfang Liu, S. Rozelle and Linxiu Zhang (forthcoming) 'Feminization of agriculture in China? Debunking myths surrounding women's participation in farming', *China Quarterly*

Giles, J. (1998) 'Off farm labour markets, insecurity, and risk aversion in China', mimeo, Department of Economics, University of California Berkeley

Huang Zongzhi (1992) *Household and Rural Development in Yangtze Delta* [in Chinese], Beijing: China Book Bureau

Jacka, T. (1997) *Women's Work in Rural China: Change and Continuity in an Era of Reform*, Cambridge: Cambridge University Press

Judd, E. (1990) 'Alternative development strategies for women in rural China', *Development and Change* 21 (1): 23–42

Li Zongmin (2002) 'Women's Land Rights in Rural China', consultant's report, Commissioned by Ford Foundation in Beijing

Parish, W., X. Zhe and F. Li (1995) 'Non-farm work and marketization of the Chinese countryside', *The China Quarterly* 143: 697–730

Rawski, T. and R. W. Mead (1998) 'On the trail of China's phantom farmers', *World Development* 26 (5): 767–781

Song, Y. and J. Jiggins (2000) 'Feminization of agriculture and related issues: Two case studies in marginal rural areas in China', working paper presented at the European Conference on Agricultural and Rural Development in China (ECARDC VI), Leiden, The Netherlands

Ye Chunhui, Yu Lerong and Zhang Linxiu (2006) 'Who can speak out for women?', proceedings (Chinese) of Gender and Land Tenure Policy Workshop, Center for Chinese Agricultural Policy, Chinese Academy of Sciences, Beijing, 21 March 2006

Part 2

Gender Interventions: Targeting Women in Sustainable Development Projects

Chapter 6

Autonomy Reconstituted: Social and Gendered Implications of Resettlement on the Orang Asli of Peninsular Malaysia[1]

Carol Yong Ooi Lin

Introduction

The Orang Asli (literally, 'first people') are known as the original inhabitants of West Malaysia, or Peninsular Malaysia. They comprise 18 ethnic sub-groups, but for administrative purposes are classified officially into three main groups, namely Negrito, Senoi and Proto-Malay. Currently, they represent approximately 0.6 per cent of the national population of Malaysia of 23.27 million (Malaysian Government Census; JHEOA, 2000). This chapter examines the social and gendered consequences of the involuntary resettlement of the Orang Asli, who have been displaced by two large dam projects, the Temenggor Dam in Upper Perak and the Sungai Selangor Dam in Kuala Kubu Bahru. Resettlement has had severe impacts on displaced Orang Asli communities because it has so drastically altered their livelihood strategies and impacted on their identity (World Bank, 1994; World Commission on Dams, 2000). The Orang Asli have been forced to move from their homelands to large state projects, and Ghai (1994) notes such projects are usually linked to powerful vested interests, resulting not only in personal losses but also in violation of the community's customary land and ancestral rights.

I start by briefly discussing some conceptual issues in dam-induced displacement and resettlement, and the research problems thus raised. The chapter next provides background information on the recent history of Orang Asli resettlement, the two dams and relocation programmes, and the methods of data collection. Against this background, I examine how loss of Orang Asli economic and social autonomy due to state-imposed dam projects and resettlement has radically reordered the pre-existing dominant normative framework on land property and access, contributing to a general loss of women's access and rights to land. The conclusion reiterates the complexity of dam resettlement processes and their inextricable links to broader questions of land rights and resource access.

Displacement and resettlement

The 20th century has been characterized as the 'century of the refugee' (Colson, 2003). Development-induced displacement remains an urgent issue, invariably affecting indigenous and tribal communities. The adverse impact of inundation on household and community livelihoods has been well documented, particularly through the 1980s, a period Dwivedi (2002, p710) called the 'decade of displacement'. Various studies have described the consequences of forced resettlement (Scudder and Colson, 1982; Goldsmith and Hildyard, 1984; Dreze et al, 1997; Mahapatra, 1999; Yong, 2003). Others have highlighted the violence and intimidation around dam and resettlement disputes (Colson, 1971; Hansen and Oliver-Smith, 1982). Those displaced are largely indigenous and tribal peoples. As the World Commission on Dams (WCD) (2000, p110) attests:

> *Due to neglect and lack of capacity to secure justice because of structural inequities, cultural dissonance, discrimination and economic and political marginalization, indigenous and tribal peoples have suffered disproportionately from the negative impacts of large dams, while often being excluded from sharing in the benefits.*

A noted expert in the field of resettlement issues is Michael Cernea (1999, 2000), the proponent of the Impoverishment Risks and Reconstruction Model. Cernea's hypothesis is that displacement with no resettlement policies or poorly handled resettlement policies results in eight main risks of impoverishment: landlessness, joblessness, homelessness, marginalization, increased morbidity, food insecurity, loss of access to common property and social disarticulation. His model assumes that resettlement policies can fail to protect those at risk, but the inadequacies and failings of resettlement can be minimized by operationalizing mitigation measures in the planning process (Cernea, 1997).

Cernea's model has been a groundbreaking influence on policies for infrastructure development, but there are weaknesses in his approach. First, his approach assumes that the dislocated community is homogeneous and thus ignores the fact that risks are borne differently by different groups within the community and that mitigating the risks for some can increase the vulnerability of others. As Dwivedi (1999) argues, social divisions such as gender, class, religion and ethnicity determine the degree of impoverishment risk faced or perceived by different displaced peoples (for example, women, men, rich farmers, landless, indigenous people and politically marginalized groups) and each has different and varied responses to involuntary resettlement. Second, in assuming that risks are built into the planning process and can be anticipated, minimized or mitigated, he ignores the argument that impoverishment is also a consequence of structural inequalities, cultural dissonance, institutional discrimination and political marginalization (World Commission on Dams, 2000).

Recent studies have linked large dam building and its consequences with historical and political circumstances (KHRP, 1999, 2003) or with social and environmental history (Isaacman and Sneddon, 2000). These studies raise questions about the broader context of authoritarian states in colonial and post-colonial times, and their use of coercive power to achieve economic, political and strategic objectives. Isaacman and Sneddon (2000, p600) argue that:

> *The Cahora Bassa dam on the Lower Zambesi River in Mozambique is about an authoritarian colonial state willing and able to use the full weight of its coercive power to achieve a set of economic and strategic objectives, which Lisbon believes would enable it to strengthen its hold over Mozambique. The deleterious social and ecological consequences of this massive, state-imposed project never figured in the colonial equation.*

Similarly, one of the central propositions of this chapter is that the exercise of state power over the Orang Asli in Malaysia is an exercise in justification. The state-imposed project, designed to integrate the rural and backward Orang Asli into national society (Hooker, 1991), provided an effective means of resettling the Orang Asli by controlling and appropriating their resources, particularly their land. As Colchester (1994) points out, 'government-directed, large-scale development projects such as plantations, dams and mines are justified as being in the national interest, and the state is therefore exercising its power of eminent domain in denying local peoples' rights' (p80). Scott's (1998) ideology of high modernism is helpful in understanding why development projects are implemented by the modern state, and at times replicated, despite it being known they are problematic. Scott claims that it is because of the quest to assume greater control over its territory and power that the state has devised numerous schemes intended to improve the human condition, but that these have 'gone tragically awry' (p4).

While there is a vast literature on gender and the environment (Joekes et al, 1994), gender is still largely missing in the dams and resettlement literature and in public debate. It is only recently that the WCD has attempted to focus on gender and dams under the thematic review process, pointing out that dam-related relocation programmes cannot be fully understood without a concern for gender. According to the WCD (2000), gender gaps have widened and women have frequently borne a disproportionate share of the social costs because they are often discriminated against in the sharing of benefits. Thus, the WCD process recommends that a comprehensive assessment be made on issues such as gender, displacement and development, which have not received the attention they deserve, and it lays down social and gender equity as one of the five principles in the process of resettlement.

The role of the state in the resettlement of the Orang Asli

A critical episode in the British occupation of Malaya was the Emergency of 1948–1960, when the colonial government was at war with the communist insurgents. Under the guise of 'national security', the colonial government embarked on the mass relocation of the 'dispersed and scattered rural population ... into barbed wire perimeter, fortified entries, look-out towers, and an armed guard of police' (Dobby, 1952–1953, pp163–164). About half a million of those resettled were of Chinese origin, whom the British suspected might be communist members or sympathizers. The Orang Asli were also forcibly resettled so that they would not support the insurgents (Dobby, 1952–1953; Public Records Office, Kew, 1952, 1953; Noone, 1972). Unlike Chinese villagers, who were allowed to plant vegetable gardens, the Orang Asli were completely cut off from their normal activities of hunting, fishing and forest foraging. Further, Orang Asli homes and food stocks were destroyed and their *ladang* (farmlands) and crops bombed. Hundreds died from the physical and psychological shock or simply lost the will to live (Dobby, 1952–1953; Noone, 1972; Carey, 1976; Hood, 1996). Some escaped by cutting the barbed wire at night and fleeing back to the deep jungle while others, though still unaffected, abandoned their villages and retreated into the jungle, or sought protection from the insurgents.

In late 1953, the British colonialists recognized that the policy of resettling the Orang Asli outside the jungle had been a failure. They devised a new tactic of winning the hearts and minds of the Orang Asli by creating forts in the jungle and bringing medical services and other amenities to them. With the success of this tactic, the post-colonial government has retained the jungle forts for Orang Asli. In 1976, the government further proposed a plan to regroup the Orang Asli settlements in the Titiwangsa region, along the central main range thought to be bases for communist insurgents (FDTCP, 1979). This culminated in the establishment of 25 regroupment schemes in the Titiwangsa area, including Air Banun, where one of the study sites is located.[2]

Officially, moving the Orang Asli into regroupment schemes is seen as a political project to protect the Orang Asli, who are assumed to be isolated from national society. The idea that the government could provide protection for the Orang Asli is supported by the scientific creation of the 'backward primitive', as Escobar (1991, 1995) has suggested, which in turn created the idea of a deficiency or underdevelopment that needed to be addressed. Dobby (1952–53) wrote that, to the colonial government, helping the Orang Asli meant bringing civilization to them and protecting them from enemies, which in the context of security meant the communist insurgents.[3] Following the protectionist policy of the colonizers, the government took advantage of the situation to continue resettling the Orang Asli, although it changed its purpose from security to infrastructure development. Building dams provides the main impetus for such development and, at the same time, justifies the project of resettling the Orang Asli and controlling and appropriating their resources, particularly land. As

Eriksen (1995, p47) reminds us, 'power-holders in any society must in one way or another legitimate their power'.

There are no current official estimates of the total number of persons displaced by dam projects in Malaysia, but new dams being built or proposed continue to affect those living in project areas. A former Minister of Works announced that 260 suitable dam sites had been identified, as another 47 dams are needed in Peninsular Malaysia by the year 2010, largely to meet the power demands of urban centres and industry (Tan, 1997). This obviously poses a threat to the Orang Asli living on ancestral lands in river ecosystems and forests.

Dam-displaced Orang Asli are most often relocated in regroupment schemes or resettlement sites with hardly any guarantee over their land tenure. The state plays a critical role in implementing its agenda and programmes with regards to the Orang Asli, given that its powers have been endorsed by both the British colonial and Malaysian governments (see Malaysian Government, 1954; Ministry of Interior, 1961) with support from vested economic interests. These projects invariably involve state appropriation of forests and rivers, in addition to the resettlement of the affected communities (Gadgil and Guha, 1994). The problem is aggravated by compensation that is not commensurate with their losses, and frequently lacking completely. The implications for women are more far-reaching, on account of the absence of security over the tenure of their lands as indigenous people, and because of unequal opportunities with regard to access and rights to land from within their own society when the application and practice of customary law has been undermined by the state (Yong, 2006).

Women are generally absent from the schemes of the state except in relation to ideologies of family and women's place within them. Seemingly obvious are models of women's roles in the broader context of society and the state through powerful mediating forces such as the family and religion (Healey, 1999). Attention is thus focused on a number of programmes that are primarily, although not exclusively, targeted at women and training them to be 'good wives and mothers'.

The Sungai Selangor Dam is a case in point. In April 2001, the dam concessionaire, Konsortium TSWA-GAMUDA-KDEB (later called Syarikat Pengeluar Air Sungai Selangor or SPLASH)[4], initiated Taklimat Rumah Sempurna, or the Familiarization Programme for Orang Asli Womenfolk, prior to their resettlement to Kampong Gerachi and Kampong Peretak. This programme 'is specifically for the womenfolk to equip them with knowledge on the use of modern house equipment and appliances, household management, cleanliness and hygiene' (www.splash.com.my). A front-page picture of a group of women being briefed on 'urban living' by a state community development officer also appeared in the daily newspaper *Metro* (27 April 2001). In contrast, the men were provided with training on building construction to prepare them for jobs at the dam site. This dominant gender stereotype is all too familiar to feminists: women being better nurturers and men being better at earning money, resulting in the extension of gender inequality in the family and in society.

The Temenggor Dam and resettlement of the Jahai

The 127m high Temenggor dam, located in Upper Perak, about 300km north of the capital city of Kuala Lumpur, was constructed in 1979 for power generation. The project involved the inundation of an area covering 15,200ha, including the houses of 266 families with an estimated 1000 individuals from 13 Orang Asli communities, who are mainly the Jahai and Temiar, with a minority of Lanoh and Semai[5] (Itam Wali, 1993). The Orang Asli living on the shores of the Temenggor Lake were relocated to the Pulau Tujuh resettlement site in the mid-1970s in preparation for the dam construction.[6] However, in 1979 it became apparent that the dam would flood the Pulau Tujuh resettlement scheme and the Jahai were moved again to the present site at Air Banun. The dam project also affected 124 Malay families who were resettled in Kampong Air Ganda in Gerik, Upper Perak, but separately from the Orang Asli. At the time of this research, there were 15 Orang Asli villages regrouped in Air Banun. However, I stayed in only one Jahai village in the area, which I refer to in this chapter under the pseudonym of Kampong Gajah.

The reservoir today is touted as a popular tourist attraction in Perak, due to the surrounding 'hidden riches' of the Temenggor and Belum Forest Reserves, the Orang Asli villages and historical towns in the vicinity such as Gerik and Lenggong.

The Sungai Selangor Dam and resettlement of the Temuan

In 1986, a study entitled 'Development of Sungai Selangor for water supplies to Klang Valley and Southern Kuala Selangor' was released, and four possible dam locations were identified (SOSS, 1999). One of these was the Sungai Selangor Dam site. In 1999, SPLASH carried out an environmental impact assessment for the proposed development, and was later awarded the contract by the Selangor State government to build the dam across the Selangor River, about 5km east of Kuala Kubu Bahru and 60km from Kuala Lumpur. The dam project was approved, even though there were 45 conditions attached to the environmental impact assessment, which the Department of Environment and the Selangor State government refused to divulge to the public (Joint Press Statement by Concerned NGOs and Individuals on the Selangor River Dam, 24 July 1999). The dam is a 114m high rock-fill dam, purportedly built to prevent a water crisis in urban centres. It inundated 600ha of land, including two well-known Temuan villages, namely Kampong Gerachi and Kampong Peretak.

The Temuan belong to the Proto-Malay group of Orang Asli, and are considered as more settled Orang Asli involved in permanent agriculture or riverine and coastal fishing. An estimated 76 Temuan families were displaced from their homes and ancestral lands around Sungai Selangor and Sungai Gerachi. Of these, 37 families (160 persons) were located in Kampong Gerachi near Sungai Gerachi and 39 families (179 persons) in Kampong Peretak, 6km upstream on Sungai Selangor. The affected families in Kampong Gerachi were resettled in August

2001 to Kampong Gerachi Jaya, a site in hilly terrain about 20km further from the old village. Kampong Peretak was relocated in October 2001, and has retained its old name. The resettlement scheme contained 41 houses in Kampong Gerachi Jaya and 43 houses in Kampong Peretak.

Method

Information was collected between September 2002 and August 2003 in two dam resettlement programmes from nine villages. Primary data was collected in Kampong Peretak and Kampong Gerachi Jaya in Kuala Kubu Bahru affected by the Sungai Selangor Dam, and only one village in the RPS Banun in Gerik affected by the Temenggor Dam, which I refer to in this chapter as Kampong Gajah. For comparative purposes, I also did a rapid observation in five adjacent Orang Asli villages and one Malay village (Kampong Air Ganda) around Gerik.

Why were these two projects and Orang Asli communities (Jahai and Temuan) chosen? The Temenggor reservoir was dammed in 1979, but the scanty information does not reflect the current situation. In contrast, voluminous data are available on the recent Sungai Selangor Dam, but the data need to be studied to reveal the rich empirical account of the two displaced communities. Moreover, the Temuan case shows a stronger sense of involvement and influence of official and unofficial groups of actors – including Orang Asli from other villages and other areas, the state, NGOs, academics and the media – while the Jahai community was almost invisible to public scrutiny. Nevertheless, in both areas, the gendered dimension of displacement and resettlement is missing and thus needs to be researched and integrated into the scholarship on resettlement and migration, as well as into mainstream national development planning, policies and programmes. Although the two dam projects were more than 20 years apart, my fieldwork data show similar patterns and processes as for the state-directed resettlement of Orang Asli.

At the village level, I used in-depth interviews with key community informants, face-to-face or small-group discussions and participant observation. At both research sites, I selected key informants by walking around the village to identify the villagers' reliability and reactions to my presence and my study. The snowballing method was used to identify individuals who were willing to participate, and who suggested further individuals to meet. This process involved chatting, sharing experiences, following them on their daily activities within and outside their homes. As a woman researcher, more women and children tended to show me around than men. I made conscious attempts to obtain information from men as well. Specific situations opened up opportunities to tackle gender-based issues. For example, I participated in several social and cultural functions, especially weddings in Kampong Gerachi Jaya, where I was frequently called upon to be the photographer. This allowed me to discuss issues related to marriage, children and so on with the bride and her escorts.

State-led dam resettlement, Orang Asli land and resources rights

Resettlement: Undermining Orang Asli land rights and identity

As noted earlier, the Jahai in Banun had to make way for the construction of the Temenggor Dam, only to be asked to move again when the dam itself flooded the initial Pulau Tujuh resettlement site. Until their resettlement, the Jahai community were territorial and moved in community groups. Claims to a specific territory for dwelling, hunting or foraging were negotiated and agreed between the male leaders of different groups. Territorial boundaries were identified by features of the landscape, such as rivers or streams, catchment areas, clumps of rattan or certain trees, legitimizing the group's rights over a particular area. In contrast to foraging communities like the Jahai, the Temuan community established their customary rights to ancestral land through the process of occupation for generations, which entitled members in the group to rights over the land and resources. The distinction between ancestral rights to lands and titling based on state-granted legal rights is important.

Thus, not all Orang Asli can successfully claim rights to land. Only those able to document their history with a link to longstanding occupation of a territory that they have inhabited and used can do so. In most cases, women's access to land is still heavily reliant on group-specific rights to ancestral lands. When the state introduced individual title to land, Orang Asli collective rights to ancestral lands and access to resources were redefined, and most Orang Asli have found it difficult to assert their claims. But as women and men come to terms with the redefinition of their land rights and access to resources, patriarchal tendencies and male-oriented bias within the state and Orang Asli society combine to marginalize women (see Yong, 2006).

Hunting, fishing and forest foraging were the main economic activities of the Jahai community, but these activities were disrupted when the Temenggor Dam project was mooted and they were removed. Today, the formal status of the Jahai community in Kampong Gajah has been defined by the state as 'settled Orang Asli communities' and as Muslims, vis-à-vis state processes of islamization and integration into the Malay culture, which occurred in the 1980s. Conversion to Islam resulted in altered gender relations. For example, conjugal relations were changed with the introduction of the concept of 'woman as keeper of the family and home', whilst men are obliged to assume responsibility for protecting and providing for wife and children. For the Jahai women in Kampong Gajah who converted to Islam, an *ustazzah* (woman Muslim missionary) visits them, primarily to teach them the Koran and to enhance their skills as mothers and wives. A resident *ustaz* (male Muslim missionary) also coaches the men in religious and ritual affairs, assuming a more visible public profile than the *ustazzah*.

As a result of the process of conversion to Islam, men's and women's roles in traditional Jahai society have been altered. Whilst at Kampong Gajah, I observed cases where the Jahai were struggling to retain their symbolic identity as nomadic peoples. They tried to continue with the practice of hunting with blowpipes and consuming forest game such as wild boar, monkeys and birds; practices severely eroded by resettlement and notions of 'indigeneity' defined according to state rules. The conversion to Islam, besides placing prohibitions on their traditional way of life, actually tends to deny the Orang Asli control over their traditional territories, as Nicholas (2000) contends. Nicholas (2000, pp102–103) argues that the state realizes that the identity of the Orang Asli is dependent on two very fundamental aspects, namely their attachment to a particular ecological niche, and a spirituality linked very much to that attachment, and therefore:

> *It is only logical that to appropriate the traditional territories of the Orang Asli, one must reduce or remove their attachment to them. This can be achieved by forcibly removing or resettling them, or by instituting strategies and programs aimed at their de-culturalization. But first, to take either course, one must destroy their political independence – their autonomy – and create a dependent community.*

The Temuan communities in Kampong Gerachi and Kampong Peretak were also dispossessed of their traditional lands and homes in the wake of resettlement following the construction of the Sungai Selangor Dam. I remember the wisdom of Mak Minah Anggong, an Asli woman activist from Kampong Peretak, who stressed that forced resettlement of the Temuan and Orang Asli caused hardship because land was so economically and socially central to the Orang Asli:

> *We Orang Asli are the most heavily sacrificed group if the dam goes ahead – we lose our ancestral land and forests which provide us with so much food, besides firewood, medicinal herbs and raw materials for building our houses and making handicrafts. We also lose our source of income from jungle produce such as bamboo, rattan, petai and forest fruits. We will be resettled. I do not want to leave this village which has been my home for so long.*

Mak Minah was exceptional in several ways. She was an Asli singer and woman healer in Kampong Peretak. When news of her talents spread in the early 1980s, she attracted a group of urban musicians to befriend her and the villagers. This suggests that the Orang Asli are not an isolated and backward community, as the state generally perceives them to be, true also of Orang Asli women. Indeed, outside actors played a significant role in the campaign against the construction of the Sungai Selangor Dam, which has added a new dimension to Orang Asli struggles for their rights.

Mak Minah continued to protest against the Sungai Selangor Dam until her last breath, on 21 September 1999. She considered the project an outright encroachment on Orang Asli ancestral territories, and the consequent loss not just of their livelihoods but also their status and identity as the original 'first peoples' of the country. The Orang Asli, like indigenous peoples and ethnic minorities elsewhere, have a special relationship with their land. Land is the foundation of their economic, social-cultural, political and spiritual way of life (Colchester, 1999). The indigenous view of land is imbued with a spirituality and sacredness that sustains their cultural identity.

In contrast to the Orang Asli worldview, land and forests are seen by the state and various private development agencies as increasingly expensive, scarce and precious commodities and resources for profit making. Accordingly, the state can revoke, and indeed has revoked, the status of Orang Asli customary rights to land, despite some degree of recognition and protection provided for in legislation (Aboriginal People's Act 1954, revised 1974). Amongst some Orang Asli communities such as the Semai, women have some rights to inherit customary land through marriage or family entitlements (Nicholas et al, 2002). Modern law, because it is founded on a different worldview, can destroy or threaten the character of Orang Asli society and its relationship with its land, and can replace it with a system where individualism, materialism and opportunism thrive. This is not to say that all Orang Asli, women or men, are victims. On the contrary, there are certain individuals with the ability to manoeuvre and take advantage of the situation for personal and familial gains, although more men than women are in a position to do so, since they are perceived to be of higher status in the community. This is especially the case when the state requires the Orang Asli to apply for individual land titles, which more often than not are granted to the men on the assumption that they head the household. In the modern land system, Orang Asli men admittedly benefit from the system more than women do. However, in the broader context of development, the Orang Asli are in a fragile situation, in which their lands can be appropriated by the state to suit its development agenda. In short, Orang Asli women are subjected to double oppression: first within the changing Orang Asli context and second within the wider society.

Clear evidence has emerged in the Sungai Selangor Dam case that the Temuan community have been squeezed into restricted and generally low potential areas in the new resettlement sites. In particular, the new site of Kampong Gerachi has no forests or other common resources needed to meet basic subsistence needs. According to Nicholas (2000; see also Meng, 1999), the areas allocated to the two resettlement sites were actually much less than the size of their original areas, and thus the Temuans lost up to 70 per cent of their traditional land. For example, 595ha of traditional land was recognized as an Orang Asli reserve by Selangor state government, but later claimed as state land in 1997.

Furthermore, the Selangor state government only offered the Temuan minimal cash compensation (for a total of 104.4ha) and land replacement in the resettlement scheme (2.4ha of land per family in Kampong Gerachi and 0.4ha in Kampong Peretak). Nevertheless, there has been some 'leniency' by the dam concessionaire, SPLASH, for the Temuan to access the forests beyond the dam site to look for food. Similarly, the Jahai were given 'special passes' to enter the Temenggor Lake site for fishing or to enter the nearby jungle to gather jungle produce. Cernea (2000) has pointed out that regaining access to productive land is an important factor for dislocated people to rebuild their livelihoods and coping strategies. Despite this, I concluded that the great majority of Jahai and Temuan households have been deprived of their traditional means of subsistence.

When traditional Orang Asli territories are acquired by the state for infrastructure development projects, it is difficult to establish ancestral ties since the state considers Orang Asli as 'tenant-at-will' (Williams-Hunt, 1990; Edo, 1998). This means that an Orang Asli is allowed to remain in an area subject to state authority, which can be reversed at the will of the state. Thus, the Orang Asli are left with little or no legal recourse if the state wishes to acquire the land (Edo, 1998). Neither is the state obligated to pay any compensation. This is contrary to international instruments, including the World Bank's recommendation that a resettlement policy framework for all cases of displacement should include 'those who have no recognizable legal right or claim to the land they are occupying' (World Bank, 2002, cited in Schmidt-Soltau 2003, p532). An elderly man from Kampong Peretak summed up the Orang Asli dilemma aptly:

> *Formerly our ancestors never had grants for their lands. We hardly dealt with government officials on matters pertaining to land. Only now we must have grants. I don't want it. The government seemed to oppress us, that's not good. I never had a grant but others know which is my land.*

Changing framework of land property and access: The effect on women's access and rights to land

Two elderly women in Kampong Gerachi told me that in traditional Orang Asli society women were able to own land or property, especially through family inheritance and marriage. By cultivating a given plot of land, either alone or assisted by family members, the community recognized her rights to use and control it. As one of them said:

> *My father gave my sister and me a piece of land to share. When I got married, we divided the land into two portions. My sister got two acres and I got three acres. I also inherited the durian orchard from my father. I have three brothers, but my father didn't consider it a hindrance to give daughters land, as long as we work hard.*

Nevertheless, their access to property rights is mediated in gendered ways – the transfer of land to a woman is still through her father or her husband. However, the situation of Kampong Gerachi is rather unusual. The community is more closely knit, and hence women's access and control over land resources is more embedded in their relations to kin groups than within the conjugal contract. Moreover, the Kampong Gerachi population is almost entirely the immediate extended family of the headman, comprising about two-fifths of the people.

Together with relatives of his siblings' spouses and his wife's siblings' spouses, they include more than two-thirds of the village population.

Even if women have rights to own land, their rights to use the land or gather forest products and food crops in the surrounding environment do not reflect any capacity to exercise power in other spheres of decision making. The larger config-urations of state forces operate primarily between men, resulting in women's loss of or reduced power to make key decisions on the forced resettlement, compensa-tion or entitlements and benefit sharing. The gender differences in the Orang Asli loss of resource access and control have to be acknowledged. Nicholas et al (2002) argue that changes in gender relations amongst the Semai people, a Senoi sub-group of Orang Asli, partly due to a depleted subsistence base, have further marginalized Semai women in the areas of leadership and authority and other spheres of their lives. For example, in the market economy, Semai women get lower pay than both non-Orang Asli workers and Orang Asli men, and are thus doubly discriminated against, first for being Orang Asli and second for being women.

The Jahai and Temuan cases show that dispossession from traditional lands decreases women's chances of obtaining land grants, leases and other forms of property rights granted by the government through the Department of Orang Asli Affairs (hereafter JHEOA). Changes have resulted from the interaction between the state and Orang Asli. In the official view, land tenure goes through the tradi-tional notion of head of household, generally perceived to be the men. Accordingly, land tenure is seen as the reserve of men. Furthermore, the village headmen and other leaders, all of whom are men, largely represent thier commu-nities in negotiations with the JHEOA, other state agencies and SPLASH. Previously, the leaders were the hereditary male leaders; today, the director of the JHEOA appoints them. Thus, newly created institutions such as the Village Security and Development Committee (JKKK) remain male-dominated. Matters are usually decided by the state and the dam concessionaire. However, the village leaders endorse these decisions on behalf of the group, and subsequently call a village meeting, which takes the form of a talk-down session by the officials.

It is not surprising then, that after their resettlement, women's access to land and other common property resources is largely governed by formal institutions headed predominantly by men. Before this shift, women, particularly older women, were consulted and enjoyed rights to decision making and advice giving under their customary law. Today, however, men with more contacts with the bureaucracy, who are often the village headman and JKKK leadership, tend to have a higher status and social bargaining power in the village than women or men from poorer households. Local leaders and policy makers, also usually men, tend to dominate decision-making processes. Hence women, as well as men from the poorer groups within the community, are often overlooked and under-repre-sented in the political decision-making structure. This situation is largely due to government officials' tendency to define the Orang Asli as homogeneous groups. It should not be assumed that women's needs and views are always expressed through their spouses.

Besides the actual loss of decision-making power of women, and particularly that of elder women, women's status in the village has also fallen due to the stereotypes created in the process. Men are assumed to be heads of households; women and children their dependents. A person's status in the community today is not seen through the eyes of knowledge and wisdom of customary law and the environment, but rather in terms of their privileged circumstances such as political and economic connections. It appears then that wider processes of development mediated through the state with assumed dominant power and interests tend to exert greater control over poorer women and men's rights to resources. It is worth repeating that the onus is on the woman to nurture and ensure the well being of the family. Moreover, at the time of my study, the Sungai Selangor Dam had curtailed access to the forests, and the immediate effects of this loss have exacerbated socio-economic pressures on families and individuals.

The notion of 'man as the household head' creates new pressures on men to be the main economic provider for the family and they have to take on additional responsibilities. They try to find waged work or seasonal employment. Some men find this economic responsibility too heavy, and this could at least partly explain the rise in alcoholism or some men abandoning their families. This has had a particularly bad effect on gender relations within the household. While I was staying at Kampong Gerachi and Kampong Peretak, I saw men venting their frustration and anger on their wives and children. In daily practice, some women acquiesce in this violence, while in other cases, they openly resist it. Women who are dependent on their husbands for support, or have many young children and are pressured to keep the family intact, tend to be silent about their circumstances. In striking contrast, village leaders' wives and wage-earning women are more daring to negotiate space to assert their agency.

Domestic violence tends to increase in situations where men struggle to cope with the indignity and frustration of enforced inactivity, as in environmental-related disasters, and the loss of authority and earning capacity. The men also experience a sense of alienation due to these new developments. However, it appears that some men do begin to become more authoritative than women, thinking that they are in power and control. Others find the economic and social responsibility too heavy and turn to alcohol or abandon their responsibilities and their families. Some villagers admit that drinking has become a more serious problem one year after moving to the resettlement sites. Similarly, in Kohadiya, India, Thukral (1996) observed that there was a rise in alcoholism among the displaced population in a resettled community. She also found that the rise in social disturbances accompanying alcoholism, prostitution, gambling and theft has also often been noted in earlier instances of displacement, for example those affected by the Hirakud Dam in Orissa, the Ukai Dam in Gujarat and the Kutku Dam in Bihar (Thukral, 1996).

For the Jahai of Kampong Gajah, forest activities are family-centred. Their social economy is based on immediate returns, gift giving and the exchange of resources between households. This has provided some sort of social capital for the community. Indeed, I witnessed my host family sharing their meals with

extended family members and immediate neighbours short of food. It is important to recognize that this practice is becoming rare in Kampong Gajah due to the
growing scarcity of food supplies. Similarly, the degraded environment around
Sungai Selangor, where the people of Kampong Gerachi and Kampong Peretak
previously lived, means an increased work burden for the families to cope with
scarce resources. Depleted forest food resources have more serious consequences
for poorer households than for richer ones. Children of poorer households experience even higher risks of hunger and malnutrition, thus affecting their well being.
Several studies (for example, Khor, 1988, 1994; Chee, 1996) on resettlement
children have revealed a high prevalence of underweight and malnourished
children.[7] For example, Khor's (1994) study on Semai children in the Betau
regroupment scheme concluded that adult women and children in resettlement
situations were malnourished or undernourished, and were at risk of higher
morbidity and acute symptoms of chronic illnesses and other health risks.

Conclusions

There is sufficient theoretical and empirical evidence to support the claim that
dam resettlement processes are linked to broader questions of Orang Asli land
rights and resource access. State projects for modernizing the Orang Asli continue
to neglect the priorities, concerns and needs of women, especially their rights to
property. This reinforces and adds to the social and gendered consequences of
Scott's (1998) proposition of 'schemes gone tragically awry'. In the two dam
relocation projects examined in this chapter, the resettlement processes have
exacerbated gender disparities among the Orang Asli communities of Jahai and
Temuan, in particular those relating to women's relative autonomy and land
rights. Women lose their autonomy and power, *inter alia*, through non-recognition
of their customary rights over land and resources and land rights or entitlements
mediated through formal institutions led by men. Therefore, a gender-based
analysis is central to understanding the Orang Asli experience of loss of autonomy
over land rights and access to resources.

Acknowledgements

This chapter draws on research findings elaborated in the author's doctoral
research at the University of Sussex, UK. The author is grateful to the British
Council for financial support to carry out the fieldwork. She also wishes to
acknowledge the contributions of Andreas Burghofer, *Gesellschaft fuer bedrohte
Voelker* (Society for Endangered Peoples), two anonymous referees and the
editors.

Notes

1　This chapter is based partly on an article that appeared in 2006 in a Special Issue entitled 'Gender and environmental governance' of *Gender, Technology and Development*, with permission of the publishers (Sage).

2　'Regroupment' was the term for resettlement adopted by the Malaysian government after 1960. Resettlement was undertaken as a military strategy during the Emergency of 1948–1960, when the British colonial government was waging war with communist insurgents. A number of Chinese and Orang Asli communities were resettled into 'jungle forts', later abandoned and replaced by 'patterned settlements'. 'Resettlement' is the new name used by the government to imply bringing facilities to the Orang Asli in the jungle without destroying their way of life. Nevertheless, regroupment and resettlement are often used interchangeably.

　　Air Banun is the Malay name for Banun Tributary in Hulu Perak district, Perak state (in the north of the peninsula). The regroupment scheme was called Air Banun since the Orang Asli communities were living around the bank of the Temenggor Lake along the Banun Tributary, and were moved out when the lake was dammed.

3　In the Ministry of the Interior document, 'Statement of Policy Regarding the Administration of the Aborigine Peoples of the Federation of Malaya' (1961), the security of Orang Asli living in and around the jungle was described as a major concern of the Malaysian government.

4　SPLASH consists of Tan Sri Wan Azmi (TSWA, 40 per cent), GAMUDA, a large construction company (30 per cent) and Kumpulan Darul Ehsan Berhad (KDEB), the investment wing of the Selangor State Government (30 percent). This consortium recently changed its name to SPLASH (Syarikat Pengeluar Air Sungai Selangor).

5　The Jahai and Lanoh are Negritos, who are largely nomadic foragers. The Temiar and Semai are Senoi.

6　This was not the first time that the Jahai have been forcibly resettled. The Orang Asli in the Upper Perak areas had been resettled in the 1950s as part of the British colonial government's military strategy to isolate them from the communist insurgents in the jungles (PRO Document Ref: CO1022/29 Resettlement in Malaya, undated; *The Straits Budget*, 3 December 1953, p7).

7　Evrard and Goudineau (2004) highlight studies that show an increase in child mortality from 133 to 326 deaths (per 1000 live births) in Akha villages in Muang Sing district after movement to lower slopes.

References

Carey, I. (1976) *Orang Asli: The Aboriginal Tribes of Peninsular Malaysia*, Kuala Lumpur: Oxford University Press

Cernea, M. (1997) 'The risks and reconstruction model for resettling displaced populations', *World Development* 25 (10): 1569–1587

Cernea, M. (ed.) (1999) *The Economics of Involuntary Resettlement: Questions and Challenges*, Washington DC: World Bank

Cernea, M. (2000) 'Risks, safeguards, and reconstruction: A model for population displacement and resettlement'. In M. Cernea and C. McDowell (eds) (2000) *Risks and Reconstruction: Experiences of Resettlers and Refugees*, Washington DC: World Bank, pp1–50

Chee Heng Leng (1996) 'Health and nutrition of the Orang Asli:The need for primary health care amidst economic transformation'. In R. Rashid (ed.) *Indigenous Minorities of Peninsular Malaysia: Selected Issues and Ethnographies*, Mountain View, California: Mayfield Publishing Co., pp48–73

Colchester, M. (1994) 'Sustaining the forests:The community-based approach in South and South-East Asia', *Development and Change* 25: 69–100

Colchester, M. (1999) 'Sharing power: Dams, indigenous peoples and ethnic minorities', *Indigenous Affairs* 3–4 (June/December 1999), Copenhagen: International Work Group for Indigenous Affairs

Colson, E. (1971) *Social Consequences of Resettlement*, Manchester: Manchester University Press

Colson, E. (2003) 'Forced migration and the anthropological response', *Journal of Refugee Studies* 16(1): 1–17

Dobby, E. H. G. (1952–1953) 'Resettlement transforms Malaya: A case-history of relocating the population of an Asian plural society', *Economic Development and Cultural Change* 1: 153–189

Dreze, J., M. Samson and S. Singh (eds) (1997) *The Dam and the Nation: Displacement and Resettlement in the Narmada Valley*, Oxford: Oxford University Press

Dwivedi, R. (1999) 'Displacement, risks and resistance: Local perceptions and actions in the Sardar Sarovar', *Development and Change* 30 (1): 43–78

Dwivedi, R. (2002) 'Models and methods in development-induced displacement (review article)', *Development and Change* 33 (4): 709–732

Edo, J. (1998) 'Claiming our ancestors' land: An ethnohistorical study of Sengoi land rights in Perak, Malaysia', unpublished doctoral thesis, Canberra: Australian National University

Eriksen,T. H. (1995) *Small Places, Large Issues: An Introduction to Social and Cultural Anthropology*, London and East Haven: Pluto Press

Escobar, A. (1991) 'Anthropology and the development encounter:The making and marketing of development anthropology', *American Ethnologist* 18 (4): 658–682

Escobar, A. (1995) *Encountering Development:The Making and Unmaking of the Third World*, Princeton: Princeton University Press

Evrard, O. and Y. Goudineau (2004) 'Planned resettlement, unexpected migrations and cultural trauma in Laos', *Development and Change* 35(5): 937–962

FDTCP (1979) 'Development Plan: Orang Asli Regroupment Scheme – Betau', Kuala Lumpur: Federal Department of Town and Country Planning

Gadgil, M. and R. Guha (1994) 'Ecological conflicts and the environmental movement in India', *Development and Change* 25: 101–136

Ghai, D. (1994) 'Environment, livelihood and empowerment', *Development and Change* 25: 1–11

Goldsmith, E. and N. Hildyard (eds) (1984) *The Social and Environmental Effects of Large Dams*, Vol 2', a report to the European Ecological Action Group (ECOROPA), Cornwall: Wadebridge Ecological Centre

Hansen, A. and A. Oliver-Smith (eds) (1982) *Involuntary Migration and Resettlement:The Problems and Responses of Dislocated People*, Boulder: Westview Press

Healey, L. (1999) 'Gender, power and the ambiguities of resistance in a Malay community of Peninsular Malaysia', *Women's Studies International Forum* 22 (1): 49–61

Hood, S. (1996) 'The plight of the Orang Asli: Constructing an equitable interpretation of rights'. In Consumers Association of Penang (ed.) *State of the Environment in Malaysia*, Penang: Consumers Association of Penang, pp59–62

Hooker, M. B. (1991) 'The Orang Asli and the laws of Malaysia with special reference to land', *Ilmu Masyarakat* 18: 51–79

Isaacman, A. and C. Sneddon (2000) 'Toward a social and environmental history of the building of Cahora Bassa Dam', *Journal of Southern African Stu*dies 26 (4): 597–632

Itam Wali bin Nawan (1993) *Rancangan Pengumpulan Semula (RPS) Orang Jahai: Kajian Kes Mengenai Perubahan Sosial di RPS Air Banun* [The Jahai: A Case Study of Social Change in the Air Banun Regroupment Scheme], Bangi: Anthropology and Sociology Department, National University of Malaysia

JHEOA (2000) *Data Maklumat Asas Orang Asli* [Basic Information Concerning the Orang Asli of Malaysia], Kuala Lumpur: Jabatan Hal Ehwal Orang Asli

Joekes, S., N. Heyzer, R. Oniang'o and V. Salles (1994) 'Gender, environment and popula-tion', *Development and Change* 25: 137–165

Khor Geok Lin (1988) 'Malnutrition among Semai children', *Medical Journal of Malaysia* 43: 318–326

Khor Geok Lin (1994) 'Resettlement and nutritional implications: The case of Orang Asli in regroupment schemes', *Pertanika: Journal of the Society for Science and Humanity* 2 (2): 123–132

KHRP (1999) *The Ilisu Dam: A Human Rights Disaster in the Making*, London: Kurdish Human Rights Project

KHRP (2003) 'This is the only valley where we live: The impact of the Munzur dams', report of the Kurdish Human Rights Project Fact-Finding Mission to Dersim/Tunceli, London: The Cornerhouse

Mahapatra, L. K. (1999) 'Testing the risks and reconstruction model on India's Resettlement Experiences'. In M. Cernea (ed.) *The Economics of Involuntary Resettlement: Questions and Challenges*, Washington DC: World Bank, pp189–230

Malaysian Government (1954) Undang-Undang Malaysia: Akta 134 – Akta Orang Asli 1954 (Disemak 1974) [Malaysian Government (1954), Laws of Malaysia: Act 134 – Aboriginal Peoples Act 1954 (revised 1974)]

Meng, Yew Choong (1999) 'Little say about compensation', *The Star Section* 2 (21 September), pp3–5

Ministry of Interior (1961) 'Statement of policy regarding the administration of the aborigine peoples of the Federation of Malaya', Kuala Lumpur: Government Printers

Nicholas, C. (2000). 'The Orang Asli and the contest for resources: Indigenous politics, Development and Identity in Peninsular Malaysia', IWGIA Document No. 95, Subang Jaya: Center for Orang Asli Concerns, and Copenhagen: International Work Group for Indigenous Affairs

Nicholas, C., Tijah Yok Chopil and Tiah Sabak (2002) *Orang Asli Women and the Forest*, Petaling Jaya: Centre for Orang Asli Concerns

Noone, R. (1972) *Rape of the Dream People*, London: Hutchinson

Public Records Office, Kew (1952) File reference: CO 1022/29. No 33 of 1952, 'Resettlement and the development of new villages in the Federation of Malaya'

Public Records Office, Kew (1953) File reference: SEA 524/1/01, 'Aborigines must be set free from reds', *The Straits Budget*, 3 December

Schmidt-Soltau, K. (2003) 'Conservation-related resettlement in Central Africa: Environmental and social risks', *Development and Change* 34 (3): 525–551

Scott, J. (1998) *Seeing Like a State: How Certain Schemes to Improve the Human Condition Have Failed*, New Haven and London: Yale University Press

Scudder, T. and E. Colson (1982) 'From welfare to development: A conceptual framework for the analysis of dislocated people'. In A. Hansen and A. Oliver-Smith (eds) *Involuntary Migration and Resettlement: The Problems and Responses of Dislocated People*. Boulder: Westview Press, pp267–287

SOSS (1999) 'Before and after', fact sheet for public education campaign against the damming of the Sungai Selangor, Selangor: Save Our Sungai Selangor

Tan Pek Leng (1997) 'Malaysia'. In Vinod Raina, Aditi Chowdhury and Sumit Chowdhury (eds) *The Dispossessed: Victims of Development in Asia*, Hong Kong: ARENA Press, pp219–255

Thukral, E. G. (1996) 'Development, displacement and rehabilitation: Locating gender', *Economic and Political Weekly*, Mumbai, 31: 1500–1503

Williams-Hunt, A. (1990) 'Law and poverty: The case of the Orang Asli', paper presented at the Conference on Law and Poverty, organized by the Malaysian Bar Council, 8–9 December 1990

World Bank (1994) 'Resettlement and Development: The Bankwide Review of Projects Involving Involuntary Resettlement 1986–1993', Environment Department Papers 032, Washington DC: World Bank

World Commission on Dams (2000) *Dams and Development: A New Framework for Decision-Making*, London: Earthscan

Yong Ooi Lin, C. (2003) *Flowed Over: The Babagon Dam and the Kadazandusun of Kampung Tampasak*, Subang Jaya, Selangor: Centre for Orang Asli Concerns

Yong Ooi Lin, C. (2006). 'Dam-based development in Malaysia: The Temenggor and Sungai Selangor Dams and the resettlement of the Orang Asli', unpublished doctoral thesis, Brighton: Institute of Development Studies, University of Sussex

Chapter 7

Do Women-Only Approaches to Natural Resource Management Help Women? The Case of Community Forestry in Nepal

Marlène Buchy and Bimala Rai

Introduction

Over the last 25 years or so, common property resource management (CPRM), or community-based resource management (CBRM) strategies have been promoted in many countries by national governments and donors programmes alike as the best way out of environmental degradation and poverty. CPRM is largely based on the principle that communities are best placed to manage the resources directly adjacent to them because they know them and use them, and therefore have an interest in maintaining the resource. In the forestry sector, different models have evolved in different countries, but in most countries the forestry department enters into partnerships with community user groups comprising community members. Legal frameworks do regulate the roles and responsibilities of user groups and the state, and typically, whilst the state provides professional support and controls the application of the rules, local people are responsible for the hands-on management in the hope of sharing the benefits from the resource harvest.

Whilst households may gain an in-kind claim to a share of the resources through their membership, the surplus of resources that may be sold on the market provides a source of funds for the community, which can then be used for community development activities (for example, a school or temple building, teachers' salaries or revolving credit). The size of a community fund depends largely on the quality of the forests and their proximity to markets. One of the biggest recent criticisms of CPRM has been the misused concept of 'community', often applied by policy makers to what are assumed to be socially and culturally homogeneous groups. In reality, communities are most usually divided along gender, economic, social and political lines. This gives some groups more power, and therefore more claim, over resources and over how they are managed and for what purpose, thus *de facto* excluding the weakest voices, typically the poor and women (Guijt and Shah, 1998).

The history of forests in Nepal over the last 200 years or so is the story of the gradual alienation of local rights to the benefit of a growing state. Successive rulers have tried to make the most of valuable timber in different parts of the country, first through privatization and then through the nationalization of forests and the gradual emergence of the Department of Forests. But throughout much of the country, such as in the mid-hills and the Terai, for example, forests have always been very much used by local people for their subsistence.[1] It is only in the latter part of the 20th century, in parallel with the 'eco-doom' scenario of the 1970s (Hobley and Malla, 1996, p77) and an acknowledgment of extreme degradation of forests (especially in the mid-hills), that local rights have started to reassert themselves, with local councils (*panchayats*) allocated responsibility for managing local forests. However, *panchayats* themselves do not necessarily represent communities' needs and interests, and forests have continued to degrade. Since the 1970s, with a particularly impressive burst of activity during the 'participatory' 1990s, Nepal has been a pioneer in developing and promoting community forestry by focusing on establishing local resource management institutions, the forest user groups (FUGs). All community members have the right to become FUG members, providing they pay a nominal membership fee. This fee, however, excludes the poorest of the poor from membership. Although typically it is the head of the household (and therefore usually a man) who becomes a member (on behalf of the household), women do become members of what are called 'mixed' FUGs. FUGs then elect an FUG committee, which is responsible for the running of the FUG and must include at least two women.

Community forestry is now operating in all 75 of Nepal's districts and has received priority support both from the state and donors. Currently, donor-supported projects exist in more than 70 districts and share about 80 per cent of the community forestry budget. Within 25 years, more than 1.5 million households (25 per cent of the total population of the country) have been organized in about 14,000 FUGs, now managing and controlling about 1 million hectares of forest (Kanel, 2004). Across the mid-hills of Nepal, many forests have been regenerated, plantation targets have mostly been achieved, and increased biodiversity in many places under community forestry has been reported. Community forests have not only resulted in increased availability of forest products but have also generated a significant amount of income locally (DOF, 1998; Kandel and Subedi, 2004; Kanel, 2004; Kanel and Niraula, 2004). However, so far, successes in terms of physical achievements are very much confined to mid-hill areas, with few forests (only 12 per cent of total forests) handed over in the Terai (Pokharel and Amatya, 2000).

In addition to conservation, CPRM strategies are believed to improve access to communal resources, especially for the poor and women whose livelihoods depend on these resources (DOF, 1998; Rai, 2002b). In the late 1990s, social justice, equity, gender balance and good governance came to dominate the community forestry agenda, and are known as 'second generation issues' (DOF, 1998; Kanel, 2004). Central to the belief that community forestry can contribute to social justice are a number of assumptions: that FUGs are all-inclusive, that the FUG committee or *samiti*, represents all the various interests groups in the community, that all users are equally affected by the rules and the regulations, and that all users will have an equal share of the benefits of the forests. Unfortunately, an increasing number of empirical works demonstrate that these assumptions do not hold. Most FUGs are exclusive in terms of participation and access to the incentives (Hunt ct al, 1995; Chhetri et al, 1996; Graner, 1997). Moreover, the three specific axes of exclusion – caste, class and gender relations – in the community result in consistently excluding women and the poor (Agarwal, 2000; Agrawal, 2001; Lama and Buchy, 2002; Rai, forthcoming). This is especially relevant for Nepal, a Hindu kingdom in which caste hierarchies and rules very much dictate people's positions and options in life.

Increasing evidence from the field and the concerns of donors on equity and sustainability issues have led policy makers to target women and enhance their visibility. To enhance the effective participation of women and to ensure their direct access and control over forestry resources, the Department of Forests and development aid-funded programmes have been promoting the formation of women-only FUGs. The assumptions are that women-only committees will be able to ensure that women's voices are heard, that their specific needs will be taken into account in the management of resources, that benefits will directly reach women in need, and that these men-free forums will encourage women to become involved in public affairs, leading to their empowerment. This approach, embedded within the women, environment and development (WED) paradigm (see van den Hombergh, 1993), we argue, is problematic because it targets women as a homogeneous group, and fails to challenge the structural constraints affecting women and the poor. It completely bypasses gender issues, still a common mistake in forest policy.

This chapter is based on empirical data from five women-only FUGs in the mid-west region of the Rapti zone.[2] It is complemented by secondary data on women-only FUGs and mixed FUGs throughout the country. We acknowledge that substantial variations may exist even between women-only FUGs, and the data presented here do not statistically represent the whole scenario. However, we aim to assess whether the goal of promoting women-only FUGs to address the gender inequity observed in mixed groups is met in reality.

The chapter questions whether the instrumental approach of promoting women-only FUGs is a wise move to address issues of gender and social inequity in community forestry. We hope to see whether in spaces in which they are in charge, women are able to exercise agency and discard the traditional hierarchies, or whether indeed traditional power relations, materialized through caste hierarchies, are maintained.

In what follows, we first discuss the socio-economic and cultural context of Nepalese society in which both mixed and women-only FUGs operate. Next we look at some empirical and secondary data of the women-only FUGs under study. This leads us to a discussion in which we focus on the value of women-only space as a strategy to improve women's participation, and in which we analyse the structural and ideological underpinning of community forestry as a policy and as a practice.

The social and research context: Community and forestry in Rapti

Agrarian societies in Nepal are internally differentiated by resource endowment (class), by caste and ethnicity, and by gender. Hinduism has traditionally been the basis of state politics and has governed the social structure and inter-caste/ethnic relations in societies. High-caste groups (such as Brahmin Chhetri) have traditionally dominated the civil and military machine of the state and enjoyed the greater share of economic resources and political power. By contrast, the majority of lower-caste groups (so-called untouchables, or *dalits*) are the poorest and most socially disadvantaged. For instance, poverty incidence among *dalits* is 46 per cent, compared to the national average of 31 per cent (Acharya et al, 2004). The same disparities are found in access to education, health and political structures, and to income-generating opportunities. The concept of untouchability can also be understood as lowering the social dignity and self-confidence of *dalits*. In Rapti, the area of the study, multiple ethnic groups live together in each district. Among them, Magars and Matwali Chhetri are the predominant groups, except in Dang, where Brahmin Chhetri form the majority. This is followed by the artisans (such as *kami, sharki, damai* and *gaine,* so-called lower and impure castes): Thakuri Chhetri, Gurung and Newars. Households tend to cluster in groups that are ethnically relatively homogeneous (or composed of at most two or three ethnic groups). This is also reflected in the ethnic composition of FUGs. Each FUG is composed of two or three ethnic groups, except in the lowland belt of Dang where settlement and FUGs are more heterogeneous. All FUGs in this study were mixed in terms of caste and ethnicity, and were relatively homogeneous in terms of religion, with Hindus predominating.

Nepal witnessed dramatic progress in cutting poverty from 42 per cent in 1996 to 31 per cent in 2004. Despite this progress, profound inequity remains.[3] The composition of poverty in Nepal has two important characteristics: first, that poverty continues to be a rural phenomenon, and second, that substantial disparities exist across ecological zones, development regions, caste, ethnicity and gender.

About 95 per cent of Nepalese live in rural areas. The village economy is critically dependent on a local agricultural and natural resource base. Subsistence agriculture is the main occupation for the rural population.[4] The distribution of land ownership is highly skewed. The bottom 47 per cent of agricultural households operate on less than 15 per cent of total agricultural land, while less than 3 per cent occupy more than 17 per cent of the total land area. Nearly 50 per cent of agricultural households operate on less than 0.5ha of land and only 4.6 per cent of households are food sufficient (CBS, 2003). Land ownership also determines access to other resources, benefits and power including access to public goods and services, creating highly unequal power relations between classes, between castes and between genders. Although villagers in Rapti supplement incomes from non-farm engagements mainly from salary, wages and business, access to non-farm engagement and the income derived vary significantly between different economic and social groups.

In such a context, common natural resources play an important role in sustaining livelihoods. Common forests are vital sources of fuelwood, fodder, leaf litter, grazing land, fruits and fibres, building materials, medicines and herbs. Land-poor households also generate small incomes by selling forest products such as fuelwood, leaf plates, mats and baskets. These forest products provide diversity to the rural economy and security in times of cash and food shortage. Although all rural households use the forests to supplement their livelihoods, their degree of dependency differs. For the poor and the *dalits*, who are often landless, forests are critical to their survival whilst landed castes who have access to alternative private sources are less dependent. Women and children, especially girls, are the main users of many forest products, and are responsible for collecting fuel and fodder and many other products used for home consumption. These highly time-consuming tasks are unavoidable because substitutes are unavailable. Thus changes in forest resource availability can have a direct impact on the livelihood and work patterns of women and children. In contrast, it is generally men who control decisions about the management of the resources, whether private or common.

Academic discussion on women and their role in natural resource management has been slow to reflect the complex realities of the field. The WED literature depicts 'women' as the main users and holders of specific environmental knowledge, as prime victims of environmental degradation and increased poverty, but also as prime managers of the resources who have been invisible to and excluded by policy makers and projects. This approach is problematic mainly because it erases the diversity between women that prevails everywhere and in specific ways in Nepal. 'Women' as a category are divided by the caste and economic class of the households they come from. Although all women provide a significant amount of labour for the rural production system, most lack control over production assets. The disparity is due to the historical gender roles and inequality, mainly in the ownership and control of family income by male household members, the absence of property rights for women, limited education, mobility and employment opportunity, and unpaid domestic work in subsistence farming. Women from poor *dalit* households suffer from triple oppression related to economic, caste and gender relations. Ethnicity does add one more dimension of discrimination: people amalgamated under 'ethnic' groups are usually (but not always) Buddhist, have historically been dispossessed from their land by the

Hindu castes, and often live in remote places, far from economic opportunities. Although women from these groups tend to enjoy more freedom within their own context, they continue to experience exclusion.

The WED approach that focuses on women being excluded and therefore needing to be included, has been at the heart of community forestry in Nepal, which is based on efficiency and not social justice (Tinker, 1993). This, Jackson (1999) has argued, is problematic because (amongst other things) it focuses on involving women on a par with men without understanding how gender relations between men and women affect the quality of their involvement. The focus on exclusion hides the fact that women are selectively excluded: women are involved in work (as users and managers) but they are often excluded from decision making and equal economic opportunities. Many women are vulnerable because the power relations are skewed against them, not because of exclusion per se. In the same way that women have been essentialized, power is often portrayed in a one-dimensional way: either one has power or one does not. Thankfully there is now a wider recognition that power is multifaceted: there is power 'over' (the power one person or group has over another), the power 'from within' (each of us has some amount of power within us), the power 'with' (the possibility to achieve collectively what cannot be achieved alone) and the power 'to' (which enables action) (Townsend et al, 1999). Gaventa (2006) has recently conceptualized three forms of power: visible (the law, the institutions), hidden (not all power is visible) and invisible (the internalized norms or stereotypes that prevent individuals from acting), which all affect simultaneously what can be done, alone or collectively. This distinction is useful when looking at FUGs as a participatory space where different forms of power are at play, affecting who participates and on what terms. Indeed Agrawal (2001) has demonstrated how participatory exclusion operates in the Nepali context where despite a discourse of involvement and participation, women and the poor have remained excluded. Gender differences in access to and control over resources are an important aspect of the rural production system throughout the country, but so is the position of the women within the family.

Despite the critique of WED offered by the gender, environment and development (GED) (Leach et al, 1995), which highlights the need to look at relations between the genders and consider closely property rights, the gendered nature of institutions, political economy and ecology, most programmes, such as the community forestry programme, still work within a WED framework, as is pointed out in the discussion below.

The arguments and the data presented here are based on both primary and secondary sources. Secondary data was obtained from the national database on community forestry maintained by the Department of Forests (DOF) at the central level and during a three-week visit and discussion with 16 FUGs, including 5 women-only groups from Rapti zone in Mid-Western Nepal using participatory methods.

Information on collective action and costs and benefits of participation in user groups and benefit distribution are based on in-depth interviews and discussions with men and women separately. Similarly, information about the quality of life, the state of forests under the groups, the control and flow of forest products and other benefits derived from user groups were cross-checked by observations in physical settlements of each group and the community forest used by that group. Secondary information about user groups, especially statistics and lessons learned from mixed user groups, is drawn from an analysis of a national database maintained by the DOF and from a review of relevant literature.

Women-only forest user groups

Of a total of about 14,000 FUGs, less than 5 per cent are women-only FUGs, spread across 61 of Nepal's 75 districts, with 82 per cent in the hills and the rest in the *Terai* (CFD, 2004). It is not clear where the idea of women-only groups originated, and though still small, their number has dramatically increased since the late 1990s. Whether this trend will continue is difficult to say, as currently formation of FUGs has slowed due to the political and security instability in the country.

The push for women-only FUGs is the result of converging interests rather than of a specific policy. First, there has been recognition by NGOs and donors of the increased need to focus community activities on women and the poor. The Agriculture Perspective Plan (1995) together with the Forestry Master Plan fed into the Ninth Five Year National Development Plan (1997–2002), in which women are recognized as primary users. The Joint Technical Review of Community Forestry (2001) also emphasizes the role of women and the need to increase their involvement. Even the second edition of the Community Forestry Guidelines (2003) includes specific mention as to how women and the poor may be involved in the formation of FUGs. The Tenth Five Year Plan (2002–2006) for the forestry sector also provides directives for the compulsory participation and inclusion of the poor, women and other disadvantaged sections of community forest management through their direct engagement in FUGs. Second, a large United Nations Development Programme (UNDP) initiative, working to sensitize institutions at all levels of administration across all sectors of governance, has increased pressure to apply a gender mainstreaming policy in all sectors in Nepal. The impact of this approach is yet to be measured but it has definitively put gender issues on the agenda. Gender focal points in ministries including His Majesty's Ministry for Forests and Soil Conservation have been appointed, and currently a Gender Working Group made up of ministry and department staff along with donor representatives is working towards the development of a gender strategy for the natural resource sector.

At the field level, some NGOs have also dedicated resources specifically targeting women, such as CARE Nepal through its Forest Afforestation Partnership Project (FPP) started in 1996. To date, in the project area (Rapti zone alone), 90 FUGs offer women a forum for experimenting with governance and forest management. Apparently women's motivation for forming and joining women-only FUGs is that 'women can manage natural resources as men do ...

[and that] ... *unity* in a women's FUG opens up their opportunities to participate in training, workshops and cross visits, which enhances their capability' (CARE, 2003, p13, emphasis ours). At first sight this initiative seems to have very positive results for women: 50 community reading centres have been opened training 1000 women; 49 women are trained as local resources persons able to prepare operational plans and facilitate awareness workshops; about 200 women from the project districts hold 'key executive positions in local government' (CARE, 2003). However, in such statements, women are essentialized as one category and the differences amongst them are being blurred (Krishna, 2001). Although the 'myth of community' (Guijt and Shah, 1998) was exposed in the late 1990s, on the ground women are still seen as one category and many practitioners fail to look critically at how women become involved, how they benefit or how they are trans-formed. Moreover, such approaches are more concerned with involving women than with the terms of their involvement (Jackson, 1999), as is discussed below.

Looking at women-only FUGs through the equity lens

The critical literature on community forestry has ascertained that gender and social differences matter mainly in three areas of forest management: governance (in particular, the mechanisms by and level of transparency through which decisions are made), management choices (i.e. decisions regarding the use and future use of the resources which satisfy some needs and priorities over others) and the distribution and use of benefits (which have direct livelihood implications for the members. Clearly if, for example, community funds are used for Hindu temple building, rather than providing cheap credit for landless non-Hindu women, there will be a different overall economic impact). To these parameters we also add the quality of the resource, because this determines to a large extent what is possible, what inputs are necessary and what benefits can be expected in the medium and long terms.

The quality of forests

One incentive to promote women-only FUGs in community forestry is the under-lying assumption that women-only space provides women with direct access to and control over common forest products. But as we look at them, the quality of forest becomes the first contentious issue as there is blatant gender discrimina-tion. The 'quality' of forests is to a certain extent relative, depending on who looks at the forests. But here we look at quality from a comparative perspective: do FUGs have more or less access to equal areas of forests per capita, and within the category 'degraded' forests (which are the forests allocated for community forestry) we make a difference between a natural degraded forest, which requires protection to enhance natural regeneration, and barren land, which requires intensive labour input for re-establishing a vegetal cover.

Table 7.1 *Quality of forests allocated to women-only FUGs*
(in five districts of Rapti zone)

District	Quality of forests
Dang	18 women-only FUGs; 9 own less than 5ha of forest. 15 out of 18 own degraded plantation and grassland (VD)
Pyuthan	19 women-only FUGs; 17 own highly degraded forest land. Remaining two are new plantations
Rukum	16 women-only FUGs; 6 own good quality forest and 10 highly degraded forest. Between them there is a combination of plantation (5), shrubby woodland (7) or both (4) (VD)
Rolpa	37 women-only FUGS; 13 FUGs own new plantation and shrub land; 24 own forests of which 12 are highly degraded (VD)
Salyan	1 women-only FUG but degraded forest (VD)

Note: DOF classifies the quality of community forest as: VG = very good, i.e. dense forest; G = good, i.e. reasonably dense forest; D = degraded, i.e. some patches; VD = very degraded, i.e. thin patches.
Source: CFD (2004)

First, the statistics show that on average per household, women-only FUG members have access to only half the forest area that households in mixed FUGs have access to. For example, in the Rapti area, mixed FUG households have access to 0.84ha per household, as against 0.42ha for women-only FUGs. At the national level, the figures are 0.73ha for mixed FUGs and 0.34ha for women-only FUGs (CFD, 2004).

Second, evidence suggests that women-only FUGs are allocated forests in much worse condition than the forests allocated to mixed FUGs. Establishing a plantation or managing a newly established one requires more labour than protecting natural forests. As it takes time for the resource to grow, the benefits one can get from these are much smaller than from established forests. National data reveal that roughly 50 per cent of forests handed over to women are of poor quality compared to 25 per cent for mixed FUGs (CFD, 2004). A close look at the quality of forests handed over to women-only FUGs in our study area also confirms the trend (see Table 7.1).

The case of the Shrijansil women-only FUG of Bijuwar, Pyuthan district, illustrates clearly how gender relations affect the allocation of resources. The FUG was formed in 1999 with the direct intervention of the District Forest Office (DFO). Before its formation, all households in the community were members of the Chhetrapal community forest, which had about 60ha of forest land (both plantation and natural pine forest). In 1999, field staff from the DOF negotiated with the mixed group the formation of a women-only group. Since all the common forest land in the community had already been handed over, the foresters discussed the possibility of splitting the mixed user group into men- and women-only user groups. Finally, a piece of newly planted area of 11ha was legally handed over to the new Shrijansil women-only FUG, while the men-only Chhetrapal FUG kept the remaining 49ha of natural pine forests.

In 1995, the Pahiro women-only FUG was given the use of 20ha of landslide-prone land on which the DOF had unsuccessfully tried to establish a plantation, and which the men of the Panakhola FUG (a mixed user group in the same village) had specifically refused to include within their community forest boundaries. The men's argument was that protecting this area 'was like pouring water on sand'. But mobilized by the Women Development Office, women worked hard to establish a plantation that has still to produce anything, and which most probably will give little return in the long term. Being in a landslide-prone area will later restrict what kind of forest management or activities are allowed.

These two cases clearly illustrate that women users have been allocated poor quality land that requires significant amounts of labour without any significant return, at least in the short run.

Exclusive and non-transparent governance

The phenomenon of elite capture in mixed FUGs has been recorded in many places: high-caste villagers constitute the bulk of FUG members, but also dominate the FUG *samitis* to the partial exclusion of low-caste people and women (Rai, forthcoming). Though a recent regulation has imposed a minimum number of women in the *samiti*, the key decision-making positions in the *samiti* are in the hands of land-rich, food-secure and relatively better-educated high-caste men. Though each user group has token representation of women and lower-caste groups, their participation in the *samiti* is merely physical (Hobley, 1996; Moffat, 1998; Lama and Buchy, 2002; CARE, 2003).

Therefore one assumption (or perhaps expectation) related to women-only groups is that women-only space reduces the weight of patriarchal power, and thus enables women to participate more effectively in public affairs. Women-only spaces should equip women with direct access to information, exposure and skills through the user groups. Compared to women in mixed groups, those in women-only FUGs have been found to be more active and effective as participants. However, women as a social group are by no means homogeneous and class, caste and ethnicity cut across women as well. Even in the women-only FUGs, not all women participate effectively.

Our data on the composition of women-only FUGs show that in mixed-caste groups, it is mainly women from land-rich, high-caste households who participate and who capture most of the decision-making seats in the *samiti* to the exclusion of the majority of women from the lower-caste group, who also often belong to the economically poorest category. In the Pahiro women-only FUG, for example, no women from the lower-caste groups (who also happen to be the ones with the lowest food security) are part of the *samiti*, although this group represents the largest number of members in the FUG. Ten of the 11 seats in the *samiti* are occupied by high-caste women. Similarly in the Shrijansil women-only FUG, a wealth ranking exercise carried out by the FUG members shows that all the *samiti* members belong to the food-sufficient category, although the majority of forest users come from food-insecure households.

The process of FUG formation is important in community forestry. The operational guidelines for community forestry (HMG/N, 1992) provide detailed steps to follow during the formation of user groups. If the steps are followed properly, there should be sufficient opportunity for individual users to be aware of their roles and rights in the FUG. However, the FUG formation process among the women-only user groups in Rapti indicates large discrepancies between what is envisaged in the guidelines and what happened in practice. In most cases, the field-based staff (mostly rangers) are given quotas to form FUGs. These are set either by NGOs such as CARE Nepal, or by the DFO. As a consequence, there is little time available to make women aware of community forest policy and relevant rules, rights and responsibilities provided by the community forest legislation, and not surprisingly little effort is expended doing so. Thus, most women members, even in some cases the *samiti* members themselves in relatively larger women-only FUGs, are unaware of their legal rights and responsibilities as FUG members. A discussion with five *samiti* members of the Dharapani women-only FUG in Rolpa district (see Box 7.1) provides evidence that even *samiti* members may have very limited knowledge and understanding of the situation, that the chairwoman is likely to be the one with the knowledge, and that the DOF has done little to share information or increase women's capacity.

In this case, none of the five *samiti* members knew the exact area of the forest they were managing. While they considered the area to be 'small', the ranger later indicated that the FUG manages 82ha of natural forest, making it the largest

---

Box 7.1 Level of awareness of rights and responsibilities in FUGs

This discussion took place between one of the researchers and five *samiti* members of the Dharapani women-only user group in Liwang Rolpa:

Researcher: How much forest land do you own?

Women: Small.

Researcher: How many members are there in the user group?

Women: All.

Researcher: When was the user group formed and how was it formed?

Women: About five years ago [in the official record, the user group was formed during 2050 BS i.e. ten years ago]. The ranger brought a letter from up (*mathi*). He sent a message that we all women in the village need to protect this forest. He asked us to form a *samiti* and we started protecting.

Researcher: How much money do you have in the FUG fund, and how do you plan to use it?

Women: We do not know. Only the chairperson and the ranger know. I think that we have supported the salary of one of the government village people as a teacher, but we do not know how much is given there.

community forest owned by a women-only FUG in Rolpa. This lack of knowledge weakens FUG members when they ask questions about their share of benefits, for example, or when they need to make decisions about different management alternatives.

The way women describe the process of group formation and the way they perceive their roles and rights in the group management process, suggest that women in fact have little choice in the matter, and also that they may in places be exploited by the DOF. Clearly, women-only FUGs are formed without women always being made fully aware of their legal rights and responsibilities, although women seem more often to know their responsibilities than their rights. In this research, similar situations were noted in other women-only FUGs. It seems that the motive to involve women is to call on their labour to carry out protection work that the government is unable to do. In such situations, it is difficult to expect that the involvement and participation of women in women-only FUGs bring any significant improvement in gender relations by empowering women.

Forest management choices

Forest management decisions made by FUGs are recorded in an operational plan that has to be approved by the DOFs, and which is supposed to represent a consensus between the needs of different constituencies in the FUGs. In practice, the elite-dominated *samiti* (supported by the conservation-oriented DOF) often makes decisions favouring its own interests or ignoring the specific conditions of women and the poor. Studies conducted in India and Nepal provide evidence that *samiti* dominated by non-poor, high-caste men tend to favour timber growing by completely closing access to the resource for the poor and the women, who then need to walk further afield to find firewood or fodder (Subedi et al, 1993; Agarwal, 1997). FUGs often set prices for forest products without considering that women and the poor may have in the past accessed these products on a daily basis free of cost (Hobley, 1996; Graner, 1997; Leach et al, 1999).

Like mixed user groups, women-only user groups are also more conservation-oriented, in addition to focusing on satisfying their livelihood needs. This conservation focus has its roots in the history of community forestry, which started essentially as a conservation programme to preserve soils and the environment. Whilst foresters are in many places reluctant to allow the exploitation of now mature plantations, many FUGs themselves want to keep the trees and allow mostly subsistence use. This is a good example of hidden power, where people have internalized the dominant conservation ideology of the state. Women groups that we visited have adopted an informal patrolling system in which two women users in rotation patrol the forest during daytime hours. The groups we visited have rationed the use of fuelwood and fodder from the community forest, have imposed prices for the products obtained from community forests, and have set specific periods of times for the collection of the products. None of these rules or actions seems to take into account the needs of specific disadvantaged groups. Such rationed use of products has resulted in increased scarcity for all, but the poor and women-headed households who own little or no private sources with which to supplement their requirement for the products pay a higher cost than most. There is no evidence that in Rapti, women-only groups have tackled equity issues in their management approach.

The share of benefits

Decisions related to the distribution of forest products tend to be based on the equality principle, not equity. Within FUGs, members are more comfortable talking about sharing equally. They consider it to be fair that all FUG members can access the forest for firewood for the same number of days per week, for example. Yet this equality often masks the fact that households with more hands can collect bigger quantities during the same time. Allowing the same access to all also overlooks the fact that some landed households would possibly need less access to the forest, because their land already provides for most of their needs. There is no targeting for addressing the needs of the poor and enhancing their livelihoods. In places where *samiti* members understand the idea of equity and even agree with it, they find it difficult to act according to the idea of equity. It is possible that *samiti* members collude with self-interest. But it is also possible that there is a fear that equitable distribution of products based on needs (which would mean less access to the common resource for wealthier and more powerful people) would only lead to conflict, which FUGs do not have the resources and capability to manage (Rai et al, 2003).

Like most of the mixed groups, women-only groups also lack an equity perspective in sharing benefits. Here also, class and caste relations determine the share of benefits that one can claim from community forests, and exclusion of the poor and lower-caste women continues. As a result, the issues raised for mixed FUGs, namely the poorest households comparatively losing out and the wealthiest gaining more (Bhattarai and Ohja, 2001), are replicated in women-only FUGs. Women who were previously highly dependent have lost access to free resources, even though the resource base may be increasing. According to one woman from Dharapani:

> *The forest condition has improved. We are happy with it. But the scarcity of fodder and* khar *(thatching material) has also increased. Now we collect it only when the forest is open. We also need to pay Rs30 ($0.74) for one* bhari *of fodder and Rs35 ($0.86) for one* bhari *of* khar. *The good thing is that we can collect dry and broken branches to use as firewood once a week free of cost. There is no fear of forest guards.*

Within the women-only user groups, some economically better-off, high-caste women in the *samiti* are well aware of the need for equitable distribution of forest products. While they admit that poor women are more dependent on communal resources, and thus need special consideration, most are reluctant to incorporate this in operational plans and product distribution rules. For example, during a group discussion in the Shrijansil women's FUG in Pyuthan, two poor women expressed interest in raising goats as one of the FUG's income generation activities. However, in order to do so, the landless women requested an increased share of fodder from the community forests. After some argument, the *samiti* rejected their request. In their view, the allocation of products based on equal amounts for each member avoids any possible conflicts within the FUG. A more equitable distribution of resources, for example giving a bigger share of fodder to poor households, might invite conflict among users and thus is largely avoided.

Poor women from the Pahiro women-only FUG also share a similar experience of curtailed access to forest products and the lack of an equity perspective even among the women. According to Pabitra Shah, a member of the Rukum women-only FUG:

> *Previously, the forest around the village was open to all, and we used to collect fuelwood and fodder as and when required. All forests have now been converted into community forest. Community forest opens only once a year for four days for people to collect fodder, fuelwood and leaf litter. Those households that have a husband at home and more family members can bring more products within this limited time. Women like me who do not have a husband at home to assist with collection of the product lose out, as all need to pay an equal price, however much can be collected within the given time. Last year also I could only bring 20* bhari *of fuelwood while others brought up to 40* bhari.

This statement illustrates that in terms of access to products from community forests, women-only groups, like mixed user groups, are prone to inequity and injustice. The inequity between women affects poor women-headed households the most. In Dharapani, for example, the women-only FUG consists of 92 households, of which two-thirds can be considered women-headed households due to the long-term absence of their husbands, mostly looking for wage labour in Indian cities. Although women from women-only FUGs can also become members of mixed FUGs, as the household is the unit for membership, the participation of women in women-only FUGs tends to restrict their participation in mixed FUGs, as there are clear (albeit informal) norms set locally that women who are part of women-only FUGs are not allowed to participate in mixed FUGs. This is so in the Rukum, Rolpa and Pyuthan women-only FUGs. This means that women-headed households, which are often also the poorest, lose out, as they cannot access the mixed FUG resource through a man, but are limited to the resources available in poorer forests.

The above also illustrates that even amongst women-only groups, members may not necessarily see or accept that better endowment should limit the claim of individuals to communal resources. If wealthier members, who are less dependent on common resources, used less of those resources, there would be more resources available for the poorer, more dependent members. More resources and more institutional support may help poorer members to improve their economic situation, and in turn perhaps decrease their dependence on communal resources. What 'outsiders' seem to forget is that 'women' is not only a created category for the purpose of an instrumental policy but also that these women come to community management with their own socialization: why should women help each other on the grounds of their gender, when their caste or social status determines the expectation that they reproduce and protect differences? Krishna (2001, p167) argues that essentializing women 'obscures the embedded ties that link a woman to her family and her kin'. One side of this argument is that women are expected to look after the interests of their family and kin. This is an issue that we have often come across in Nepal (although not necessarily in Rapti): women are often 'allowed' to be involved on the understanding that the family will benefit. Although this study does not explore this issue, questions include: how much is a woman's agency in a public sphere constrained by her degree of agency within her own household? How can women who are weak in their households challenge the accepted social order in public? In other words, how can women alone overcome hidden and invisible power?

The use of community funds

In terms of use of funds, as we illustrated earlier, most women-only FUGs own either degraded or newly planted forest land that offers few opportunities to raise income from selling the products. However, each FUG sets an annual compulsory membership fee and also raises small amounts from firewood and fodder sale. Four out of five FUGs were found to use FUG funds to cover all or part of the salary of the government schoolteacher. While this shows that women are prepared to invest in education, this is also an example of the wider community benefiting from women's labour.

Two of the five women-only FUGs (Pahiro and Shrijansil) also invested FUG funds in providing loans to members. However, the interest charged was found to be exceptionally high at 36 per cent per annum, compared to the 18 per cent per annum charged by formal banking institutions. The FUGs justify this by claiming that the high interest rate:

> *encourages users to pay back the loan as soon as possible ... it helps to increase the amount of fund so that it can be invested elsewhere.*
> (Chairperson, Shrijansil women-only FUG, personal communication)

Poor women face specific constraints in their ability to benefit from collateral loans from the FUG funds. Because of the immediate need for consumption, poor women may not be able to invest the loans that they obtain in productive activities. Evidence to support this finding came from Rukum, Salyan and Pyuthan, where poor women took loans but spent the money to meet immediate consumption needs leading to a more vulnerable indebted situation in the long run. The pressure to meet immediate needs (mainly for food and medical treatment) is sometimes so great among poor women that they are not able to utilize credit obtained from user groups for productive investment. One woman in the Pahiro women-only FUG told us that:

> I borrowed Rs1500 ($37) from the women-only user group to buy a goat. But I had to spend it on buying food grains, as there was nothing to feed children. I paid the amount after three years. The interest rate made the loan amount more than double. When the user group frequently asked me to pay the loan so that others can borrow it, I had to sell my only buffalo to repay the loan amount.

The lack of productive investment makes it almost impossible for repayment of the loan. Here also, class and caste relations determine the share of the benefits one can claim from community forests.

What is the value of women-only spaces?

As Pandey (1999) argues, empowerment is a process of building capacities and confidence for taking decisions about one's own life at the individual and collective levels, and gaining control over productive resources.

One of the arguments for creating space for women is that away from the intimidating glance of men, women might slowly be able to build up their confidence, their leadership skills and more generally their capacity to engage in public affairs. Creating women-only spaces would help to develop a critical mass (Agarwal, 1997) and allow women to ascertain their power to act, mobilizing the power from within.

Observation and discussion indicate that women-only FUGs in Rapti lack information and exposure to pre- and post-formation services available for FUGs from government and non-government service providers, and thus are lagging behind in capacities and confidence building for resource management and utilization compared to the men (and women) of mixed user groups.

Women are sidelined at the local level within their communities by having access only to lower quality resources, but also at the more strategic level, by not being able to engage more in the national debate, as the following discussion demonstrates. Ironically, therefore, by getting involved, women are losing out and pay a high cost for their involvement (Jackson, 1999).

Women's low representation and participation in users' federations also illustrates that women-only FUGs have little to contribute to confidence and leadership skill building specific to women. The Federation of Community Forest Users, Nepal (FECOFUN) is a national federation of forest users across Nepal, dedicated to promoting and protecting users' rights by linking FUGs throughout the country and lobbying for FUGs in policy matters. Of the 16 women members on the national executive committee of FECOFUN, only one comes from a women-only FUG. Women-only FUGs comprise only 5 per cent of the total number of FUGs in the country. However, one might have expected that women-only forums should have proportionally produced more women in leadership or decision-making positions. This has not proved to be the case. According to the secretary of FECOFUN:

> *In the last national assembly, when women from the women-only FUG could not compete with women from mixed groups who were more outspoken, we had to nominate women from women-only FUGs for executive committee. Women from mixed groups may have found it difficult in the first few years to participate effectively in the presence of men, but later they become used to it. Women from women-only groups lack exposure and linkages. They also lack the experience of speaking in front of men compared to women from mixed groups, and thus can not compete with women from mixed user groups in an election.*

Networking among FUGs (including at the Federation and local-level networks) is found to have important positive impacts among the FUGs: it increases users' awareness and understanding about roles, rights and opportunities (Kafle, 2001). It also opens up multi-stakeholder forums for sharing opportunities and resources, leading to capacity building of groups and members, and synergistic efforts for advocacy and lobbying for collective benefits (Rai, 2002a).

Yet because of their restricted mobility, lack of sufficient time to get involved in community affairs and their limited exposure, most women-only FUGs are unaware of the need for and the usefulness of networking. Only a few women-only user groups are members of the Federation, and even among members, involvement in the networks and Federation is limited mostly to those making regular payment of membership fees. As a result, women-only user groups lag behind mixed user groups in getting access to information and opportunities, and thus tend to be left out of the process of mutual learning and capacity building.

Women-only FUGs present two problems for women, and especially for poor women. First, they are what Cornwall (2004, p78) has described as spaces for 'regularized relations' that are set up for instrumental purposes ('let the community take charge of what the State may not be capable of undertaking'), and for which the rules and agenda are set by outsiders rather than members of the group. Second, they are spaces 'made available by the powerful' (Cornwall, 2004, p78). Women-only FUGs exist in most cases *only* because outsiders (donors or the FOD) have created them with the agreement of mixed FUGs, not because women or poor women wanted them. Nothing in the women-only FUGs was specifically set up to address gender or social equity issues; they are just an exclusive group assigned to manage a portion of (degraded) resource following the same rules and regulations as the mixed FUGs, but with more constraints.

Why isn't community forestry a gender-transformative policy?

An individual's ability to participate, or not to participate, in forest management is shaped by incentives that emerge from the physical, technical, economic and institutional circumstances in which they are embedded (Jeffery and Vira, 2001). The social, familial and personal subordination of women within the households further determines their ability to engage in community forestry. Similarly, an individual's ability to claim a share of the benefits depends on her initial resource endowments, her bargaining power in the group and her perception of power relations (Leach et al, 1999; Rai, forthcoming). The question then is whether community forestry as a policy and as a process can critically address these constraints at community level, and whether it can do so specifically for women and for the poor?

What does the policy say?

The current forest policy (including the Revised Master Plan 1990, forest policy and directives) clearly mentions women as primary users of communal forests and stresses the need to facilitate their effective participation in decision making. However, because these plans and policy documents do not provide a clear programme and policy directives to address the immediate and strategic gender needs and priorities, the policy recommendations are not internalized in practice. The plan does not make explicit that existing unequal gender roles and relations that need to be transformed in order to enable more sustainable and equitable gender development (Bhatia, 1995; Rai, 2002b). The policy suffers because it does not distinguish between gender issues and women issues, terms it uses interchangeably (Cornwall, 2003). This refers back to what we said earlier about the instrumental approach, which tries to make women more visible in order to reach targets rather than consider and challenge the barriers inherent to gender relations. But also it is very clear from our own experience in the field that practitioners and policy makers still have a limited conceptual understanding of gender as constructed and mostly defined by the relationships between men and women. For many people, gender still means women's issues.

The community forestry policy documents lack proper assessment and analysis of the gender-specific constraints and opportunities that entangle both men and women. The lack of such analysis undermines the value of policy statements and weakens mechanisms to implement changes in practice. For example, although the master plan provides directives to promote women's active decision making at all levels, the rules and procedures of the DOF do not have any specific mechanisms to achieve women's involvement. This is due to practical procedures and mechanisms, organizational incentives and the absence of women staff, but also to a deep inability to recognize gender as a form of power relations, itself linked to a lack of understanding, overlapping with the fact that foresters and policy makers are themselves entangled in their own gendered behaviour. The

Community Forestry Guidelines (2002) can be considered a practical instrument for the implementation of the policy. They focus on the process of FUG formation, yet do not include any analysis of the specific constraints faced by women and the poor during FUG formation. 'Gender' or 'equity' as concepts are not mentioned, and 'women' and 'the poor' are mentioned only as categories of users with different needs.

What do implementers do?

Unfortunately, the DOF, which is in charge of the management of community forests, has traditionally been ill-equipped to deal with social and gender equity issues (Malla, 2001). Government departments in general are largely dominated by staff from higher castes and women staff in His Majesty's Ministry of Forests and Soil Conservation (MoFSC), are conspicuously absent, especially at the field level. The DOF overall is ill-equipped with staff possessing appropriate skills and incentives to go out of their way to mobilize communities for social change. Most foresters have limited awareness and interest in these issues. Gender and social discrimination are ingrained in Nepali society, and anybody who addresses these issues in their work also needs to address them in their personal lives. From our discussions in the field with many government officials, it is clear that gender issues equal women's issues, and that women should be confined to the domestic sphere (despite their ubiquitous presence in the landscape). Data from the field also show that few efforts are made during FUG formation to reach poor and disadvantaged groups, with the result that the elite dominate FUG affairs.

Foresters are more interested in forests and their protection than in facilitating sustainable community-based use and management of forests (Malla, 2001). Although community forestry is essentially about empowering communities, in practice this does not happen. Few rangers believe that communities are capable of taking a leading role in their own development, and few are committed to the creation of self-reliant groups. Although the policy clearly states that FUGs can manage their own affairs and that the district forest officer need only approve the operation plan, in practice the DFO informally controls every decision made by the FUGs, from the harvesting and sale of every log to the use of FUG funds. This makes forest management costly and bureaucratic, and community empowerment a farce.

Clearly the role of foresters needs to change from one of policing to one of facilitating. During formation of a FUG, when the FUG is preparing its rules and regulations, foresters can support communities in tackling embedded gender and social inequity in a straightforward way. Though users may not necessarily be against introducing equity measures in the FUG constitution, they fear that the social cohesion of the group may not be able to survive internal conflicts. Concrete support from the policy makers and the implementers is needed to help communities to constructively address conflicts.

Conclusions

It seems that women-only FUGs, as in the case of mixed FUGs, are so far giving voice to economically better-off and high-caste women who may have little interest in benefiting the poor and lower-caste women. Such institutions 'can serve to reproduce existing relations of inequality between "women" and "men" and strengthen compacts between particular kinds of women and their men folk, rather than build the basis for more equitable gender relations' (Cornwall 2003, p1329). Our data show that most shortcomings recorded in mixed FUGs in terms of gender and social inequity are reproduced in women-only FUGs. This, we argue, will continue as long as community forestry addresses solely the practical needs of environmental protection rather than tackling head on the strategic need for social change.

The objective of promoting women's effective participation in CPRM should not be confined to their participation in the management of resources (which they are doing anyway), but should ensure increased access to and control of the resource in parallel with concrete measures to increase their capability. Unless efforts are made to address class-, caste- and gender-based exclusion at community level through specific policies but also through explicit directives for implementation, the formation of women-only space in community forestry will be counterproductive, isolating women and further marginalizing them.

In addition to creating women-only spaces, it is also important to ensure that gender equity is structured into all FUGs. Sarin (1999) suggests that gender equity can be structured in FUGs by making women visible both in a general body and the executive committee, as well as by ensuring that women members are clearly, and independently of male members, entitled to resources in specified ways. More importantly, there is a need to work for a more accountable, committed and responsive policy environment and structures to encourage and accommodate gender equity at all levels through gender mainstreaming. Making policy and structure gender-sensitive at all levels would be a wiser move than creating women-only spaces without a clear commitment and responsiveness to change towards gender equality. But as we have demonstrated elsewhere (Buchy and Subba, 2003), community forestry is a gender-blind technology, so the issue is not so much which type of groups will best serve the needs of women, but rather that a much more thorough analysis of the policy from a gender perspective is needed in order to weed out structurally embedded constraints. Krishna (2001, p167) has talked about 'engendering community rights' but she also warns that a 'gender balance of community rights cannot be sustained without gender balance within families'. This then brings us back to the ongoing struggle and discussion about gender relations, which have to be addressed and resolved at the personal level as well as at the collective level, through gendered policies and practices.

Notes

1 The mid-hills represents the areas from the Siwaliks foothill range north to the Tibetan border. The Terai area is adjacent to the foothills to the Gangetic plains of the south.

2 Administratively, Nepal is divided into five geographic development regions: Eastern, Central, Western, Mid-Western and Central, 14 zones and 75 districts. Rapti zone falls in the Mid-Western development region and consists of five districts, namely Dang, Rukum, Rolpa, Salyan and Pyuthan.

3 Poverty is defined in Nepal as the proportion of the population living in households in which per capita expenditure for food and non-food items is beneath that required to purchase the minimum calorific requirement and other basic needs (Nepal Living Standard Survey, 2003/2004).

4 Although there are numerous variations across the country, agriculture throughout Nepal is based on a combination of crop production, livestock rearing and the utilization of forest resources.

References

Acharya, M., C. Subba, H. Regmi and S. Aryal (2004) *Analysis of Caste, Ethnicity and Gender Data from 2001 Population Census*, Kathmandu: Tanka Prasad Memorial Foundation

Agarwal, B. (1997) 'Environmental action, gender equity and women's participation', *Development and Change* 28 (1): 1–44

Agarwal, B. (2000) 'Conceptualising environmental collective action: Why gender matters', *Cambridge Journal of Economics* 24: 283–310.

Agrawal, A. (2001) 'Collective action, property rights and decentralisation in resource use in India and Nepal', *Politics and Society* 29 (4): 485–514

Bhatia, K. S. (1995) *Swasni Manchhe, Logne Manchhe Ra Jungle (Women, Men and Jungle): Gender analysis of Dolkha Ramechhap Community Forestry Project*, Kathmandu: Nepal Australia Community Forestry Project

Bhattarai, B. and H. Ojha (2001) 'Distributional impact of community forestry: Who is benefiting from Nepal's community forestry?', Kathmandu: Forest Action

Buchy, M. and S. Subba (2003) 'Why is community forestry a social- and gender-blind technology? The case of Nepal', *Gender, Technology and Development* 7 (3): 313–332

CARE (2003) 'CARE Nepal Fact Sheet', Kathmandu: Care Nepal

CBS (2003) 'National Sample Census of Agriculture Nepal, 2001–2002', Kathmandu: His Majesty's Government, National Planning Commission Secretariat, Central Bureau of Statistics

CFD (2004) 'National Database', Kathmandu: Community Forestry Division, Department of Forest

Chhetri, G., S. Rana and D. Hinchley (1996) 'Nepal Australia Community Forestry Project ACFP Gender Workshop Report', Kathmandu: Nepal Australia Community Forestry Project

Cornwall, A. (2003) 'Whose voices? Whose choices? Reflections on gender and participatory development', *World Development* 31 (8): 1325–1342

Cornwell, A. (2004) 'Spaces for transformation? Reflections on issues of power and difference in participation in development', in S. Hickey and G. Mohen (eds) *Participation – From Tyranny to Transformation*, London: Zed Books

DOF (1998) 'Community forestry for everybody forever', proceedings of the Third National Community Forestry Workshop, Department of Forests, Ministry of Forest and Soil Conservation, Kathmandu, 2–4 June

Gaventa, J. (2006) 'Perspectives on participation and citizenship'. In R. Mohanty and R. Tandon (eds) *Participatory Citizenship, Identity, Exclusion and Inclusion*, New Delhi: Sage, pp51–67

Graner, E. (1997) *The Political Ecology of Community Forestry in Nepal*, Saarbrücken: Verlagfur

Guijt, I. and M. K. Shah (eds) (1998) *The Myth of Community: Gender Issues in Participatory Development*, London: Intermediate Technology Publications

HMG/N (1992) 'Operational Guidelines for Community Forestry', Kathmandu: Department of Forest, Ministry of Forest and Soil Conservation

Hobley, M. (1996) *Participatory Forestry: The Process of Change in India and Nepal*, London: Overseas Development Institute

Hobley, M. and Y. Malla (1996) 'From forests to forestry – the three ages of forestry in Nepal: Privatisation, nationalisation, and populism'. In M. Hobley (ed.) *Participatory Forestry: The Process of Change in India and Nepal*, London: Overseas Development Institute, pp65–91

Hunt, S. M., W. J. Jackson and K. B. Shrestha (1995) 'Income generation through community forestry in Nepal', paper presented at a seminar on Income Generation through Community Forestry, RECOFTC, 18–20 October 1995, Bangkok, Thailand

Jackson, C. (1999) 'Social exclusion and gender: Does one size fit all?', *European Journal of Development* 11 (1): 125–146

Jeffery, R. and B. Vira (2001) 'Introduction'. In R. Jeffery and B. Vira (eds) *Conflict and Co-operation in Participatory Natural Resource Management Part II*, New York: Palgrave Macmillan, pp1–16

Kafle, G. (2001) 'Platforms for learning: Experiences with adaptive learning in Nepal's community forestry programme'. In E. Wollenberg, D. Edmunds, L. Buck, J. Fox and S. Brodt (eds) *Social Learning in Community Forests*, Bogor: Center for International Forestry Research, pp45–63

Kandel, B. and R. Subedi (2004) 'Pro-poor community forestry: Some initiatives from the field', Fourth National Workshop on Community Forestry, Community Forestry Division, Department of Forest, Kathmandu, 4–5 August

Kanel, K. R. (2004) 'Twenty-five years of community forestry: Contribution to Millennium Development Goals', Fourth National Workshop on Community Forestry, Community Forestry Division, Department of Forest, Kathmandu, 4–5 August

Kanel, K. R. and D. R. Niraula (2004) 'Can rural livelihood be improved in Nepal through community forestry?' *Banko Jankari* 14 (1): 19–26

Krishna, S. (2001) 'Introduction: Towards a 'genderscape' of community rights in natural resource management', *Indian Journal of Gender Studies* 8 (2): 151–174

Lama, A. and M. Buchy (2002) 'Gender, class, caste and participation: The case of community forestry in central Nepal', *Indian Journal of Gender Studies* 9 (1): 27–42

Leach, M., C. Joekes and C. Green (1995) 'Editorial: Gender relations and environmental change', *IDS Bulletin* 26 (1): 1–8

Leach, M., R. Mearns and I. Scoones (1999) 'Environmental entitlements: Dynamics and institutions in community-based natural resource management', *World Development* 27 (2): 225–247

Malla, Y. B. (2001) 'Changing policies and the persistence of patron–client relations in Nepal', *Environmental History* 6 (2): 287–307

Moffat, M. (1998) 'A gender analysis of community forestry and community leasehold forestry in Nepal within a Macro-Meso-Micro Framework', unpublished MPhil dissertation, University of Manchester

Pandey, D. R. (1999) *Nepal's Failed Development: Reflections on the Mission and Maladies*, Kathmandu: Nepal South Asian Centre

Pokharel, B. K. and D. Amatya (2000) 'Community forestry management issues in the Terai'. In Ministry of Forest and Soil Conservation (ed.) *Joint Technical Review of Community Based Forest Resource Management*, Kathmandu: Ministry of Forests and Soil Conservation, pp139–164

Rai, B. (2002a) *An Assessment of ActionAid Nepal's support to FECOFUN and TECOFAT: Achievements and Challenges*. Kathmandu: ActionAid Nepal

Rai, B. (2002b) 'Contribution of forestry sector in addressing gender equity in 10th five year development plan of Nepal', report prepared for Department of Forests, Kathmandu

Rai, B. (forthcoming) 'Agrarian structures and distributive outcomes of community forestry in Nepal', doctoral thesis to be submitted to Institute of Social Studies (ISS), The Hague

Rai, B., D. Ojha and B. K. Shrestha (2003) *Design Report for the Rapti Zone Districts*, Kathmandu: Livelihoods and Forestry Programme

Sarin, M. (1999) 'Should I use my hands as fuel?'. In R. Subrahmanian (ed.) *Institution, Relations and Outcomes: Framework and Case Studies for Gender Aware Planning*, London: Zed Books, pp231–265

Subedi, B. P., C. L. Das and D. Messerschmidt (1993) *Tree and Land Tenure in the Eastern Terai: A Case Study from the Siraha and Saptari Districts, Nepal*, Community Forestry Case Study Series No. 9, Rome: Food and Agriculture Organization of the United Nations

Tinker, I. (1993) 'Women and community forestry in Nepal: Expectations and realities', *Society and Natural Resources* 7: 367–381

Townsend, J., E. Zapata, J. Rowlands, P. Alverti and M. Marcado (1999) *Women and Power: Fighting Patriarchies and Poverty*, London: Zed Books

van den Hombergh, H. (1993) *Gender Environment and Development: A Guide to the Literature*, Amsterdam: International Books

Chapter 8

Gender, Legitimacy and Patronage-Driven Participation: Fisheries Management in the Tonle Sap Great Lake, Cambodia

Bernadette P. Resurreccion

Introduction

The Tonle Sap Great Lake is the largest freshwater body in Southeast Asia and is often referred to as a unique hydrological phenomenon, where local people fish and farm its rich fishing grounds, floodplains and inundated forests in seasonal cycles. The Tonle Sap Great Lake area includes the Great Lake, the Tonle Sap River, the adjacent floodplain and the affluent rivers that feed the lake. The region is home to nearly 3 million people, most of whom derive their livelihoods directly from its natural resources.

In order to conserve fishery resources in the Tonle Sap region, the Royal Cambodian Government has recently recognized the role of local communities in managing common property freshwater and forest resources through the formation of community institutions known as community fisheries (CFs).[1] Community fisheries management groups have been created throughout villages in the Tonle Sap region, where women's participation is increasingly being recognized as a key component by state and non-state organizations in community-wide efforts to use and manage fishery and forest resources in sustainable ways (RCG, 2001). Stewardship and quasi-property rights have been granted to community groups over the extractive reserves found in the Tonle Sap.

This chapter aims to examine community fisheries management as a newly state-created and community-based institution in the Tonle Sap region as it operates against a historically conflict-ridden and patronage-driven context in which intense competition for fishery resources has been commonplace and prevalent. The study explicitly employs a gender perspective in order to explore the experiences of women and men in fisheries management, and to pry open a different type of socio-political order based on backdoor power, legitimacy and status – often rendered invisible in studies of state–society relations.

Cambodia is a society undergoing transition after years of conflict and strife. In the absence of any liberal democratic state tradition, adequate civic culture and publicly tested opportunity structures for participation are only just evolving alongside state structures. This is due to the overriding presence of a traditional elite and anti-development oligarchs who oppose and/or capitalize on growing subsidiarity and the decentralization of state authority that seems to be the currency of development practice and natural resource management today (Le Billon, 2000, 2002; Persoon and Van Est, 2003; Keskinen et al, 2007).

The literature on Southeast Asia has numerous accounts of how patronage, clientelism and traditional affiliations capture and constitute state programmes, define market activities, and more recently, pervade efforts to enhance participatory democracy for development goals (Rigg, 1991; Hefner, 1997; McCargo, 1998; Trocki, 1998; Sidel, 1999; Le Billon, 2000, 2002; Case, 2002; Phatharathananunth, 2002; Charuvichaipong and Sajor, 2006). Generally speaking, existing development programmes may end up serving the needs of traditional elite interests rather than their intended redistributive and participatory goals. The situation is exacerbated by the lack of plurality of genuinely autonomous organizations (Yamamoto, 1995; Bierling and Lafferty, 1998; Charuvichaipong and Sajor, 2006).

This chapter discusses conflicts surrounding Tonle Sap's fishery resources in order to shed light on the kinds of social relations that actually constitute access and control rights, and which likewise define the legitimacy of those who can play an active role in the new institutions represented by the community fisheries management programmes. In particular, the study employs a gender optic that serves to illumine the embeddedness of these new institutions within traditional and existing social relations of kinship and patronage, especially since development organizations active in the Tonle Sap region emphasize the role of women in community fisheries. That said, the study therefore asks: how do relations of power constitute the actual rights to fishery resources in the Tonle Sap? How then do women in the study site deal with traditional male domains of fisheries management and participate in community fisheries management? How have development organizations conceptualized the presence of women in these newly formed institutions?

Data collection for this chapter proceeded in two stages. The first stage, in late 2004, was a scoping study to review recent academic and policy literature on community fisheries in the Tonle Sap. The second stage was field-based. Data was collected in November–December 2005 in the village of Kanleng Phe, Kork Banteay Commune in Kampong Chhnang province. Focus group discussions were organized among 25 male and female villagers of Kanleng Phe on village history, major livelihoods, organization of the CF and people's involvement in CF activities. A survey was conducted through a purposive sampling technique among the 15 most involved women and 17 least involved women in CFs in order to draw out the factors that may explain differences in women's involvement.[2] In-depth interviews were carried out with three types of women – the most involved women and the least involved women in CF activities, and women from female-headed households. These interviews aimed to learn more about the nature of their involvement or non-involvement in CFs, their livelihoods, resource use practices and how they generally perceive participation in CFs.

What follows is a discussion on local institution building, as it is currently conceptualized by its framers in new subsidiary development programmes, as a means to build trust and redress malfeasance in the management of resources. It is argued that current conceptualizations embarking on this route sidestep more complex relations of gender and other types of social relations such as those currently at play in the Tonle Sap, a region marked by a long history of resource conflict and competition.

Gender-embedded institutions

Creating local institutions has come to be regarded as the means by which risks of over-exploitation of resources can be minimized. In the case of the Tonle Sap, the creation of CFs and the dismantling of the fishing lot system in the Tonle Sap in 2000 were supposed to reduce commercial exploitation and increase the fishing area available to local communities, mostly the poor. These ideas were largely drawn from foundational literature on governance and institutions (Uphoff, 1986; Ostrom, 1990, 1992; Keohane and Ostrom, 1995) that views local people and governments as being able to successfully co-manage common property resources through the creation of local institutions and rule making as potential platforms for building trust, reciprocity and cooperation. In natural resource management in particular, the creation of institutions is considered to be crucial in ensuring sustainability of the use of resources, economic production and to some degree, 'empowerment' of communities. By creating institutions, planners aim to 'craft' formalized community structures for purposive agendas (Ostrom, 1990).[3] Desirable results from the formation of such institutions at the local level, for example, include a clearly defined group and its boundaries, a system of sanctions and rules imposed on those who violate publicly designed regulations and an array of conflict resolution mechanisms (Ostrom, 1990). There is also an emphasis on participation in these newly created structures through democratic representation and the election of representatives.

Various critiques have been levelled at this type of formalistic institutional approach. First, commentators have pointed out its lack of attention to the complexity of social relationships and practices that actually characterize and shape resource management rights (Mehta et al, 1999; Ahlers and Zwarteveen, 2006). Second, this approach also tends to gloss over the fact that unclear boundaries define informal and formal institutions, and are often managed in ways that blur such boundaries. Migdal (1994), for instance, highlights the concept of 'state in society,' arguing that in many state-run programmes devolved to local institutions, state or quasi-state actors remain major and influential players in these programmes, rather than the intended subsidiary non-state actors. Third, institutions are often viewed as static and ahistorical, rather than being rooted in people's actual and even *ad hoc* practices that shift or continue according to the ebb and flow of circumstances under which they live, and that these do not necessarily conform to project 'rules' and activities (Mosse, 1997; Cleaver, 1998, 1999; Long, 2001). Fourth, the approach is ensconced within the three neo-liberal 'recipes,' namely decentralized decision making,[4] private property rights and markets, which are intended to solve poverty and resource depletion problems in the South but which do not recognize power and politics as being constitutive of resource rights and realities. Current devolution reforms share a problem analysis influenced by models of privatization, new institutionalism and rational choice theory where 'undersocialized' or atomized individuals are envisaged to generate rules in order to level the playing field and efficiently allocate rights to resources (Mosse, 2001a; Boelens and Zwarteveen, 2005). In a study of people and markets, for instance, Mark Granovetter (1985) compellingly argued that far from being products of atomized-actors' actions, institutions are usually embedded in concrete social relations. This is the track that the study intends to pursue.

This study employs a gender analysis to demonstrate the embeddedness of local institutions. Three key conceptual frames serve to examine the workings of gender in conventional, male-exclusive resource management institutions. First, the recognition that, other than in formal, state-defined spaces, institutions interface with informal domains such as households and other gendered networks through which women's access to resources may be determined and decided. Second, women's presence in formal organizations and programmes is legitimized by their relations with certain types of men. Third, in many parts of Southeast Asia, men's prestige is less tied to money-mindedness; thus money making, considered a less status-earning task, is socially ascribed to women. Despite intentions to effect empowering and participatory opportunities for women in these emerging institutions, state and NGO programmes may paradoxically re-traditionalize women's status by assigning them conventional roles, spaces and tasks that constrain these opportunities.

In conventional male-exclusive domains of resource management such as in water governance bodies (irrigation facilities, community fisheries or river basin organizations), women often elude researchers and policy makers since they are not visible, vocal or active members in these organizations. Meinzen-Dick and Zwarteveen (2001), however, make the case for female non-members of irrigation committees succeeding to get their needs met 'from the rear', by negotiating with male kin outside public scrutiny. They argue that not all irrigation management decisions pass through formal organizations, but that these may be decided in overlapping domains of interaction, such as the household. The dynamics of resource management cannot be properly understood when attention is limited to the formal organization, so researchers need to shift their attention to the 'backstage', 'where the story of those who are muted elsewhere can be heard' (Brunt, 1992, p78). Magdalena Villareal (1994) in her study of female beekeepers in a Mexican *ejido* drew attention to special 'housewife' strategies employed by the beekeepers to assure their husbands that their involvement in the beekeeping project did not prevent them from dutifully performing their domestic tasks. This allowed them to 'wield power by yielding to power'. In addition to the overlapping domains of formal and informal institutions, social ties with specific types of men may legitimize women's presence and involvement in formal institutions or their access to vital resources and information. For instance, female farmers in Sri Lanka and Nepal have forged good relations with male leaders, and often rely on them for their water-related needs and questions (Zwarteveen and Neupane, 1996). Women therefore safeguard their ties with men, by which means they are able to indirectly secure access to resources, which puts into question the conventional feminist emancipatory norm that seeks to gain individual and independent control rights over resources as a 'one size fits all' goal for women despite the nature of their relations and diversity of social contexts (Meinzen-Dick and Zwarteveen, 2001; Jackson, 2003).

In Central Maluku in Indonesia, the continuity of *sasi* – the set of rules that regulate traditional fishery resource use and social behaviour – flourishes since they are highly valued by the traditional village leader who is still considered legitimate by villagers, despite his collaborations with contemporary non-*sasi* institutions like the Christian church, police and higher state authority (Harkes and Novaczek, 2003). Legitimacy therefore drapes people with stature and authority, serving to justify and firm up the social acceptability of their presence and actions in public spaces. In many instances, women's relations with powerful and influential men serve to legitimize their own status and presence in formal organizations, and the absence of such ties may render them with less legitimacy and rights to be visible in public community activities or programmes. In her accounts of rural women transgressing the social boundary between themselves and men in their claims to land, Brunt (1992) says that it is only when women 'use' and accommodate men within their range of social acquaintances that they are able to make contact with people high in the state bureaucracy and to get their claims heard. Women will use this 'verticalism' – so salient in hierarchical societies such as those in Southeast Asia – to support their goals and aims. For instance, in her book on influential women in the Philippines, Mina Roces (1998) argues that unofficial women's power is resourced through kinship politics, but because it is exercised behind the scenes, it makes women vulnerable to criticisms that they are wielding power illegally. Alternatively, apart from their kin relations with powerful men, women's presence in formal politics is also legitimized by discourses on their traditional gendered roles as moral guardians.

While capitalizing on vertical relations to insert themselves in formal organizations, women themselves may create a social identity (Brunt, 1992) by reproducing and affirming conventional gendered discourses on acceptable roles and spaces of women. They may tactically use these discourses to legitimize their presence in otherwise male-influenced organizations because not to do so will effectively edge them out.

Southeast Asian ethnographies throughout the 1990s revealed that money making tends to be seen as an unflattering trait among men who wished to claim high social status, whereas women were seen as more money-minded and as a result, were conferred lower status (Ong and Peletz, 1995; Hefner, 1997). Male violence, bossism and gangsterism, by contrast, were political implements used to assert power over transactions and claims to resources (Trocki, 1998: Sidel, 1999). Many contemporary state organizations and NGOs reproduce these gendered norms and roles by demarcating programmes deemed appropriate for women and for men,[5] indeed chiming with what Ong and Peletz (1995) refer to as development's 'retraditionalization' of gendered spaces, norms and obligations. Mosse (2001b) echoes these ideas as he observed development projects that reconstitute and capitalize on patronage and gender relations in order to comply with the needs for efficiency in local programme management and timeliness in delivery of project outputs and results.

The preceding discussions attempted to centralize the informal and backstage negotiations – a key defining feature of how institutions are embedded in complex gender relations. I refer to these insights later when I discuss the accounts of men in fishing lot operations in the Tonle Sap and women in CFs in the village study site.

The next section is a brief discussion on the recent history and dynamics of fisheries management that embody complex *de facto* networks and transactions among predominantly male actors, and their creation of a violent fisheries environment in the Tonle Sap region.

History of patronage, resource conflict and rights in the Tonle Sap

For over a century, fishing lots in the Tonle Sap covered the largest and the most productive parts of floodplain containing flood forest habitats essential for the feeding and spawning of many aquatic species. The fishing lot system was an official system where lots were auctioned for exclusive use by the highest bidders for a period of two years. Fishing lot operations were interrupted and completely abandoned from 1975–1981 under the Khmer Rouge regime. After the downfall of the Khmer Rouge, the system of *krom samaki* ('solidarity or collective group')[6] was introduced, where fishing lots were run by a selected small group of local people under the Vietnamese-backed People's Republic of Kampuchea (1979–1989). This system ended when the privatization of fishing lot operations was restored in 1989 and resumed full operations in the early 1990s under the auspices of the Department of Fisheries (Sina, 2003; Sithirith et al, 2004).

In the years following the restoration of the private fishing lot system, an environment of violence erupted in the Tonle Sap region, with fishing lot owners, local authorities, military, police and local fishers resorting to armed force as they competed for rights to fishing grounds and floodplains. Villagers began to clear the inundated forest for rice cultivation, dug wells for drinking water or pumped water from ponds for irrigation, and applied chemical pesticides that poisoned the fish, thus ultimately affecting fishing activities in the fishing lots. In turn, violent encounters took place during the dry season, when fishing lot owners prevented local people from further degrading forest and water resources that threatened to diminish the richness of these habitats for fish species. Those living by river embankments complained that boats navigating their rivers threatened the fish that they needed for food and sale.

For their part, fishing lot owners, uncertain whether their lease agreements would extend beyond two years, intensified their catch, often by using illegal fishing gear. In turn, villagers, threatened by the intensity of fishing by lot owners, also started to use illegal and dangerous fishing methods, such as electro-fishing, and were threatened or shot at by fishing lot guards and paramilitary personnel. These guards also threatened illegal poachers and guarded lots even when lot owners had illegally extended their boundaries.

In general, the main sources of conflicts were the sale and bequest of common access areas by lot owners and military to loyal friends, extending the fishing lot boundary and thereby restricting fishing in the extended areas, poaching inside fishing lots, and agricultural activities inside the fishing lots (cf. Degen et al, 2000; Vuthy et al, 2000; Swift, 2001; FACT, 2002; Sithirith et al, 2004).

As the situation worsened, the Cambodian government was forced to address the escalating violence and growing local protests. Responding to what he perceived as an 'anarchy in fisheries', Prime Minister Hun Sen announced the release of 8000ha out of the 84,000ha under the fishing lot system in Siem Reap province for community fisheries management in 1999 and the creation of CFs as local management units made up of local villagers and stakeholders (RCG, 1999). The following year, the government released an additional 536,000ha for CF grounds, or about 56 per cent of the entire area earlier classified as private commercial fishing lots.

As a result of the state's fisheries reforms, use rights in inland fisheries in the Tonle Sap are theoretically divided according to: (a) private rights in commercial fishing lots, (b) community rights in community fisheries-designated areas, and (c) open access rights in portions of the lake and floodplains where there are no private fishing lots or CFs. However, in practice, transactions on the use of resources are still patronage-driven. They continue to involve a complex clientelist and predominantly male network of state authorities, military, businessmen and retinues of loyal henchmen who exercise these rights in ways that are premised on exclusion, loyalty and patronage. In practice, differences between the three rights blur, especially since actors exercise them arbitrarily.

Figure 8.1 illustrates how fishing lots operate in reality. Informal and *de facto* management of fisheries operates beyond the control of the Department of Fisheries (DoF). Access and rights to fishery resources are apparently legitimized by combined military, political and economic power. In the 'burden book' (articles

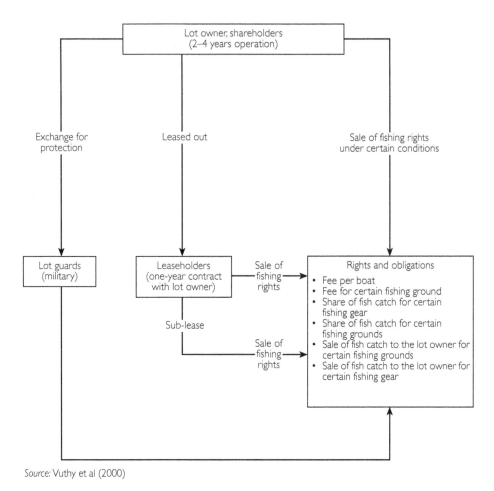

Source: Vuthy et al (2000)

Figure 8.1 *Informal ownership and rights structure of a fishing lot*

of rules) of fishing lot owners, areas outside lots are considered common or open access areas for villagers. However, 'open access' has become an erroneous assumption since many of these areas have come under some type of informal ownership by powerful individuals. For example, the military often collaborate with lot owners in selling 'open access' areas to individuals or groups for a fee, which includes general armed and guarded protection of their exclusive use rights to fishing grounds. Local political leaders or army commanders frequently lease out 'open access' areas, for which a seasonal 'licence' has been purchased from the local fisheries inspectors, but which is not recognized in official accounts. Parts of the lake officially designated as CFs are also still under the control of the military and businessmen who rent these areas out for seasonal licences. Some fishing lot owners have also extended their lots to cover CF areas, open access areas and fish sanctuary zones. Fisheries officials are said to provide protection for lot owners and allow the use of illegal fishing gear. Lot owners are also known to buy electrocution gear for villagers and buy fish back from them at a cheap price. People who produce or sell illegal gear (such as electrocution equipment) are also not arrested (Degen et al, 2000; Vuthy et al, 2000; Sithirith et al, 2004; Heng Samay, 2005; Keskinen et al, 2007; Sithirith, personal communication).

Indeed, established mosaics of social and power relations have determined fishing rules and rights in the Tonle Sap for a fairly long time. Le Billon (2000, 2002) similarly observes these patterns in the exploitation of forest resources in Cambodia, demonstrating also how pre-existing networks of patronage and local interests that preserved informal and illegal entitlements were the means by which Cambodians generally gained access to natural resources. He draws particular attention to the elite's 'shadow state' practices for securing resources, which paradoxically capitalize on the currency of international discourses on the sustainable development of forests.

These arrangements and networks reveal strong patron–client relations in the fishing lot system, involving strongmen who coalesce with state officials and are backed up by state forces such as military men, local officials and loyal henchmen. This echoes James Scott's description of informal and personal alliance networks in Southeast Asia three decades ago: 'consisting of a power figure who is in a position to give security, inducements, or both, and his personal followers who, in return for such benefits, contribute their loyalty and personal assistance to the patron's designs. Such vertical patterns represent an important structural principle of Southeast Asian politics' (Scott, 1972, p92).

Community fisheries management

The CF programme emerged in response to mounting violence in Tonle Sap region and to the management needs for areas newly classified as CFs. Its programme included instituting mechanisms of conflict resolution and sustainable use of existing freshwater, land and forest resources through local community management.

There are over 160 designated CFs in Tonle Sap, comprising 300 management units or councils (Sithirith et al, 2004). However, commercial enterprises still account for a high proportion of the total fish catch. In the catchment areas, commercial logging, mostly illegal, has eroded the evergreen inundated forest by around 15 per cent in ten years. It is believed by both the government and development organizations that the sustainability of common property resources in the Tonle Sap region hinges on equitable access, which is best advanced by community management through the CFs programme.[7]

Early accounts of the CF programme cite instances where actions and interests of the state and traditional elite mesh, such as when commercial fishing lot owners were elected to CF councils (Cheam, 2003), demonstrating the preponderance of former personal alliances and networks pervading the new domain of CFs. The authority of CF officers is also often questioned locally. Prior to the reform in 2000, fisheries inspectors derived part of their incomes from exacting fines from illegal fishers. While patrolling river and lake areas today, CF teams –

many of them former government inspectors – arrest fishers using illegal fishing gear (Cheam, 2003; Heng Samay, 2005). In a study conducted by Oxfam GB (2005), 21 per cent of CF councils were accused of supporting illegal large-scale fishing activities by issuing fishing permits. They are not able to effectively prohibit these large-scale fishers. Fisheries management in the Tonle Sap thus continues to be a domain of blurring lines between state and elite men and loyalist groups, indeed one which is also a predominantly male domain in which women are least visible.

Against this male-dominated backdrop of both the commercial fishing lot system and the newly state-created community-based fishery management institutions, where actors continuously engage in informal transactions shaped by a history of patronage, conflicts and competition over fishery resources, the CF programme has nevertheless increasingly emphasized the important role of women in CF management. How then do women participate in CF management, given that rights for and competition over fishery resources have traditionally been a male domain?

Institutional responses to local women's apparent absence in fishery management have positioned women in the CF programme (ADB, 2002; CCD, 2003; CFDO-DoF, 2004). Planners, however, have glossed over the complex template of rules, roles and rights in fisheries management in the Tonle Sap.[8] Development organizations and programmes on resource management and poverty alleviation[9] have legitimized the involvement of women in CFs, but overlook their linkages with past and existing social relations of kinship, class and patronage.

The following section demonstrates how the CF programme in Kanleng Phe village is also embedded within power and gendered social relations and practices pervading the fishing lot system described earlier.

Women's participation in community fisheries management

There are two major seasons in Kanleng Phe village and in the Tonle Sap region as a whole: the flooded and non-flooded seasons. The flooded season runs from August to November, and the non-flooded season from December to July. Fishing is the main livelihood activity of Kanleng Phe villagers during the flooded season. Farming, some fishing and wage labour are the main livelihood activities of villagers during the non-flooded season. Throughout both seasons, some villagers maintain a general supplies store, pharmacy, small rice mill, hardware supply store and there is a tailor. Caring for livestock is a year-round activity and is regarded as an additional source of income by almost all village households. Wage employment is an important source of additional income for medium and poorer households in which both men and women are involved following the gender-specific arrangements in fishing and farming in the village.

Rice is the main staple crop in Kanleng Phe, but at the same time villagers also grow corn, chilli, watermelon and cucumber to augment their incomes.

During the dry and non-flooded season of December to July, villagers prepare the land, transplant rice seedlings, weed and harvest rice crops. From August to November, the flooded season, villagers earn by selling selected farm and fish products and fishing gear when the village comes under 1–2m of floodwater.

Women are exclusively responsible for reproductive work and trade but they also engage in productive activities such as farming and some fishing. Women also usually engage in fish-related activities, such as processing *prohok* (fish paste), preparing bait and assembling fishing implements such as gill nets, shrimp traps and fish long lines. Men, for their part, do most of the fishing. As a third occupation during the flooded season, women may also fish right at their homes using single fish lines and hooks. Women in the study site are more heavily reliant on land and farming, since fishing is generally considered a male activity.[10]

They are also chiefly responsible for taking short-term loans of rice and/or transacting cash loans with middlemen that tie their household's future fish catch as loan repayments. Cash debts are needed for the purchase of fishing gear or for emergencies such as sickness in the family. When there are shortfalls in rice supply, rice loans are usually taken from kin. Labour shortages in land preparation due to the absence of draught animals and land preparation implements compel women to exchange their labour with households who loan these implements out to them.

As part of the CF programme in Kanleng Phe that began in 2001, the DoF together with an NGO, Community Capacities Development (CCD), conducted various types of training for women dealing with 'conventional' gender issues such as domestic violence, HIV/Aids and health care. Group interviews revealed that only women attended these training sessions. Activities in CFs also included 'leadership training and provision of small loans to (women) clients to be invested in a small business or used to buy an asset' (CCD, 2003, p5). As a result of the programme, two groups of women were organized. One group, organized for poorer women, was the Self-Help Group that operated a group savings scheme. The other, Women's Self-Improvement Group, managed a group credit project.

In the Self-Help Group, each member was required to deposit 1000 riels (US$0.3) a day with the group leader. Members of this group could withdraw or take a loan from the group savings at any time for whatever need. In the Self-Improvement Group, CCD provided a loan of 30,000 riels (US$8) to each member to be repaid without interest. Members are required to use this money to purchase fishing gear or to use it to cover the costs of setting up an enterprise. Each member also has to repay 5000 riels (US$1.3) every month to service their earlier loans, and upon completion of payment in six months, CCD provides a fresh loan of 30,000 riels (US$8). At the time of the study, the Self-Improvement Group had 15 members and the Self-Help Group had 20 members, out of a total of 385 women in Kanleng Phe. Of these, five women were found to be most involved in the CF programme and were individually interviewed for this study. Apart from microfinance activities, awareness-raising sessions were held for both women and men on fishing laws for the protection of fishery resources and the role of CFs in this effort. For instance, in such sessions they were told that villagers are not required to apply for fishing licences unlike fishing lot owners, and that they can fish as much as they like in designated CF areas provided that they use legal fishing gear. Outsiders who fish in designated CF lake areas are only allowed to take one boat and to use 300m hook lines, as well as having to pay 3000 riels (US$0.8) to the CF council in charge of the areas. Patrol teams were organized to enforce these regulations in designated CF areas. Only a few women have joined patrol teams, however, since these teams usually operate at night.

Overall, the CF programme has raised awareness of the principles of fisheries co-management and protection, but clearly mainly involved women only in poverty-alleviation activities, through group credit and savings schemes. Ong and Peletz (1995) have referred to the tendency of development programmes to re-traditionalize gender roles according to dominant money-making ascriptions commonly found for women in Southeast Asia. Influential men also mobilized their wives and other female kin to participate in the CF programme. This capitalizes on patronage and gender networks in order to ensure efficient project management, as Mosse (2001b) similarly observed in a tank irrigation management project in India.

The most and least involved women in the CF programme were surveyed and interviewed in order to examine the factors prompting women's participation or the lack of it (see Table 8.1).

Descriptors in Table 8.1 were derived from the fieldwork household survey (total = 32) and key differences between the two groups of women. All other variables such as age, education, farmland size and how farmland was acquired

Table 8.1 *Selected descriptors of differences between the most involved and least involved women in CFs in Kanleng Phe*

	Primary household livelihoods	Range of household size	Household income per year	Number of livelihood sources
Most involved women in CF (N = 15)	8 out of 15 are engaged in fishing*	4–6 members	13 out of 15 have incomes of between 101,000 and 1 million riels (US$27–267)	11 out of 15 engage in 3–4 livelihood sources
Least involved women in CF (N = 17)	15 out of 17 are engaged in rice farming	4–9 members	15 out of 17 have incomes of between 1,001,000 and 7 million riels (US$267–1867)	15 out of 17 engage in 3–4 livelihood sources

Note: *The six remaining households were engaged in various types of farming (rice, lotus and orchard) while one household earned income by trading farm products.

Source: Author's research data

were more or less equal. The extrapolated descriptors indicate that the least involved women in CFs have bigger households, are engaged primarily in farming rather than in fishing, and earn more income yearly than the most involved women in CFs.

The findings also suggest that women who are involved in many livelihoods may have no time for CF activities, especially if they have larger households.[11] It is also noteworthy that fishing is the primary livelihood in households of the most involved women in the CF programme, while those least involved are primarily engaged in farming.[12] This denotes that the interest women may have in CFs may be strongly premised on their primary livelihood stakes and interests.

Apart from factors of time, household sizes, and number and types of livelihoods, women's disposition to be involved in CFs may also be governed by more political factors and social relations.

Interviews and group discussions revealed that the most involved women in CFs have husbands or male relatives who occupy positions of leadership in the village. For instance, Tearn, one of the five most involved women, confirmed that her husband is the village chief and that she herself is head of the women's Self-Help Group initiated by CCD. Another is Ream, whose brother is chief of the CF in the village and is linked to a powerful commercial fishing lot owner in the Tonle Sap region. Chantha is involved in the Self-Improvement Group, and it helps that her husband is the chairman of the rice distribution unit of the Agricultural Bank that distributes seeds to villagers for rice cultivation and was a former village chief. Ib, whose uncle is the village chief of Kanleng Phe, reluctantly joined the CF largely due to the persuasion of her relatives but was enticed much more by the possibility of loans in the women's group. By contrast, some of the least involved women in CFs are wives of minor employees or members in patrol groups, working as assistants of CF leaders, such as in the cases of Leng, Channara, Ley and Chheng Han.

Chheng Han, for her part, has a family of nine, and her husband, a member of the CF, has fallen ill and can no longer fish. Ley's husband is disabled and she is the sole breadwinner, although she does not know how to fish. However, she grows rice, corn, beans and water hyacinth, and is also hired seasonally as a farm worker during harvests. The husbands of Channara and Leng are assistants to the CF council members and they often join patrol teams. Both maintain that the involvement of their husbands is sufficient to represent the interests and participation of their households. These accounts suggest that these women's involvement in CFs is mediated largely by their workloads and their husbands' social positions in the village.

Apart from the legitimacy of their social position within the CF programme due to their relationships with male kin village leaders, the most involved women in CFs believe that the core activity of fishery resource protection and preservation remains the men's responsibility. Here are some of their thoughts on this issue:

Men should guard in and around the CF since this kind of work requires strong labour. Women, on the other hand, can use a more peaceful method in resolving conflicts caused by violations of rules in the community. Our interest is really the microcredit project since it provides me with 10,000 riels (US$2.7), for which I only need to pay an interest rate of 300 riels (US$0.08). (Chantha, 43 years old, involved in CF through the Self-Improvement Group)

I think that women should join training courses on community fisheries since attendance by itself does not require too much physical effort. We learn to be aware of the need to protect our natural resources. Men, however, should actively join the patrolling team. This is very difficult work. (Kimly, 43 years old, once involved in CF through a daytime patrol team)

I received a lot of encouragement from my brother to join the community activities. I have learned a lot about the need to conserve our environment; this is good for us women to know. Men should guard the community fishing grounds so that they are able to punish those who violate the law. Men are more courageous than women. (Ream, 45 years old, involved in CF through the Self-Help Group)

I think that the most appropriate activity for women is training on domestic violence and taking loans for business. Men should guard the CF and catch those who conduct illegal activities and use illegal fishing gear in our lake. (Ib, 32 years old, involved in CF through the Self-Improvement Group)

Women's involvement in CF activities was determined by livelihood types, workloads and availability, household sizes and their relations with influential men. Least involved women were related to less influential village men, practised more farming than fishing or had heavy workloads, since they were chiefly responsible for subsistence and incomes. By contrast, strong kin relations with influential men in the community legitimize involved women's involvement in the CF programme. The women also had fairly clear ideas about which types of activities were most suitable for them and affirmed men's important role in patrolling and protecting fishery resources in designated CF areas. In order to maintain their social positions within CF management, women affirm their ascriptive 'places' within these structures. As Brunt (1992), Villareal (1994) and Jackson (2003) have observed, women themselves may create a social identity by reproducing and affirming conventional gendered discourses on acceptable roles and spaces of women in order to insert and legitimize themselves in public spaces.

Apart from the most and least involved women in CF, the study was also able to identify those who were not at all involved in the CF programme. They were the women from female-headed households.

Table 8.2 *Selected socio-economic descriptors of female-headed households in two sets of survey data, Tonle Sap region*

	Ahmed et al, 1998 Siem Reap province (N = 523 households)		Heng Samay (2005) Kanleng Phe, Kampong Chhnang* (N = 31 households)
Population of FHHs	N=162 FHHs (100% or 31% of total sample households)		N=5
Widows	63%		2
Married	28%		0
Divorced	6%		2
Single	3%		1
Rice farming	Primary occupation (83%)		Primary occupation (3 of 5)
Trade	Secondary occupation (23%)		(0)
Fishing/fish-related activities	Tertiary occupation (14%)		Tertiary occupation (3 of 5)
Selling labour	Fourth occupation (14%)		Fourth occupation (1 of 5)
Housing	Male household heads	Female household heads	Female household heads
Bamboo and cane with palm leaves roof	74%	64%	4
Wooden house	22%	29%	1
Education	Female household heads	Male household heads	Average number of years of schooling
No education	47%	18%	FHHs: 1.6 years
Primary education	4%	13%	Male-headed households: 6 years

Note: This study was complemented by Heng Samay's research at the Asian Institute of Technology.
Source: Resurreccion (2006)

Gender-related research in Cambodia has repeatedly drawn attention to the fact that there are slightly more women than men in the country due to the huge numbers of men killed in over a decade of armed conflict. The phenomenon of female-headed households (FHHs) has much to reveal regarding vulnerability due to the absence of men in the context of farming and fishing (see Table 8.2).

Table 8.2 indicates that, in general, FHHs are usually less educated, are mostly widows and tend to live in houses constructed from substandard material, compared to those of male household heads. A number of them make shrimp traps and catch shrimps, fish using a single hook, cut fuelwood, process fish and sell their labour as fishers. They also sometimes accompany their sons fishing and help row their sons' boats. In both databases, most women are farmers, but sometimes engage in fishing and trade. FHHs also rely heavily on available lakeshore aquatic resources, and also resort to hiring out their labour for income.

Under the CF management programme, households are entitled to use rights and extractive rights over fishery resources provided that they patrol designated CF areas at night to curb illegal fishing, and that they attend regular community meetings and training sessions organized by the government or NGOs. Conversations with key informants in Kanleng Phe revealed that in order for households to secure use rights to fishery resources, they have to maintain linkages with an informal network that wields influence beyond the formal and legal authority of CF councils and the DoF. FHHs are unable to link up with such networks and to observe membership obligations in the CF programme due to the absence of men in their households who broker women's involvement and legitimize their use rights and participation. Additionally, CF membership legitimizes access rights to resources within the designated CF areas. Under such circumstances, women from FHHs are constrained from taking part in community management of fishery resources, unlike women of male-headed households.

In Kanleng Phe, women heads of households expressed their current difficulties with respect to access to forest resources. Under the new community management system of fishery resources, fuelwood extraction from the nearby swamp forest has been banned in order to conserve the forest as an area for fish spawning. However, informants claim that households with close links to CF council officers are able to gather fuelwood from the forest despite the restriction. As sole heads of their households and widows, the following women share their accounts of a growing problem:

> *Since the introduction of CF management in our village in 2001, the community has been prohibited from cutting in the flooded forest. Like others I cannot collect wood from the forest, which I could do in the past. Now it is very difficult to cook food. Everyday, I cut a kind of grass called* Banla Yuon *to use as alternative fuel. This grass is getting scarcer by the day. I have to walk a long distance to find this grass.* (Num, 58 years old)

> *The new regulations of CF have not affected life so much because I am not involved in fishing. But the problem is collecting fuelwood for cooking. The new law does not allow the collection of wood from the flooded forest. You know, I do not have any boat to venture outside the restricted fisheries area to collect fuel wood. I have to buy fuel from the market. In the rainy season the price of fuelwood goes up to 10,000 riels (US$2.7) per cubic metre. This is really a growing problem among those of us who do not have boats or husbands who will travel further to collect alternative fuelwood or negotiate with the village community heads who may be their bosses.* (Roen, 37 years old)

> *Nowadays, I have to cut* doem banlayuon – *a kind of grass for cooking instead of using firewood from the flooded forest. But to collect this grass, I have to go to places that do not belong to our village. I have to cut the*

plant secretly; otherwise I will have great difficulty cooking our daily meals. The village heads may catch me if they see me. My son has married and no longer lives with me so there is no one to ask permission for me to enter the flooded forest. (Chouen, 54 years old)

Without falling into reductionist views that frequently assume vulnerability and poverty (Chant, 2005) or attach heteronormative ascriptions[13] (Blackwood, 2005) to FHHs, it was found that these widowed women are not legitimate actors in the CF programme under the prevalent conditions of patronage, personal alliances and the arbitrary use and control rights of fishery and land resources that pervade the fishing lot system and CF institutions. They do not have the necessary means – influential male relatives – to legitimize themselves. This contrasts with the women most involved in CF microfinance and microcredit programmes, whose male kin are influential individuals in their community and in CF councils. In many hierarchical societies, legitimacy through influential male brokers offers access to significant resources and privileges. In the context of fisheries management in the Tonle Sap, resource use is a site where decisions are made daily on the basis of patronage relations and 'shadow state' practices: transactions that fall beyond the purview of formal state sanctions but instead are simultaneously legitimized and subjected to more complex markers of personal loyalty, armed power, favouritism and social prestige. Thus, the women closest to these powerful alliances have the legitimacy to access resources and keep themselves involved in state-created programmes.

Conclusions

This chapter has drawn attention to the embeddedness of formal state-initiated institutions, such as CFs and its programmes, within concrete, often informal, social relations and practices by existing networks of gendered actors in the Tonle Sap. In so doing, the study underscores in particular the insufficiency of current neo-liberal conceptualizations on institutions, which posit that by their formal creation in communities, they enable successful co-management of resources through rule making, trust building and cooperation. These conceptualizations depoliticize institutions and sidestep historical and existing power relations that constitute people's actual rights to resources.

Gender has been highlighted as a means of demonstrating the inevitable embedding of formal institutions such as CFs within traditional and existing informal relations of power and practices of patronage that also characterized earlier private fishing lot operations. Complex clientelist alliances and networks of male businessmen, state officials, military and loyal henchmen persistently engage in 'shadow state' transactions, commandeering almost exclusive rights to fishery resources, even through violent means.

Women in CF programmes, by contrast, legitimize their presence through their close ties with powerful men in the community – a practice that re-enacts patronage ties in fishing lots and in the region as a whole. Apart from nurturing kinship ties with influential men, they align themselves with the powerful by way of creating a social identity for themselves that affirms their conventional roles in 'money making', instead of associating themselves with the task of patrolling lake areas that marks the masculine stereotype in this conflict-ridden region. They also comply with tendencies of development programmes to retraditionalize women's roles by involving them in microfinance projects for poverty alleviation.

Women who are less involved in CFs are usually less well off, shoulder heavier workloads in farming, and are not related to influential men. Female heads of households for their part are compelled to access resources for their subsistence in the Great Lake's marginal areas that are not under the control of the region's influential networks. They are the least resourced and do not have influential male relatives who can broker their needs with the powerful networks, either within community fisheries councils or among private fishing lot owners' henchmen.

The Tonle Sap case has demonstrated that patron–client relations are cultural moulds that have endured as a pattern in resource politics in Cambodia. This pattern ostensibly extends to community-based management programmes that emerged from Cambodia's contemporary engagements with international development. Both women and men in this study 'inserted' themselves into newly created formal development institutions through simultaneous backstage and public means: the 'shadowy' mélange of male patronage alliances that meshes the state with private resource interests, and women's open compliance with retraditionalized identities and use of kinship ties to legitimize their presence in these development institutions. But both reproduce political mechanisms for social exclusion in fishery resources in the Tonle Sap region – and demonstrate that rights and institutions are indeed constituted by relations of power.

Acknowledgements

The author is deeply grateful to the generous assistance of Hor Sophea in data collection for this research, and to Heng Samay and Mak Sithirith for sharing their intimate knowledge of the Tonle Sap region and its political history.

The research was supported by the Academy of Finland, and was previously presented at two conferences organized by the Helsinki University of Technology (HUT) on *Integrated Water Resources Management on Tonle Sap Lake as a Part of the Mekong System* in Phnom Penh (February 2005) and on *Modern Myths on the Mekong* in Vientiane, Lao PDR (February 2006). The author is grateful for this support.

Notes

1   Sometimes referred to as the Community Fisheries Co-Management Program (CFP).

2   Eight key informants in a focus group discussion identified the most involved and least involved village women in community fisheries activities, as well as those not involved at all in CF activities.

3   The result of this planning has been a proliferation of new water user associations, water user groups, community fisheries, village user associations, community forestry groups, village development councils and community-based natural resource management programmes.

4   Decentralization studies often denote a strong state that devolves power to fairly visible local structures already in place. Cambodia seems still to be evolving such structures, and therefore the 'local' is often marred by unclear boundaries between strongmen in power and state rule.

5   The same phenomenon pervades the microcredit and microfinance programmes ubiquitously present in development programmes targeting poor women.

6   The *krom samaki* had one leader, and was created by the Kampuchean regime to enable people to help each other, especially disabled people and widows, in fisheries and agriculture. One *krom samaki* consisted of about 50 members from about 12 households. The *krom samaki* was also envisaged as a mechanism for redistribution of resources.

7   The DoF was designated as the lead institution and the chief implementer of this programme, with the assistance of various international and national non-government development organizations.

8   Some commentators have drawn attention to the lack of understanding of the social and political conditions under which women are compelled to participate in the CF programme (Cleaver, 1998; Jackson, 1998).

9   Gender-responsiveness in the fisheries sector has been expressed in the context of poverty reduction goals: 'Reduce the incidence of poverty among vulnerable groups of society, including women, in fisheries communities'. This is Goal No. 3 in the Master Plan for Fisheries, 2001–2011 of the DoF (RCG, 2001).

10   Keskinen (2003) points out that in some Tonle Sap villages, there may be overlaps in the fishing and farming seasons, with possibly severe labour bottlenecks occurring during these periods. In another study, Chou Meng Tarr (2003) reported that the late rice harvest and the start of the fishing season is a very busy period for women, since they participate in harvesting as well as preparing fishing implements and traps, in addition to their regular domestic tasks. Women are expected to manage cash and labour debt transactions with kin and middlemen as they perform post-harvest tasks, and fishing implements have to be purchased for the approaching fishing season.

11   This may also explain why their incomes are higher, since they would have to earn more to feed more household members, and thus have more expenses.

12   Farmers in these parts often do not have a direct interest in managing fishery resources. Often they clear the inundated forest to maximize returns from agriculture. There is in fact an inherent conflict between those (often landless) villagers dependent on fisheries and those whose primary occupation is farming.

13   'Heteronormative ascriptions' refers to the assumption that men are a necessity and presupposes heterosexual relations as being the universal norm, thus positing that men's absence would cause a sense of weakness or vulnerability to women and their households.

References

ADB (2002) 'Report and recommendation of the President to the Board of Directors on a proposed loan and technical assistance grant to the Kingdom of Cambodia for the Tonle Sap Environmental Management Project', Manila: Asian Development Bank

Ahlers, R. and M. Zwarteveen (2006) 'The water question in feminism', paper presented at the International Conference on Land Policies, Poverty, Social Justice and Development, Institute of Social Studies, The Hague, 9–14 January

Ahmed, M., H. Navy, L. Vuthy, and M. Tiongco (1998) *Socio-economic Assessment of Freshwater Capture Fisheries Cambodia*, Phnom Penh: Department of Fisheries–DANIDA-Mekong River Commission Project for Management of Freshwater Capture Fisheries of Cambodia

Blackwood, E. (2005) 'Wedding bell blues: Marriage, missing men, and matrifocal follies', *American Ethnologist* 32 (1): 3–19

Bierling, J. and G. Lafferty (1998) 'Pressures for change: Capitalist development and democracy'. In R. Maidment, D. Goldblatt and J. Mitchell (eds) *Governance in the Asia-Pacific*, London and New York: Routledge and Open University, pp275–300

Boelens, R. and M. Zwarteveen (2005) 'Prices and politics in Andean water reforms', *Development and Change* 36 (4): 735–758

Brunt, D. (1992) *Mastering the Struggle: Gender, Actors and Agrarian Change in a Mexican Ejido*, Amsterdam: Center for Latin American Research and Documentation

Case, W. (2002) *Politics in Southeast Asia: Democracy or Less*, London and New York: Routledge Curzon

CCD (2003) *Program for the Development of Community Fisheries Phase II*, Kampong Chhnang Province: Community Capacities for Development

CFDO-DoF (2004) *CFDO Strategic Plan*, Phnom Penh: Community Fisheries Development Office, Department of Fisheries

Chant, S. (2005) 'Dangerous equations? How female-headed households became the poorest of the poor: Causes, consequences and cautions', *IDS Bulletin* 35 (4): 19–26

Charuvichaipong, C. and E. Sajor (2006) 'Promoting waste separation for recycling and local governance in Thailand', *Habitat International* 30: 579–594

Cheam, Pe-A (2003) 'Community-based fisheries management: Case study of Phat Sanday community fisheries in Kompong Thom Province', unpublished masters thesis, Bangkok: Asian Institute of Technology

Chou Meng Tarr (2003) 'Fishing lots and people in Cambodia'. In M. Kaosa-ard and J. Dore (eds) *Social Challenges for the Mekong Region*, Chiang Mai: Chiang Mai University, pp347–367

Cleaver, F. (1998) 'Incentives and informal institutions: Gender and the management of water', *Agriculture and Human Values* 15 (4): 347–360

Cleaver, F. (1999) 'Paradoxes of participation: Questioning participatory approaches to development', *Journal of International Development* 11: 597–612

Degen, P., F. Van Acker, N. Van Zalinge, N. Thuok and L. Vuthy (2000) 'Taken for granted: Conflicts over Cambodia's freshwater fish resources', paper presented at the 8th IASCP Conference, Bloomington, Indiana, 31 May–4 June

FACT (2002) *Feast or Famine? Solutions to Cambodia's Fisheries Conflicts*, Phnom Penh: Fisheries Action Coalition Team, in collaboration with the Environmental Justice Foundation

Granovetter, M. (1985) 'Economic action and social structure', *American Journal of Sociology* 91 (3): 481–510

Harkes, I. and I. Novaczek (2003) 'Institutional resilience of marine *sasi*, a traditional fisheries management system in Central Maluku, Indonesia'. In D. M. E. Van Est, P. E.

Sajise and G. A. Persoon (eds) *Co-management of Natural Resources in Asia: A Comparative Perspective*, Copenhagen: Norway Institute of Asian Studies, pp63–86

Hefner, R. W. (1997) *Market Cultures: Society and Morality in the New Asian Capitalisms*, Boulder: Westview Press

Heng Samay (2005) 'Gender issues in a fishing community of ex-fishing Lot No. 13, Kampong Chhang Province, Cambodia: A case study of Kanleng Phe village', unpublished masters thesis, Bangkok: Asian Institute of Technology

Keohane, R. and E. Ostrom (eds) (1995) *Local Commons and Global Interdependence*, London: Sage

Keskinen, M. (2003) *The Great Diversity of Livelihoods? Socio-economic survey of the Tonle Sap Lake*, WUP-FIN Socio-Economic Studies on the Tonle Sap 8, Phnom Penh: Cambodia

Keskinen, M, M. Kakonen, P. Tola and O. Varis (2007) 'The Tonle Sap Lake, Cambodia: Abundant water, abundant conflict', *The Economics of Peace and Security Journal* 2 (2): 41–51

Long, N. (2001) 'Demythologising planned intervention'. In N. Long (ed.) *Development Sociology: Actor Perspectives*, London and New York: Routledge, pp30–48

Jackson, C. (1998) 'Gender, irrigation and environment: Arguing for agency', *Agriculture and Human Values* 15 (4): 313–324

Jackson, C. (2003) 'Gender analysis of land: Beyond land rights for women?', *Journal of Agrarian Change* 3 (4): 453–480

Le Billon, P. (2000) 'The political ecology of transition in Cambodia 1989–1999: War, peace and forest exploitation', *Development and Change* 31: 785–805

Le Billon, P. (2002) 'Logging in muddy waters: The politics of logging in Cambodia', *Critical Asian Studies* 34 (4): 563–586

McCargo, D. (1998) 'Elite governance: Business, bureaucrats and the military'. In R. Maidment, D. Goldblatt, and J. Mitchell (eds) *Governance in the Asia-Pacific*, London and New York: Routledge and Open University, pp126–145

Mehta, L., M. Leach, P. Newell, I. Scoones, K. Sivaramakrishnan and S. A. Way (1999) 'Exploring understandings of institutions and uncertainty: New directions in natural resource management', IDS Discussion Paper 372, Falmer: Institute of Development Studies

Meinzen-Dick, R. and M. Zwarteveen (2001) 'Gender dimensions of community resource management: The case of water users' associations in South Asia'. In A. Agrawal and C. Gibson (eds) *Communities and the Environment: Ethnicity, Gender and the State in Community-Based Conservation*, New Brunswick, New Jersey and London: Rutgers University Press, pp63–88

Migdal, J. (1994) 'The state in society: An approach to struggles for domination'. In J. S. Migdal, A. Kohli and V. Shue (eds) *State Power and Social Forces*, Cambridge: Cambridge University Press, pp7–34

Mosse, D. (1997) 'The symbolic making of a common property resource: History, ecology, and locality in a tank-irrigated landscape in South India', *Development and Change* 28 (3): 467–504

Mosse, D. (2001a) *The Rule of Water: Statecraft, Ecology and Collective Action in South India*, New Delhi: Oxford University Press

Mosse, D. (2001b) 'People's "knowledge" participation and patronage: Operations and representations in rural development'. In B. Cooke and U. Kothari (eds) *Participation: The New Tyranny?*, London: Zed Books, pp16–35

Ong, A. and M. Peletz (1995) 'Introduction'. In A. Ong and M. Peletz (eds) *Bewitching Women, Pious Men: Gender and Body Politics in Southeast Asia*, Berkeley: University of California Press, pp1–18

Ostrom, E. (1990) *Governing the Commons: The Evolution of Institutions for Collective Action*, Cambridge: Cambridge University Press

Ostrom, E. (1992) *Crafting Institutions for Self-Governing Irrigation Systems*, San Francisco California: Institute for Contemporary Studies Press

Oxfam GB (2005) *Report on Assessment and Learning from Community Fisheries Management Process*, Phnom Penh: Oxfam GB

Phatharathananunth, S. (2002) 'Civil society and democratization in Thailand: A critique of elite democracy'. In D. McCargo (ed.) *Reforming Thai Politics*, Copenhagen: Nordic Institute of Asian Studies, pp125–142

Persoon, G. and D. M. E. Van Est (2003) 'Co-management of natural resources: The concept and aspects of implementation'. In D. M. E. Van Est, P. E. Sajise and G. A. Persoon (eds) *Co-management of Natural Resources in Asia: A Comparative Perspective*, Copenhagen: Norway Institute of Asian Studies, pp1–24

RCG (Royal Government of Cambodia) (1999) *The Proclamation on the Management and Elimination of Anarchy in Fisheries*, No. PROR KOR, 10 May, Phnom Penh

RCG (2001) *Master Plan for Fisheries, 2001–2011*, Phnom Penh: Department of Fisheries

Resurreccion, B. (2006) 'Rules, roles and rights: Gender, participation and community fisheries management in Cambodia's Tonle Sap region', *Water Resources Development* 22 (3): 433–447

Rigg, J. (1991) 'Grass-roots development in rural Thailand: A lost cause?', *World Development* 19 (2): 199–211

Roces, M. (1998) *Women, Power, and Kinship Politics*, Westport CT: Praeger Publishers

Scott, J. (1972) 'Patron–client politics and political change in Southeast Asia', *The American Political Science Review* 66 (1): 91–113

Sidel, J. T. (1999) *Capital, Coercion, and Crime: Bossism in the Philippines*, Stanford: Stanford University Press

Sina, L. (2003) *Cambodia Fisheries Conflicts in the Post-War Era and the Creation of Fishing Communities: A Case of Fishing Lot Conflicts around Tonle Sap and the Great Lake*, Nagasaki: Nagasaki University Graduate School of Science and Technology

Sithirith, M., Vann Piseth and Te Sokhoeun (2004) 'Communication strategies for fisheries conflict management: A case study in Cambodia', paper presented at the International Workshop on Developing Communication Strategies for Conflict Management in Fisheries, 7–8 July 2004 at the Mitraniketan Center Vellanland, Thiruvanathapuram, Kerala, India

Swift, P. (2001) 'An approach to overcoming the conflict between fishing and farming for sustainable fisheries management', Cambodia Technical Papers Series Vol. III, Phnom Penh: MRC/DANIDA, Program for Fisheries Management and Development Cooperation

Trocki, C. A. (1998) 'Democracy and the state in Southeast Asia'. In C. A. Trocki (ed.) *Gangsters, Democracy and the State in Southeast Asia*, Ithaca: Cornell University Press, pp7–16

Uphoff, N. (1986) *Local Institutions and Participation for Sustainable Development*, Sustainable Agriculture and Rural Livelihoods Programme, Gatekeeper Series No. 31, London: International Institute for Environment and Development

Villareal, M. (1994) 'Wielding and yielding: Power, subordination and gender identity in the context of a Mexican development project', unpublished doctoral thesis, Wageningen: Wageningen Agricultural University

Vuthy, L., Yin Dara and P. Degen (2000) *The Management of the Freshwater Capture Fisheries in Cambodia: Legal Principles and Field Implementation*, Phnom Penh: MRC/DANIDA—Program for Fisheries Management and Development Cooperation

Yamamoto, T. (1995) *Emerging Civil Society in the Asia Pacific Community*, Singapore: Institute of Southeast Asian Studies

Zwarteveen, M. and N. Neupane (1996) *Free-Riders or Victims: Women's Non-Participation in Nepal's Chhattis Mauja Irrigation Schemes*, Colombo: International Water Management Institute

Chapter 9

Gender, Microcredit and Conservation at Caohai: An Attempt to Link Women, Conservation and Development in China

Melinda Herrold-Menzies

Introduction

Microcredit, especially in developing countries, has been championed as a way both to alleviate poverty and to empower women. With the year 2005 dedicated as the United Nations Year of Microcredit, followed by the awarding of the 2006 Nobel Peace Prize to Muhammad Yunus, the founder of the Grameen Bank, the most well known of microcredit ventures, microcredit as an engine of economic development has achieved international approbation from NGOs, multilateral organizations, donors, governments and the general public. As a development strategy, microcredit meshes well with neo-liberal ideologies that champion individual initiative, self-reliance, and 'pulling yourself up by your bootstraps', squarely putting the onus of development on the individual without challenging the distribution of wealth, patriarchy, racial and ethnic discrimination, and other structural sources of inequality. Incorporating women into microcredit programmes fits neatly with the objectives of what has become known as the 'women in development' paradigm, notably set forth by Boserup (1970), which promotes Western-style modernization. Microcredit programmes encouraging women to develop market-oriented microenterprises have been seen as a way to further national goals of economic development while enabling women to better provide for their families' needs.

In the 1980s and 1990s, as microcredit ventures were expanding in the developing world, so too were efforts to link environmental conservation with economic development around national parks and nature reserves. These efforts, collectively referred to as integrated conservation and development projects (ICDPs), were developed to reduce local people's use of natural resources in and around protected areas. ICDPs were seen as a way to overcome perceived conflicts between environmental protection and economic development, creating a win–win situation where promoting development in local communities would actually lead to better conservation. A few of these projects introduced microcredit as one component of a development programme designed to reduce the dependence of the poor on natural resources.

Both microcredit programmes and ICDPs have their critics who challenge the effectiveness of these programmes in achieving their much vaunted goals. For example, several scholars have questioned whether women are truly empowered by microcredit programmes and have critiqued the essentialized constructions of gender embedded in assumptions about women as borrowers and as providers for their families (see Goetz and Gupta, 1996; Rahman, 1999; Isserles, 2003). Researchers examining efforts to integrate conservation and development have likewise questioned the effectiveness of ICDPs in reducing resource exploitation and promoting environmental protection (see Barrett and Arcese, 1998; Redford et al, 1998; Newmark and Hough, 2000; van Schaik and Rijksen, 2002).

This chapter examines a project at Caohai Nature Reserve, a wetland in southwestern China that provides an important wintering habitat for rare black-necked cranes (*Grus nigricollis*) and other protected species of birds. The project has used microcredit, with some efforts targeted toward women, to link environmental conservation with economic development. What makes this programme unique is that it was one of the first to attempt to link microcredit with the conservation of natural resources. This conservation and development programme, which I have been studying since 1997, was designed to reduce local farmers' dependence on natural resources and reduce violent conflicts between farmers and nature reserve staff over access to fishing resources by providing farmers with microcredit loans as start-up capital for the establishment of small businesses. The assumption underlying this programme was that farmers, once involved in their microenterprises, would be less likely to over-tax the natural resources of the nature reserve. Although the majority of microcredit borrowers in this programme have been men, with the creation of specific microcredit groups for women being something of an afterthought, the programme has affected women's lives in many ways, increasing their work burden while offering them new opportunities for work, travel and socializing. What the microcredit programme has not done is meet its goal of substantially reducing women's and men's dependence on natural resources in the nature reserve. In this chapter, I focus on the use of microcredit funds by women, the impact of microcredit on women's work, and the relationship of microcredit to natural resource use by both men and women.

This chapter is based on extensive interviews with nature reserve managers, group interviews and over 200 in-depth semi-structured household interviews conducted at Caohai Nature Reserve between 1997 and 2005. In general, interviews were conducted with both the female and male heads of households. Because the original study was focused on microcredit use and its connection to natural resource management, some nuances related to gender have probably been lost because of the lack of separate interviews with women.

Microcredit

'Capitalism combined with heart' is how Dokmo (2000, p476) describes microcredit, an increasingly popular tool for poverty alleviation. Microcredit has attracted a wide range of support from a diverse array of organizations. The enthusiasm of multilateral banks, foundations, development organizations and NGOs for microfinance led to the Micro-Credit Summit of February 1997, at which participants pledged to expand microcredit resources in order to reach 100 million of the world's poorest people by 2005 (Al-Sultan, 1997). With Muhammad Yunus, the founder of the Grameen Bank, receiving the Nobel Peace Prize in 2006 and the year 2005 dedicated as the United Nations Year of Microcredit, this intervention looms larger in the public consciousness than ever before.

As Sue Wheat (1997) has pointed out, the focus of microfinance on women's empowerment, poverty alleviation and financial sustainability, while making use of market principles, has wide appeal. Advocates depict microfinance as a win–win undertaking where lenders profit because of high interest and repayment rates, while poor borrowers engage in 'self-help', using their entrepreneurial skills and hard work to improve their own lives. Rankin (2001) notes that the new emphasis on microcredit is often characterized as part of a trend away from state-led economic development toward market-led approaches.

Microcredit institutions, which are often quite varied, aim to provide credit to the poor who, because of their extreme poverty and lack of conventional collateral, are not served by more mainstream credit institutions. Microcredit institutions, which generally make small short-term loans, enable the poor to increase their income-generating opportunities by providing them with the capital to develop microenterprises or to improve agricultural production (Al-Sultan, 1997). The traditional requirement for collateral is replaced with alternative arrangements such as expected returns from investment in a microenterprise or group responsibility for repayment, what Bornstein (1997, p45) refers to as 'social collateral'. In the Grameen Bank, for example, traditional collateral is replaced by social collateral in that borrowers are grouped into units where each group member is jointly responsible for the loans taken out by any group member. This makes for tremendous peer pressure to repay a loan. In many microcredit programmes, borrowers repay their loans in a public space near their homes at regular intervals, ensuring public knowledge of who repays and who defaults on their loans (Hulme and Mosley, 1996).

While many microcredit programmes trumpet their high repayment rates as evidence of how successful microcredit has been, some scholars have suggested that high repayment rates indicate little about the impact of the loan on the borrower's financial situation (Buckley, 1997; Brett, 2006). Brett (2006) found that in two microcredit programmes in Bolivia, women were not earning enough money through their enterprises to make payments on their loans. Many women had to borrow money from their husbands or cut household expenses to make their payments. Additionally, group responsibility for loans imposes numerous burdens. The peer pressure may mean that borrowers struggling to repay a loan will have to borrow money from other sources to repay the loan. Woolcock (1999) found that in one Grameen group examined, borrowers were forced to take loans from moneylenders in order to repay their Grameen loans.

Other scholars have critiqued the notion that microcredit is the panacea for poverty alleviation. Buckley (1997) raises the concern that funds that might be better channelled to other forms of development projects are being diverted into microcredit programmes. Park (1999) notes that credit might not always be the major constraint on economic development in rural areas. Investment in health and education programmes could possibly bring greater benefits in some cases.

One of the great successes of many microcredit programmes has been their ability to reach out to impoverished women, giving them access to credit to start up their own microenterprises. The targeting of women has been touted as a way to empower women while making sure that the benefits of poverty alleviation funds improve the economic, health and education situation of the entire family. Microcredit, with its neo-liberal foundations and emphasis on the development of individuals as entrepreneurs, often falls within the women in development (WID) paradigm. Boserup (1970) and others associated with WID advocate the incorporation of women into the project of modernization in order to promote national development efforts while improving the status of women (Tinker, 1997). Srivastava (2005, p46), writing in the *UN Chronicle*, asserts that microcredit, in addition to empowering women, has 'made women productive', betraying the belief that somehow women were less productive before they became immersed in market-oriented enterprises funded by microcredit loans. This values women's productivity in terms of income-generation and not in terms of the many activities (for example, farm work, household chores and child-rearing) women engage in to reproduce the household. This approach, while promoting improvements in the status of women, fails to challenge the way capitalist enterprises have exploited patriarchal relations and women's subordination for greater capital accumulation with a female workforce (Mies, 1985; Benería and Sen, 1997).

Several studies have challenged the optimistic views on empowering women expounded by microcredit's proponents. Goetz and Gupta (1996) found that many loans taken out by women in Bangladesh were actually destined for the women's male relatives. Although the women were the official borrowers, the loans or a substantial percentage of the loan often went to men. Since women's repayment rates on loans in Bangladesh are substantially higher than men's, this ensured that the loan was likely to be repaid. Rahman (1999), examining the

Grameen Bank, points out that women are more likely to succumb to pressure to repay their loans because of their subordinate position in society, with women being more manageable and easier to extract payments from.

In China, the implementation of the microcredit programme at Caohai by international NGOs coincided with a period of decentralization in the 1990s. Harvey (2006, p120) characterizes this decentralization and retreat of the Chinese state as 'neoliberalism with Chinese characteristics', with the state maintaining an important presence in the economy.[1] Microcredit found a convenient niche for itself, with the burden for development resting on the individual during this period of state retreat, when even government agencies such as nature reserves were expected to engage in market activities for greater self-funding (see Harkness, 1998).

Microcredit, conservation and development

Following a period of intense wildlife exploitation in national parks in several developing countries during the 1970s and 1980s, many conservation practitioners began to question the effectiveness of traditional approaches to nature conservation, in which local people in and around parks were excluded from resources on which their livelihoods depended (Gibson and Marks, 1995). The integration of conservation with economic development for local communities was championed as a way to alleviate poverty, reduce local resource dependency and encourage community support for conservation efforts (IUCN et al, 1991; Wells and Brandon, 1992). ICDPs, which have become the embodiment of this drive to couple community development with environmental protection, can take a wide variety of forms with diverse components such as the promotion of businesses that cater to tourists, the sharing of revenues from tourism and hunting, the provision of alternative income strategies, and the development of community infrastructure including schools, roads, and health and sanitation services (Wells and Brandon, 1992; Newmark and Hough, 2000).

Following the implementation of a wide range of ICDPs, researchers found that many of their expectations were not being met. Brandon and Wells (1992) point out that households generally attempt to maximize total income, so that they will not renounce an illegal activity just because they have begun to engage in legal activities, especially if labour is not completely absorbed by the new activities. Barrett and Arcese (1998) note that increases in income from ICDPs may provide more disposable income that may increase demand for resources.

In my research at Caohai Nature Reserve, I have found evidence that supports both positive and negative assessments of ICDPs. Although the community development programmes have not led to major reductions in resource use by project participants, the programmes have been successful in transforming a violent relationship between male reserve residents, particularly fishers, and nature reserve managers into a more cooperative one (Herrold-Menzies, 2006).

One of the distinctive aspects of the effort to integrate conservation and development at Caohai Nature Reserve is its use of a microcredit programme to promote economic development and environmental protection. A few other ICDP-type programmes have employed microcredit as a conservation and development strategy, including several projects in East Africa in which village banks have been created with funds derived from revenues from ecotourism or sustainable resource use, directly linking the availability of microcredit with the protection of natural resources (Nicholas K. Menzies, pers. comm.).

The story of Caohai Lake

Since the founding of the People's Republic of China in 1949, Caohai Lake has been the site of sweeping anthropogenic changes that have dramatically transformed the lives of local people. In the 1950s, Caohai Lake was a shallow lake with a surface area of approximately 45km^2. During Mao's Great Leap Forward in 1958–1959, campaigns to reclaim 'wastelands' were initiated, and the wetlands and lake area of Caohai were partially drained. In a follow-up drainage effort in the early 1970s, the lake was almost completely drained. Local collective farms turned the lake bottom into agricultural fields of corn and potatoes. In the early 1980s, however, in order to reverse microclimate changes resulting from the drainage of Caohai Lake, the provincial government decided to restore Caohai Lake to half of its pre-1958 size.

While planning was underway for lake restoration, the central government was implementing new policies that would change agricultural production and land rights in rural areas. With Deng Xiaoping coming to power in the late 1970s, a new system of agricultural production and procurement was promoted in the countryside. Communes were disbanded as use rights to land and production quotas were contracted to households as part of the Household Responsibility System (*baochan dao hu*). This was part of the beginning of China's move toward more market-oriented economic policies.

As the county government was disbanding communes, most farmers were unaware of the plan to restore the lake – a plan that would flood much of their newly contracted land. With partial restoration of Caohai Lake, local farmers lost much of their cropland. Most households lost between 30 and 70 per cent of their land. The restoration of the lake meant that per capita farmland immediately decreased from 2.5 *mu* (0.17ha) to 1 *mu* (0.067ha), leaving many households without enough land to produce sufficient quantities of food to feed their families. As the population has grown, many who had 1 *mu* (0.067ha) of farmland remaining after the restoration are today trying to support a family of five or more on that small parcel of land.

In order to make up for the shortfall in crop production wrought by the inundation of their farmland, many farmers took advantage of the newly restored lake for fishing and trapping waterfowl. Some were able to drain small amounts of land by digging trenches and raising the soil level of their flooded land. Many households immediately turned to clearing secondary forests on the hillsides around the lake. After these hillsides were cleared, the highly erosive slopes were planted with crops.

Following the restoration of the lake, rare birds, including the endangered black-necked crane, started to winter at the lake after many years of absence. To protect these birds, a provincial-level nature reserve including Caohai Lake was established in 1985. With the establishment of the nature reserve, however, farmers' livelihood activities of fishing, hunting and land reclamation were criminalized. While farmers were allowed to continue to live in the reserve, the hunting or trapping of waterfowl, the draining of wetlands, the clearing of wooded hillsides and fishing during the spawning season were banned. In spite of these prohibitions, land-poor farmers have continued to engage in these activities. Violent conflicts, primarily between nature reserve officials and male farmers, formerly erupted whenever reserve officials enforced a ban on the netting of fish during the spawning season.

Caohai Nature Reserve is located in Weining county, one of the poorest counties in Guizhou province, one of the poorest provinces in China. Today there are some 33,000 people, mostly farmers, living within Caohai Nature Reserve in 89 natural villages (what I will call 'hamlets' in this study). Thirty-two hamlets lost land with the restoration of the lake. It is these hamlets that border the lake where residents have engaged in practices that conflict with nature reserve regulations.

Most hamlets in Caohai Nature Reserve have access to markets. The reserve borders the town of Weining (with an estimated population of 50,000) where there are markets several times a week. Many hamlets are within walking distance of Weining or accessible by a short bus or boat ride. Opportunities for off-farm labour in construction in the town have steadily increased over the years.

Most hamlets in Caohai Nature Reserve are single surname villages in which marriage is patrilocal. Most men are related, being brothers or cousins, while women leave their families behind in their natal village for marriage into another. In general, land is contracted to men. Wives work their husband's contracted land and do not have their own land. Hamlets in Caohai generally have between 300 and 500 people. Annual per capita income is around US$75 (Herrold-Menzies, 2006).

The principal crops grown in the reserve are corn, potatoes, beans and cabbage. Most farmers are able to grow only enough food to support their families for six to nine months a year. Most residents have had little formal education and illiteracy is widespread, especially among women and the elderly. The average number of years of elementary education for male interviewees was approximately four years. For female interviewees, the average education was less than one year. Of interviewees' male children of school age (ages 7–16) 84 per cent attend school. Of their female children, only 50 per cent attend school. Many of these girls are only able to attend school because of the nature reserve's 'One Helps One Programme', a smaller component of the overall project to integrate conservation and development at Caohai, which finds individuals in the US to donate money to cover a girl's school fees. Both mothers and fathers have said that they would be squandering scarce funds if they paid school fees for a daughter since girls marry into another village. Educating daughters is not considered to be an investment in the parents' future nor a security for their old age.

Integrating conservation and development: Microcredit at Caohai

With the enforcement of restrictions on resource use following the establishment of the nature reserve, reserve managers frequently found themselves in violent confrontations with angry farmers over fishing regulations. Reserve officials also found it difficult to stop farmers from reclaiming wetland, woodland and grassland. In order to reduce these conflicts over resources, the International Crane Foundation and the Trickle Up Program (TUP), launched a microcredit programme in 1993 with the support of the nature reserve and provincial environmental protection bureau. The first component of the development programme was to give small grants to farmers who were deemed 'the poorest of the poor' so that these individuals would have a chance to launch a microenterprise. These grants, which do not have to be repaid, are not intended to replace microcredit but to complement microcredit programmes. In general, 10–20 TUP recipients were selected in each participating hamlet. A typical TUP group would consist of three adult family members, including women, who would receive some training in business design and bookkeeping.

After TUP recipients in a hamlet had had several months to demonstrate that they were able to manage an enterprise, revolving microcredit funds (community trust fund, CTF) were established for farmers, regardless of wealth. The size of the CTF groups varies. In general, a CTF would comprise 10–20 members from different households within the same hamlet. A few CTF groups were established that were the size of the number of households in the hamlet, with the male head of a household as the CTF member. The programme allocated 200 yuan (US$25) per member to the fund. The use of funds would revolve between the members of a CTF. Usually at one time, three or four members of the CTF would borrow around 500 yuan (US$62.5) for a three-month period, pay back the money with 2 to 3 per cent interest per month, and then the next group of three or four members would borrow the money. The interest would accrue to the CTF group, either to be loaned out or to be spent on community projects. In one hamlet the interest was used to improve village wells, while in another the interest was used to hire a schoolteacher.

From the beginning, reserve staff responsible for implementing the TUP and CTF programmes emphasized the empowerment of farmers made possible by these programmes. Farmers, without being told what to do by the state, could decide for themselves what activities they would do and carry out those activities as they saw fit. The language used reveals implementers' interests in participatory democracy with neo-liberal undertones. Basically, the programmes would allow one to express her/his 'inner entrepreneur' without interference from what was seen as a cumbersome (and corrupt) state.

The microcredit programmes at Caohai stand in contrast to the general format of microcredit institutions as described by Sun (2005). Caohai farmers do not meet weekly to pay instalments on their loans, nor does an outside financial institution such as a bank, with agents to make sure loans are repaid, oversee the money. CTF funds at Caohai, in theory, are always in circulation in the hamlet. When farmers pay off their loans in a single instalment (in contrast to many programmes with weekly payments), the money is immediately loaned out to the next group of borrowers. The CTF group itself administers the loan. If there are problems with repayment, the group decides how to manage the problem. There is no larger financial institution to which farmers repay the money. The fact that there is no institution in which to store the money if no one has immediate need of funds has proved to be problematic for the sustainability of the CTF groups. There are public meetings at which loans are repaid and made to the next set of borrowers, but over time, the meeting process has become time-consuming and burdensome, especially, for those in charge of bookkeeping.

Caohai's microcredit programme is distinct from some of the more famous microcredit programmes in that it was not mostly targeted toward women. When the CTF programme was initiated, the reserve had not thought about creating women's microcredit groups. Reserve staff assumed that the men involved in the microcredit groups would engage in activities that would benefit the entire household. However, following the success of many female-headed TUP enterprises, the reserve – with prompting from their foreign donors – developed CTFs for women. There are only five (later seven after groups subdivided) women's CTF groups, with approximately 70 women, out of a total of 73 CTF groups. While the first women's CTF groups were established with much fanfare, as the reserve moved away from establishing small CTF groups to establishing hamlet-size groups, the idea of targeting women was de-emphasized. In the hamlet-size CTF groups, as noted above, men usually represent their household as the CTF member.

One of the disincentives to creating more women's CTF groups was the lack of literate women who could keep the books. In four of the women's CTF groups all of the members are illiterate. In three of these, men help with the accounting books. In the fourth a girl in high school helps with the books. In the fifth CTF, the only literate woman is the bookkeeper.

Women, microcredit use and natural resources at Caohai

Loan use

One of the interesting findings in this study was that women members of CTF groups tend to use their loans for their own entrepreneurial activities while male members actually use more of their loans for their wives' activities than for their own. Women's business activities include pig raising, the production of liquor, tofu and sweets, and small-scale trade in beans, corn, tree nuts and fruit. Using a subsample of interviewees for which I have complete loan-use data, of 41 loans taken by women CTF members, 66 per cent went to the borrower's non-crop-based entrepreneurial activities, 10 per cent for planting the household's fields, which both men and women work and includes production of both subsistence crops and market-oriented vegetables, and 24 per cent went for general household expenses including food, children's school fees and home improvements. Of 162 loans taken by male CTF members, 34 per cent went to support their wives' activities (usually pig raising, liquor production or small-scale trade), 20 per cent went to the borrower's non-crop-based entrepreneurial activities, 23 per cent went to planting expenses (usually for fertilizer and seeds), and 23 per cent to general household expenses.

When many of the CTF groups were first established, both men and women often chose to use their loans for pig raising, an activity that was already being practised by households. Pig raising is primarily the women's responsibility. The wife, with the children, gathers the pig food, much of which has to be cooked to make it more digestible for the pig. Both men and women sell piglets or meat in the market. When borrowers take loans to raise more pigs, a heavier work burden is placed on the women. In some cases, men borrow money to buy corn so that their wives could make liquor. The corn mush leftover from the process can then be used to feed the pigs. This venture produces both liquor and pigs for sale.

Developing enterprises by both men and women that involve small-scale trade is one of the most significant changes brought about by the CTF programme. At the beginning, a few villagers had had some experience working in the market, buying beans from more remote locations and then selling them in the market near Caohai. Their neighbours quickly followed suit, with many borrowers starting to use loans for products that could be sold in the market. Women sought out other women who were engaged in market enterprises and learned marketing skills from them. While men were also engaged in small-scale trade, men believed that women were more successful at small-scale trade because the women actually brought home more money as they did not purchase cigarettes or liquor.

The women credit the funds with having given them the opportunity to learn new skills. Many have expressed sentiments such as, 'I didn't know I could do business'. Women told me that they would have never tried to begin an enterprise had start-up capital not been available through the microcredit funds. Women have also said that they had visited new places because of their engagement in small-scale trade. Most live relatively circumscribed lives, but travelling to purchase and sell goods has expanded their world.

During a brief period, roughly from 1997 to 1999, women's market earnings in a few hamlets exceeded those of men's, according to interviewees. During this period, when profits from the market were high, men in these hamlets were actually spending more time at home with the children[2] while their wives were doing well at the market. A few men even joked that there had been something of a role reversal, with women out in the market making money and men more often at home feeding the pigs, cooking and doing the housework.

Nature reserve officials have touted this as a breakthrough for women in Caohai, saying that men were staying at home taking on the burden of the women's work while the women were at the market. When I investigated the situation in the two hamlets cited most often by nature reserve officials as places where roles have been reversed, I found that the nature reserve's picture was not completely accurate. Men may have been at home more so that someone was at home with the children, but I found that the men were only taking on a small part of the women's responsibilities. Men were spending very little time cooking, cleaning, and feeding the pigs. It was their older daughters who had taken over this work, though the men were paying attention to the children. In general, men used their time at home to work in the fields, check their fishing nets, or do building projects around the house. It should be noted that the so-called 'role reversal' trumpeted by the nature reserve only occurred in a few hamlets that were relatively close to the town of Weining.

For a few years, women's earnings in the market were relatively high. However, as more people started to engage in market activities, women's profit margins were reduced. By the early 2000s, as the area started to develop economically, local economic conditions were changing and more opportunities for men to do part-time construction work appeared in the town of Weining. Once men started going into town for day work, the women had to stay home to be with the children, with only occasional forays to the market. The money in the microcredit funds was no longer needed on a regular basis for entrepreneurial activities such as small-scale trade. Since the microcredit funds needed to be constantly in circulation, because there was nowhere to deposit the money, both men and women used their loans to meet household consumption needs. The loans and interest were then paid off with the husband's earnings from construction. Since the loans were not being used for any income-generating activities, paying back loans and interest using men's earnings became burdensome. Eventually CTF members in many hamlets found it much easier to divide up the fund than to go on managing it when it no longer served the same purpose. The nature reserve made efforts to get dissolving CTFs to reorganize by threatening to take back the money. Many CTFs said that they had reorganized, but it was clear from my interviews in 2001 and 2005 that the money had been divided up while the books were being made to show that loans were still being made.

By 2002, only 11 CTF groups were still functioning (Liu, 2004). It was not until late 2004, after the three staff members who had been responsible for overseeing the programmes had acquired new jobs elsewhere and new staff members had replaced them, that reserve staff acknowledged that most of the microcredit groups had ceased to function. During my last visits in 2005, I was unable to find anyone who had continued to use the microcredit funds. Many women were still working in the market but not nearly as often as they had done in the late 1990s before their husbands had so many more opportunities to work in construction.

Microcredit use and natural resource management at Caohai

Disaggregating changes in natural resource use due to the community develop-ment programmes with regard to gender is difficult because both spouses engage in most natural resource use activities. When I asked who made decisions about production activities, husbands usually said they made production decisions but consulted their wives. If the partners disagreed, the wife would follow her husband's lead. I do not want to dismiss women's agency in their activities and imply that women always submissively acquiesce to their husband's wishes. It should be noted, however, that women have no contracted land and usually have no relatives in the village into which they marry. Women would find it a humilia-tion for themselves and a dishonour to their parents if they returned to their natal village because of an unsuccessful marriage. Women, therefore, find it worthwhile to invest in the household and their children, especially their sons, who will honour them and take care of them in old age. Both husband and wife work the husband's land and reclaim land. The most clearly gendered natural resource use is pig raising. Many women said that although their husbands might have initially encouraged them to increase pig production for the market, many women chose to continue the enterprise after finding it profitable. Women involved in trade said they usually made their own decisions about what items to sell. Decisions about fishing were made by men, while it was seen as the 'obvious' obligation of the wife to sell the fish in the market.

Wang (2000) found that those who used microcredit loans, in comparison with those who did not, had higher incomes. The increase in income has had some unintended consequences, which may be harmful for the environment, including increases in pig raising and the use of chemical fertilizers.

Pig raising can potentially have substantial impacts on the local ecosystem because of water plant collection to feed the pigs and because of increased animal wastes that run off into Caohai Lake. Pig raising has increased more in CTF households than in non-CTF households. Sixteen per cent of CTF households (n = 134) said that they had increased the number of pigs they were raising, while less than 7 per cent of those who do not participate in a CTF (n = 44) are raising more pigs. Those who are raising more pigs are usually raising between one and three more pigs. One major issue concerning pig raising is the increased utiliza-tion of water plants to feed livestock. Water plants in Caohai Lake are dense and an important component of the ecosystem, providing cover for spawning fish and other organisms. The name of the lake itself, Caohai, means 'Sea of Grass', because the plants emerging from the lake during the summer make parts of the lake look like a field of plants. Overall, a majority of informants who are raising more pigs say that they have increased their use of water plants. However, this increase has not been measured, nor have biologists studied the impact of water plant harvesting on the ecosystem of Caohai. Not all farmers, however, rely exclu-sively on water plants to feed their pigs. For some who raise pigs with microcredit loans, corn is purchased as feed. The relatively small proportion of households involved in the distillation of liquor usually does not rely on water plants to feed their pigs.

Of greater importance for Caohai Lake might be the number of farmers who have increased their use of chemical fertilizers since participating in the programmes. Forty-one per cent of CTF participants said that they were purchasing more chemical fertilizer than before, while only 14 per cent of those who had not participated in any development programme (n = 28) said that they were using more fertilizer than they had a few years ago. To date, there has been no measurement of what this added fertilizer might mean for water quality in Caohai Lake. Because of erosion problems and farming on steep hillsides, there is reason to believe that increased use of fertilizer will lead to an increase in fertilizer runoff into the lake. Caohai Lake is experiencing increasing eutrophication. Nature reserve officials attribute this to the inflow of household wastewater from the town of Weining and the increased use of chemical fertilizers by local farmers.

Woodland and grassland conversion by microcredit users in the main area where woodland and grassland remain has continued, in spite of the community development programmes. In general, most natural woodland has already been cleared for cultivation. A few scattered remnants are found in a couple of hamlets. I witnessed three people (two women and one man) who are themselves participants or whose husbands are participants in the microcredit programme, engaged in converting the remaining pockets of woodland in this area into cropland. When I asked if woodland reclamation was prohibited in their environmental contracts, all three said yes. All three also said that the programme money was still not enough for them to feed their families. They needed more cropland to meet their household needs.

There has been a slight decrease in the number of microcredit participants who are raising soil levels on plots around the lake. One problem for the wetland is that farmers dig ditches around the plots that border the lake and pile soil from the ditches onto their plots to raise the soil level above the water level. The digging of ditches creates deeper channels that are destructive to the wetland. Six of the 68 CTF households (9 per cent) that had regularly drained wetland along the edge of the lake said that they were either no longer maintaining their plots of drained land or were maintaining less, allowing some of the drained land to revert to wetland habitat, mostly because members of these households were too busy with their microenterprises to continue draining the wetland.[3] Of non-CTF, non-TUP households (n = 18), 55 per cent said that they currently ditched and raised soil levels on their cultivated plots, while none had stopped or scaled back this activity in the past few years.

Although farmers interviewed by Chinese researchers claim to have given up fishing, when I visited homes in several fishing hamlets, nets were hanging both inside and outside the home. After spending time with farmers and asking them to explain the presence of the nets, they would concede to me that they still fish. Many men and women said that the CTF and TUP programmes do not provide enough money to offset the need to fish. In one hamlet, four interviewees told me that they had stopped fishing because of the CTF programme. However, when I visited two of these interviewees some months after our first interview, they had small tubs of freshly caught fish in their homes. Another interviewee said that he had given up fishing because he had dug a fishpond to raise his own fish. The nature reserve discourages the digging of fishponds because this destroys wetlands. In another hamlet, three programme participants (two CTF and one TUP) said that they had in recent years stopped fishing. Two of these intervie-wees had houses filled with fishing nets that were being prepared for use. Two programme participants from another hamlet said that they had given up fishing because they had joined the CTF programme. Months later, as I was being punted across Caohai Lake, I passed one of these interviewees as he was punting a boat filled with fish that he had caught.

During the spawning season ban of 1999, several market women had their fish confiscated. At least two of these women, who were selling fish caught by their husbands, were in CTF households. One woman was a member of the women's CTF in her hamlet. She had used loans for liquor-making and small-scale trade. In spite of this, she said that she needed to sell fish so that she could feed her children. The other woman, who was from a different hamlet, was married to a CTF member who regularly used his loans to transform used oil barrels into stoves for the market. She said that his profits were fairly good but that they still needed income from fish sales in order to feed the family.

Although uses of natural resources have not been radically changed by the programmes, 71 per cent of interviewees (both men and women) who had participated in a TUP or CTF group (n = 147) believe that their understanding of environmental issues around Caohai has increased as a result of the programme. Only 21 per cent of those who were neither CTF nor TUP members (n = 28) said that their knowledge of the environment had increased in the past few years.

Most CTF and TUP households said that relations between the nature reserve and their hamlet have improved because of the community development programmes. A total of 59 per cent (n = 147) said that relations have improved with another 9 per cent saying that relations had always been good. Only 5 per cent (and all from one specific site) said that relations were still bad or had become worse. Sixteen per cent said they do not know. Of the 28 interviewees who were neither CTF members nor TUP recipients only 4 per cent said relations were better.

The most significant change following the implementation of the programmes has been the reduction of violence between male farmers/fishers and nature reserve staff. During the late 1980s and early 1990s, before the programmes were imple-mented, there was approximately one violent confrontation a year between farmers and reserve staff. When reserve staff would confiscate and burn fishers' nets during the spawning-season ban, farmers would angrily confront reserve officials, make death threats and come to blows. Since the programmes started, nature reserve officials are no longer threatened when they visit fishing hamlets, even though officials still intermittently confiscate and destroy fishing equipment during the spawning season (Herrold-Menzies, forthcoming).

Conclusions

The microcredit programmes at Caohai Nature Reserve have had numerous complex and contradictory impacts on women's work, household natural resource use and the environment. While the idea behind the microcredit programme at Caohai Nature Reserve was to reduce dependence on natural resources, thereby reducing harmful environmental impacts, there is no overwhelming evidence that the use of microcredit loans has led to less use of natural resources. In some cases the opposite may be happening. There were unintended consequences associated with the programmes, which could probably have been foreseen by reserve staff, but were not. The use of chemical fertilizers and the number of pigs a household raises has increased more among CTF households than non-CTF households since the inception of the programme. However, the magnitude of these increases is unclear, and no scientific data are available on what impacts the increases in the use of chemical fertilizers and the harvesting of water plants are having upon Caohai Lake. The major question here is whether a neo-liberal, market-oriented intervention such as microcredit, in which funds available to borrowers do not come from activities related to sustainable natural resource use, can promote reduced natural resource use. Around Caohai, this kind of intervention did not change resource uses in the ways that project developers and implementers had hoped.

The incorporation of women into the microcredit programme was very much in the tradition of WID interventions, while the microcredit programme itself is open to critiques similar to those levelled at conventional development projects by writers within the 'women and development' and 'gender and development' (GAD) approaches. Following conventional WID, project implementers recognized the importance of women's participation in the market and the fundamental role women can play in making economic development happen, and understood that without women's participation the pace of economic development would be hindered. One major problem with this approach is that it assumes that if women are not directly incorporated into a modernization or development activity, the women are somehow not a part of the development process, when in reality, even if women are apparently only engaged in conventional homestead-based occupations, economic development does dramatically affect women's lives. For women whose husbands are involved in development-related activities around Caohai, whether the men are using microcredit loans to produce stoves and water basins for the market or doing construction work in town, the women make their spouses' participation possible by shouldering an increased burden of work on the homestead. When women increase their engagement in market-oriented activities, their subordinate positions to their husbands do not change, especially since women lack rights to land and live in villages with their husbands' kin and not their own.

Overall, the microcredit programmes have had mixed impacts on women, only empowering women to a limited extent, while increasing their work burden without really reducing their dependence on natural resources. A large percentage of men's microcredit loans were used so that their wives could raise pigs for the market, an activity that husbands initially decided their wives would do. When women used their own loans to raise pigs, the idea originated from their husbands. Microcredit-inspired involvement in pig raising has increased women's work burden and most likely increased their dependence on the lake's water plants, something that could have significant consequences for the Caohai Lake ecosystem.

The microcredit programme has offered women opportunities to expand ongoing enterprises and start new enterprises that they have said that they would never have embarked upon without the start-up capital provided by the CTF. Many women became involved in small-scale trade, travelling to buy goods in one place to sell elsewhere. Women who engaged in food production or livestock raising for the market were able to increase their production, which meant that they spent more time in the market in the town of Weining. Many women seemed to relish the opportunity to meet new people, observe new things, socialize with friends and do something different from their usual household chores. At the same time, both men and women agree that women are busier than they were before the CTF programme, juggling household responsibilities and farm work with their new or expanded enterprises.

Ideally, the microenterprises that borrowers engaged in would have occupied so much of their time that they would not have time for activities that the reserve and donors wanted to discourage. However, only a few microcredit borrowers became so involved in their enterprises that they reduced their use of local natural resources. For the majority of borrowers, resource use continued as before as long as the microenterprise did not absorb all of the borrower's time. A small number of project participants did say that they were too busy to fish or maintain their wetland-edge plots because they were occupied with CTF-supported activities. While these are positive results with regard to reducing dependency on natural resources, the numbers are quite small.

While ICDP components are often designed to provide the target population with an increased array of activities to participate in so as to distract them from engaging in resource activities deemed harmful to the environment, the microcredit programme at Caohai simply increased women's work burden without reducing dependence on resources. In the end, the programme did not fundamentally address the real grievances that farmers have with the loss of access to natural resources. Without offering real land reform, real compensation for land lost or justice for inequities, other things have been offered that have helped to silence opposition, but not reduce resource dependency.

Notes

1   The extent to which one can characterize the Chinese state as 'neoliberal' is controversial, with different levels of 'state retreat' seen in different provinces. While there has been increased marketization throughout the country, the state, whether as the central government or as local governments, still plays a prominent role in the economy.

2   Most families, although they are Han Chinese, have several children, since the one child policy is not strictly enforced in this area.

3   The drained plots along the edge of the lake need regular maintenance. Most farmers said that they needed to re-dig ditches along the plots and add more soil to the top of the plot about every three years.

References

Al-Sultan, F. H. (1997) 'Micro-finance for macro-results', *UN Chronicle* 34 (1): 36–37

Barrett, C. B. and P. Arcese (1998) 'Wildlife harvest in integrated conservation and development projects: Linking harvest to household demand, agricultural production, and environmental shocks in the Serengeti', *Land Economics* 74 (4): 449–465

Benería, L. and G. Sen (1997) 'Accumulation, reproduction and women's development: Boserup revisited'. In N. Visvanathan, L. Duggan, L. Nisonoff and N. Wiegersma (eds) *The Women, Gender and Development Reader*, New Jersey: Zed Books, pp42–51

Bornstein, D. (1997) *The Price of a Dream: The Story of the Grameen Bank and the Idea that is Helping the Poor to Change Their Lives*, New York: Simon & Schuster

Boserup, E. (1970) *Women's Role in Economic Development*, New York: St Martin's Press

Brandon, K. E. and M. Wells (1992) 'Planning for people and parks: Design dilemmas', *World Development* 20 (4): 557–570

Brett, J. A. (2006) '"We sacrifice and eat less": The structural complexities of microfinance participation', *Human Organization* 65 (1): 8–20

Buckley, G. (1997) 'Microfinance in Africa: Is it either the problem or the solution?', *World Development* 25 (7): 1081–1093

Dokmo, C. L. (2000) 'Microcredit: Ending poverty on our planet', *Vital Speeches* 66 (15): 476

Gibson, C. C. and S. A. Marks (1995) 'Transforming rural hunters into conservationists: An assessment of community-based wildlife management programs in Africa', *World Development* 23 (6): 941–957

Goetz, A. M. and R. Sen Gupta (1996) 'Who takes the credit? Gender, power, and control over loan use in rural credit programs in Bangladesh', *World Development* 24 (1): 45–63

Harkness, J. (1998) 'Recent trends in forestry and conservation of biodiversity in China'. In R. L. Edmonds (eds) *Managing the Chinese Environment*, New York: Oxford University Press

Harvey, D. (2006) *A Brief History of Neoliberalism*, Oxford: Oxford University Press

Herrold-Menzies, M. (2006) 'Integrating conservation and development: What we can learn from Caohai, China', *Journal of Environment and Development* 4 (15): 382–406

Herrold-Menzies, M. (forthcoming) 'Violence in the marsh: Enclosure, community development, and changing patterns of resistance around Caohai Nature Reserve'

Hulme, D. and P. Mosley (1996) *Finance Against Poverty*, New York: Routledge Press

Isserles, R. G. (2003) 'Microcredit: The rhetoric of empowerment, the reality of "development as usual"', *Women's Studies Quarterly* 31 (3 & 4): 38–57

IUCN, UNEP and WWF (1991) *Caring for the Earth: A Strategy for Sustainable Living*, Gland, Switzerland: International Union for the Conservation of Nature and Natural Resources, United Nations Environment Programme and World Wildlife Fund

Liu Wen (2004) 'Caohai cunzhai fazhan jijin xiangmu de xiankuang he zhengdun' ('The current status and reorganization of Caohai's Village Development Funds Program'), unpublished report to the International Crane Foundation

Mies, M. (1985) 'The dynamics of the sexual division of labour and integration of rural women into the world market'. In L. Benería (ed.) *Women and Development: The Sexual Division of Labor in Rural Societies*, New York: Praeger Publishers, pp1–26

Newmark, W. D. and J. L. Hough (2000) 'Conserving wildlife in Africa: Integrated conservation and development projects and beyond', *BioScience* 50 (7): 585–592

Park, A. (1999) 'Banking for the poor', *Chinabrief* 2 (2): 9–15

Rahman, A. (1999) 'Micro-credit initiatives for equitable and sustainable development: Who pays?', *World Development* 27 (1): 67–82

Rankin, K. N. (2001) 'Governing development: Neoliberalism, microcredit and rational economic woman', *Economy and Society* 30 (1) 18–37

Redford, K., K. Brandon and S. Sanderson (1998) 'Holding ground'. In K. Brandon, K. H. Redford and S. E. Sanderson (eds) *Parks in Peril: People, Politics, and Protected Areas*, Washington, DC: The Nature Conservancy and Island Press, pp455–463

Srivastava, P. (2005) 'Reducing poverty and empowering communities', *UN Chronicle* 3: 45–46

Sun Yanyan (2005) 'A comparison of microcredit and individual development accounts: Implication for China', *Social Development Issues* 27 (3): 49–60

Tinker, I. (1997) 'The making of a field: Advocates, practitioners and scholars'. In N. Visvanathan, L. Duggan, L. Nisonoff and N. Wiegersma (eds) *The Women, Gender and Development Reader*, New Jersey: Zed Books, pp33–42

van Schaik, C. and H. D. Rijksen (2002) 'Integrated conservation and development projects: Problems and potential'. In J. Terborgh, C. van Schaik, L. Davenport and M. Rao (eds) *Making Parks Work: Strategies for Preserving Tropical Nature*, Covelo, CA: Island Press, pp15–29

Wang Sangui (2000) 'Economic impact assessment of the Caohai project'. In S. L. Hong, J. Harris and W. Y. Wang (eds) *Community-based Conservation and Development: Strategies and Practice at Caohai*, Guiyang, China: Guizhou Nationalities Publishing House, pp194–221

Wells, M. and K. Brandon (1992) *People and Parks: Linking Protected Area Management with Local Communities*, Washington DC: World Bank, WWF, USAID

Wheat, S. (1997) 'Banking on the poor', *Geographical Magazine* 69 (3): 20–22

Woolcock, M. (1999) 'Learning from failures in microfinance: What unsuccessful cases tell us about how group-based programs work', *American Journal of Economics and Sociology* 58 (1): 17–43

Part 3

Responding to Intervention: Gender, Knowledge and Authority

Chapter 10

Insider/Outsider Politics: Implementing Gendered Participation in Water Resource Management[1]

Kathleen O'Reilly

Introduction

Gendered participatory approaches have grown popular as project planners seek ways to incorporate women's knowledge and labour into natural resource management and development projects. Often these projects seek to build on or change existing gendered relationships to natural resources. For example, the project featured in this chapter is a large-scale drinking water supply scheme in northern India. The village-level activities of the NGO that is facilitating community and women's participation components are based on extending gendered roles around water to include management, payment and operation of the new drinking water supply.

Corresponding with the rise of gendered participatory approaches to environmental management and planning, women have been recruited into projects as facilitators of women's participation components. Once hired, however, these women fieldworkers often find themselves at the margins of their organizations (Garcia, 2001; O'Reilly, 2003), or discover that they too are the targets of development efforts (Springer, 2001; O'Reilly, 2004). Thus, women's participation raises two problems in overlapping spheres: first, how to interest and include local women; and second, how women fieldworkers will (and will be allowed to) participate inside their own organizations. In the case of the first, women fieldworkers are seen as the solution. Planners assume a natural communication between all women, despite socio-economic differences between women fieldworkers and their clients. Women fieldworkers, simply because they are women, are expected to enable local women's participation (O'Reilly, 2004). For example, according to the Project Social Side (PSS) Feasibility Report (PSS, 1993, p8), 'it is essential that at least two persons of [each field] team are women.[2] Otherwise the work ... with the rural women as [the] target group could be neglected.' In the case of the second problem, women fieldworkers create it. Their presence within male-dominated NGOs immediately requires social and spatial changes in order to accommodate women as full-fledged members (O'Reilly, 2004). A woman fieldworker, in order to do her job, must make sense of the contradiction that surrounds her position (O'Reilly, 2003). She is necessary to the implementation of women's participation, but sidelined within her NGO.

In this chapter, I seek to fill a gap in current literature on participation by exploring, first, the positionality of women fieldworkers within NGOs; and second, how gendered relations of power influence meanings of participation that are produced in villages. I argue that women fieldworkers' practices in the field reflect the contradictory position they occupy within their NGOs as both problem and solution to women's participation. I find that their actions result in subversive meanings of participation that circulate alongside more hegemonic definitions. From previous research we have learned that project outcomes do not often reflect project plans (Ferguson, 1990). We know that meanings of participation are not directly put into action by field staff, which then leads to the success or failure of a project (Crewe and Harrison, 1998; O'Reilly, 2002). But to date, attention to participatory policies, practices and results has disregarded interconnections between gendered relations of power, the positionality of fieldworkers and individual practices in the field.

Feminist studies have come far in their explorations of the gendered dynamics of participatory approaches for women who are the targets of development and environmental interventions (Agarwal, 2001; Cleaver, 2001; Cornwall, 2003; Coles and Wallace 2005). However, far less attention has been given to fieldworkers as active agents during the implementation process of projects.[3] Emma Crewe and Elizabeth Harrison (1998) illustrate how a low-level male fieldworker is embedded within community relations and makes choices based on constraints and opportunities presented by both the organization that he works for and the community that provides him with social and professional support. Far from being whimsical, the choices he makes are shaped by the relationships and discourses in which he is immersed. Fieldworkers choose what to foreground or mute during interactions with villagers, which often results in contradictions within a single fieldworker's field-level practices (O'Reilly, 2003). In her study of male agricultural extension workers in India, Jenny Springer (2001) shows the degree to which workers identify with state-sponsored meanings of development has bearing on their practices with local farmers. Springer demonstrates the ways in which the state is constructed as separate from society by the efforts of local officials to align themselves with development or progress, acts that happen at the expense of local farmers. Such research moves beyond a view of fieldworkers as instruments, mechanically implementing plans, and explores the power relations in which they are embedded for the production of meanings. To these accounts I add the critical aspect of gender because of its importance for fieldworkers' experiences of power. By turning toward those doing the implementing, I seek to further erode what has become a staple of critiques of participatory approaches: the attempt to discover what formulas for participation are operative within projects and then offer suggestions for better implementation, training and so on (see also Cooke and Kothari, 2001). My research shows that participatory approaches are complex and negotiated during every interaction among staff, and between staff and local people.[4] Simple suggestions of techniques for implementation cannot begin to cope with the range of power dynamics experienced (and created) by fieldworkers on a daily basis.

Bill Cooke and Uma Kothari, in their edited volume *Participation: The New Tyranny?* (2001), turn to Michel Foucault and address participatory approaches as a form of power. Foucault (1990, p100) holds that the world of discourse is 'a multiplicity of discursive elements that can come into play in various strategies'. This conceptualization allows Cooke and Kothari (2001, p4) to frame participation as discourses that contain 'the potential for an unjustified exercise of power'; that is, participation can be tyrannical. Discourses of participation are suffused with power – what they contain and omit have important ramifications (see also Crush, 1995; Escobar, 1995; Kothari, 2001). Different meanings of participation may serve similar purposes, while similar meanings may serve different purposes. Because identical discourses, like those of participation, may be deployed to both further and hinder power, Foucault argues that it is necessary to take seriously individual actors and the context in which discourses are created and operationalized.

Power, for Foucault, is exercised through a net or web; it is not something that is possessed by any single individual. On the contrary, individuals are 'simultaneously undergoing and exercising this power' (Foucault, 1980, p98). Instead of criticizing staff practices, I direct my attention to the micro-level where individual practices of participation depict the reproduction and subversion of existing gendered power relations. By tracing the circulation of power during the activities of NGO staff, this chapter provides a detailed illustration of how participation operates as a form of power. I ask the following questions: first, what do discourses of women's participation mean for women fieldworkers' positionality within their employing NGO? Second, how do women fieldworkers deploy meanings of participation as an exercise of power? And finally, what conditions enable this exercise? My findings indicate that women fieldworkers create fluid meanings and engage in shifting practices of participation that reflect the multilayered power dynamics in which they are embedded.

In the following sections, I discuss my methods and describe the drinking water supply project. I then turn to discuss the inherent tensions contained within participatory approaches. The third section is a deconstruction of the term and image of women fieldworkers in project texts. I suggest that the ways women fieldworkers are represented in PSS discourses position them as 'not quite' village women and 'not quite' male fieldworkers. This insider/outsider status has implications for field-level practices that are ethnographically illustrated in the subsequent section. Finally, I offer an analysis of relationships between women fieldworkers, NGOs' gendered, internal practices and participatory approaches.

Methods and case study

Between 1997 and 2002, I studied a drinking water supply project in northern Rajasthan, India. As I travelled with field staff (both men and women) while they implemented a participatory approach to water management, it became clear that they were involved in highly nuanced negotiations among themselves over meanings of women's participation and the limits of associated practices. Women fieldworkers played a pivotal but controversial role as staff struggled with an increasing focus on women's significance to the project over the years. Some staff openly denigrated women's involvement; others publicly celebrated women field-workers' capabilities. But a majority of staff, both programme officers and fieldworkers, both men and women, engaged in practices that signalled ambiva-lence about women fieldworkers' importance in the project (O'Reilly, 2003). One thing was unequivocal, however; women fieldworkers' positionality within the NGO had direct bearing on the women's participation component in villages.

Over the course of intermittent visits, each lasting between two months and one year, I collected project literature and conducted participant observation with the 70 staff (management, consultants and fieldworkers) working on the project. I wrote daily field notes about fieldworkers' interactions and conversations in the main office and in villages. With the assistance of Tasneem Khan, I interviewed staff and villagers in Hindi, Marwari and English. Of the 50 fieldworkers in the PSS, only 14 were women. In the interest of anonymity due to the small numbers of women staff, I attribute all quotations and actions of PSS women fieldworkers to two composite women fieldworkers, whom I call Vidya and Kavita. The composites, Vidya and Kavita, represent two common strategies deployed by women fieldworkers as they tried to make sense of their position as both solution and part of the problem of women's participation.

The drinking water project that I studied is funded by a large German devel-opment bank and the Government of Rajasthan (GOR). Engineers and contractors affiliated with the GOR designed and built the vast supply system infrastructure. A group of five Rajasthani NGOs compose the PSS, which focuses on community participation for the purpose of system sustainability. The NGOs making up the PSS all had previous experience running a variety of education and health projects in the area and were on solid financial ground. None of them had a strong commitment to gender mainstreaming or participatory approaches before the onset of the drinking water project, although some staff had received gender training. The PSS self-consciously acts as a single NGO, separate from the GOR (that is, as a non-state body). The PSS's participatory approach was written into early project plans, reflecting planners' beliefs that if villagers invest their time, effort and money in the drinking water supply system, they will use it properly (i.e., not waste water) and maintain it. Villagers are expected to pay for water, which they previously got for free from the GOR. They also must agree to assist in the care and maintenance of the system inside village boundaries. The work of PSS field staff involves organizing these two primary activities as well as providing health education, constructing latrines and facilitating public tap site selection. Community participation in the case of the PSS has less to do with gaining local knowledge in order to tailor project plans to circumstances (Crewe and Harrison, 1998) and more to do with setting up bureaucratic mechanisms for the payment of water tariffs and village-level governance of the system. Women's participation was initially understood more as a means to achieve water system sustainability, but over the years I studied the project, women's participation emerged as part of a larger gender mainstreaming agenda. The presence or absence of gender-trained staff and consultants influenced the attention given to the incorporation of women staff as full participants at any given time.

An unquestioned relationship between women and water underlies themes for women's participation in the project. Project plans indicate an assumption that women will see to it that public standposts (that is, taps) and the system are maintained because women need a reliable water supply in order to fulfil their roles as mothers and household managers (O'Reilly, 2006). As stated in the PSS *Women's Participation Handbook* (PSS, no date), 'Women are the ones who will gain most from the project being accepted in the village and from the continued smooth functioning of the new facilities. Those who benefit most can also be expected to be most committed.' Social change is hinted at in suggestions that women's groups might eventually proceed to solve other problems besides that of drinking water supply:

> *Women's groups must first and foremost serve the purpose of making the water supply system sustainable in the long run, i.e. women must be mobilized to take responsibility for the water management of their village. The health and hygiene education objective and the empowerment and self-help objective are important but should be subordinate to this overriding goal.* (PSS, no date)

Women's participation as stated in PSS documents means drawing on women's labour as mothers and housewives to facilitate the long-term viability of the system (O'Reilly, 2002). Health education and empowerment take place as secondary goals.

All women who work for the PSS work solely on the issue of women's participation. A women's participation programme officer directs their activities; she is the sole woman in a group of seven programme officers. While I was doing fieldwork with the PSS, considerable turnover occurred in the ranks of the women fieldworkers.[5] Women fieldworkers with PSS are a remarkably diverse group, although all are Hindu. They range in age from early 20s to mid-30s, come from all over India (for example, Rajasthan, Karnataka and Bihar), and have a variety of education levels from tenth standard (that is, tenth grade) to MSW degrees. Some speak the local language as native speakers; others learn it on the job; others never learn it. This variety of backgrounds means that field staff come to the organization with very different experiences and occasionally contradictory ideas. Their work involves covering anywhere between 15 and 30 villages a month. In villages, they are expected to, first, involve women as representatives to village committees overseeing water use and decision making, second, form women's groups, third, establish microcredit groups, and finally, instruct women on hygiene at home and safe water handling practices. Women fieldworkers are also responsible for recruiting caretakers for public taps and facilitating additional women's participation activities if they have time.

In this chapter, I am simultaneously interested in deconstructing images of women fieldworkers created by project discourses and reconstructing, through ethnographic data, our notions of who women fieldworkers are and what it might be like to be one. Chandra Talpade Mohanty (1991) calls for a deconstruction of the category *third world woman* for the purpose of recognizing the agency of all women, especially those in the global South. But Mohanty cautions us that if we are going to deconstruct, then we must ask ourselves what we are reconstructing in its place. Here I seek to contribute to a reconstruction of individual women fieldworkers' agency and the implications of their agency for women's participation in natural resource planning and management. I want to highlight fieldworkers' political savvy as they decide for themselves the usefulness or uselessness of performing certain tasks. I seek to dislodge critiques of NGOs and participatory approaches that call for technical solutions transferable among NGOs (Garcia, 2001; Cornwall, 2003) or personal transformation (Chambers, 1997). In this chapter, I shift the scale of my investigation away from an ethnography of NGOs as units to individual fieldworkers and the relations of power in which they are embedded. A focus on organizations and groups obscures the ways that individual actors personally negotiate the social relations that embody participatory approaches on the ground. An extended ethnographic method allows for revelations about the micro-politics surrounding participatory approaches and suggests what specific constellations of power mean for individual actions, and therefore, for participation in general (see Buroway et al, 2000). I now turn to discuss contradictions within approaches to women's participation.

Tensions within participatory approaches

Participation is popular both as a method of acquiring local knowledge and as a way to encourage project sustainability. Proponents laud participatory approaches for producing local actor investment in projects through increased sensitivity and attention to local people's desires for certain kinds of environmental and economic interventions (Chambers, 1983, 1997). Participation frequently appears as a framework for gathering local knowledge to facilitate sustainability and actor investment in a project (Mosse, 2001). Supporters argue that previous top-down approaches to environmental management and development failed because they did not concern themselves with local knowledge or interests

(Chambers, 1983, 1997; Cornwall, 2003). Local civil society is celebrated as already having the answers to resource conservation and sustainable use. The use of local knowledge purportedly facilitates empowerment of target populations and creates projects that serve the needs of villagers, thereby increasing success rates compared to those of top-down planned projects. Additionally, local involvement in project tasks hypothetically results in cost and time efficiency.

Whether participatory approaches are any more or less successful than top-down development approaches is subject to debate, and a substantial literature of critique has emerged following participation's rise in popularity. Participation, as read from project texts, takes a top-down approach toward existing human–environment relationships and corresponding roles, with significant gendered implications (Schroeder, 1999; O'Reilly, 2003). Critics argue that participatory approaches cloak what is really business as usual: donor-driven, predetermined categories of people and activities that do not allow much flexibility for changing existing power imbalances (Crewe and Harrison, 1998; Blaikie, 2000). As David Mosse (2001, p32) states, participation 'remains a way of talking about rather than doing things'. Others charge that participatory approaches have become a mechanism for efficiency of service delivery (for example, water supply) or for continuing maintenance (for example, of system standposts) that reduces state responsibility (Kabeer, 1996; Rahnema, 1997; Paley, 2001; O'Reilly, 2002).

Participation prevails as a term that is multiply deployed to validate any number of activities, including legitimizing expenditures, reducing operation costs, improving public image and creating new markets (Mosse, 2001). Mosse (2001, p32) writes, 'theory of participation separate from analysis of the meaning of the concept in specific organizational practices would be impossible'. Any analysis of meanings of participation within an NGO becomes further complicated when that organization reflexively begins to take note of its own practices of inclusion and exclusion. For my Rajasthani case study, women's participation began as a gendered element of community participation, which was intended to ensure the project's long-term sustainability. But validating women's participation became a concern when staff began reflexively evaluating the marginal inclusion of women fieldworkers in project decision making. As one male fieldworker said to me, 'So even here in the PSS there is no equal participation [for women]. How will she be able to create it in villages?'. His words emphasize that women's participation is not only an effort to involve village women in project activities but also a process of negotiating how women fieldworkers will participate in their NGO. I explore below how these dual meanings of participation intersect, and what they indicate about gendered, social relations within NGOs.

Elsewhere (O'Reilly, 2002, 2003) I have illustrated how PSS staff actively produce contradictory logics of participation in their everyday practices. On the one hand, village women are represented in project discourses as a category with immutable, essential characteristics: traditional, powerless and without agency (Mohanty, 1991). Women are targeted as a category, which does not call existing gender roles into question, nor does it interrogate the variety of individual circumstances of individual women (class, caste, religion, ability, age and family status). Plans are laid for women, all of whom (including women fieldworkers), it is assumed, need to be empowered. On the other hand, the PSS's participatory approach depends on women's agency; the fulfilment of PSS plans for sustainability depends on women to take an active role in reporting problems with public taps or misuse of the system. However, this agency should have limits. For example, women should *not* be organizing to discuss their dissatisfaction with a delay in the onset of the clean water supply. Women's participation not only creates a contradictory positionality for women fieldworkers, but contains as a concept multiple meanings that serve different purposes (O'Reilly, 2003).

Women as a general development category influences constructions of women fieldworkers, who find themselves discursively placed in a tenuous position of being like village women but not like village women. This situation is made all the more precarious when we consider that some fieldworkers are in fact village women hired from the PSS project area. I discuss below the creation of women fieldworkers as a development category, before exploring some illustrative incidents in the field.

Who is a woman fieldworker?

Following the work of Rosemary Pringle (1989) on meanings of *secretary* (in a First World context), I am interested in unpacking the multiple, contradictory meanings contained within the construction *woman fieldworker*. By deconstructing the tasks, images and demands of women fieldworkers,[6] we can explore the relations of power that influence the implementation of women's participation in drinking water supply. Women fieldworkers are hired into an organization that has stated participatory goals, but they also arrive with their own ideas about women's participation, and these are further negotiated in the field with villagers' and co-workers' ideas.

Trying to understand *woman fieldworker* as a static figure will not work, for her position both in villages and in the NGO is constantly shifting. Nor is she a singular category. Besides differences in class, caste, religion, age, family status and so on, women fieldworkers are surrounded by contradictions within participation and demands of staff and constituents. They also contribute to the fluidity of circulating meanings and an abundance of contradictory practices. They labour at the centre of gendered tensions that converge in her (as a person) and on her (as a figure). Nevertheless, the burden of resolving the multifaceted and multilayered contradictions of women's participation ultimately falls on them. Just as meanings of participation are multiple and contested, so also are meanings of *woman fieldworker* and her work as flexible, situational and struggled over. Like participation, the category of *woman fieldworker* is produced and reproduced during daily practices of fieldwork in a variety of spaces (O'Reilly, 2002). I suggest that a woman fieldworker is a new type of female figure – not quite *gaanv mahiilaa* (village woman) because she is more modern, not quite male fieldworker because she is not as mobile or powerful.[7] Her position on both the outside of the PSS (and yet occasionally the focus) and the outside of villages where she works (see Trinh, 1997) compounds tensions a *woman fieldworker* faces in her job, and they add complexity to her decisions and practices.

Trinh T. Minh-ha (1997, p418) suggests in reference to difference that negotiations occur not only between outsider and insider but they 'are also at work within the outsider herself, or the insider herself – a single entity'. Not only do those who are not women fieldworkers produce conflicting meanings for the construct of *woman fieldworker*, but conflicting meanings are also at work within women fieldworkers and are constitutive of women fieldworkers engaging in ambiguous practices.[8] A woman fieldworker may at times identify with her village-level constituents at the expense of the PSS (for example, she may agree that PSS demands on women's time are too great) and at other times distance herself from village women and side with project meanings of modern woman-hood (for example, wear a 'modern' sari instead of a traditional local dress). Trinh (1997, p418) explains a parallel situation for post-colonial women:

> *Not quite the same, not quite the other, she stands in that undetermined threshold place where she constantly drifts in and out. Undercutting the inside/outside opposition, her intervention is necessarily that of both not quite an insider and not quite an outsider. She is, in other words, this inappropriate 'other' or 'same' who moves about with always at least two gestures: that of affirming 'I am like you' while persisting in her difference and that of reminding 'I am different' while unsettling every definition of otherness arrived at.*

While some women fieldworkers come from urban, middle-class backgrounds and others come from rural, agricultural backgrounds, all negotiate a delicate position of working with village women with whom they supposedly share much in common because they are women.

But the women's participation programme officer (and others in PSS management) expects women fieldworkers to distinguish themselves from village women through their behaviour, for example by attending mixed-gender night-time puppet shows. Their position as not quite the same, not quite the other creates tensions for individual women fieldworkers. Vidya says, 'We used to go to the field late at night, it is not that we did not go, but it would always come to my mind, "what will villagers say?" since we are moving around with men late at night. Even in daytime it is in their minds.' In an area where women's seclusion is practised and women veil themselves in front of elders and in-laws, women field-workers feel the pressure of social mores held by those with whom they live and work.

Within the PSS, women fieldworkers also occupy an ambivalent position. During day-long meetings held in the main office, women fieldworkers often remained on the sidelines in the main meeting room while male fieldworkers sat in small groups with the various programme officers in their offices. These circumstances gave men opportunities to reinforce their dominance as project actors by planning their activities without considering women's input. Women fieldworkers may not have wanted it differently – they could sit and talk freely among themselves while men were out of the room. At other times, women made it plain that they wanted responsibilities beyond their limited roles. For example, Kavita publicly demanded that project management provide equal opportunities for women in the PSS leadership ranks. Thus, the PSS's lack of reflexivity about its participatory approach was called into question by a woman fieldworker frustrated at her position outside the organization's power structures.

Women fieldworkers, trained by the PSS about the benefits of gendered participation at the village level, acted out directly and indirectly a critique of their marginal participation in PSS decisions that affect their lives and work. It is from an awareness of their marginalization within their NGO that women fieldworkers make decisions about their practices in the field. In the next section, I use examples of women fieldworkers' practices in villages to illustrate the negotiated meanings of participation. Each woman draws from her unique position within the organization to inform her decisions in the field.

Politics of participation

Field teams organized by the PSS work anywhere between two and five hours away from the main office, which means that most of their work is unsupervised by programme officers or consultants. Field team leaders are responsible for the activities of teams, but they do very little supervising. This arrangement gives women fieldworkers a degree of freedom to decide for themselves on which activities they want to spend time and on which they do not. An activity known as social mapping illustrates beautifully a disjuncture between management's plans and women fieldworkers' ideas about women's participation activities. Programme officers designed the social mapping activity to facilitate the process of public tap site selection. Based on standard participatory and rural appraisal (PRA) techniques, women fieldworkers gather village women's local knowledge of village paths, neighbourhoods and existing water points by having them draw a map. Ideally, village women are encouraged to express themselves creatively by designing a map of their village or neighbourhood from locally available materials, such as coloured powders, lentils, leaves and sticks. They decide as a group what materials should represent what and, finally, determine the best locations for new public taps. This three-dimensional map is then transferred onto paper with pens and pencils. The exercise is intended to raise awareness of village surroundings, create solidarity by involving women in a group effort, and boost women's self-esteem through pride in their created map.

When Vidya led this exercise, she and two village women used pencils and paper to draw a map, with Vidya occasionally grabbing the pencil and instructing the women to show a tree like this or a house like that. The rest of the group of about a dozen village women and many children looked on in amusement and gave occasional suggestions or pointed out locations. After about an hour and a half, Gopal (a male fieldworker) came and asked if we were done. Vidya, finishing, said, '*bas*' (enough), picked up the map in its unfinished state, and left without saying anything to the women about what would become of it. She said to me, '[it] wastes time (*time waste kartaa hai*) – other field teams do it with sand (*ret*), but here we shouldn't waste time (*time waste na ho*)'.

It is possible to listen to this narrative and analyse the event as an example of a fieldworker with a bad attitude not doing her job. Or that this fieldworker has adopted the behaviour of lazy government workers whose behaviour she knows well from other everyday contexts. She is a social worker employed by an NGO that has been contracted by the GOR, so her actions could be taken to reflect her interest in creating some distance between herself and the civilians with whom she works (Springer, 2001). Her rudeness certainly indicates her disregard for her village clients, which may derive from PSS discourses of women as objects. It could be argued that Vidya needs training; if she had proper training she would under-stand what is required and why (Pigg, 1992), and she would perform her tasks correctly in full knowledge of the reasons for a step-by-step, time-consuming process. Such potential views of Vidya's practices assume that she justifies her choices neither completely within nor without project discourses of participation. Vidya's choices of which women's participation activities are and are not worth an effort make sense, given her knowledge and experience with the PSS.

Vidya's fieldwork is embedded within discourses circulating among project staff as to whether women's participation is important to the project. Like others in the project, including some programme officers, her actions indicate that she believes that women's participation does not matter in the project, at least not in terms of social mapping. Her choices about how to run the social mapping activ-ity reflect a logical decision not to spend more time than is necessary on an activity that will not amount to anything later. She says that social mapping for women is a waste of time; after five years' experience she has learned that decisions women make about the location of public taps rarely amount to anything – the men of the village or the GOR engineers make the final decisions anyway. Vidya may believe that far from being an empowering activity, social mapping is actually disempowering – as women would make maps and choose public tap locations only to have their decisions overridden by men. If she is going to waste her time and other women's time, she is going to waste as little of it as possible. Within the constraints of the PSS's social mapping activity, she exercises her agency by minimizing what she might call the harmful effects of women's participation.

In an October 2000 interview, Kavita told me that on her first day in villages with her co-workers, she learned that they considered women's participation a mechanism for getting funds from the German donor bank (O'Reilly, 2004). She said, 'from conversations with [management] and team leaders (unofficially) I came to learn this goal'. Kavita understood that neither men nor women senior fieldworkers take women's participation seriously, but she had a different concern. She told me, 'For me the primary concern was the village women and not the [German bank] fund. So I only tried to concentrate on the village women. But at times, I had realized I was cheating with them.' Village women wanted free health treatment, medicine and some income generation activities, she said, which she could not provide. Her feelings of cheating derived from her inability to offer women the help they wanted. But Kavita also said:

> *From the very beginning most of the village women used to trust me a lot because I never told them a lie and never tried to make false promises. I always told them the truth, and that's why I always had a clash with my colleagues and my team leader. I gave village women a clear picture of the project's objectives and also told them what we expect out of them.*

Kavita's early disillusionment led her to apply a no-nonsense approach to her work. She wanted women to know without sugar-coating that women's participation in the new water supply system meant new tasks for them: collecting payment for water usage and cleaning the public taps. Her decision to present women's participation in this way made her unpopular with her supervisor and co-workers. Kavita felt deeply the clashes she had with her male co-workers, and she cited 'non-cooperation from [field team] staff (mainly senior staff)' as a reason why she eventually quit her job. Her truth-telling also made her job with village women difficult at times, and more difficult still when she had to report in monthly meetings the trouble she was having in villages.

What Kavita learned about women's participation on her first day galvanized her will to take the component seriously, to find out what women wanted and to tell them honestly that their concerns were only going to be partially and occasionally considered by project staff. For Kavita, women's participation needed to be put to women without empty promises – they were going to receive a 24-hour supply of clean water; in return, they needed to pay for it and keep the new public taps clean. When women asked to be paid for cleaning public taps, she told them frankly that it would not happen. She admitted to me that she was not altogether successful in getting these tasks accomplished, but she had very clear ideas about what women's participation was and was not. Like Vidya, she knew it was only a minor project element and made no promises. She gave straight answers, much to the dismay of her male colleagues.

As a woman fieldworker informed about how senior employees viewed women's participation, Kavita was empowered to dispense with lies and postponements of solutions. Instead, she took the time to get to know women and listen to their problems, offering herself as at least one person willing to hear women's voices. She made it her business to know what women's concerns were and what village politics meant for their everyday lives. Kavita protected her own integrity. Having learned the truth, she chose to tell it to her women clients so they were equipped with the knowledge of what the project could not do for them and what the project required from them. In contrast to Vidya's distance, Kavita's outsider status within her field team led her to seek closeness with village women.

Analysis

Instead of dismissing Vidya's actions as those of a bad fieldworker or celebrating (or condemning) Kavita for her honesty, we must explore their behaviour for what it tells us about their own positionality within the organization, the status of women inside the PSS, the PSS's gendered structures of control, and conflicts within the NGO about implementing women's participation. The staff practices of the PSS reflect staff members' personal responses to the socio-political circumstances in which they find themselves. Fieldworkers change their practices, language and behaviour to accommodate the different demands made on them by co-workers, their field team supervisors and local constituents (see also Springer, 2001). Although they are not performing as some might think they should, given that they are paid to do a job, Vidya and Kavita's actions demonstrate their embeddedness within PSS power dynamics as marginalized women fieldworkers performing a low-status job. More broadly, their words and behaviour indicate how power circulates through their practices.

Women fieldworkers simultaneously exercise, and are influenced by, participation as a form of power. They have the ability to disrupt dominant meanings of participation that PSS management and consultants would like to see implemented. Management in response tries to create schedules and procedures to constrain the variability of meanings that fieldworkers are putting in place, or refusing to put in place. Springer (2001) shows in a case of state extension workers that behaviours like Vidya's and Kavita's led to increased attempts to regulate them (for example, Kavita's co-workers' non-cooperation may be seen as an attempt to discipline her), although the extension workers' practices made the most sense, given the socio-political circumstances. Similarly, women fieldworkers do not need increased regulation. They do not escape the discourses signalling that water work is women's work; they rarely engage women in some topic or activity completely unrelated to the project's overall aims of drinking water supply. They may not follow the topical script in discussions with village women (for example, how to carry water pots), but their topics seldom stray radically (for example, how women labour while men play cards). Their behaviour is controlled; they must implement social mapping or standpost cleaning instead of some other activity that they think is better, so that they can report and prove that they have done so.

The above examples of Vidya and Kavita (compositely illustrating many women fieldworkers' remarks and practices) demonstrate how participatory practices in villages grow out of gendered power dynamics within NGOs. Women fieldworkers' refusal to perform as expected by management reflects their understanding of the insignificance of women's participation in the PSS. For example, Vidya has sufficient experience in her organization to realize that maps village women make do not end up determining where project standposts will be located. Creating a participatory venue such as map making for women's knowledge and opinions does not mean that when women speak they will be heard (Cleaver, 2001). From their position as women fieldworkers, women employees of the PSS

have learned that women's participation may be talked about in terms of its criti-
cality to the new drinking water system's sustainability but it remains something
that many staff feel at the very least conflicted about.

The behaviour of fieldworkers must be taken in context; blaming women
fieldworkers does not move beyond a technical-fix logic into the messy realm of
social relations. A perception of Vidya or Kavita as a bad fieldworker must shift
when either's practices are considered from the point of view of their
insider/outsider status within the NGO and in villages. Crewe and Harrison
(1998) suggest considering resistant responses as hybrid resolutions to conflicts
or selective internalization of dominant notions of development. Importantly,
these responses are gendered. A woman fieldworker's actions reflect her position
as influenced by an ambivalence within the PSS about the importance of women's
participation in the drinking water system's sustainability and, therefore, women
fieldworkers. Women's participation in natural resource management is further
influenced by women fieldworkers' own power to create women's participation in
a way that makes sense to them. The examples of Kavita and Vidya given here are
ambiguous, which is exactly why they are worth exploring. They indicate that
participatory practices are not pure – mixed messages in the field spring from
power dynamics (for example, hierarchy and gendered discrimination) within
organizations. Participation begins with contradictory discourses of women's
participation, taken-for-granted understandings of relationships between women
and natural resources, and opposing images of village women and women fieldworkers. It remains ambiguous through staff practices. From women's ambivalent
positionality within their organizations and in their complicated relationships with
villagers, multiple meanings of participation emerge and are created.

Participation as a form of power circulates through women fieldworkers.
Whether they subvert meanings or reproduce project norms of participation,
women fieldworkers' words and activities always carry power with them
(Foucault, 1980). The above examples of women fieldworkers' practices show the
role that women fieldworkers play in recreating, subverting and hybridizing
meanings of women's participation. Vidya does not have much interest in village
women's knowledge regarding standpost selection, nor does she give them much
information regarding their construction. However, in not wasting her own time,
she also saves them time and arguably frustration, and a potential demonstration
of powerlessness. (Although perhaps this frustration would eventually lead to
feminist revolution.) Kavita, on the other hand, listens to women's problems and
concerns in an atmosphere of mutual trust and respect; for her, the best she can
do is to subvert those who consider women's participation superfluous.

Participatory approaches to natural resource management may make a difference if they challenge assumptions about gender and power (Cornwall, 2003), but
a set of rules or a single definition of participation will not solve these problems.
Whether the PSS or individual actors themselves fix a definition, a variety of
forces lead women fieldworkers to make on-the-spot decisions about what will
and will not be participation at any given place or time. In one village, Vidya met
with many women's groups, but she refused tea at every house except where the

family was that of her caste; during the extra time we spent there, she expanded on latrine usage and benefits in ways she did not at other households. Mosse (2001) suggests that project activities tend to settle on a fixed set of interventions, which limit the creativity of potential solutions. I find, however, that fieldworkers act creatively when given the chance and that even fixed interventions can be modified on the spot. Approaches to participation in environmental decision making and resource management remain fluid due to the dynamic socio-political context within which NGO staff work.

Conclusions

In the preceding pages I have steered my enquiry and analysis away from logistical and functional questions about problems with participatory approaches to natural resource management. Instead I have tried to answer the question: how do gendered social relationships, constructed categories and development discourses within an NGO influence the meanings of participation that staff members produce? Drawing on Foucault's (1980, 1990) concepts of power and Cooke and Kothari's (2001) framing of participation as a form of power, I advance debates on participation in natural resource management by offering a detailed portrayal of how participation can be a form of power, by tracing women fieldworkers' individual words and practices. I have shown that women fieldworkers create meanings of participation that both reproduce and subvert existing gendered relations of power among staff and between staff and villagers. I argue that the actions of women fieldworkers make sense when viewed within the context of project discourses of participation and mixed messages about women fieldworkers' significance to the project.

Too often in environment and development literatures, fieldworkers' agency and the power dynamics surrounding them within their organizations are overlooked. Critics mistakenly assume that fieldworkers simply implement plans, instead of interrogating their unique position moving between their NGOs and their village constituents. This chapter fills a gap in participatory literatures by exploring women fieldworkers' contradictory positionality within their employing NGO and the importance of that positioning for field-level practices. I have depicted women fieldworkers as agents, actively producing and challenging meanings of participation. Participation is shown as a form of power that interacts with other operations of power within NGOs, such as the marginalization of women. Bearing this in mind, efforts at finding technical solutions or seeking greater control over field staff are certain to fail. Tensions within participation and the context of fieldwork itself (for example, women working alone when in villages) enable women fieldworkers to facilitate meanings of participation that fit under the circumstances. They work knowing that limitations to women's participation constrain their field activities, and they use that knowledge to put in place their own ideas about what constitutes meaningful forms of participation.

Women fieldworkers are hired by the PSS to implement the women's participation component, making them insiders and different from women in villages
who do not have the backing of a multimillion-dollar foreign-sponsored project
behind them. But women fieldworkers do not fully participate within the PSS,
that is, men and women do not play equal roles. As women, they are expected to
have a natural affinity with women in the field, but to hold more 'modern' beliefs
about health, water and sanitation. While undoubtedly aware of project definitions
of participation, women fieldworkers negotiate the meanings of participation
within a context of their own contested status in their NGO and limited room to
manoeuvre. An examination of their practices in the field illustrates participation
as a form of power whose shape reflects and interconnects with other gendered
relations of power within NGOs. Participation as a form of power travels through
agents, including fieldworkers. Their interactions in the field lead to the creation
of subversive meanings and the recreation of dominant meanings of participation
that defy technical solutions.

Notes

1   This chapter is based partly on an article that appeared in the journal *Signs*, with
    permission of the publishers (copyright © 2006 The University of Chicago Press).
2   Over the period that I was conducting fieldwork, each field team comprised two men
    and one woman. Two teams worked together out of one field office based in a village
    in the project area.
3   Notable exceptions include Arce and Long (1992), Villareal (1992), Crewe and
    Harrison (1998), Nagar (2000), Springer (2001) and O'Reilly (2002, 2003, 2004).
4   Mutersbaugh (1998), Schroeder (1999), Mosse (2001) and O'Reilly (2003).
5   The reasons for high turnover are numerous. Most frequently, women left the project
    because of pregnancy or a stated need to be at home with family.
6   Note that *woman fieldworker* is a marked category; a male field staff member in the
    PSS is known simply as a *fieldworker*.
7   Tensions due to prospective social change intensify around the issue of gender
    because of associations of men with modernity and women with tradition
    (Chatterjee, 1993; McClintock, 1997; O'Reilly, 2003). Gendered participatory
    approaches such as the PSS's that encourage village women's participation within
    traditional gender roles balance some of these tensions. By contrast, women field-
    workers are cast as modern.
8   As a researcher, I have only a partial understanding of how women internally process
    the decisions that they make.

References

Agarwal, B. (2001) 'Participatory exclusions, community forestry, and gender: An analysis
    for South Asia and a conceptual framework', *World Development* 29 (10): 1623–1648
Arce, A. and N. Long (1992) 'The dynamics of knowledge: Interfaces between bureau-
    crats and peasants'. In A. Long and N. Long (eds) *Battlefields of Knowledge: The*

Interlocking of Theory and Practice in Social Research and Development, London: Routledge, pp211–246

Blaikie, P. (2000) 'Development, post-, anti-, and populist: A critical review', *Environment and Planning A* 32 (6): 1033–1050

Buroway, M., J. Blum, S. George, Z. Gille, T. Gowan, L. Haney, M. Klawiter, S. H. Lopez, S. Riain and M. Thayer (2000) *Global Ethnography: Forces, Connections, and Imaginations in a Postmodern World*, Berkeley: University of California Press

Chambers, R. (1983) *Rural Development: Putting the Last First*, London: Longman

Chambers, R. (1997) *Whose Reality Counts?: Putting the First Last*, London: Intermediate Technology Publications

Chatterjee, P. (1993) *The Nation and its Fragments: Colonial and Postcolonial Histories*, Princeton, NJ: Princeton University Press

Cleaver, F. (2001) 'Institutions, agency and the limitations of participatory approaches to development'. In B. Cooke and U. Kothari (eds) *Participation: The New Tyranny?*, London: Zed Books, pp36–55

Coles, A. and T. Wallace (eds) (2005) *Gender, Water and Development*, Oxford: Berg

Cooke, B. and U. Kothari (eds) (2001) *Participation: The New Tyranny?*, London: Zed Books

Cornwall, A. (2003) 'Whose voices? Whose choices? Reflections on gender and participatory development', *World Development* 31(18): 1325–1342

Crewe, E. and E. Harrison (1998) *Whose Development? An Ethnography of Aid*, London: Zed Books

Crush, J. (ed.) (1995) *Power of Development*, London: Routledge

Escobar, A. (1995) *Encountering Development: The Making and Unmaking of the Third World*, Princeton, NJ: Princeton University Press

Ferguson, J. (1990) *The Anti-politics Machine: 'Development', Depoliticization, and Bureaucratic Power in Lesotho*, Cambridge: Cambridge University Press

Foucault, M. (1980). *Power/Knowledge: Selected Interviews and Other Writings, 1972–77* (edited and translated by Colin Gordon), New York: Pantheon Books

Foucault, M. (1990) *The History of Sexuality: An Introduction*, New York: Vintage

Garcia, V. V. (2001) 'Taking gender into account: Women and sustainable development projects in rural Mexico', *Women's Studies Quarterly* 29(1–2): 85–98

Kabeer, N. (1996) *Reversed Realities: Gender Hierarchies in Development Thought*, New Delhi, India: Kali for Women

Kothari, U. (2001) 'Power, knowledge and social control in participatory development'. In B. Cooke and U. Kothari (eds) *Participation: The New Tyranny?*, London: Zed Books, pp139–152

McClintock, A. (1997) '"No longer in a future heaven": Gender, race, and nationalism'. In A. McClintock, A. Mufti and E. Shohat (eds) *Dangerous Liaisons: Gender, Nation, and Postcolonial Perspectives*, Minneapolis: University of Minnesota Press, pp89–112

Mohanty, C. T. (1991) 'Under western eyes'. In C. Talpade Mohanty, A. Russo and L. Torres (eds) *Third World Women and the Politics of Feminism*, Bloomington: University of Indiana Press, pp51–80

Mosse, D. (2001) '"People's knowledge", participation and patronage: Operations and representations in rural development'. In B. Cooke and U. Kothari (eds) *Participation: The New Tyranny?*, London: Zed Books, pp16–35

Mutersbaugh, T. (1998) 'Women's work, men's work: Gender, labor organization, and technology acquisition in a Oaxacan village', *Environment and Planning D: Society and Space* 16 (4): 439–458

Nagar, R. (2000) 'Mujhe Jawab Do! (Answer me!): Women's grass-roots activism and social spaces in Chitrakoot (India)', *Gender, Place and Culture* 7 (4): 341–362

O'Reilly, K. (2002) 'Creating contradictions, recreating women: Struggles over meanings and spaces of women's participation in a Rajasthan (India) drinking water supply project', unpublished doctoral dissertation, University of Iowa

O'Reilly, K. (2003) 'Competing logics of women's participation in a Rajasthan Development project'. In S. Singh and V. Joshi (eds) *Institutions and Social Change*, Jaipur, India: Rawat, pp272–291

O'Reilly, K. (2004) 'Developing contradictions: Women's participation as a site of struggle within an Indian NGO', *The Professional Geographer* 56 (2): 174–184

O'Reilly, K. (2006) '"Traditional" women, "modern" water: Linking gender and commodification in Rajasthan, India', *Geoforum* 37: 958–972

Paley, J. (2001) *Marketing Democracy: Power and Social Movements in Post-Dictatorship Chile*, Berkeley: University of California Press

Pigg, S. L. (1992) 'Inventing social categories through place: Social representations and development in Nepal', *Comparative Studies in Society and History*: 34 (3): 491–513

Pringle, R. (1989) *Secretaries Talk: Sexuality, Power, and Work*, London: Verso

PSS (Project Social Side) (1993) 'PSS Feasibility Report. Volume E', PSS

PSS (no date). 'Women's Participation Handbook', PSS

Rahnema, M. (1997) 'Participation'. In W. Sachs (ed.) *The Development Dictionary: A Guide to Knowledge as Power*, New Delhi, India: Orient Longman, pp155–175

Schroeder, R. A. (1999) *Shady Practices: Agroforestry and Gender Politics in the Gambia*, Berkeley: University of California Press

Springer, J. (2001) 'State power and agricultural transformation in Tamil Nadu'. In A. Agrawal and K. Sivaramakrishnan (eds) *Social Nature: Resources, Representations, and Rule in India*, New Delhi, India: Oxford University Press, pp86–106

Trinh T. Minh-ha (1997) 'Not you/like you: Postcolonial women and the interlocking questions of identity and difference'. In A. McClintock, A. Mufti and E. Shohat (eds) *Dangerous Liaisons: Gender, Nation, and Postcolonial Perspectives*, Minneapolis: University of Minnesota Press, pp415–419

Villareal, M. M. (1992) 'The poverty of practice: Power, gender and intervention from an actor-oriented perspective'. In N. Long and A. Long (eds) *Battlefields of Knowledge: The Interlocking of Theory and Practice in Social Research and Development*, London: Routledge, pp247–267

Chapter 11

Gathered Indigenous Vegetables in Mainland Southeast Asia: A Gender Asset

Lisa Leimar Price and Britta M. Ogle

Introduction

Women farmers in mainland Southeast Asia collect indigenous food plants from a host of anthropogenic environments associated with farming. These include field boundaries, roadsides, irrigation canal edges, ponds, swamps and well sides. Gathering plants that are commensals to agriculture and agricultural practices takes place in fields when crops are growing, in fallow fields and in areas of secondary growth. The collection of indigenous vegetables, 'weeds', fruit and the edible leaves of trees by women farmers is common for both domestic consumption and for sale in markets. These activities are important from a nutritional and food security standpoint and as a source of income.

Many of the growth locations in the agricultural landscape can be considered what Rocheleau and Edmunds (1997, p1355) term 'in-between spaces' (such as roadsides, field boundaries and irrigation ditches), spaces that may be of little interest to men but that contain essential resources such as wild food plants, medicinal plants or grasses that women use to fulfil a range of household responsibilities. The use of edible plants from agricultural environments and in-between spaces appears to be common practice around the world (Wilken, 1970; Galt and Galt, 1976; Ogle and Grivetti, 1985; Huss-Ashmore and Curry, 1991; Scoones et al, 1992; Dufour and Wilson, 1994; Etkin and Ross, 1994; Nordeide et al, 1996; Price, 1997, 2000, 2003, 2006; Pieroni, 1999, 2003; Vainio-Mattila, 2000; Ogle, 2001a; Pieroni et al, 2002; Daniggelis, 2003; Ertug, 2003; Malaza, 2003).

Across cultures, it appears that farming women predominate as wild food plant gatherers. Attention to gathered food plants as a part of farming systems, however, has only slowly become visible in the agricultural research, development and policy arenas. Until the last ten years or so, a cloak of invisibility was cast over these commensals to agriculture despite their growing visibility in academic research. This invisibility was partly due to the prominence of economists as the key social scientists in agricultural research and development with an emphasis on productivity of crops and cash earnings. In addition to disciplinary bias, gender blindness must also be considered as a partial cause for this obscurity (Dufour and Wilson, 1994; Etkin, 1994; Price, 2000; Howard 2003). At present, a number of UN agencies (FAO, UNDP, WHO), national development cooperation bodies (IDRC), and international agricultural research centres such as the International Plant Genetic Resources Institute (IPGRI) are showing a noticeable interest in wild food plants gathered and used by rural farming households. Despite this growing attention, however, gathered plants and their gatherers receive marginal attention with respect to other natural resources, their management in agriculture and the role these plants have in rural well being.

This chapter examines the gathering of wild plants, mostly as food but also as medicinal ('functional') foods, and to a lesser extent as animal feed, and explores the links between women, gender and these important resources. The foundation for the chapter is our own fieldwork in mainland Southeast Asia, specifically in Vietnam and Thailand. We expand our chapter based on the literature of other researchers for Laos, and selected material from other countries as appropriate to particular issues.

We faced some challenges in writing this chapter. First and foremost, the number of studies on the gathering of wild food plants in mainland Southeast Asia is not substantial, nor are there many studies addressing women or gender with regard to these resources. Second, we use a number of different studies that had different original objectives and were conducted at different times in different locations. The evidence we have on women's gendered resource rights, differences between women in a given community and the empirical research on gendered knowledge and management of the resources comes from Thailand. The richness in botanical, nutritional and multi-use value of plants gathered by women is from Vietnam. Studies from Lao PDR show differences in valuation of environment types and resources, and differences between women farmers who have access to old growth forest and those that do not, in relation to time spent gathering, selling at market and forming gathering groups. Another limitation is the lack of empirical evidence on the overlapping use of selected species between men and women and the complementarity or tension this involves and how these are negotiated.

In all cases, it is clear that women are the gatherers. It should be understood, however, that when we talk about women in this chapter, we are talking about women as socio-culturally constructed. The work, activities and knowledge of women are inseparable from this construct. While there are similarities among women within mainland Southeast Asia as a broad culture area, there are also cultural differences as well as intra-cultural and individual variations. We use the terms 'women' and 'gender' throughout this chapter, but not as if they are inter-changeable. We make some leaps of faith, however. For example, the evidence from empirical studies conducted in Northeast Thailand shows that women and girls know more wild food plants than boys and men. We make the assumption that women's greater plant knowledge is associated with their predominance in gathering through the gendered division of labour. We assume this competency in women's knowledge for other agricultural contexts where women predominate culturally as gatherers of wild plant foods, as in the case of the Lao PDR and Vietnam (Howard, 2003). In other aspects, selected assumptions are based on the literature and our own fieldwork observations regarding women and culture on mainland Southeast Asia.

An additional aspect of this chapter introduced under the section 'Forest to field' provides some insight into the transition from dependence on foraged food plants from forests to gathered plants in the agricultural environment. The current evidence, though scant, points to the centrality of women in this transition.

Woman the gatherer and the sexual division of labour

Anthropologically, it is an empirical fact that across cultures women predominate as food plant foragers, whereas men predominate in hunting large game (Waguespack, 2005). While there are well-documented exceptions to this, where women hunt large game (Estioko-Griffin and Griffin, 1981), this is not a common pattern. Examination of the gendered division of labour illustrates that the greater reliance the hunter/gatherer culture group has on wild meat in their diet, the less dependence there is on gathered plants from female labour. Ultimately, Waguespack (2005) found that the actual minutes per day spent foraging by women (exclusive of processing time) increases as reliance on large hunted game diminishes. She makes the point that women in groups that hunt big game, while spending less time gathering, do not have a reduced overall work burden, as they apply their time to other tasks such as constructing shelters, hauling goods and facilitation activities; women's foraging generally continues, however, but focuses on 'high return plant foods' (p672).

Too little research has been done on sedentary farmer/gatherer-hunter systems for us to fully comprehend the gendered division of labour. Contemporary horticulturalists and agriculturalists are deemed to have hunter/gatherer forbears, and there are some papers that thematically address the bridge between hunter-gatherer ways of life and a move to agriculture (Bender, 1978; Layton et al, 1991; Arnold, 1993; Keeley, 1995). Feminist anthropologists since the 1970s have worked to theorize the role female gathering may have played in hominid/human behavioural evolution. This is exemplified by the landmarks in feminist anthropology: *Woman the Gatherer* edited by Dahlberg (1981), *Gathering and Hominid Adaptation* by Zihlman and Tanner (1978) and *The Woman that Never Evolved* by Hrdy (1981). Feminist archaeologists like Colley (2000) continue to work on making gathering and women visible both in theory and the archaeological record, attempting to counter the many years of women's invisibility in this scholarly arena. As Waguespack (2005, p667) notes, it is a struggle against 'the incredible shrinking prehistoric women'.

While we can observe that there is this division of men predominating in hunting and women in gathering, explanations of why this is so remain in the realm of theory. The current state of affairs is summarized by Winterhalder and Smith (2000, p57):

> *Quantitative, ethnographic studies of time allocation have illuminated the work patterns and subsistence contributions of different sex-age groups, … but a satisfactory explanation for male-female division of labour seen in foraging and forager-horticulturalist societies has remained elusive*

Gender and gathering

The stance that women have a natural affinity with the environment, and thus can be seen as custodians or the target of conservation initiatives has had a number of influential proponents and critics (see Jackson, 1993 for an overview). While we cannot answer the question 'why' women predominate as gatherers, we take the position that gathering is 'feminine' only in the sense that it is grounded in the gendered division of labour to the extent to which a given culture attributes social rationality, with associated meanings, to the categorizations of what is feminine or masculine behaviour. These rationalities are socio-cultural products, and as such negate biologically deterministic and essentialist notions about women and gathering.

This pattern of women's predominance as gatherers is not common to all contemporary circumstances. Gendered patterns, as part of culture, are subject to change. Two cases illustrate this point.[1] Nancy Turner's work (2003) illustrates that gathering was the traditional work of women among indigenous societies of northwestern North America. Her work with Helen Clifton (Turner and Clifton, 2006), however, shows that currently men and women, most notably elderly men and women, in those societies gather seaweed together. The changes have in part been brought on by the younger generation not having time to pursue this traditional activity and there being fewer people interested in the consumption of seaweed. The entrance of men into what was previously only women's work has also been accompanied by technological changes, including the use of speedboats rather than cedar-wood dugouts.

The research of Allison Goebel (2003) on Zimbabwean woodlands also illustrates that wild food plant gathering is not always women's work and she also provides some insight as to why this may be the case. In her study, only men listed wild vegetables (women listed other plants, such as medicinal herbs). Part of this may have to do with the reliance on the 'bush', rather than agricultural environments, for gathered food plants. The contemporary bush (or forest) is not a woman-friendly place. As Goebel (2003, p121) notes:

> *Women are often fearful of venturing alone into such areas because of*
> *the danger of rape or theft. Indeed, within a three-year period, a number*
> *of women were assaulted while walking alone in the bush in Sengezi*
> *resettlement area. The bush therefore emerges as a predominantly male*
> *sphere, not only because of divisions of labour, but as an expression of*
> *male dominance and power over women.*

Resources, spaces and assets

Wild food plants in mainland Southeast Asian rice systems consist not only of herbaceous and aquatic species such as weeds in rice paddy fields, swampy areas and irrigation canals, but also of products from trees found on paddy dikes, field hillocks and roadsides.[2] Thus, these food plants are comprised of multiple species scattered throughout the agricultural landscape.

The physical spaces in the landscape that men and women use overlap, but by virtue of their exploitation of different resources in those spaces, both the species and the spaces have distinct gender elements. This is further nuanced by gender-based intersections with regard to men and women gathering the same species but for different specific purposes. For example, different uses of the same species occur in the study by Ogoye-Ndegwa and Aagaard-Hansen (2006) among the Luo of Western Kenya. They illustrate that while collecting vegetables is women's and girl's work culturally (and not culturally acceptable for men), both men and women can collect the same species for medicinal use. The plants as vegetables are prepared as food only by women, whereas medicinal preparations of these same species are made by both male and female herbalists.

Gathering a given species for a particular use also interfaces with the space from which it is collected. Evidence from Thailand illustrates that the right to gather a given species depends on the culturally perceived rarity of the species, in addition to its market and taste value and where the species grows. This interfaces with land tenure and concepts of private property, whereby it is forbidden to gather specific species for market sale (rare, tasty, high market-value wild food plants) from the private property of others. But customary usufruct rights for gathering these same species for domestic consumption from the private property of others can be much more lenient. For example, collecting a handful to eat on the spot or only enough to feed your family might be acceptable practice. Given that these gathering restrictions are conditioned on perceived rarity coupled with valuation, it also means that the rights and prohibitions to gather a species for specific purposes are also changeable (Price, 1997, 2003).

The examples given above indicate that any given individual's portfolio of assets surrounding wild food plants can include differences in rights of access and tenure between (and among) men and women in different contexts and over time, and are thus not fixed. Not all species are available to all, not all people are equal in their entitlements, and not all spaces are equally endowed with the range of species. Rocheleau and Edmunds (1997) propose that there is a need to look beyond the two dimensional maps of ownership in order to more fully understand property and customary rights in agriculture. The examination of land ownership or tenure alone is clearly insufficient to capture the complexity of plant resource use.

Chambers and Conwey (1992) and Swift (1993), in their early discussion on food security and sustainable livelihoods, have brought into the food security debate the two concepts of material and social assets. More recently, Bebbington (1999) has used the concept of capital (human, social, natural) in a similar capacity as assets, thus broadening the understanding of intangible assets such as gender-based environmental knowledge.

Gender has been identified as a non-material asset on a number of levels. This includes the non-material on both an individual and sub-group level. On the individual level, there is gender-based knowledge and experience. While women in a given culture may hold more or less knowledge than men in a given domain, there will be differences in competencies between women based on aptitude and interest as well as their own life trajectories.

In focusing on gender as an asset (entitlements and knowledge) interfacing with gathered indigenous vegetables in the lower Mekong basin countries of Thailand, Lao PDR and Vietnam, we have come to focus on women farmer-gatherers. Culturally, women's activities in this area are primarily through their collection, management and preparation of plants for domestic consumption, for animal feed and for sale. There is thus a direct gender link to understanding women's assets, that is, their engendered assets of knowledge and entitlements and activities and the various values of the indigenous vegetables. Women's knowledge of the environment and their material assets such as access to land on which these plants grow, are part and parcel of the gendered assets of women. The vegetables themselves are an asset for women as well as their families with regard to the income women generate from the sale of these food plants. Additionally, these food plants make an important nutritional contribution to women's diets and the diets of women's family members, and are a vital aspect of food security. Ultimately, women's wild food plant work and knowledge is an asset to food security for rural farm families.

Women's gathering activity and rights are linked to space and tenure and usufruct rights as nested dynamic gender-based entitlements and privileges. On the larger group level, gender can determine entitlements to land and other material assets as well as the rights to control the fruit of one's labour, depending on the society in which one lives (Niehof and Price, 2001). While we can general-ize about gender-based assets, not all women in a given context will have the same assets or degree of an asset in their portfolio. The variables may be either material and tangible, such as relative wealth, or intangible and non-material, such as relative knowledge level.

In this chapter, we consider three forms of value with regard to indigenous wild food plants and, to a lesser extent, the overlap of these foods with medicinal properties and animal feed as a gender asset. For the most part, this includes direct use value, but also some consideration is made of indirect use value and option value. The utilitarian valuation of biodiversity using the concepts of direct use value, option value and so on is perhaps more common to economics and conservation biology (More et al, 1996; Perlman and Adelson, 1997; Primack, 2002; UNEP, 2006) than the frameworks of anthropology and nutrition that we use here. Nonetheless, we find these concepts useful in thinking about gathered food plants and pinpointing different kinds of importance. Our modification of these values for this chapter regarding women, gender and gathered plants is as follows:

- *Direct use value* refers to the benefit for actual use from vegetables for food and market sale. We also touch on the overlapping use of these wild vegetables for medicinal purposes and as animal fodder.
- *Indirect use value* is discussed with regard to the cultural and social value of the diversity of the indigenous wild vegetables.
- *Option value* is the value of having and managing the species as a form of insurance, that is, as an asset for the future.

Social contexts

In this section we clarify which populations in Thailand, Vietnam and Lao PDR we are addressing. In Lao PDR, there are many ethnic groups, but the primary studies on gathering used in this chapter are specific to the lowland Lao, who live mainly in the provinces bordering the Mekong River (Ireson, 1997; Denes, 1998), who are speakers of Lao and who represent slightly over 52 per cent of the country's population (according to the 1995 population census). The lowland Lao are the dominant ethnic group in the country's government and national culture. Women and men are actively engaged in agriculture, which is centred on wet rice cultivation (paddy fields), particularly the cultivation of glutinous rice as the staple crop. The cited study by Foppes and Ketphanh (1997) was conducted on the Nakai Plateau, where villagers engage in upland rice cultivation, livestock raising and rely also on wild foods. The populations in this region are indigenous minority groups living in the uplands (NTCP, 2005).

Thailand, like Lao PDR, has many ethnic groups. The dominant ethnic group in the running of the country and the overall national culture are the Thai. This chapter, however, focuses on Northeast Thailand, where the Thai-Lao are the majority. The rural population has as its mother-tongue the Lao language, with some influence from the Thai language. Culturally, they can best be viewed as poor farmers rather than an indigenous minority given that they are not tribal and to a high degree they identify with the nation state, although they are certainly one of the largest minority populations in the country. The predominantly rural Northeast is known as the poorest region of Thailand, comprising one third of the country's area. Women farmers are actively engaged in the cultivation of glutinous rice along with men. The studies on Lao speakers of the Northeast used in this chapter centre on the research of Price, but include numerous publications of other researchers who have also investigated women, gender and wild foods in this region (Moreno-Black and Price, 1993; Lyndon and Yongvanit, 1995; Moreno-Black et al, 1996; Somnasang, 1996; Price, 1997, 2000, 2003, 2006; Somnasang et al, 1998; Moreno-Black and Somnasang, 2000).

The lowland Lao and the Thai-Lao of Northeast Thailand have a pattern of customary inheritance of land by women and a pattern of matrilocal residence. In both the Lao PDR and in Thailand, the state has, in contemporary times, challenged the customary systems of female control and inheritance of property. This includes the authority of male heads to sign contracts and the lack of authority of women under state marriage laws in Thailand (ADB, 1998). In Lao PDR, a large national land titling initiative showed much land being registered in the name of the male head only. These state attempts to undermine women's control of economic resources and women' authority have been successfully challenged on many levels by women's movements (Schenk-Sandbergen et al, 1997; ADB, 2004).

The focus in Vietnam centres on the research of Ogle and a number of her colleagues with whom she has co-authored publications. Vietnam is also a multi-ethnic society. The Vietnamese (also known as Kinh) are the centre of national identity, national culture and politics. The Kinh engage in paddy rice cultivation and predominate in the lowlands. Some Kinh also live in the uplands due to the state's past resettlement programmes. Tribal ethnic minorities reside primarily in the highlands. The research conducted by Ogle and her colleagues in Vietnam and reported here includes the Mekong Delta region (Kinh being 100 per cent of their sample) and the highlands of Central Vietnam (Kinh representing 43 per cent of their sample) and the two ethnic minorities of Pako (also spelled Pacoh) being 27 per cent and the Ca Tu at 30 per cent of the sample. Spoken Pako and Ca Tu are in the Mon Khmer language family. In both regions, among all ethnic groups in this research, women are engaged in the cultivation of rice along with the men. Highlanders engage in the cultivation of dry seeded rice but some now engage in the cultivation of wet paddy rice, cassava and fruit, and livestock production. Until recent times, highlanders were engaged in shifting cultivation. Lowlanders engage in wet paddy rice cultivation, sugar cane production and livestock husbandry (Ogle et al, 2001a, 2001b, 2201c, 2001d, 2001e).

In Vietnam, the customary holding of land among the Kinh is patrilineal and residence is patrilocal, as is so for the Pako and Ca Tu groups. Thus, the historical antecedents and customary law are the opposite of those described above for Laos and Thailand. Under contemporary state law, farmers are holders of land use certificates. The 1993 land law allowed land use certificates to be transferable and inheritable (Price and Palis, 1998). As of 2002 , only 11 per cent of land use certificates were registered in the wife's name and only 3 per cent in both names (General Statistics Office Vietnam, 2002). Amendments to the marriage and family law now require land use certificates to have the names of both spouses on them (UN Volunteers, 2004).

Food security and nutrition

For more than three decades, food security has remained a major development concern and an important area for research and conceptual development. While wild food resources are given some recognition, especially as famine foods and use in crisis situations, their role and contribution have largely remained undervalued in the food security debate. This picture is now changing and the ability to make use of such local food resources is on the development agenda and included in some food security frameworks (Midmore et al, 1991; Scoones et al, 1992; Balakrishnan, 1999; Heywood, 1999; FAO and UNDP, 2004).

The contribution to nutritional adequacy may be direct, through diversification of diets, but can also be indirect as a source of income, as livestock feed, an integrated element in a farming system or as a component in traditional medical systems (Grandstaff et al, 1986; Moreno-Black and Price, 1993; Etkin, 1994; Heywood, 1999; Nakahara and Trakoontivakorn, 1999; Nakahara et al, 2001; Ogle et al, 2003; Pieroni and Quave, 2006; Price, 2006).

Wild foods in food resource systems and nutrition security

Many wild vegetables are important sources of micronutrients and play an important role in nutrition, especially for women as women have high demands for micronutrients (Grivetti and Ogle, 2000). Women in low-income households are more vulnerable to nutritional deficiencies where the food budget is limited and the diet restricted. Diversifying the family diet through the use of wild plants enables women in poor households to improve their nutrient intake at little or no additional cost (Ogle et al, 2001d, 2001e).

Research indicates bio-active substances with potential disease-preventing or health-promoting mechanisms in many traditional food plants (Craig, 1999; Lampe, 1999). These include substances that have antioxidant activities that stimulate the immune system, or have antibacterial, antimutagenic or antiviral activities, for example flavonoids, tannins, pectins and saponins (Borchers et al, 1997; Beecher, 1999; Nakahara and Trakoontivakorn, 1999; Nakahara et al, 2001; Price, 2006). Many medical plants may also have direct nutritional benefits of which we know little. The practice of using herbal infusions may add small daily quantities of trace-minerals and vitamins to the intake of sick or malnourished individuals that is sufficient to alter the metabolic uptake or restore the balance between nutrients and thereby improve body functioning (Golden, 1996; Xiu, 1996; Chandra, 1999; Pardo de Santayana et al, 2006). Thus, women's knowledge and use of local wild vegetables increases their power over both their personal health and family welfare whether they are poor, landless or have limited access to markets.

In local Southeast Asian food markets, women overwhelmingly predominate as market sellers. Research from Lao PDR and Thailand has shown that from the marketing perspective, knowledge of locally accepted and culturally valued foods increases the economic freedom of women as they can market wild food plants for income. The knowledge of edible wild plants also strengthens their social space as it enables them to carry forward culinary traditions, bring gifts to members of their social network or exchange wild plants for transplanting and use (Moreno-Black and Price, 1993; Ireson, 1997; Price, 2000). Moreno-Black and Price (1993) illustrate in their study of wild food marketers in Kalasin province in Northeast Thailand that women marketers have full control of their earnings and use part of them to publicly make merit at the village temple through donations and thereby increase their community status.

Forest to field

The relationship between gathering wild food plants from forests and gathering them from agricultural environments is not well understood. One proposal suggests that as forest resources diminish, the time it takes to travel to forests to gather forest food products increases and farmers increasingly begin to use the resources closer to home. These resources are in the form of agricultural 'weeds' and other species in nearby environments, including vegetable plants gathered from roadsides and other nearby anthropogenic micro-environments. This pattern was identified as the *botanical dietary paradox* by Ogle and Grivetti in 1985. The paradox is that despite a reduction in forest food plant species available, there is an increase in the consumption of gathered plant foods. This is because new plant species are brought into the diet. Women's time constraints are noted as an important factor in the transition to the increased use of agricultural weed species. As forests become increasingly remote from the village, collection of plant foods for domestic consumption becomes too time-consuming, and so a shift begins to occur to areas closer to home.

Wiersum (1996, 1997) has suggested that there is also a trend toward increased management of trees in the agricultural landscape as forests decline. Activities include freeing trees from competition and intentional dispersal of seeds or seedlings of trees with cultural value into agricultural fields as well as home gardens. It should be noted here that people consume the leaves of many tree species as vegetables.

We have very limited documentation about how this transition from dependence on forests to dependence on fields for wild food plants occurs. Scudder (1971) provides us with the best evidence that women are central to the process through their experimental consumption of new food plants. African Savannah cultivators during a relocation programme had a high incidence of female death in their relocated community compared to the indigenous population in the area. After extensive medical and anthropological research into the cause of these deaths it was ultimately concluded that the deaths could best be attributed to poisoning due to test consumption of unfamiliar wild plant foods. This evidence may indicate a pattern that women, wherever they are gatherers, may also be the bearers of a great responsibility and vital knowledge not to be taken lightly.

Laos

A study by Foppes and Ketphanh (1997) illustrates that farmers use multiple environments for the collection of non-timber forest products (NTFPs) in Laos. This may be an example of the transition from dependence on forests to dependence on fields and secondary growth, although we cannot say with certainty. In their study of 26 villages, collection was done mainly for subsistence. The farm women and men considered vegetables, bamboo shoots, fish and wildlife the most important items. Despite the fact that their study focused on forest products, the researchers discovered that farmers used multiple land types and that 60 per cent of the NTFP products were collected from fields (paddy, dry grass and fallow), streams and ponds (see Table 11.1).

According to the authors, there was a difference in the priorities of men and women with regard to placing relative importance on resources. Women place more importance on vegetables (plant food gathering) and men on wildlife and fish. These priorities can be taken to reflect the gendered division of labour and gendered domains of food procurement activities and environments. What is also noteworthy is that there is an overlap of the actual physical environments deemed important to both men and women who use the spaces to serve their own ends.

Carol Ireson's (1997) research in Laos sheds further light on the relationship between forest and field use in the collection of indigenous food plants (fruit, vegetables and mushrooms). Her research sample included villages with and without access to old growth forests, and with access to secondary growth. Ireson's findings indicate that women farmers in both kinds of villages show no difference in the use of wild gathered products but did show some other striking differences. Women with access to old growth forests reported that they visited the forest every day, while the women from the villages without close access to the old growth forests were more likely to have visited the forest at intervals longer than two weeks. Further, women with access to secondary growth areas were more likely to sell what they gathered, an income opportunity mainly used by women rather than men. Ireson (1997, p23) notes that 'most village women do not go

Table 11.1 *Collection areas for NTFPs, ranked according to relative importance by men and women in three villages on the Nakai Plateau, Lao PDR, March 1997*

Land type important for gathering of NTFPs		Perceived importance,		
Land type (Lao language)	Land type (English translation)	by sex of villager		
		men	women	overall
dong/pou	evergreen forest/mountains	24%	25%	25%
kok	dry diptocarp/pine forests	15%	16%	16%
pa lao	fallow regrowth	14%	20%	17%
houay/nong	streams/ponds	32%	28%	30%
thong/naa	grass fields/paddy fields	15%	11%	13%
		100%	100%	100%

Source: Foppes and Ketphanh (1997)

great distances into the forest; they always come home by dark'. She further notes that the majority of women gather with only one or two other people, that all the women gathered at least once a week (with 25 per cent gathering daily), and that these small groups of women usually gather from fallow fields or secondary growth areas. Those women having access primarily to secondary growth, rather than old growth forests, were more engaged in the marketing of forest products.

It is theorized that the shifts that induce the *botanical dietary paradox* are linked to the reduction in the availability (increased distance) of old growth forests, and as a concomitant, have increased the time it takes to reach the forests. This was first proposed by Ogle and Grivetti (1985) and is further substantiated by the work of Ireson (1997).

Some of the most vulnerable villages in terms of food security may well be those that are verging on transitions in the paradox from reliance on forest plant foods to greater reliance on plant foods that are in the anthropogenic environments of agriculture. Research conducted by Alexandre Denes (1998) on foraging in several villages in Salavan province in the Laos among the lowland Lao documents a pattern of paddy cultivated rice and foraged foods. This includes a variety of leafy greens, bamboo shoots, mushrooms, fruit, frogs, freshwater fish, freshwater shrimp and insects. The results indicate that all the villages are experiencing both rice and foraged food shortages. These shortages are relatively recent and the shortage of gathered foods has reached a critical state. Women spend more time gathering than men as they gather on a daily basis. Women also forage for a wider range of products compared to men. Denes (1998, p115) notes that 'It is also evident from the seasonal timeline that women must increase time spent for daily consumption during the dry season, as well as go further from the village as resources become more scarce.'

Thailand

Forest, field and garden wild food plants

Threatened food security as well as nutritional stress due to reduced availability of wild food plants from forests is reported for minority populations in Northern Thailand (Johnson and Grivetti, 2002). Forest cover in Thailand has gone from 62 per cent in 1940 to 30 per cent in 1992 (Ganjanapan, 1992). As of 2002, forest cover in Thailand was 28.9 per cent of the total land area, of which just 3 per cent is forest plantation (FAO, 2005).

Johnson and Grivetti (2002), in their study among Karin women living in the hills of the north, make a number of important observations. The researchers examined 47 key species. They found that wild food plants from the forest have gone into serious decline over the last decade and that certain species have even disappeared. They also found that multiple environments are in use for wild food plant gathering, including forests, rice fields, fallow agricultural areas, river banks and open/transition areas. Some of the species studied have been transplanted into home gardens, and eight wild species grown in home gardens no longer exist in the wild.

Most of the intensive research on wild plants has been conducted in Northeast Thailand. Women farmers there are the key to important aspects of wild food plant gathering. They gather for their own consumption and household provision, and for selling at market, and are owners of the agricultural land and gardens in which these plants grow. Ultimate decision-making authority and veto power over land as well as major economic decisions rest with the female head. Villages are thus made up of networks of female blood-kin. Because of the pattern of matrilocal residence, which is still the norm, women also stay in their natal villages or return to them after a period of labour migration as adults, and so have deep knowledge of their physical and social environments.

In this region, woman farmers gather extensively from agricultural land and other anthropogenic environments, mostly private but also public land. They also engage in transplanting desirable species from distant dry land fields to their closer paddy field areas, and also into their home gardens. The women transplant onto their own lands although source material can come from their own property, kin, public lands and the market. Price (1997) documented 77 species gathered and used by farmers in a village in Kalasin province, with the majority occurring in paddy fields or the village environs, 23 species of which were either trans-planted or seed planted. A survey of 49 home gardens in the same village as the Price (1997) study showed that 95 per cent of the sampled gardens contained a total of 17 species of both naturally occurring and transplanted non-domesticated food plants (Moreno-Black et al, 1996). These transplanting and home gardening activities are both for the sake of convenience and a form of insurance to help guard against periods of food scarcity (Moreno-Black and Somnasang, 2000).

Marketing wild food plants

Women farmers in Northeast Thailand have been shown to make a statistically significant contribution to overall household income through earnings from the local marketing of wild food plants (Moreno-Black and Price, 1993; Price, 2000). They are central to the movement of local wild food plants onto the market for both urban and rural consumers, and thus to the transformation of these plants into income-generating commodities. In their 1993 study, Moreno-Black and Price only observed women selling wild plant foods at the market in the Kalasin provincial capital; they documented 567 women sellers and 39 men on a market day.

The income earned by female marketer-farmers is used in many ways, includ-ing the purchase of meat and other food, medicines, school fees for children, clothing and agricultural expenses. The money earned is theirs to use as they see fit, and is a statistically significant portion of household income, providing for material needs as well as enhancing their social status in the community. The market is not only a place to purchase wild food plants for direct consumption, but is also a place where other women farmers obtain planting materials (Price, 1997, 2000).

Gendered knowledge

Several studies conducted in Northeast Thailand examine gender-based knowledge of wild food plants. Somnasang (1996) documented how farm women and girls are more likely to correctly identify wild food plants than men and boys. In a study by Lyndon and Yongvanit (1995) of 307 men and 483 women, women were found to be more able to identify and name wild food plants than men, who nonetheless knew some of the plants. This area of knowledge is therefore not mutually exclusive and there are some overlaps. These overlaps can to a certain degree be anticipated, the degree varying, based on the society. It may also be a function of food plants being eaten by both male and female villagers, and may also be that selected species have multiple functions, some of which may fall into the domain of men's work and knowledge.[3] Somnasang et al (1998) provide the only indication of male expertise in this region. In a study of 20 villages, their evidence confirms that women are the primary gatherers and men and boys are engaged in hunting small game that includes birds, rats and rabbits. Men also engage in fishing, especially in deeper waters.

Price (2006), based on recent field research in the Northeast, observed that men gather lotus stems from deep waters at the request of their wives; women explained that they do not like to go into the deep swamp water because it is full of leaches. It should also be noted that women also collect protein foods such as freshwater shrimp, snails, paddy field crabs and various insects from the paddy fields. Somnasang et al (1998) attribute the differences they uncover in knowledge between males and females to the gendered division of labour. Men and women not only pass down their knowledge in a gendered manner to the young but also their tools (both how to make and use them) and specialized techniques.

In addition to gender, age and education and class have been shown to be factors in knowledge of wild food plants. Women aged 30–50 in a village in Northeast Thailand could name more plants that they had transplanted and could discuss management methods better than older women. Many of the species known to older women were unknown to women aged 30–50, as they had disappeared from the landscape or were too rare (Moreno-Black and Somnasang, 2000). This indicates both that the nature of the resource has changed and that there has been an increase in the management intensity. The research findings of Lyndon and Yongvanit (1995) with regard to education level, mobility and class, provide indications that knowledge of wild food plants is linked to traditional rural life. Lyndon and Yongvanit (1995, p84) state that:

> *Knowledge of traditional food plants, as measured by a plant identification test, was almost the exact opposite of results of most standardized tests. People who scored the highest had the least formal education. Those who did poorest where the most mobile or urbanized of the subjects and had the largest number of middle class credentials.*

Gathering entitlements

The issue of rights to collect wild food plants from privately owned land in rural Northeast Thailand has been extensively documented (Price, 1997, 2000, 2003, 2006). Female farmers have a complex system of gathering rights based on land ownership, usufruct rights and the nature of the intended use of the species and the species status. The status of a species is based on its perceived rarity in the environment, how desirable its taste and its market value. Gathering rights, coupled with land entitlements, have shifting boundaries as perceptions change about species rarity and whether those species are being over-exploited. Thus, species can move in and out of a protected status. The restrictions are for plants on privately owned land. Rights and restrictions applicable to the private property of others have a range: (1) gathering all you want for any purpose; (2) gathering enough for a meal; (3) taking only what you can eat on the spot; (4) asking permission to gather for consumption; (5) total prohibition for gathering for sale but some degree allowed for personal or home consumption; and (6) full prohibition of gathering for consumption and sale. Thus, private property is a critical asset given women's central role as land owners, gatherers and market sellers.

There are no formal meetings held on changing a plant's gatherability status on private property that does not belong to the gatherer. Women report that community consensus on which species has what restriction is based on general agreement through informal discussions. This process of reaching consensus may be facilitated by people's life-long knowledge of the environment, and of each other (Price, 2003). While this process has been reported by many women, it has never been observed by a researcher, nor has there been an analysis of the different stakeholders in this process (land-holding women compared to landless people, for example).

Grandstaff et al (1986) document several communities that had almost eliminated gathering rights to any items on privately owned land in the Northeast. The most recent research of Price (2006) shows that of the 77 wild food plants documented in 1990 and restudied in 2006, the collection for market sale from the land of others of 32 wild plant foods is strictly forbidden. Of these 32 species, 23 also have some gathering restriction for domestic consumption (for example, only enough for one meal can be taken). Six of the 32 also have absolute prohibitions on gathering from other people's land. In 1990, in the same village and for the same plant species, only 21 were not allowed to be gathered for market sale, with 13 having some restrictions on gathering for consumption. Only four plant species were forbidden completely from both consumption and sale. Thus, gathering prohibitions and restrictions now encompass up to 11 new species (see Table 11.2). It should be noted that a species with restrictions for gathering for consumption always has a corresponding prohibition for gathering for market sale. Overall, the pattern is one of increased privatization between 1990 and 2006 in the village.

Increasing implementation of concepts of privatization may provide protection of valued species, particularly when combined with increasing management

Table 11.2 *Wild food plant species with gathering restrictions on privately owned land (N = 38)*

	1990		2006	
	For eating	For sale	For eating	For sale
Non-restricted	21	12	9	6
Restricted	13	5	23	
Forbidden	4	21	6	32

Source: Price (2006)

such as transplanting. There are, however, no quantitative studies on species abundance to prove this. The effects on poor women and their families, particularly the landless, are yet to be studied.

There are, however, tensions between the protective management of plants engaged in by women and the contemporary needs for cash income that plant sales can bring. This may, in part, explain the observations of Moreno-Black and Somnasang (2000) that younger women in their sample could name more plants that they had transplanted compared to older women, and did not know many of the plants that the older ones knew. In a way, privatization and increasing management intensity are indicators of the race against extinction and over-exploitation for market sale of a species.

Nutrition, health and food security

Wild foods were attracting attention from Thai nutritionists in the late 1980s. Somnasang et al (1987) estimated that wild food (plants, fish, frogs and insects) made up 50 per cent of the diet of farmers in Northeast Thailand, with most of the remainder being rice. The early documentation of the importance to the diet of farmers of gathered foods is also to be seen in development-oriented nutritional publications of the 1980s (Pradipasen et al, 1985; Tontisirin et al, 1986; Ngarmsak, 1987). There is growing evidence that many of these food plants not only provide nutritive value but also serve as functional foods (Nakahara and Trakoontivakorn, 1999; Trakoontivakorn, 2002; Price, 2006).

Vietnam

Vietnam provides interesting examples of the role of gathered food plants from a gender asset viewpoint. There is a wealth of known edible wild plant species in Vietnam (Bui Minh Duc, 1986; Nguyen Tien Ban and Bui Minh Duc, 1994), of which many continue to be used (Gessler and Hodel, 1997; Ogle, 2001a) and which have multiple economic functions (Ogle et al, 2003). The research by Ogle et al (2003) in the Mekong Delta and in the highlands of Central Vietnam illustrates how women continue to add diversity and value to family food security and

Table 11.3 *Frequency of consumption of individual species of* rau dai

Scientific name	1-y FFQ* % women using 3–7 species /week	
	N=101	N=103
	Mekong Delta	Central Highlands
1. Aquatic plants		
Eleocharis spp[1]	49	–
Ipomoea aquatica[2]	64	46
Limnocharis flara[1]	32	–
Nasturdium officinale	–	37
Nymphea lotus	68	–
2. Terrestrial plants		
Basella rubra[3]	17	16
Centella asiatica	32	59
Commelina communis	21	–
Diplazium esculentum	–	10
Eryngium foetidum	–	20
Forma rubra	12	–
Gynura crepidioides	–	11
Homalomena occulta	–	17
Houttuynia cordata	–	26
Passiflora foetida	10	–
Piper sarmentosum	–	49
Plantago major	–	12
Portulaca oleraceae	–	15
Sauropus androgyn [4]	28	28
Schismatoglottis calyp	–	22
Schizostschyum avicul	–	61
Solanum nigrum	–	15

Note: * 1-y FFQ, 1-year food frequency questionnaire.
Additionally, *Ageratum cynozoides*, *Costus speciosus* and *Neptunia oleraceae* were reported. 1) Used almost universally in one village, but not at all in the other village. 2) Cultivated by approximately one third of households in the Mekong Delta, and mostly purchased in the highlands. 3) Often cultivated yet listed as *rau dai*. 4) Mostly cultivated in Mekong sites, yet grouped with gathered plants by women

Source: Ogle et al (2003)

nutrition directly or indirectly through their knowledge of edible wild plants. Over 90 species of wild plants were used as vegetables in the four villages in the study.

About one third of the natural vegetables identified in this survey were recognized for their specific therapeutic or curative properties, 40 per cent were also used as livestock feed and one fifth had multiple uses as foods, feed and medicines. Table 11.3 shows the frequency of consumption of the most popular species in two villages in the Mekong Delta and two villages in the highlands of Thua Thien Hue in central Vietnam.

These vegetables were harvested from many types of environments and ecological niches. Many were gathered from fields, dikes, home gardens, roadsides or commons and in the highland sites also from complex forest or agroforestry systems. Many of the growth locations in the agricultural landscape can be considered what Rocheleau and Edmunds (1997) term *in-between spaces* (roadsides, field boundaries, irrigation ditches) that contain essential resources such as wild food plants, medicinal plants or grasses that women use, but are spaces of marginal interest to men. Chambers (1990), accurately labelled these *micro-environments unobserved* and included home gardens, backyards, trenches, gullies, roadsides, river banks, groves, hedges and sheltered corners where women find many of the indigenous wild species that they use to diversify and enrich the family diet.

In the Central Highlands, a large number of wild food plants growing in forests were known to the population yet only a few were in regular use. Frequently these plants were transplanted to the more anthropogenic environments closer to their homes. Women said one reason for this was that the forest was too far and when they did gather there it was normally in combination with activities for other purposes. Women farmers of the Mekong Delta had the largest number of gathered plants coming from the paddy field dikes but aquatic plants were among those most abundant. Marketing of selected species also occurred.

With respect to multiple functions, many were used also as livestock feed (Nguyen Nhut Xuan Dung, 1996; Ogle et al, 2003). Livestock management, especially pig and poultry raising, is largely the responsibility of women. Women in the Mekong Delta would say 'plants for livestock are free, if not we would be lost', indicating that wild plants are a valuable and free supplementary resource, commonly used as an essential part of animal diets. These resources enable poor households to include livestock in their farming activities, thereby both improving their economy and getting direct access to animal products in the diet. The nutritional advantages from such indirect use of edible wild plants is considerable, especially for children and for women, as the bioavailability of many nutrients from animal products is better than that from plant products.

Among the popular species used as feed is *Alternanthera repens*. This has a relatively high protein content and is commonly given raw or cooked to pigs, ducks, chickens and buffaloes (Nguyen Nhut Xuan Dung, 1996). Whole plants are cooked with broken rice and rice bran into a thick soup that is fed to local breed sows three times a day after farrowing. Women say that such feed stimulates lactation and their piglets grow quickly. *A. sessilis*, *Amaranthus caudatus* and *A. viridis* are also widely used for pigs and ducks. Other species included *Commelina* spp as ration ingredients for pigs, ducks and chickens. Women consider these as 'cold' feeds for animals, and use them especially in the hot season. *Commelina* species grow well in homestead areas in the Mekong Delta and women collect and feed them fresh to the pigs without expending too much labour and time. For ducks, the plant is chopped into small pieces and mixed with other plants such as *Passiflora foetida* and *Alternathera sessilis*, and with rice bran.

Ogle et al (2003) also illustrate links between therapeutic plants and nutrition (see Table 11.4). For the wild vegetables used in the study areas, recent phyto-medical research has shown the antibacterial effects of pectin from *Plantago major* (Hetland et al, 2000), wound healing properties of *Centella asiatica* (Brinkhaus et al, 2000), acute pain reduction and antibacterial properties of *Ageratum cynozoides* (Perumal et al, 1999; Sampson et al, 2000; Silva et al, 2000), anti-inflammatory effects of *Portulaca oleracea* (Chan et al, 2000), antiviral activities of *Basella rubra* (Bolognesi et al, 1997) and liver-protective activities from aucubin, a glycoside found in *Plantago major* (Chang, 1998).

Many indigenous therapeutic regimes include herb teas and infusions made from a mixture of several plants, but there are no published data on nutritional benefits. The therapeutic use of plant material needs to be viewed also from a nutritional viewpoint. Several of the treatments include daily doses of 30–50g of vegetable matter in the form of juices or extracts, or mixtures of several types of green leafy vegetables (Le Van Truyen and Nguyen Gia Chan, 1999).

Discussion and conclusions

The direct use value of gathered plants has come through clearly in this chapter in terms of nutrition from their consumption, income that women earn from their market sale, and their overlapping functions in support of livestock feed and as functional foods. These foods add diversity to the diets of women and support women's livelihood enterprises. The indirect value of the plants, that is, their social and cultural value, rests not only in the vital position they have in the livelihood system but in their value as part of a gendered cultural heritage, both tangible (environment and cuisine) and intangible (women's knowledge). The plants are socially valued, not stigmatized, and thus this social value is extended to their use not only as daily fare (cuisine) but also for trade. Wild food plants known and managed by women also have important option value in that they are managed as an asset for the future through women's work in transplanting them. In the case of Northeast Thailand, this option value includes restricting open access gathering of valued wild food plants species that the community of village women perceive as rare and valued, particularly for market sale.

The current evidence points to the fact that women are pivotal in the following ways:

- Women's time is the important factor in a move from gathering forest food plants to gathering food plants from agricultural in-between spaces. As forests diminish, gathering in forests becomes too labour intensive, and so women turn to environments that are closer, most of which are agricultural micro-environments.
- Women bring these food plants to the tables of their families, and to consumers through food preparation and marketing of wild food plants.

Table 11.4 *Some examples of therapeutic uses of wild vegetables and reported phytochemical constituents*

Name of vegetable	Applications according to respondents and key informants	Reported phytochemical constituents
Centella asiatica *rau ma*	Many applications, both boiled and fresh: as a diuretic, to reduce fever, as an antibiotic, for bleeding gums, nose bleeds, to increase breast milk, to improve liver function	Alkaloids, (hydrocotylin), glucosides, (asiaticosid), centellosides, saponins
Sauropus androgynus *bo ngot* *	Many applications, leaf as well as stem and root: as a diuretic, to relieve fever, fungi on tongue. Infusion of the root can cause abortion and be used to remove placenta after birth	Alkaloid (papaverine)
Limnocharis flava *keo neo*	Used against back ache	
Commelina communis *rau trai*	Cooked vegetable extract is used for diarrhoea and dysentery. Also to treat flu, ARI and to relieve fever. Also as a diuretic in heart complaints and as a remedy for insect bites	Glucosides, delphin, commelinin, flavocommelin, awobanin
Passiflora foetida *nhan long*	Used for tiredness and for sleeping well. Used in heart complaints	Flavonoids
Basella rubra *mong toi*	Multiple uses: to strengthen bones, to reduce temperature, to improve digestion, to increase breast milk. Also as a laxative and as a diuretic	Saponins and pectins
Enyndra fluctuans *rau ngo*	Cooked leaves eaten against discharge, vaginal itching and infections in the uterus	Enhydrin, fluctuadin, melampolides
Ageratum cynozoides *cõ cùt heo*	Raw vegetable used as cough medicine; cooked extract used to relieve pain and improve kidney function. Also anti-inflammatory, antihistamine	Cadinen, caryophyllen, geratocromen, demetoxygeratocromen, alkaloids, saponin.
Neptunia oleraceae *rau nhut*	Used to relieve uterine infections and discharge, fever and dysentery, and as a diuretic	
Glinus oppositifolius *rau dang dât*	Used in uterine infections and discharge, to reduce temperature, and as a diuretic, icteric, and to treat convulsions	Saponins
Bacopa monnieri *rau dang biên*	Extract used for diabetes, as a laxative, to improve liver function	
Premna integrifolia *lá cách*	To relieve pain, part of treatments for many liver conditions, dysentery, improves digestion, relieves fever, diuretic	
Plantago major *mã dê*	In kidney disorders, diuretic, kidney stone	Glucosides (aucubin and rinantin)
Portulaca oleracea *rau sam*	Antihistamine, vasoconstriction, dysentery, salmonella, removes worms (helminth), antibiotic, laxative, persistent cough, and for blood in urine	Saponins
Piper sarmentosum *lá lôt*	Relieves pain, leaf and stem used for kidney trouble, root used for toothache, to improve the digestion system, for diarrhoea, vomiting and acidic stomach	

Note: *Consumption of raw juice extract associated with severe respiratory distress (Ruay-Sheng et al, 1996; Luo-Ping et al, 1997).

Sources: WHO and Institute of Materia Medica (1990); Doan Du Dat et al (1992); Gessler and Hodel (1997); Magalães et al (1997); Chang (1998); Perumal et al (1999); Shukla et al (1999); Brinkhaus et al (2000); Chan et al (2000); Hetland et al (2000); Sampson et al (2000)

- Women in both Thailand and Vietnam are engaged in the management of these species through transplanting. Such transplanting activities not only provide for daily domestic consumption needs but also, as the Thailand research shows, consciously ensures their availability in times of scarcity.
- The foods themselves provide valuable nutrition for households through direct consumption, through their use as functional foods, and indirectly as animal feed.
- The income that women earn from their sales of wild plants supports agricultural activities (purchase of inputs and equipment), purchases of meat and other food supplements, provides for their own personal needs, and supports or enhances their domestic and community social standing. This is evident in Northeast Thailand, where women's income is a statistically significant contribution to the income of farming households.

While women are central to understanding this aspect of rural food systems in Thailand, Vietnam and Lao PDR, clearly understanding the gender nuances with regard to women and wild food plants is difficult given the scarcity of empirical studies in the area. However, the evidence we do have leads us to make some important observations.

Land ownership is shown to be an important factor in the intensification of management of wild food plants in Northeast Thailand and the increasing restrictions placed upon gathering for market sale as well as domestic consumption from private property. Women's gendered authority over agricultural land, extended to wild food plants that grow on that land, is tied to a long culture history of matrilineal land ownership and inheritance. The cultural consensus among village women in determining which valued species are rare and thus should be restricted for collection from privately owned land for consumption and sale is a product not only of authority over the land and plants, but also of the intimate social knowledge of other women in the village, and their intimate environmental knowledge, fostered by a configuration of matrilineal inheritance of land, matrilocal residence, freedom of movement and freedom to market and control cash, among other factors. Women gatherers in contexts that are patrilineal with male control over land and patrilocal residence may show a very different pattern of access rights and a process of privatization of valued rare species. Currently there is no research available on this issue.

The studies available show that women within both kinds of cultures, male or female control and ownership of agricultural land, gather from fields. However, many of the micro-environments in the contexts from which women gather are indeed 'in between spaces', such as roadsides. The research from Northeast Thailand illustrates, however, that it is not only the spaces but the species that are important to understanding who has access rights. Spaces such as paddy dikes are private property and are restricted spaces only for selected species and for gathering for selected purposes. For example, collecting a plant deemed valuable and rare for market from land owned by others is strictly prohibited, even though one can gather that same species in the same place for domestic consumption. When the species is too rare, even collection for domestic consumption of a given species from private property (community usufruct rights) can be strictly prohibited. In the northeast of Thailand, the system is one of complex layers of rights and prohibitions. We do not know the extent to which such complexity exists in other contexts, as it is yet to be determined. However, it does illustrate the importance of understanding gender-based rights and management of natural resources on a deeper contextualized level.

The research presented shows that wealth is a vital aspect when considering the interface between gender and wild food plant resources. Relative wealth (land owned) is also linked to authority over resources and access rights. As this chapter has shown, the boundaries of community usufruct rights with regard to gathering from private property are also shifting, as evidenced through increased privatization and gathering prohibitions on selected species between 1990 and 2006. To gather selected species, land-poor women in Northeast Thailand may have to rely more on the spaces that have no recognized land owner. But given that rarity is a key factor in bringing a plant into a more privatized status, it is unlikely that the restricted species occur in any abundance in public access micro-environments, such as roadsides. While we do not yet have studies available on the actual impact of such restrictions on the poor, it is clear that there is a probable reduction in availability of restricted items. Areas of impact on the poor (cash- and land-poor women) would include the reduction and elimination of selected species in their diet, with possible nutritional implications, restricted ability to earn cash from these valued species through their market sale, and restricted use of valued species in upholding culinary traditions in their own homes and social circles. This would result not only from a lack of access to gather directly but also from a lack of sufficient cash to purchase from the market, as these species have high market values and are thus relatively expensive.

Clearly, there may be social costs attached to privatization. A loss for women farmer-market sellers from this source of income can mean the difference between buying a plough, sending a child to school or using cash to enhance one's social status in the community. It is a difference that matters. Alternatively, privatization may be a way to limit cost-shifting to the environment that gathering for market sale can bring on, helping to preserve rare species now and for the future. There are many potential trade-offs.

In conclusion, the research cited and presented in this chapter illustrates that increased distances to gathering locations serve as a motivation to bring many new species into the diet of farmers. We do not yet understand the trial and error process involved, nor do we understand fully the risks women take in eating unfamiliar species in broadening their dietary repertoires. There is much to be learned from women's wild plant knowledge and work in understanding such transitions. Likewise, a more detailed and nuanced examination of values, use and management of plants is warranted for a better understanding of the processes of social and environmental change that interface with wild food plants. For Thailand, Vietnam and Lao PDR, rural women's cultural heritage surrounding wild food plants is comprised of bundled assets and value manifests itself differently in many varied, often subtle, ways.

Notes

1 Although neither deals with gathering in agricultural environments, the two cases illustrate that gathering is part of a larger cultural system of which gender is a component, is not always women's work, and like other cultural features, is subject to change.
2 In addition to the fruit and seeds of trees, leaves are commonly consumed as vegetables.
3 Among Luo women gatherers in western Kenya, for example, where men do not culturally gather vegetables, 'the availability of certain vegetables in specific procurement sites is a secret treasured by the women' (Ogoye-Ndegwa and Aagaard-Hansen, 2006, p331). In such circumstances, we can expect to find a greater difference between the knowledge of women and men as well as potentially a greater degree of variation between women themselves.

References

ADB (1998) 'Women in Thailand', country briefing paper produced by Pawadee Tonguthai, Suteera Thomson and Maytenee Byongsung, Manila: Asian Development Bank, www.adb.org/Documents/Books/Country_Briefing_Papers/ Women_in_Thailand/women_thailand.pdf (accessed 25 May 2007)

ADB (2004) 'Lao PDR: Gender, poverty and the Millennium Development Goals', country gender strategy produced by the Mekong Department and the Regional and Sustainable Development Department of the Asian Development Bank. Prepared by the consultant, Eugenia McGill. Manila: Asian Development Bank, www.adb.org/Documents/Reports/Country-Gender-Assessments/cga-women-lao.pdf (accessed 25 May 2007)

Arnold, J. E. (1993) 'Labour and the rise of complex hunter-gatherers', *Journal of Anthropological Archaeology* 12: 75–119

Balakrishnan, R. (1999) *Gender Dimensions in Biodiversity Management and Food Security: Policy and Programme Strategies for Asia*, Bangkok: FAO Regional Office for Asia and the Pacific

Bebbington, A. (1999) 'Capitals and capabilities: A Framework for analyzing peasant viability, rural livelihoods and poverty', *World Development* 27 (12): 2021–2044

Beecher, G. R. (1999) 'Phytonutrients' role in metabolism: Effect on resistance to degenerative processes', *Nutrition Reviews* 57: S3–S6

Bender, B. (1978) 'Gatherer-hunter to farmer: A social perspective', *World Archaeology* 10 (2): 75–119

Bolognesi, A., L. Polito, F. Olivieri, P. Valbonesi, L. Barbieri, M. G. Batteli, M. V. Carusi, E. Benuveto, F. Blanco, F. Delvecci, A. Di Maro, A. Parente, M. D. Loreto and F. Stirpe (1997) 'New Ribosome-inactivating proteins with polynucleotide: Adenosine glycosidase and antiviral activities from *Basella rubra* L. and *Bougainvillea spectabilis* Willd.', *Planta* 203: 422–429

Borchers, A. T., R. M. Hackman, C. L. Keen, J. S. Stern and M. E. Gershwin (1997) 'Complementary medicine: A review of immuno-modulatory effects of Chinese herbal medicines', *American Journal of Clinical Nutrition* 66: 1303–1312

Brinkhaus, B., M. Lindner, D. Schuppan and E. G. Hahn (2000) 'Chemical, pharmacological and clinical profile of the East Asian medical plant *Centella asiatica*', *Phytomedicine* 7: 427–448

Bui Minh Duc (1986) 'Study on the nutritive value and the utilization of wild vegetables in Vietnam'. In *Proceedings of the International Conference on Applied Nutrition*, Hanoi: The National Institute of Nutrition and UNICEF, pp326–334

Chambers, R. (1990) *Micro Environments Unobserved*, IIED Gatekeeper Series No 22, London: International Institute of Environment and Development

Chambers, R. and G. Conwey (1992) *Sustainable Rural Livelihoods: Practical Concepts for the 21st Century*, IDS Discussion Paper 296, Falmer: Institute of Development Studies

Chan, K., M. , W. Islam, M. Kamil, R. Radhakrishnan, M. N. Zakaria, M. Habibullah and A. Attas (2000) 'The analgesic and anti-inflammatory effects of *Portulaca oleracea* L.', *Journal of Ethnopharmacology* 73: 445–451

Chandra, R. K. (1999) 'Nutrition and immunology: From the clinic to cellular biology and back again', *Proceedings of the Nutrition Society* 58: 681–683

Chang, I. M. (1998) 'Liver-protective activities of aucubin derived from traditional oriental medicine', *Research Communications on Molecular and Pathological Pharmacology* 102: 189–204

Colley, S. (2000) 'Sisters are doing it for themselves? Gender, feminism, and Australian "aboriginal" archaeology'. In M. Donald and L. Hurcombe (eds) *Gender and Material Culture an Archaeological Perspective*, New York: Macmillan Press, pp20–32

Craig, W. J. (1999) 'Health-promoting properties of common herbs', *American Journal of Clinical Nutrition* 70: S491–S499

Dahlberg, F. (ed.) (1981) *Woman the Gatherer*, New Haven: Yale University Press

Daniggelis, E. (2003) 'Women and "wild" foods: Nutrition and household security among Rai and Sherpa forager-farmers in eastern Nepal'. In P. L. Howard (ed.) *Women & Plants: Relations in Biodiversity Management and Conservation*, New York and London: Zed Books and St Martin's Press, pp83–97

Denes, A. (1998) 'Exploring the links between foraging and household food security: A gender-based study of foraging activities in Salavan Province, Lao PDR', unpublished masters thesis, University of Oregon, Eugene

Doan Du Dat, Nguyen Ngoc Ham, Doan Huy Khac, Nguyen Thi Lam, Phan Tong Son, Nguyen Van Dau, M. Grabe, R. Johansson, G. Lindgren and N. E. Stjernström (1992) 'Studies on the individual and combined diuretic effect of four Vietnamese traditional herbal remedies (*Zea mays, Imperata cylindrica, Plantago major* and *Orthosiphon stamineus*)', *Journal of Ethnopharmacology* 36 (3): 255–231

Dufour, D. L. and W. M. Wilson (1994) 'Characteristics of "wild" plant foods used by indigenous populations in Amazonia'. In N. Etkin (ed.) *Eating on the Wild Side*, Tucson and London: University of Arizona Press, pp114–142

Ertug, F. (2003) 'Gendering the tradition of plant gathering in Central Anatolia (Turkey)'. In P. L. Howard (ed.) *Women & Plants: Gender Relations in Biodiversity Management and Conservation*, New York and London: Zed Books and St Martin's Press, pp183–196

Estioko-Griffin, A. and P. B. Griffin (1981) 'The Agata'. In F. Dahlberg (ed.) *Woman the Gatherer*, New Haven: Yale University Press, pp121–151

Etkin, N. (1994) 'The cull of the wild'. In N. L. Etkin (ed.) *Eating on the Wild Side*, Tucson and London: University of Arizona Press, pp1–21

Etkin, N. and P. J. Ross (1994) 'Pharmacological implications of "wild" plants in the Hausa diet'. In N. L. Etkin (ed.) *Eating on the Wild Side*, Tucson and London: University of Arizona Press, pp85–101

FAO (2005) *State of the World's Forests 2005*, Rome: Food and Agriculture Organization

FAO and UNDP (2004) *African-Asian Agriculture against AIDS. Consultation on Agriculture, Development and HIV-vulnerability Reduction*, Food and Agriculture Organization & United Nations Development Programme, Bangkok: UNDP and Rome: FAO

Foppes, J. and S. Ketphanh (1997) 'The use of non-timber forest products in Lao PDR', paper presented at the workshop on Protected Area Management, Xishuangbanna, 3–8 November, www.mekonginfo.org/mrc_en/doclib.nsf/0/EEC6C5A20B599D 37802566FF005A61B5/$FILE/FULLTEXT.html (accessed 25 May 2007)

Galt, A. H., and J. W. Galt (1976) 'Peasant use of some wild plants on the island of Pantelleria, Sicily', *Economic Botany* 31: 20–26

Ganjanapan, A. (1992) 'Community forestry in northern Thailand: Learning from local practices'. In H. Wood and W. H. H. Mellink (eds) *Sustainable and Effective Management Systems for Community Forestry*, Proceedings of workshop, Bangkok, Thailand, January, Bangkok: Regional Community Forestry Training Center, pp83–88

General Stastics Office Vietnam (2002) Vietnam Living Standards Survey (VHLSS), Hanoi: General Statistics Office of Vietnam, www.gso.gov.vn (accessed 16 June 2007)

Gessler, M. and U. Hodel (1997) *In Situ Conservation of Plant Genetic Resources in Home Gardens in Southern Vietnam*, Selangor Darul Ehsan, Malaysia: International Plant Genetic Resources Institute

Goebel, A. (2003) 'Gender and entitlements in the Zimbabwean woodlands: A case study of resettlements'. In P. L. Howard (ed.) *Women & Plants: Relations in Biodiversity Management and Conservation*, New York and London: Zed Books and St Martin's Press, pp115–129

Golden, M. (1996) 'Severe malnutrition'. In *Oxford Textbook of Human Health*, Washington: Island Press, pp1278–1296

Grandstaff, S., T. B. Grandstaff, P. Rathakette, D. E. Thomas, and J. K. Thomas (1986) 'Trees in paddy fields in northeast Thailand'. In G. E. Marten (ed.) *Traditional Agriculture in Southeast Asia*, Boulder: Westview Press, pp273–292

Grivetti, L. E. and B. M. Ogle (2000) 'Value of traditional foods in meeting macro and micro nutrient needs: The wild plant connection', *Nutrition Research Reviews* 13: 31–46

Hetland, G., A. B. Samuelsen, M. Lovik, B. S. Poulsen, I. S. Aaberge, E. C. Groeng and T. E. Michelsen (2000) 'Protective effect of *Plantago major* L. pectin polysaccharide against systemic *Streptococcus pneumoniae* infection in mice', *Scandinavian Journal of Immunology* 52: 348–355

Heywood, V. (1999) *Use and Potential of Wild Plants in Farm Households*, FAO Farm Systems Management Series 15, Rome: FAO, www.fao.org/documents/show_cdr.asp?url_file=/DOCREP/003/W8801E/w8801e00. htm (accessed 25 May 2007)

Howard, P. (2003) 'Women and the plant world: An exploration'. In P. L. Howard (ed.) *Women & Plants: Gender Relations in Biodiversity Management and Conservation*, New York and London: Zed Books and St Martin's Press, pp1–48

Hrdy, S. B. (1981) *The Woman that Never Evolved*, Cambridge, Massachusetts and London England: Harvard University Press

Huss-Ashmore, R. and J. J. Curry (1991) 'Diet, nutrition, and agricultural development in Swaziland. Part 2: Patterns of food consumption', *Ecology of Food and Nutrition* 26:167–185

Ireson, C. (1997). 'Women's forest work in Laos'. In C. E. Sachs (ed.) *Women Working in the Environment*, Washington DC and London: Taylor & Francis, pp15–29

Jackson, C. (1993) 'Doing what comes naturally? Women and environment and development', *World Development* 21: 1947–1963

Johnson, N. and L. E. Grivetti (2002) 'Environmental changes in northern Thailand: Impact on wild edible plant availability', *Ecology of Food and Nutrition* 41: 373–399

Keeley, L. (1995). 'Protoagricultural practices among hunter-gatherers: A cross-cultural survey'. In T. Douglas Price and A. B. Gerbauer (eds) *Last Hunters First Farmers: New*

Perspectives on the Prehistoric Transition to Agriculture, Santa Fe: New School of American Research Press, pp95–126

Lampe, J. W. (1999) 'Health effects of vegetables and fruit: Assessing mechanisms of action in human experimental studies', *American Journal of Clinical Nutrition* 70: S475–S490

Layton, R., R. Foley and E. Williams (1991) 'The transition between hunting and gathering and the specialized husbandry of resources', *Current Anthropology* 32, 3: 255–274

Le Van Truyen and Nguyen Gia Chan (1999) *Selected Medicinal Plants in Vietnam*, Volume I-II, National Institute of Materia Medica. Hanoi, Vietnam: Science and Technology Publishing House

Lyndon, W. and S. Yongvanit (1995) 'Biological diversity and community lore in northeastern Thailand', *Journal of Ethnobiology* 15 (1): 71–87

Luo-Ping, Ger, Ambrose A. Chiang, Ruay-Sheng Lai, Su-Mei Chen and Ching-Jiunn Tseng (1997) 'Association of *Sauropus androgynus* and bronchiolitis obliterans syndrome: A hospital case control study', *American Journal of Epidemiology* 145: 842–849

Magalães, J. F. G., C. F. G. Viana, A. G. Aragao Jr., V. G. Moraez, R. A. Ribeiro and M. R. Vale (1997) 'Analgesic and antiinflammatory activities of *Ageratum conyzoides* in rats', *Phytotherapy Research* 11: 183–188

Malaza, M. (2003) 'Modernization and gender dynamics in the loss of agrobiodiversity in Swaziland's food system'. In P. L. Howard (ed.) *Women & Plants: Relations in Biodiversity Management and Conservation*, New York and London: Zed Books and St Martin's Press, pp243–257

Midmore, D. J., V. Niñez and R. Venkataraman (1991) *Household Gardening Projects in Asia: Past Experience and Future Directions*, AVRDC Technical Bulletin No. 19, Taiwan: Asian Vegetable Research and Development Center

More, T. A., J. R. Averill and T. H. Stevens (1996) 'Values and economics in environmental management: A perspective and critique', *Journal of Environmental Management* 48 (4): 397–409

Moreno-Black, G. and L. L. Price (1993) 'The Marketing of gathered food as an economic strategy of women in northeast Thailand', *Human Organization* 52: 398–404

Moreno-Black, G. and P. Somnasang (2000) 'In times of plenty and times of scarcity: Nondomesticated food in northeastern Thailand', *Ecology of Food and Nutrition* 38: 563–586

Moreno-Black, G., S. Prapimporn and S. Thamathawan (1996) 'Cultivating continuity and creating change: Women's home garden practices in northeast Thailand', *Agriculture and Human Values* 13 (3): 11

Nakahara, K. and G. Trakoontivakorn (1999) 'Antioxidative and antimutagenic properties of some local agricultural products in Thailand'. In M. Suzuki and S. Ando (eds) *Highlight of Collaborative Research Activities between Thai Research Organizations and JIRCAS*, JIRCAS Seminar, Bangkok, pp141–143

Nakahara, K., M. Onishi-Kameyama, H. Ono, M. Yoshida and G. Trakoontivakorn (2001) 'Antimutagenic activity against Trp-P-1 of the edible Thai plant, *Oroxylum indicum* vent', *Biosciences, Biotechnology, and Biochemistry* 65: 2358–2560

Ngarmsak, T. (1987) 'Status and nutritional importance of unconventional food crops in Thai diets', report submitted to the FAO Regional Office for Asia and the Pacific, Bangkok: Food and Agriculture Organization

Nguyen Nhut Xuan Dung (1996) 'Identification and evaluation of noncultivated plants used for livestock feed in the Mekong Delta of Vietnam', unpublished masters thesis, Uppsala: Swedish University of Agricultural Sciences pp1–84

Nguyen Tien Ban and Bui Minh Duc (eds) (1994) *Wild Edible Vegetables in Vietnam*, Hanoi: People's Army Publishing House

Niehof, A. and L. L. Price (2001) 'Rural livelihood systems: A conceptual framework', No. 5, UPWARD Working Paper Series, Wageningen University and User's Perspective in Agricultural Research and Development (CIP-UPWARD), Wageningen: Wageningen University

Nordeide, M. B., A. Hatloy, M. Folling, E. Lied and A. Oshaug (1996) 'Nutrient composition and nutritional importance of green leaves and wild food resources in an agricultural district, Koutiala, in Southern Mali', *International Journal of Food Sciences and Nutrition* 6: 455–468

NTCP (2005) 'Ethnic groups on the Nakai Plateau'. In *Vol. 2: Nakai Plateau-EMDP and RAP, Social Development Plan Final Draft*, March 2005, Vientiane: Nam Theun 3 Power Company Limited [NTCP], www.namtheun2.com/gallery/libr_sdp/ newversion/Volume%202/Chapter%203%20Ethnic%20Groups%20on%20the% 20Nakai%20Plateau.pdf (accessed 25 May 2007)

Ogle, B. M. (2001a) 'Wild vegetables and micronutrient nutrition: Studies on the significance of wild vegetables in women's diets in Vietnam', doctoral dissertation, Uppsala University Sweden, http://publications.uu.se/abstract.xsql?dbid=694 (accessed 25 May 2007)

Ogle, B. M., Ha Thi Anh Dao, G. Mulokozi and L. Hambraeus (2001b) 'Micronutrient composition and nutritional importance of gathered vegetables in Vietnam', *International Journal of Food Science and Nutrition* 52: 485–499

Ogle, B. M., M. Johansson, Ho Thi Tuyet and L. Johanneson (2001c) 'Evaluating the significance of dietary folate from wild vegetables in Vietnam', *Asia Pacific Journal of Clinical Nutrition* 10 (3): 216–221

Ogle, B. M., N. N. Xuan Dung, T. T. Do and L. Hambraeus (2001d) 'The contribution of naturally occurring vegetables to micronutrient intakes among women: An example from the Mekong Delta, Vietnam', *Ecology of Food and Nutrition* 40: 159–184

Ogle, B. M., Pham Huang Hung and Ho Thi Tuyet (2001e) 'The significance of wild vegetables in micronutrient intakes of women in Vietnam. An analysis of food variety', *Asia Pacific Journal of Clinical Nutrition* 10 (3): 21–30

Ogle, B. M. and L. E. Grivetti (1985) 'Legacy of the chameleon: Edible wild plants in the Kingdom of Swaziland, southern Africa. A cultural, ecological, nutritional study. Part IV – nutritional analysis and conclusions', *Ecology of Food and Nutrition* 17: 41–64

Ogle, B. M., H. T. Tuyet, H. N. Duyet and N. N. X. Dung (2003) 'Food, feed or medicine: The multiple functions of edible wild plants in Vietnam', *Economic Botany* 1: 103–117

Ogoye-Ndegwa, C. and J. Aagaard-Hansen (2006) 'Dietary and medicinal use of traditional herbs among the Luo of western Kenya'. In A. Pieroni and L. L. Price (eds) *Eating and Healing: Traditional Food as Medicine*, Binghamton, New York: Haworth Press, pp323–344

Pardo de Santayana, M., E. San Migueal and R. Morales (2006) 'Digestive beverages as a medicinal food in a cattle-farming community in northern Spain'. In A. Pieroni and L. L. Price (eds) *Eating and Healing: Traditional Food as Medicine*, Binghamton, New York: Haworth Press, pp131–148

Perlman, D. L. and G. Adelson (1997) *Biodiversity: Exploring Values and Priorities in Conservation*, Malden, Massachusetts: Blackwell Science

Perumal Samy, R., S. Ignacimuthu and D. P. Raja (1999) 'Preliminary screening of ethnomedicinal plants from India', *Journal of Ethnopharmacology* 66: 235–240

Pieroni, A. (1999) 'Gathered wild food plants in the upper valley of the Serchio River (Garfagnana), Central Italy', *Economic Botany* 3: 327–341

Pieroni, A. (2003) 'Wild food plants and Arbëresh women in Lucania, Southern Italy'. In P. L. Howard (ed.) *Women & Plants: Relations in Biodiversity Management and Conservation*, New York and London: Zed Books and St. Martin's Press, pp66–82

Pieroni, A. and C. L. Quave (2006) 'Functional foods or food medicines? On the consumption of wild plants among Albanians and southern Italians in Lucania'. In A. Pieroni and L. L. Price (eds) *Eating and Healing: Traditional Food as Medicine*, Binghamton, New York: Haworth Press, pp101–130

Pieroni, A., S. Nebel, C. Quave, H. Munz and M. Heinrich (2002) 'Ethnopharmacology of *Liakra*: Traditional weedy vegetables of the Arbershe of the Vultura area in southern Italy', *Journal of Ethnopharmacology* 81: 165–185

Pradipasen, M., R. Charoenpong, P. Temcharoen and Y. Porapakkham (1985) *Nangrong Dietary Survey*, Nakorn Pathom, Thailand: Institute for Population and Social Research, Mahidol University

Price, L. L. (1997) 'Wild plant food in agricultural environments: A study of occurrence, management and gathering rights in northeast Thailand', *Human Organization* 2: 209–221

Price, L. L. (2000) 'The fields are full of gold: Women's marketing of wild foods from rice fields in Southeast Asia and the impacts of pesticides and integrated pest management'. In A. Spring (ed.) *Women Farmers and Commercial Ventures: Increasing Food Security in Developing Countries*, Boulder: Lynne Rienner Publishers, pp191–207

Price, L. L. (2003) 'Farm women's rights and roles in wild plant food gathering and management in northeast Thailand'. In P. L. Howard (ed.) *Women & Plants: Relations in Biodiversity Management and Conservation*, New York and London: Zed Books and St Martin's Press, pp101–114

Price, L. L. (2006) '"Wild" food plants in farming environments with special reference to northeast Thailand, food as functional and medicinal, and the social roles of women'. In A. Pieroni and L. L. Price (eds) *Eating and Healing: Traditional Food as Medicine*, Binghamton, New York: Haworth Press, pp65–100

Price, L. L. and F. Palis (1998) 'Transformation in entitlements: Land ownership and farming culture in Vietnam', *Culture and Agriculture* 20 (1): 12–20

Primack, R. B. (2002) *Essentials of Conservation Biology*, Sunderland, Massachusetts: Sinauer Associates

Rocheleau, D. and D. Edmunds (1997) 'Women, men and trees: Gender, power and property in forest and agrarian landscapes', *World Development* 8: 1351–1371

Ruay-Sheng Lai, A. A., M. T. Chiang, J. S. Wu, N. S. Wang, J. Y. Lai, L. P. Lu and V. Roggli (1996) Outbreak of bronchiolitis obliterans associated with consumption of *Sauropus androgynes* in Taiwan, *The Lancet* 348: 83–85

Sampson J. H., J. D. Philipson, N. G. Bowery, M. J. O'Neill, J. G. Houston and J. A. Lewis (2000) 'Ethnomedicinally selected plants as sources of potential analgesic compounds. Indication of in vitro biological activity in receptor binding assays', *Phytotherapy Research* 14: 24–29

Schenk-Sandbergen, L., H. Rodenburg and C. Phengkhay (1997) 'Land, gender and social issues in Lao PDR: Towards gender sensitive land titling', background study funded by AusAID for the Land Titling Project, Vientiane: AusAID

Scoones, I., M. Melnyk and J. N. Pretty (1992) *Hidden Harvest: Wild Foods and Agricultural Systems. A Literature Review and Annotated Bibliography*, International Institute for Environment and Development and Swedish International Development Agency

Scudder, T. (1971) *Gathering Among African Woodland Savannah Cultivators: A Case Study: The Gwembe Tonga*, No. 5, Zambian papers, Manchester: Manchester University Press, Manchester [for] University of Zambia, Institute for African Studies

Shukla, A., A. M. Rasik, G. K. Jain, R. Shankar, D. K. Kuhlshrestha and B.N. Dhawan (1999) 'In vitro and in vivo wound healing activity of asiaticoside isolated *Centella asiatica*', *Journal of Ethnopharmacology* 65: 1–11

Silva, M. J., F. R. Capez and M. R. Vale (2000) 'Effects of water soluble fraction from leaves of *Ageratum cynozoides* on smooth muscle', *Phytotherapy Research* 14: 130–132

Somnasang, P. (1996) 'Indigenous food use: Gender issues in rural northeast Thailand', unpublished doctoral dissertation, Department of Anthropology, University of Oregon

Somnasang, P., P. Rathakette, P. and S. Rathanapanya (1987) 'The role of natural foods in northeast Thailand'. In S. Subhadira, G. Lovelace and S. Simarap (eds) *Rapid Rural Appraisal in Northeast Thailand: Case Studies,* Khon Kaen University, Khon Kaen, Thailand: KKU-FORD Rural Systems Research Project, pp78–103

Somnasang, P., G. Moreno-Black and K. Chusil (1998) 'Indigenous knowledge of wild food hunting and gathering in northeast Thailand', *Food and Nutrition Bulletin* 19 (4): 359–365

Swift, J. (1993) 'Understanding and preventing famine and famine mortality', *IDS Bulletin* 24 (4): 1–16

Tontisirin, K., J. Yhoung-aree, S. Chantapiromsuk, K. Chuncherd, P. Tontiwattanasatien, X. Srianujata and A. Suksangpleng (1986) *Annual Report 1985/1986: Thailand Food Habits,* Bangkok: ASEAN Sub-Committee on Protein: Food Habits, ASEAN-Australian Economic Cooperation Program

Trakoontivakorn, G. (2002) 'Application of value-adding technologies in Thailand', Proceedings of the 9th JIRCAS International Symposium 2002 Value-Addition to Agricultural Products, pp130–134

Turner, N. (2003) 'Passing on the news': Women's work, traditional knowledge and plant resource management in indigenous societies of north-western North America'. In P. L. Howard (ed.) *Women & Plants: Relations in Biodiversity Management and Conservation,* New York and London: Zed Books and St Martin's Press, pp133–149

Turner, N. and H. Clifton (2006) '"The Forest and the seaweed": Gitgaát seaweed, traditional ecological knowledge, and community survival'. In A. Pieroni and L. L. Price (eds) *Eating and Healing: Traditional Food as Medicine,* Binghamton, New York: Haworth Press Project, pp153–178

UNEP (2006) 'Biological diversity, nutrition and health – a cross cutting initiative', *Convention for Biological Diversity,* www.biodiv.org/programmes/areas/agro/food-nutrition/default.shtml (accessed 9 June 2007)

UN Volunteers (2004) 'Vietnamese land use certificates must now bear both husband and wife names', *Volunteer Voices,* http://dynamic.unv.org/infobase/voices/2004/vietnam.htm (accessed 25 May 2007)

Vainio-Mattila, K. (2000) 'Wild vegetables used by the Sambaa in the Usambara Mountains, NE Tanzania', *Annales Botanici Fennici* 37 (1): 57–67

Waguespack, N. M. (2005) 'The organization of male and female labor in foraging societies: Implications for Early Paleoindian archaeology', *American Anthropologist* 4: 666–676

Wiersum, K. F. (1996) 'Indigenous exploitation and management of tropical forest resources: An evolutionary continuum in forest-people interactions', *Agriculture, Ecosystems & Environment* 63: 1–16

Wiersum, K. F. (1997) 'From natural forest to tree crops, co-domestication of forests and tree species: An overview', *Netherlands Journal of Agricultural Science* 45: 425–438

Wilken, G. (1970) 'The ecology of gathering in a Mexican farming region', *Economic Botany* 24: 286–295

Winterhalder, B. and E. A. Smith (2000) 'Analyzing adaptive strategies: Human behavioral ecology at twenty-five', *Evolutionary Anthropology* 9: 51–72

WHO and Institute of Materia Medica (1990) 'Medical plants in Vietnam', WHO Regional Publications, Western Pacific Series No. 3, Manila, Hanoi: Institute of Materia Medica

Xiu, Y. M. (1996) 'Trace elements in health and diseases', *Biomedical Environmental Sciences* 9: 130–136

Zihlman, A. L. and N. Tanner (1978) 'Gathering and hominid adaptation'. In L. Tiger and H. Fowler (eds) *Female Hierarchies*, Chicago: Beresford Book Service, pp163–194

Chapter 12

Religion, Gender and the Environment in Asia: Moving Beyond the Essentialisms of Spiritual Ecofeminism?

Emma Tomalin

Introduction

Development research, policy and practice have typically avoided engagement with considerations of religion and spirituality (Sweetman, 1999; Ver Beek, 2002; Selinger, 2004); this is so of major world religions and indigenous religions alike. While the persistence of religious forms across the globe would seem to challenge versions of secularization that predict the disappearance of religion with modernization, social scientists working in the field of development have tended to overlook the influence of religion on individuals and societies. They tend to 'see in religious conviction an eclipse of reason and in religious motivation a constraint on enlightened social behaviour' (Candland, 2000, pp129–130) and instead focus on 'practical, technical, or material' concerns (Sweetman, 1999, p3). Underlying this avoidance is the implicit assumption that religion will decline as communities modernize, and a wariness of engaging with religious issues that are frequently political and potentially socially divisive.

Nevertheless, the relevance of religion to development is arguably substantial, having both a positive and negative impact. For instance, faith-based organizations are often relied on to provide basic services in situations where the private sector and the state have failed. They can provide a source of social capital formation through linking people together in a common belief as well as supporting initiatives that may generate 'higher levels of education, literacy, health, employment, and other public goods that increase social opportunity' (Candland, 2000, p357). Moreover, the emphasis that the contemporary development project places on material or economic development is often criticized for ignoring the importance of 'spirituality' for human flourishing. Nussbaum (2000, p179), for instance, points towards the way in which religious belief and practice can enhance the search for 'an understanding of the ultimate meaning of life', whereas Verhelst and Tyndale (2002, p3) suggest that 'as all religions would confirm, to become fully human is more than a matter of improving one's material condition'.

But religion can also have a negative influence on social and economic development where religious values play a role in shaping and maintaining social hierarchy and exclusion. The extent to which religion can limit women's empowerment, for instance, has been well documented, from the reluctance of some forms of religion to allow women to assume positions of responsibility within religious and social institutions, to the ways in which religious values often define women in terms of their domestic responsibilities. Nevertheless, such studies of religion and gender have also attracted criticism from those who argue that the existence of 'difference' between the genders is not necessarily problematic.

The argument that men and women are 'equal yet different' is articulated by some 'religious feminists'.[1] They argue that according to their religious traditions, men and women are intended to have different social roles but that these roles are considered to be equally important.[2] This understanding of feminism presents difficulties to the dominant approach within gender analysis that maintains the social constructedness of all gendered difference and that tends to emphasize the ways in which difference can be used to justify oppression or subordination. However, the type of gender equality pursued by Western, secular feminists is often perceived as a post-colonial imposition that fails to account for local and varied socio-cultural systems, often underpinned by religious norms (see Donaldson and Pui-Lan, 2002).

The complexity and sensitivity of such debates around gender and religion is perhaps another reason why development has avoided engagement with religious issues. It has proved difficult and controversial enough for Western social scientists to challenge gender hierarchies in non-Western contexts, frequently attracting charges of imperialism and lack of cultural sensitivity. However, to directly engage in a debate that might imply that religious traditions are errant in their understandings of the roles and status of the sexes, is to challenge what many people take as divine ordinance (a 'given') rather than constructions emerging from patriarchal interests. Nevertheless, an understanding of religious traditions as reflecting patriarchal interests (in terms of promoting particular understandings of texts and traditions that subordinate and may lead to the oppression of women) is voiced from various women's movements in both developed and developing countries. While there has perhaps been a tendency for 'secular feminism' to reject religious traditions when they are considered to oppress women, we also find the emergence of styles of 'religious feminism' where women seek to transform their religious traditions as a source of empowerment. Although various expressions of religious feminism have directed their attention to development issues there is still a relatively undeveloped research interest within this area.

One place, however, where issues of gender, religion and development have been explored is within ecofeminism. Although ecofeminism is not a unified system of thought, reflecting different feminist perspectives (such as liberal, Marxist or socialist), its various expressions do share the view that 'there are important connections between the domination of women (and other human subordinates) and the domination of nature, *and* that a failure to recognize these connections results in an inadequate feminism, environmentalism, and environmental philosophy' (Wilson, 2005, pp333–334; see also Warren, 1996).

For the purposes of this chapter, I am interested to explore the contribution of 'spiritual' or 'cultural' ecofeminism[3] to understandings of the relationship between women and the environment. Whereas liberal feminism, for instance, considers that gender difference is socially constructed, cultural feminism views men and women as essentially different in personality and nature as well as biology. Its emancipatory vision is based on the notion that female empowerment should involve the celebration of female difference rather than its erasure (as in liberal feminism). Cultural/spiritual ecofeminists draw attention to the fact that cross-culturally, women's physiology and social roles have tended to bring them into closer contact with nature than men. However, this closeness of women to nature is considered to be inherent rather than socially constructed and, as Merchant (1992, p191) writes, one way of reclaiming both women and nature from patriarchal oppression is thought to be 'the revival of ancient rituals centered on goddess worship, the moon, animals, and the female reproductive system'. So a key feature of cultural ecofeminism is the promotion of distinct styles of female spirituality associated with nature.[4]

This type of ecofeminism has been criticized for promoting an essentialism that locks women into particular roles and relationships associated with their biology. While spiritual ecofeminists are wont to look to religio-cultural traditions that lie outside the Christian West (which stress the imminence of the divine, particularly the worship of the Goddess including various expressions of 'Mother Earth'), as evidence for the existence of matriarchal religion, this reasoning has been challenged. Moreover, some critics have argued that spiritual ecofeminism is actually a reflection of 'white' feminist religiosity: the confluence of a romanticized post-materialist environmentalism with modern styles of 'deregulated' feminist spirituality (Smith, 1997).[5] Detailed critiques have been made elsewhere (see for instance, Biehl, 1991; Jackson, 1994, 2001) and in the following section I only outline some of the main contours of the debate. Despite the existence of rigorous critique of cultural ecofeminism, from the point of view of this volume, the key assumption that women have a special bond with nature has shaped and continues to influence approaches to women and environmental resource management within mainstream development theory and practice (Green et al, 1998; Leach, 2007).

My main interest in spiritual ecofeminism is that it has captured discussions about the relationship between women, religion and environmental resource use and management. There has been little attempt in other academic, activist or policy literature to consider the ways in which gendered natural resource use and management is cross-cut by issues of religious and cultural attachment. The discussion presented in this chapter is therefore more conceptual and reflective than other contributions in this volume. While I draw on existing empirical studies where relevant, I aim to discuss the theoretical usefulness of religion for understanding the actual relations of women and men with their environment rather than focusing on new empirical material. I conclude with some suggestions for the directions that an informed research agenda on gender, religion and the environment could take.

If ecofeminism really is a 'white feminist' discourse then it is important to find ways of moving beyond the narrow essentialisms of spiritual and cultural ecofeminism to find alternative ways of thinking through the relationship between religion, gender and environmental resource management. I argue here that women's religious identities are significant to a gender analysis of natural resource management in a variety of ways. Thus, a rejection of the ecofeminist assumption that women are spiritually 'in tune' with the natural world ought not to result in a rejection of the significance of religion to understanding the gendered nature of resource management.

Spiritual and cultural ecofeminism: Characteristics, critiques and influence

In his seminal article, 'The historical roots of our ecological crisis', Lynn White Jr (1967) argued that the displacement of paganism by Christianity led to the 'desacralization' of nature. Whereas paganism was intimately tied to nature through the worship of immanent forms of the Goddess, the Christian God was seen as transcendent to creation and humanity and was granted dominion over the natural world. This monumental shift, he argued, opened the way for humans to begin the domestication and transformation of nature. On the one hand, the growth of science was predicated on the desire to understand God's 'mind' and, on the other hand, the development of technologies to manipulate the natural world were an 'Occidental, voluntarist realization of the Christian dogma of man's transcendence of, and rightful mastery over, nature' (White, 1967, p1206). In tracing the roots of the contemporary environmental crisis to the union of science and technology in the 19th century, which created the conditions for the industrial revolution, White (1967, p1206) concludes that 'more science and more technology are not going to get us out of the present ecological crisis until we find a new religion, or rethink our old one'. He suggests that Eastern religious traditions, such as Zen Buddhism, hold a holistic view of the humanity–nature relationship (Callicott and Aimes, 1991), or that a stewardship model, which draws on the example of St Francis of Assisi, subverts and challenges dominant attitudes towards nature, which are 'deeply grounded in Christian dogma' (White, 1967, p1207).

Spiritual/cultural ecofeminists would agree with much of White's argument, but specifically aim to 'revive' a woman-focused or feminist religiosity.

Consequently, cultural ecofeminism draws on various expressions of 'nature religion' involving the worship of immanent forms of the feminine divine. This is a source of women's empowerment as well as a strategy for environmental protection. Cultural ecofeminists are concerned not only that patriarchal religion, modes of production and technological developments have been devastating for nature, but also for women. The work of feminist archaeologists and historians such as Marija Gimbutas (1982, 1989) and Gerda Lerner (1986) provides some of the groundwork for this analysis through their reconstructions of the historical record as providing evidence for Neolithic, Earth Goddess matriarchies that were eventually deposed by militaristic, patriarchal cultural systems. Anthropological studies that are concerned with goddess or nature worshipping tribal or indigenous cultures are similarly interpreted as providing evidence of societies that have not quite lost or given up their matriarchal origins (Wilson, 2005). Thus, within this spiritual ecofeminist literature, there is also a tendency to assume that goddess worship is a vestige of matriarchy, of cultures that afforded a high status not only to the feminine divine but also to females. This reasoning has been vigorously challenged. Jackson (2001, pp32–33) argues that:

> *Cultures where goddesses have been prominent have hardly been matricentric... Furthermore, ecofeminist interpretation of goddesses selectively emphasizes harmony and nurturance ... although a widely known aspect of goddess cultures is that 'human sacrifice is everywhere characteristic of the worship of the Goddess'.*

While this feminist version of history has been widely discredited (Meskell, 1995), it continues to inform spiritual ecofeminist understandings that women have a special or 'spiritual' bond with nature. With respect to the Hindu tradition, the Indian ecofeminist Vandana Shiva (1988, p38) makes this link explicit in her writing when she argues that 'women in India are an intimate part of nature, both in imagination and in practice. At one level, nature is symbolized as the embodiment of the feminine principle, and at another, she is nurtured by the feminine to produce life and provide sustenance.' Shiva considers that women are closer to nature because nature (*prakriti*) is seen as feminine in the Hindu tradition. Hindu philosophical traditions consider that there are two principles in the universe: *purusha*, which is male/non-material/'self' or 'soul'/static, and *prakriti*, which is female/nature/dynamic.[6] For Shiva, the 'death of the feminine principle' is equated with 'mal-development', the introduction of Western modes of development into the 'Third World', particularly intensive agriculture. Many ecofeminists, thus, re-evaluate what they see as a myth of patriarchal progress and instead envisage a return to small-scale, agricultural communities that worship the Earth Goddess, and in which women's natural inclination to work with nature rather than against it is permitted to flourish. Even where the antipathy towards modern progress is less extreme there is still a tendency to see non-Western religious traditions as 'free of the nature–culture dualism which is believed to underpin the oppression of both women and nature in Western history and thought, and the absence of which is thought to engender positive and sustainable relations between peoples and their environments in many non-Western societies' (Jackson, 2001, p23; see also Merchant, 1982; Plumwood, 1986; Warren, 1987).[7]

This tendency to oversimplify the way that religion informs people's relationship to the environment has been widely criticized for sustaining an unhelpful orientalist construction of the myth of primitive ecological wisdom (Milton, 1996) that 'tells us far more about the Western commentator and his [sic] desires than about the East' (Guha, 1989b, p77; see also Inden, 1986; Tomalin, 2002, 2004). If cultural ecofeminism, then, is also a style of what Baviskar (2002), has called 'bourgeois environmentalism', its usefulness as a model with which to approach the relationship between religion, gender and the environment is limited. Nevertheless, the hegemony of discourses about poor women's 'primitive ecological wisdom' is also apparent within development approaches to women and the environment. As Leach (2007, p67–68) argues:

> *The woman carrying firewood across a barren landscape has become an environment and development icon. Reproduced in policy reports, NGO glossies and academic books alike, her image encapsulates powerful and appealing messages... These material dimensions were bolstered by fables about women's natural, cultural or ideological closeness to nature; varieties of 'earth mother' myths which could be, and were, used to justify women's roles, as well as to give cultural and political appeal to the notion of global environmental sisterhoods.*

While Leach considers that such myths are receding, it is no longer *de rigueur* to depict women as natural carers, a view that has permeated development thinking to such a large degree that it is still evident in policy and programmes to this day. For instance, UNEP's manual 'Women and Environment' (2004) promotes the tapping of women's and local people's productivist and participatory potentials to ensure efficient and supposedly sustainable use of resources (Mosse, 2003). While this type of development discourse does not directly invoke the religious and spiritual symbolism that underpins cultural ecofeminism, it is uncritical about the extent to which portrayals of poor women as having shared concerns about 'sustainable' resources, for which they are inherently inclined to collectively mobilize or cooperate, are myth or fact. However, the virtual normalization of the notion of women as natural carers is arguably a product of the cultural ecofeminist tendency to embed this blatant biological determinism within vague and decontextualized interpretations of Eastern or pagan religio-cultural traditions.

Leach (2007) and others have drawn attention to the failure of this dominant WED approach to accommodate thinking about gender. Pearson (2000, p392) writes that:

> *The WED approach highlights the specific relationship women have with the environment as the main users and managers of natural resources at the local level. It starts with an acceptance of gender roles and gender*

division of labour and focuses on women who are hewers of fuelwood and haulers of water and who play a major (if unacknowledged) role as cultivators. Like WID itself, WED focuses on women rather than on gender relations.

WED interventions have typically involved an emphasis on women-centred environmental/conservation projects, including women-focused social forestry, agroforestry, soil and water conservation projects, fuel-efficient stoves and solar cookers (see chapter by Buchy and Rai in this volume). However, as Jackson (1994) points out, these projects tend to treat women's time and labour as flexible and inexhaustible, and often just add to their other tasks. Fuel-efficient stoves, for instance, may create more work for women, as they need tending and are unsafe for small children (Jackson, 1994). Moreover, there is an assumption that women are naturally in favour of 'sustainable development', when women in many cases have benefited from the Green Revolution. WED has been criticized for treating traditional gender roles as natural and for rarely involving women in decision-making processes. Women are commonly depicted as bearing the brunt of environmental problems but also as having a 'natural' inclination towards environmental conservation.

Since the 1980s, there has been a shift from thinking about 'women in development' to 'gender and development'.[8] But Leach (2007) argues that there has not been a parallel shift with respect to considerations of women and the environment. She expresses concern that although the 'women as natural carer' approach is no longer *de rigueur* (at least in principle) it seems to have been replaced by 'gender-blind environment and development work ... and there is rather little evidence of a more politicised, relational perspective on gender and environment taking root' (Leach, 2007, p68). A 'gender environment development' approach to looking at women and the environment would draw back from essentializing women as natural carers, and instead focus 'on the ways in which women's and men's relationship with the environment are seen to emerge from the dynamic social context of gender relations' (Pearson, 2000, p392). However, once we adopt a gender perspective, rather than one that posits essential differences between the sexes, it becomes crucial to examine the range of forces that shape gender relations and includes religion and culture. Moreover, both ecofeminism and WED have tended to focus on essentialized notions of women. A GED approach, by contrast, is concerned with the roles and relationships experienced by both women and men, and how this impacts on their interaction with the natural environment. The rest of this chapter, therefore, considers the relevance of religion to a GED approach, without falling into the ecofeminist trap.

Despite the role that religion plays in contributing to the definition of gender identities, there has been little attempt in academic, activist or policy literature to consider the ways in which that gendered natural resource use and management is cross-cut by issues of religious and cultural attachment. To date, ecofeminism has captured this issue. I argue that the limitations of cultural/spiritual ecofeminism should not mean that religious identities and faith traditions are excluded from discussions about gender and natural resource management.

While I have argued against essentialisms such as those found in ecofeminism, a number of scholars have noted their potential strategic value. Sturgeon (1999, p255), for instance, argues that the criticism of Western ecofeminists 'for appropriating the environmental activism of Third World & Native American women as "ecofeminist" and for using essentialist conceptions of these women as being closer to nature' has meant that all forms of ecofeminist discourse have been dismissed as racist and sexist. By contrast, he suggests that ecofeminism has benefited WID discourse and that 'credit should be given to Third World activists who have made use of Western ecofeminist interventions to build coalitions both horizontally and vertically in the international political arena of post-Cold-War globalizing environmentalisms' (Sturgeon, 1999, p255). Similarly, Brosius (1999) suggests that we need to distinguish between 'strategic' and 'romantic' essentialisms since 'historically marginalized communities have begun to recognize the political potency of strategically deployed essentialisms' (p281).

Having already provided a discussion about what a nexus of religion-gender-environment-development *shouldn't be* (i.e. ecofeminism), I will now examine what it could be.

Beyond the essentialisms of 'spiritual ecofeminism'

In this section, I first suggest that an understanding of how religion feeds into the ways in which a society 'genders' men and women is useful in assessing the differential use of natural resources, the differential impact of environmental degradation as well as the various options and limitations with respect to managing environmental resources. Whereas an ecofeminist position considers that women have a 'special' relationship to nature, and that this is reflected in their cultural and religious practices, a gender analysis views the situation from the opposite direction. Women are often 'locked' into a particular relationship with the natural environment due to powerful cultural beliefs about how women should behave and what their proper job is in the family. In their discussion of GED, Green et al (1998) suggest a number of ways in which women's gendered relationship to the natural environment is relevant to considerations of research and policy. They point out that 'if certain women are closely involved with natural resources, this may reflect gender-divided roles and lack of any other economic opportunity, rather than any inherent caring relationship' (Green et al, 1998, p276). Thus, an examination of the role that religio-cultural traditions play in shaping the types of social and economic activities that women and men typically engage in, within particular contexts, would aid our understanding the nature of particular gender relations that define people with respect to their biological role. Women have a relationship to the natural environment in many societies that is a reflection of their reproductive role in the household, and the recourse to religious values is one way in which this role is defined and sustained. Moreover, as Green et al (1998, p277) suggest, 'relations of tenure and property, control over resources, products, and decision-making' can also have an impact on 'people's environmental interests and opportunities'. Religio-cultural norms can be similarly active in many situations in influencing these factors.

Thus, in thinking about the nexus between religion-gender-environment-development, the first area that could usefully be investigated is the role of religion in gendering people's relations with environment. How do religio-cultural traditions inform gender relations that in turn influence the differential use of natural resources, the differential impact of environmental degradation, and the various options for and limitations on managing environmental resources? Such knowledge has both explanatory and strategic importance for environment–development initiatives. It can help account for gender differences in people's relationships to natural environment use and also guide the nature and implementation of policy and practice. In addition to this broad question, which is concerned with the ways in which religion influences land inheritance patterns or the different roles that men and women perform, it is also useful to look at the significance of particular religious beliefs and practices to both men and women's relationship with nature.

Wilson's study (2005) amongst the Anishinabek Canadian Aboriginal community suggests a role for grounded anthropological research in different contexts to understand women's (and men's) religious connections with the environment, which may not fit with the 'women as close to nature' narrative of spiritual ecofeminism nor with the tendency of social ecofeminism (and other styles of 'Western' feminism) to see women's closeness to nature as inherently oppressive. She argues for an informed ecofeminism that would 'provide some insight into women–nature connections by listening to and learning from' women as they discuss their relations to the land (Wilson, 2005, p338). Wilson is critical of spiritual ecofeminism for its unreflexive embrace of the women–nature connection. But she is also critical of social ecofeminism, which wishes to deconstruct and disrupt it. Her study draws two important conclusions that problematize both extremes within ecofeminism. First, *both* women and men are seen as spiritually close to nature 'an issue that has yet to be acknowledged within spiritual ecofeminism' (Wilson, 2005, p348). This suggests scope for further research in other contexts that investigates men's religious identification with the natural world. However, it also suggests the absence of the man–culture/woman–nature dualism on which social ecofeminism bases its critique. Thus, her second conclusion demonstrates that since the Anishinabek do not make the hierarchical distinction between men–culture/women–nature, the maintenance of an essentialist connection between women and nature does not necessarily result in a devaluation of women and their roles. In fact, she tells us that although men and women have different roles they are not seen in terms of an oppositional hierarchy. She argues that her case study of the Anishinabek actually reconciles spiritual and social ecofeminism: it 'emphasizes the maintenance of an essentialist connection between women and nature' yet 'does not reinforce a culture–nature dualism ... or a hierarchical relationship between culture and nature' (p349).

Wilson (2005, p349) emphasizes that her study should not imply that biological essentialism, which reinforces the woman–nature connection, is never oppressive, nor that all Aboriginal peoples are 'ecologically noble' (p349). But her study also illustrates that in this example religious beliefs and practices relating to the Earth do coincide with the expression of respect for nature. In response to the romanticism and essentialism associated with much literature on religion and environmentalism, however, there are now many studies (see for example, Tomalin, 2004) that point to a disjuncture between beliefs and practices associated with nature and people's actual environmental behaviour. One study that takes women's enviro-religious practices as its starting point is Nagarajan's work (1998, 2000) on 'embedded ecologies' in India. In common with ecofeminist literature, Nagarajan's research focuses on a nature-related ritual that only women engage in, yet avoids the narrow essentialism of 'Hinduism equals environmentalism' that we find in much literature on religion and the environment. She is concerned to understand the significance of the daily ritual followed by many women of drawing a *kolam* at the entrance to their homes (these are elaborate patterns traditionally made from rice flour). When women draw the *kolam* they invoke *Bhu Devi*, the Earth Goddess, who is seen as 'the physical earth, a large living being with a soul, and as the particular soil at a woman's feet' (Nagarajan, 1998, p273). However, Nagarajan writes (1998, p275) that she 'was puzzled by the contradiction between women's reverence for *Bhu Devi* and their seeming disrespect for her throughout the day, as they threw trash and garbage on the earth, the very place that they considered to be sacred'. In attempting to resolve this contradiction she makes a number of points. First, although one reason for invoking and praising Hindu deities is to purify oneself of sin, she points out that 'waste, sin and pollution collapse into a category that is seen to be absorbable by *Bhu Devi*' (p275). Thus, just as *Bhu Devi* can absorb and cope with human sin, she can also deal with material waste and pollution.[9] Second, Nagarajan observes that the sacrality of the Earth is intermittent for these women. *Bhu Devi* is sacred while they are performing their rituals, but throughout the rest of the day that sacrality is not significant.

We can conclude that although from the point of view of modern environmental concerns, the worship of nature may seem to coincide with environmentally friendly behaviour, in fact it does not. The worship of *Bhu Devi* does not mean women are environmentalists in the modern, Western or ecofeminist sense. Nagarajan asks us to contrast her view with the conclusion of Shiva (1988, p282) who assumes that, because of such behaviour, 'Hindu women have been and continue to be naturally and culturally ecological'. Shiva seems to assume uncritically that when a natural object is worshipped as divine then it will result in ecological lifestyles. The implications of Nagarajan's research are rather more pessimistic: the idea of nature as sacred does not mitigate the destruction of the environment. In fact the idea that *Bhu Devi* can cope with all forms of pollution actually acts against the interests of environmental protection. Nagarajan is not saying that practices of nature worship are irrelevant to the promotion of environmentalism but that we cannot assume that they are the same thing.[10] While 'embedded ecologies', such as the drawing of the *kolam*, do not reveal that Indian women are inherent environmentalists, they can tell us something about the ways in which women's relationship to the natural world is mediated through religious belief and practice. Spiritual ecofeminism is also concerned with this. However, it theorizes the relevance of religion to understandings of how women relate to the environment by relying on essentialisms that reflect particular Western feminist agendas, rather than an informed understanding of the various ways that religion, gender and the environment interact in different cultures (Smith, 1993, 1997; Wilson, 2005).

Both Wilson (2005) and Nagarajan (1998, 2000) suggest the importance of grounded anthropological research to understanding the ways in which religious cosmologies inform how women and men see their relationship to nature. While anthropologists have turned their attention to this type of research, it is rarely directly related to development-environment thinking, nor is it reflected in development policy and practice. Hence, the third and final area that I have selected for discussion is concerned with the role that religion plays in women's responses to environmental change, including ecological activism as well as strategies to cope with changing ecological roles and environmental disaster. It is common within cultural ecofeminist literature to find examples of women taking part in environmental protests portrayed as evidence of their spiritual bond with nature. Most notable here is the Chipko movement, which is often termed a 'woman's movement', or specifically an 'ecofeminist movement' (Shiva, 1988, p3). Other scholars have been critical of this interpretation of the movement, arguing instead that it is a struggle over resources, in which both men and women participated, and not primarily an expression of women's religious environmentalist wisdom or indeed any other ideology (Jain, 1984; Guha, 1989a; Mawdsley, 1998; Peritore, 1999). While such essentialisms are to be rejected, the role that women's religious identities can play in the struggle over natural resources is worthy of consideration. Examples include the participation of Christian women in the Keralan movement against deep sea trawling (Tyndale, 2003), or the Sarvodaya Women's Movement in Sri Lanka. The latter is based on Gandhian and Buddhist principles, and has the aim of community regeneration through the use of appropriate technology and bottom-up development. Within such movements women are not participating because as women they have an innate desire to protect feminine nature, but because their religio-cultural traditions offer models to negotiate and secure more favourable socio-economic conditions or to resist the introduction of unfavourable patterns of resource use.

However, religion can also provide strategies to cope with changing ecological roles. For instance, Dolan (2002) describes the situation of women in Kenya who have become economically disadvantaged when men take control of cash cropping. Part of their coping strategy has involved both conversion to Christianity, which they consider to be empowering and consoling, and the use of traditional occult practices to put spells on their husbands to punish them for their economic exclusion. Thus, while religion can serve to reinforce traditional gender roles, women may also use religion as a means of empowerment and to renegotiate and challenge normal gender relations. Moreover, religion can also play an important role in consoling women when they experience various forms of environmental disaster such as floods and earthquakes. The psychological and spiritual support that religious belief provides can be crucial in enabling women to cope with the deaths of family members, loss of possessions and threat to livelihoods, as well as to begin to rebuild their lives. However, the combination of natural disaster and religious belief can also act against women's interests. Following the Asian tsunami in 2004, for instance, women in Aceh, Indonesia, were blamed by a prominent Sharia judge because their 'bad' behaviour had caused Allah to send the tsunami in revenge. Women are now routinely punished by the Sharia police for not veiling or for mingling with members of the opposite sex. According to Fatimah Syam, of Indonesian Women for Legal Justice, 'they seek out women without headscarves or unmarried girls meeting boys in private and parade them through the streets in an open car... The Sharia police say the tsunami happened because women ignored religion. We never heard of this parading before the tsunami' (Meo, 2005).

Conclusions

This discussion illustrates the complexity of the interactions between religion, gender and the environment and some of the ways in which this nexus is relevant to development policy and practice. Consideration of this topic is timely since, despite the typical avoidance of religious issues in development (including GAD), there are signs that interest in promoting a research agenda on religion and development is beginning to emerge. This reflects concerns from donors that they are poorly informed about the intersection between faith and development as well as an escalating interest in religio-cultural issues more broadly in Western nations, largely stemming from the panic engendered by religiously based terrorism. The subject of this chapter itself reflects this incipient turn to religion within development studies. However, in embracing religion as a valid and important field of enquiry, it must avoid the narrow essentialisms and romanticization of non-Western religio-cultural traditions that have beleaguered both ecofeminism, and more broadly, religious environmentalism.[11] Moreover, it is important to emphasize that a research agenda that aims to 'mainstream' considerations of religion into development is not one that promotes religion or endorses any particular religious position. It recognizes the impact of religion in shaping social norms and values and uses those insights, where relevant, to inform policy and practice.

This chapter has drawn attention to the failure of gendered approaches to environmental resource use and management to consider the impact of religion and culture. I have argued that considerations of women, religion and the environment have been captured by ecofeminist discourse but that a rejection of the ecofeminist assumption that women are spiritually 'in tune' with the natural world ought not to result in a rejection of the significance of religion to understanding the gendered nature of resource management. Ecofeminism is perhaps valuable in highlighting the significance of women's religious identification to the natural world and the value of religiously inspired eco-activism within an academic milieu that otherwise fails to engage with religion. However, its tendency to essentialize and generalize across cultures from a Western perspective means that its final analysis is a rather dangerous and limited basis on which to found policy. By contrast, the mainstreaming of religion into development research, policy and planning that is concerned with gendered use and management of natural resources is to be welcomed. My suggestion is that development studies should encourage a research agenda that moves beyond spiritual ecofeminist essentialisms, yet supports a greater awareness of women's religious identities as well as the ways in which religion informs gender relations.

Notes

1 This general description is intended to refer to feminists who seek to reinterpret their religious traditions in order to promote female empowerment. The definition of 'empowerment' is broad and does not necessarily coincide with liberal feminist understandings of the erasure of gender difference.

2 Not all religious feminists articulate this view – it is just one religious feminist position. Others stress the social constructedness of gender roles and the potential for gender differentiation to lead to discrimination, and therefore to come closer to a 'Western' feminist perspective.

3 I use 'spiritual' and 'cultural' ecofeminism interchangeably in this chapter.

4 Liberal, social, Marxist or socialist traditions of ecofeminism do not draw upon notions of religion and spirituality and as such are not the focus of this chapter. Those traditions consider gender difference to be socially constructed and hence reject the biological essentialism typical to cultural feminism. Even so, critics such as Janet Biehl, who was once a proponent of social ecofeminism, consider that ecofeminism as a whole has become tainted by essentialism and what she sees as the irrationalism of cultural ecofeminism, with its emphasis on goddess worship, metaphors and myths (Biehl, 1991).

5 By 'deregulated' feminist spirituality, I am referring to contemporary styles of religiosity that take place outside traditional religious systems where (normally Western) spiritual seekers appropriate or borrow features of non-Western religio-cultural traditions. Beckford (1990) suggests that the contemporary environmental movement is one such context where, through a process of 'bricolage' (Lévi-Strauss, 1966), individuals select, borrow and interpret diverse religious symbols and ideas for novel purposes. An emergent post-colonial critique of such 'cultural theft' is concerned with the 'misrepresentation' that occurs through such a process (Smith, 1997).

6 In India, rivers are associated with the feminine. This is often understood as a reflection of their association with fertility and the sustenance of life, qualities linked with the female sex. See also the work of Apffel-Marglin (1994) on links between women's menstruation and the Earth in Indian religio-cultural traditions.

7 Sherma (1998) points out that Shiva's interpretation is at odds with that provided by the schools of Hindu philosophy of *Samkhya, Yoga* and *Advaita Vedanta*, where *prakriti*, the manifest universe, is seen as entirely separate from *purusha* and the aim of spiritual practice is to overcome attachments to the material world, to life itself. For

example, within *Advaita Vedanta*, the manifest universe is considered to be an illusion, *maya*, in the sense that it does not represent reality.

Reality, by contrast, is the realization that the divine self, *atman/purusha*, within the individual is identical with the impersonal absolute, *brahman* or *purusha*, and has nothing to do with material creation. She argues that Shiva's interpretation 'is only viable from the standpoint of Tantra, where the Goddess as *prakriti/shakti* is . . . identified with the highest spiritual principle, and there is, ultimately no dualism. Without this qualification, however, Shiva's praise of the *purusha/prakriti* doctrine is somewhat misleading' (p105). It is within Tantra that various bodily techniques, including sexual, are utilized in order to realize the unity between the changing and creative feminine principle and the static godhead, the masculine principle.

8   Ester Boserup's book *Women's Role in Economic Development* (1970) is widely heralded as marking the beginnings of a recognition that women are central to the development process and that without considering the subordinate position of women, poor countries were likely to remain poor. This was the first study to highlight the negative effect of development processes on women's lives in many contexts and was accompanied by an interest within the international development community to find ways that women could be integrated more effectively into development processes. The WID approach began to challenge the 'trickle down' theory of development, since women did not seem to be benefiting greatly from development initiatives.

The WID approach is commonly contrasted with GAD. WID did not challenge existing development paradigms, which reflected Western interests and were themselves not gender neutral. WID analysis failed to tackle the underlying structural reasons for gender oppression in different contexts, relying instead on the assumption that increasing educational and employment opportunities to women would be sufficient to end gender discrimination (see Rathgeber, 1990; Moser, 1993; Pearson and Jackson, 1998; and Pearson, 2000 for a discussion of the limitations of WID).

9   This observation has also been made with respect to the Ganges. Alley (1998) conducted her fieldwork at Dasasvamedha Ghat in Varanasi, particularly amongst the *pandas*, pilgrim priests, working there. Her basic argument is that whereas environmentalists in Varanasi are concerned to clean the Ganga because it is becoming polluted with wastes, which are a threat to human health as well as biodiversity, the *pandas* are more concerned about ritual purity and do not consider physical pollution to threaten the spiritual purity of Ganga: it is not a contradiction for something to be ritually pure but physically dirty. She does not intend to imply that the *pandas* are unconcerned about the material pollution of Ganga but that they see this in terms of wider social degeneracy rather than in terms of population growth, urbanization and industrial and technological development, all of which have contributed to ecological imbalance. The *pandas*' aim is to keep Ganga happy through the performance of *arati* and *puja* so that she will continue to purify the cosmos, soul, body and heart, thereby avoiding complete collapse of the current moral order.

Alley suggests that the separation of ideas of ritual purity (*shuddha* or *pavitra*) from physical pollution (*gandagi*) mean that people tend not to be as interested in projects to clean the Ganges as one would hope. However, if the priests can be persuaded to incorporate environmental cleanliness into their ritual activities, she suggests, then they could act as a conduit to transmit these environmentalist ideas to local people.

10   Although it is not useful for Western environmentalists to assume that 'nature religion' is identical to 'religious environmentalism', there are many examples around

the world of local environmental NGOs thinking about environmental issues in terms of familiar practices and customs. See, for instance, the Alliance of Religions and Conservation website at www.arcworld.org/ (accessed 31 May 2007).

11   'Religious environmentalism' here describes the conscious and reflexive process of applying religious ideas to the issue of the destruction of the environment. This fundamentally modern phenomenon, which arose alongside the emergence of the environmental movement since the 1960s, is distinct from ancient religious practices of worshipping features of the natural world, which exist across many cultures.

References

Alley, K. (1998) 'Idioms of degeneracy: Assessing Ganga's purity and pollution'. In L. Nelson (ed.) *Purifying the Earthly Body of God*, New York: SUNY Press, pp297–330

Apffel-Marglin, F. (1994) 'The sacred groves: Menstruation rituals in rural Orissa', *Manushi* 82: 22–32

Baviskar, A. (2002) 'The politics of the city', seminar, www.india-seminar.com/2002/516/516%20amita%20baviskar.htm (accessed 31 May 2007)

Beckford, J. (1990) 'The sociology of religion and social problems', *Sociological Analysis* 51 (1): 1–14

Biehl, J. (1991) *Rethinking Ecofeminist Politics*, Boston, MA: South End Press

Boserup, E. (1970) *Woman's Role in Economic Development*, London: Allen and Unwin

Brosius, P. J. (1999) 'Analysis and interventions: Anthropological engagements with environmentalism', *Current Anthropology* 40 (3): 277–309

Callicott, J. B. and R. T. Aimes (1991) *Nature in Asian Traditions of Thought: Essays in Environmental Philosophy*, Delhi: Sri Satguru Publications

Candland, C. (2000) 'Faith as social capital: Religion and community development in Southern Asia', *Policy Sciences* 33 (3/4): 355–374

Dolan, C. S. (2002) 'Conflict and compliance: Christianity and the occult in horticultural exporting', *Gender and Development* 7 (1): 23–30

Donaldson, L. E. and Kwok Pui-Lan (eds) (2002) *Postcolonialism, Feminism and Religious Discourse*, New York and London: Routledge

Gimbutas, M. (1982) *Goddesses and Gods of Old Europe*, London: Thames and Hudson

Gimbutas, M. (1989) *The Language of the Goddess*, London: Thames and Hudson

Green, C., S. Joekes and M. Leach (1998) 'Questionable links: Approaches to gender in environmental research and policy'. In C. Jackson and R. Pearson (eds) *Feminist Visions of Development*, London and New York: Routledge, pp259–283

Guha, R. (1989a) *The Unquiet Woods: Ecological Change and Peasant Resistance in the Himalaya*, Berkeley: University of California Press

Guha, R. (1989b) 'Radical American environmentalism and wilderness preservation: A Third World critique', *Environmental Ethics* 11: 71–83

Inden, R. (1986) 'Orientalist constructions of India', *Modern Asian Studies* 20 (3): 401–446

Jackson, C. (1994) 'Gender analysis and environmentalisms'. In M. Redclift and T. Benton (eds) *Social Theory and the Global Environment*, London: Routledge, pp113–149

Jackson, C. (2001) 'Gender, nature and trouble with anti-dualism'. In A. Low and S. Tremayne (eds) *Women as Sacred Custodians of the Earth? Women, Spirituality and the Environment*, New York and Oxford: Berghahn Books, pp23–44

Jain, S. (1984) 'Women and people's ecological movement: A case study of women's role in the Chipko Movement in Uttar Pradesh', *Economic and Political Weekly* 19 (41): 1788–1794

Leach, M. (2007) 'Earth mother myths and other ecofeminist fables: How a strategic notion rose and fell', *Development and Change* 38 (1) 67–85

Lerner, G. (1986) *The Creation of Patriarchy*, New York: Oxford University Press

Lévi-Strauss, C. (1966) *The Savage Mind* (*La Pensée Sauvage*, 1962), Chicago: University of Chicago Press

Mawdsley, E. (1998) 'After Chipko: From environmental to region in Uttaranchal', *Journal of Peasant Studies* 25 (4): 36–54

Meo, N. (2005) 'Tsunami was God's revenge for your wicked ways, women told', *Times Online*, 2 December, www.timesonline.co.uk/article/0,,25689-1952823,00.html (accessed 2 June 2007)

Merchant, C. (1982) *The Death of Nature: Women, Ecology and the Scientific Revolution*, London: Wildwood House

Merchant, C. (1992) *Radical Ecology: The Search for a Liveable World*, London and New York: Routledge

Meskell, L. (1995) 'Goddesses, Gimbutas and [New Age] archaeology', *Antiquity* 69 (262): 74–86

Milton, K. (1996) *Environmentalism and Cultural Theory: Exploring the Role of Anthropology in Environmental Discourse*, New York: Routledge

Moser, C. (1993) *Gender Planning and Development: Theory, Practice and Training*, London: Routledge

Mosse, D. (2003) *The Rule of Water: Statecraft, Ecology and Collective Action in South India*, New Delhi, Oxford, New York: Oxford University Press

Nagarajan, V. (1998) 'The Earth as Goddess Bhu Devi: Toward a theory of "embedded ecologies" in folk Hinduism'. In L. E. Nelson (ed.) *Purifying the Earthly Body of God: Religion and Ecology in Hindu India*, New York: State University of New York Press, pp269–296

Nagarajan, V. (2000) 'Rituals of embedded ecologies: Drawing kolams, marrying trees and generating auspiciousness'. In C. K. Chapple and M. E. Tucker (eds) *Hinduism and Ecology: The Intersection of Earth, Sky and Water*, Harvard: Harvard University Press, pp453–468

Nussbaum, M. C. (2000) *Women and Human Development: The Capabilities Approach*, Cambridge: Cambridge University Press

Pearson, R. (2000) 'Rethinking gender matters in development'. In T. Allen and A. Thomas (eds) *Poverty and Development into the 21st Century*, Oxford: The Open University in Association with Oxford University Press, pp383–402

Pearson, R. and C. Jackson (1998) 'Introduction: Interrogating development: Feminism, gender and policy'. In R. Pearson and C. Jackson (eds) *Feminist Vision of Development*, London and New York: Routledge, pp1–16

Peritore, N. P. (1999) *Third World Environmentalism: Case Studies from the Global South*, Gainsville: University Press of Florida

Plumwood, V. (1986) 'Ecofeminism: An overview and discussion of positions', *Australian Journal of Philosophy* 64: 120–138

Rathgeber, E. M. (1990) 'WID, WAD, GAD, trends in research and practice', *Journal of Developing Areas* 24: 489–502

Selinger, L. (2004) 'The forgotten factor: The uneasy relationship between religion and development', *Social Compass* 51 (4): 523–543

Sherma, R. dasGupta (1998) 'Sacred immanence: Reflections of ecofeminism in Hindu Tantra'. In L. E. Nelson (ed.) *Purifying the Body of God: Ecological Concern in Hindu India*, Albany: State University of New York Press, pp89–132

Shiva, V. (1988) *Staying Alive: Women, Ecology and Nature*, New Delhi: Kali for Women and London: Zed Books

Smith, A. (1993) 'For all those who were Indian in a former life'. In C. Adams (ed.) *Ecofeminism and the Sacred*, New York: Continuum Publishing Company, pp168–171

Smith, A. (1997) 'Ecofeminism through an anticolonial framework'. In K. Warren (ed.) *Ecofeminism: Women, Culture, Nature*, Bloomington: Indiana University Press, pp21–37

Sturgeon, N. (1999) 'Ecofeminist appropriations and transnational environmentalisms', *Identities: Global Studies in Culture and Power* 6 (2–3): 255–279

Sweetman, C. (1999) 'Editorial', *Gender and Development* 7 (1): 2–6

Tomalin, E. (2002) 'The limits of religious environmentalism for India', *Worldviews: Environment, Culture, Religion* 6 (1): 12–30

Tomalin, E. (2004) 'Bio-divinity and biodiversity: Perspectives on religion and environmental conservation in India', *Numen* 51 (3): 265–295

Tyndale, W. (2003) 'National Forum of Fish Workers: A spiritually inspired movement for alternative development', *World Faiths Development Dialogue*, www.wfdd.org.uk/programmes/case_studies/fishworkers.pdf (accessed 2 June 2007)

United Nations Development Programme (2004) *Women and the Environment*, Nairobi, Kenya: UNEP

Ver Beek, K. A. (2002) 'Spirituality: A development taboo'. In D. Eade (ed.) *Development and Culture*, Oxford: Oxfam GB, pp60–77

Verhelst, T. and W. Tyndale (2002) 'Cultures, spirituality, and development'. In D. Eade (ed.) *Culture and Development*, Oxford: Oxfam GB, pp1–24

Warren, K. (1987) 'Feminism and ecology: Making connections', *Environmental Ethics* 9 (3): 3–20

Warren, K. (1996) *Ecological Feminist Philosophies*, Bloomington: Indiana University Press

White Jr, L. (1967) 'The historical roots of our ecological crisis', *Science* 155: 1203–1207

Wilson, K. (2005) 'Ecofeminism and First Nations peoples in Canada: Linking culture, gender and nature', *Gender, Place and Culture* 12 (3): 333–355

Index

Printed and bound by CPI Group (UK) Ltd, Croydon, CR0 4YY

08/05/2025

01864351-0002